Alliance of Adversaries

Historical Materialism Book Series

The Historical Materialism Book Series is a major publishing initiative of the radical left. The capitalist crisis of the twenty-first century has been met by a resurgence of interest in critical Marxist theory. At the same time, the publishing institutions committed to Marxism have contracted markedly since the high point of the 1970s. The Historical Materialism Book Series is dedicated to addressing this situation by making available important works of Marxist theory. The aim of the series is to publish important theoretical contributions as the basis for vigorous intellectual debate and exchange on the left.

The peer-reviewed series publishes original monographs, translated texts, and reprints of classics across the bounds of academic disciplinary agendas and across the divisions of the left. The series is particularly concerned to encourage the internationalization of Marxist debate and aims to translate significant studies from beyond the English-speaking world.

For a full list of titles in the Historical Materialism Book Series available in paperback from Haymarket Books, visit:
https://www.haymarketbooks.org/series_collections/1-historical-materialism

Alliance of Adversaries

The Congress of the Toilers of the Far East

Edited by
John Sexton

Haymarket Books
Chicago, IL

First published in 2018 by Brill Academic Publishers, The Netherlands
© 2018 Koninklijke Brill NV, Leiden, The Netherlands

Published in paperback in 2019 by
Haymarket Books
P.O. Box 180165
Chicago, IL 60618
773-583-7884
www.haymarketbooks.org

ISBN: 978-1-64259-040-1

Distributed to the trade in the US through Consortium Book Sales and Distribution (www.cbsd.com) and internationally through Ingram Publisher Services International (www.ingramcontent.com).

This book was published with the generous support of Lannan Foundation and Wallace Action Fund.

Special discounts are available for bulk purchases by organizations and institutions. Please call 773-583-7884 or email info@haymarketbooks.org for more information.

Cover design by Jamie Kerry and Ragina Johnson.

Printed in the United States.

10 9 8 7 6 5 4 3 2 1

Library of Congress Cataloging-in-Publication data is available.

For Soraya

Contents

Acknowledgements XI
Note on Texts and Sources XII
Illustrations XIII

Introduction 1

Preface to the 1970 Hammersmith Reprint 43

Opening Session: 21 January 1922, Moscow 45
   Opening address by Zinoviev, chairman of the Central Executive Committee of the Comintern. Election of Congress Presidium. Speeches by Katayama on behalf of the Comintern, Kalinin on behalf of All-Russia Central Executive Committee, Lozovsky on behalf of the Red Trade Union International, Yoodzu (Mizutani Kenichi) of the Japanese delegation, Tao (Zhang Qiubai) of the Chinese delegation, Pak-Kieng (Kim Kyu-sik) of the Korean delegation, Wong (Huang Bihun) of the Chinese women's delegation, unnamed Mongolian delegate, Simpson (Semaun) of the Java delegation, Schiller (Richard Schüller) on behalf of the Young Communist International, M.N. Roy from India, Carr (L.E. Katterfeld) from the United States.

Second Session: Morning of 23 January 1922, Moscow 65
   Election of mandate commission and adoption of standing orders. Report by Zinoviev on the international situation and the results of the Washington Conference.

Third Session: Evening of 23 January 1922, Moscow 88
   Report on the situation in China by Li-Kieng (Zhang Guotao). Report on Chinese workers by Wong-Kien-Ti (Deng Pei).

Fourth Session: Morning of 24 January 1922, Moscow 99
   Report on the economic situation of China by Ping-Tong (Yu Shude). Greetings from the Nizhny Novgorod division of the Red Army. Report on the political situation in China by Tao (Zhang Qiubai).

Fifth Session: Evening of 24 January 1922, Moscow   118
Report by Wong (Huang Bihun) on the position of Chinese women. Report on the Washington Conference by Wong-Kieng of Korean delegation. Report by Pak-Kieng (Kim Kyu-sik) on the Korean revolutionary movement.

Sixth Session: Morning of 25 January 1922, Moscow   159
Report on Mongolia by Din-Dib (Dendev). Report on the economic situation in Korea by Kho (Cho Tongho). Report on the political and economic problems of Japan by Katayama. Report on the Japanese Communist Party by Yakiwa. Report on the Japanese labour organisation Rodosha by Kato (Yoshida Hajime).

Seventh Session: Evening of 25 January 1922, Moscow   202
Debate on Zinoviev's report. Speakers: Yodoshu (Yu Shude), Katayama, Flore (Kim Won'gyŏng), Tao (Zhang Qiubai), Kim-Khu (Rim Wŏn-gŭn/Im Wŏn-gŭn), Booyan-Manhu (Sonombaljiryn Buyannemekh). Reply by Zinoviev. Motion to draw up a manifesto.

Eighth Session: Morning of 26 January 1922, Moscow   220
Report on the national-colonial question by G.I. Safarov.

Ninth Session: Morning of 27 January 1922, Moscow   240
Debate on Safarov's report. Speakers: Din-Dib (Dendev), Kor-Khan (Ch'ae Tongsun), Khwong (Kwon Aera), Kim-Chow (Yi Chaegon), Tao (Zhang Qiubai), Koo, Kolokolov, U-An, Nagano, Yakova, Kato (Yoshida Hajime).

Tenth Session: Evening of 27 January 1922, Moscow   259
Safarov replies to discussion. Report of the credentials committee.

Eleventh Session: Evening of 30 January, Moscow   268
Speeches by Ker of the French Communist Party and Walter (Walcher) of the German Communist Party. Ker and Walter (Walcher) elected to Presidium. Discussion and voting on draft resolutions on the reports of Zinoviev and Safarov. Speakers: Sun, Katayama, Kho-Syl-Mon, Din-Dib (Dendev). Invitation of delegates to Petrograd. Election of committee to revise draft manifesto. Text of resolution on Zinoviev's report *The Results of the Washington Conference and the Situation in the Far East*. Resolution on Safarov's report.

The Results of the Washington Conference and the Situation in the Far East   275
   Resolution on Zinoviev's report. Resolution proposed by Chow on Safarov's report.

Final Session: Evening of 2 February 1922, Petrograd   283
   Speeches by Smirnov on behalf of Petrograd Committee of the R.C.P., Evdokimov of the Petrograd Trade Union Council, Naumov of the Revolutionary Military Council of Petrograd and the Baltic Fleet, Nikolaevna on behalf of the working women of Petrograd, Lang-Tsa-Sin, Katayama, Tan-Zam (Danzan), Wong (Huang Bihun), Khem, Li, Ker, Carr (L.E. Katterfeld). Manifesto read by Safarov. Closing address by Zinoviev.

Manifesto of the Congress   299
   Manifesto of the First Congress of the Communist and Revolutionary Organisations of the Far East to the Peoples of the Far East.

Greetings to the President of the All-Russian Central Executive Committee M.I. Kalinin   304

Report of the Credentials Committee   305

Classification of Delegates   307

Appendix 1: Organisations Represented at the Congress   313
Appendix 2: Timeline of Events   319
Appendix 3: Congress Delegates   322
Bibliography   337
Index   347
Illustration Section   360

Acknowledgements

Professor Gregor Benton read the entire text more than once and made many valuable suggestions as well as advising and encouraging me throughout the entire project. Jamila Djoudi read and corrected the introduction and also translated several German language Comintern documents. Dr Pavel Toropov generously spent many hours helping me decipher Russian handwriting. Pang Li did the same for handwritten Chinese documents and even painstakingly retyped some of them. Dr Owen Miller transliterated many Korean names and gave me biographical material on several of the Korean delegates. Gregor Kneussel helped me many times with the names of Korean organisations. Professor Louise Edwards explained the history of the women's liberation movement in southern China. Professor Alexander Pantsov introduced me to and guided me through the Comintern archive. Professor Christopher Atwood unstintingly answered my many questions about the Mongolian delegates. Professors Yang Kuisong and Yao Jinguo responded most helpfully and courteously to my questions on the Chinese delegation. Professors Steve McKinnon and Edward Rhoads helped me identify Chinese politicians from the Qing dynasty and early Republican period. Without all their help I would not have been able to complete this volume and I am immeasurably grateful to them. No doubt there are mistakes and shortcomings in my work, for which they, naturally, bear no responsibility.

Note on Texts and Sources

The text in this edition is adapted from the 1970 Hammersmith reprint of the 1922 English edition of the Congress minutes printed in Petrograd. I used the Russian and Chinese versions of the minutes held in the Comintern archive to correct mistakes in translation and resolve ambiguities. Information on the speakers, delegates and the organisations that sent them to the Congress is mainly taken from the Comintern archive, but also from other published sources, including the German language version of the minutes.

A major problem with the source text was the distortion of Asian proper names. The minute takers seem to have used no particular transliteration standard. Where, as in most cases, I have been able to identify the person, organisation or place referred to, I have inserted modern transliterations and put the original form in a footnote. For some well-known names I have stuck with older, commonly used forms – so I use Syngman Rhee not Yi Sŭng-man, Chiang Kai-shek rather than Jiang Jieshi, Sun Yat-sen rather than Sun Yixian or Sun Zhongshan. I have used the more familiar term Kuomintang rather than Guomindang to refer to the Chinese Nationalists, and Ming Pao rather than Ming Bao to refer to their newspaper. The city of Guangzhou is usually referred to as Canton in the literature of the period, including in the Congress minutes, and I have followed this usage.

Another problem was the Comintern practice of using pseudonyms which made it difficult to identify the speakers. Where I have been able to identify the people referred to, I have put their real names in brackets beside their pseudonyms (except where they are better known by their pseudonyms as in the case of Zinoviev). I have included a list of delegates to the congress as an appendix, along with short biographies where I could find material. For the most part, I identified delegates from the conference mandates and the questionnaires they filled in. But some mandates are missing from the archive, in particular several from the Japanese delegation, so I included some names from secondary sources. An odd result of this is that for the Chinese and Japanese delegations I have listed one more delegate than the number counted by the credentials committee. Another outstanding anomaly is that I have so far been unable to identify one of the main Korean speakers who is referred to as Wong-Kieng in the English minutes, Pak Chen in the Russian minutes, Piao Ren in Chinese, and Pak Tachen in a German language list of speakers.

I have corrected straightforward spelling mistakes and obvious printing errors – for example, *religious sects* was written as *religious seels* – without marking them. Where I have made small changes to the wording to clarify the meaning, I have indicated this with square brackets.

Illustrations

All illustrations can be found in the separate Illustration Section following the Appendices.

1. Katayama Sen speaks while Zinoviev reads a document   360
2. Delegates listen to a session of the congress   361
3. A group of delegates to the congress   362
4. Delegates to the congress   363
5. Delegates leaving the congress venue   364
6. Members of the Chinese delegation in their dormitory   365
7. The Chinese feminist-anarchist delegate Huang Bihun who was shot by the KMT the year after the congress   366
8. M.N. Roy's request to attend the Far East Congress as a delegate from India   367
9. Letter to the congress mandate commission, signed by the leader of the Korean delegation, Kim Kyu-sik   368
10. Comintern order, signed by Grigori Voitinsky, directing the Chinese Communist Party to move its HQ to Canton, base of the KMT, and follow the advice of the Dutch Comintern agent Henk Sneevliet   369

Introduction

> Revolutions in Russia, Persia, Turkey and China, the Balkan wars – such is the chain of world events of our period in our 'Orient'. And only a blind man could fail to see in this chain of events the awakening of a whole series of bourgeois democratic national movements.
> – LENIN 1914[1]

∴

Origins of the Congress

The Communist International or Comintern, which staged the congress this volume presents and analyses, was founded in 1919 in response to the failure of the Second International to resist war in 1914. Its aim was the overthrow of world capitalism and the creation of an international Soviet Republic. It held seven congresses before it was wound up in 1943, as Stalin's sop to his World War Two allies. The Comintern was a relatively small organisation in terms of staff and cadres, but it was highly influential in steering world communism through the crises of the 1920s and 1930s. At its heart sat Russian communism, for it was born in Moscow on a Soviet initiative, funded by Moscow, and Moscow ran the agents sent overseas to spread the Comintern's message and enforce its decisions. Within a few years, the Comintern had become more an arm of Russia foreign policy than the 'General Staff' of the world revolution.

Although the Comintern aspired to centralism from the outset, it was far less monolithic in its early years than after Stalin's rise to power, when 'Bolshevisation' (meaning a regime of 'iron discipline') was imposed on communist parties throughout the world. Early Comintern congresses tolerated non-orthodox opinions and were marked by fierce controversies. A striking example was the debate at the Second Congress on Lenin's famous theses on the national and colonial questions, which identified revolution in Asia as a key to world revolution. Lenin's strategic vision was of an anti-imperialist alliance of the proletariat of the advanced capitalist countries, the Soviet state and nationalist revolutionaries. As when he later advocated a united front with the parties

---

1 'The Right of Nations to Self-Determination', in Lenin 1977, Vol. 20, p. 406.

of the Second International, Lenin faced opposition from those who opposed any dealings with 'bourgeois' forces. The debate crystallised around the views of the young Indian revolutionary Manabendra Nath Roy who argued that the masses were not 'fired with a national spirit', and that Communists should focus on economic and social issues. Lenin prevailed, but Roy presented supplementary theses which were approved by the congress along with Lenin's.

Within a year and a half of the Second Congress, the Comintern assembled two international conferences – the Baku Congress of the Peoples of the East, held in September 1920, and the Congress of the Toilers of the Far East which opened in Moscow on 21 January 1922 and closed on 2 February in Petrograd.[2] The Far East Congress was much smaller than the Baku congress; it attracted fewer than 150 delegates, almost all of them from four countries, China, Japan, Korea and Mongolia, as against the nearly 2,000 from 37 nationalities who assembled in Baku. And although it produced some fierce rhetoric, the Moscow congress failed to produce a moment to equal the Comintern chairman Grigori Zinoviev's call from the rostrum in Baku for a holy war against capitalism.[3] However, the Far East Congress seems to have had more lasting practical influence, perhaps because it attracted authentic overseas nationalist and communist organisations whereas ad hoc groups from Soviet territory were the majority in Baku. The leader of the Chinese Communist Party delegation, Zhang Guotao, credited the congress with decisively shifting the party from its original, propagandist emphasis on proletarian revolution to a predominantly anti-imperialist line. A year after the congress, the Chinese Communists formed an alliance with the nationalist Kuomintang.

Lenin had been paying increasing attention to the national question and colonial revolutions in the decade before the Far East Congress. In 1912, following the overthrow of China's imperial dynasty, he extravagantly praised the nationalist leader Sun Yat-sen as a 'revolutionary democrat, endowed with the nobility and heroism of a class that is rising, not declining', adding that 'in Asia, there is *still* a bourgeoisie capable of championing sincere, militant, consistent democracy, a worthy comrade of France's great men of the Enlightenment and the great leaders of the close of the eighteenth century'.[4] In 1913, he instructed Stalin to set out Bolshevik policy in the pamphlet *Marxism and the National*

---

2   Hereafter the Far East Congress. The Congress was also known as the First Congress of Communist and Revolutionary Organizations of the Far East.
3   The *Times* correspondent mocked Zinoviev and Béla Kun as 'two Jews, one of them a convicted pickpocket, summoning the world of Islam to a jihad'. Cited in Hopkirk 2001, p. 108. For a full account of the Baku Conference see Riddell (ed.) 1993.
4   'Democracy and Narodism in China', in Lenin 1975, Vol. 18, p. 165.

Question. In 1914, he penned a polemic against Rosa Luxemburg, who regarded demands for national self-determination as obsolete or even reactionary in an age when capitalism had outgrown the nation state. In May 1917, he called for systematic work 'to bring about an uprising among all peoples now oppressed by the Great Russians, all colonies and dependent countries in Asia (India, China, Persia, etc.)'.[5] Two months after the October Revolution, the Russian government issued an appeal to 'the Moslems of Russia and the East', calling on 'Persians, Turks, Arabs and Hindus' to overthrow the imperialist 'robbers and enslavers' of their countries.[6]

The Washington Conference

Although the Far East Congress was the direct political descendant of the Second Comintern Congress, it originated as a countermove by the People's Commissariat for Foreign Affairs to the Washington Conference – an intergovernmental conference convened by the United States in late 1921. On the Washington agenda was a naval arms race that had developed among the victorious powers of World War One, and tensions in the Pacific where Japan was becoming increasingly assertive. In the summer of 1921, the newly-elected President Warren Harding issued invitations to America's wartime allies, Britain, France, Italy, Japan, Belgium, Portugal and China, and to neutral Netherlands, which was a Pacific power because of its possession of the Dutch Indies (Indonesia). The defeated central powers were not invited. Soviet Russia was pointedly excluded, despite its clear territorial interests in the Pacific region.

The People's Commissar for Foreign Affairs, Georgy Chicherin, protested against Russia's exclusion. Since Russia and the United States had no diplomatic relations, he sent his note to the us ambassador to Sweden. The us State Department replied indirectly in a press statement declaring that the former territory of the Russian Empire should be considered under the 'moral trusteeship' of the powers invited to Washington until such time as a single Russian government was established.[7] The Soviet view was that it was due to the intervention of the 'moral trustees' in the Russian civil war that no unitary government had yet been established. While the United States, France and Britain had withdrawn their armies, Japan still had tens of thousands of troops in

---

5 *Pravda*, no. 56, 26 May (13) 1917, in Lenin 1977, Vol. 24.
6 *Appeal of the Council of People's Commissars to the Moslems of Russia and the East*, 23 December 1918.
7 Dukes 2004, pp. 3–5.

Siberia. In November, Chicherin addressed another note to the United States, Britain, France and Japan, ridiculing the suggestion that Russia's 'interests are to be guarded by the same Governments that have been bleeding her, sending the Tsar's generals against her, trying to strangle her by a ruthless blockade'.[8]

Moscow's claim to a seat at Washington was weakened by the fact that, at the time, most of its territory east of Lake Baikal belonged to the nominally independent Far Eastern Republic (FER). The FER was a temporary by-product of the civil war, ruled by a coalition of Communists and moderate socialists. It was essentially a buffer state created by the Soviets to rally patriotic non-communists against the interventionists while avoiding outright war with Japan. Its democratic trappings and private property rights were also intended to encourage the United States to press for the withdrawal of Japanese forces from Siberia. Since it answered to the Soviet government, the FER had ceded the Kamchatka peninsula to Russia precisely to secure Moscow a place at any negotiations regarding the Pacific region.[9]

The initial Soviet plan was to convene a rival intergovernmental conference. In the 2 August 1921 edition of *Izvestia*, a foreign affairs official, V.D. Vilensky, proposed a four-sided conference of Russia, China, Mongolia and the FER. While the attendance of Mongolia and the FER was guaranteed, to have attracted China would have been a diplomatic coup for Moscow. Russian hopes lay with General Wu Peifu, leader of the Zhili clique of warlords that had recently ousted the pro-Japanese Anhui clique from power. Wu was, mistakenly as it turned out, believed to hold 'progressive' views. But the Beijing government accepted the invitation to Washington and the plan for an intergovernmental conference had to be abandoned.

Instead it was decided to assemble a congress of East Asian revolutionary organisations under the banner of the Communist International. The call to attend the Congress was drafted by a young Chinese revolutionary, Zhang Tailei. 'Comrades of Korea, China, Japan and Mongolia! ... On November 11, 1921, a surgical operation, known as the Washington Conference, will be performed on the peoples of the Far East. It is on that day that we will convene a Congress of the Toilers of the Far East in Irkutsk, the purpose of which is to unite

---

8 Chicherin 1922, p. 11.
9 The Far Eastern Republic comprised the Siberian provinces of Transbaikal, Amur, the Maritime Province, and northern Sakhalin. It was formed in April 1920 after the collapse of the White government of Admiral Kolchak and absorbed into Soviet Russia in November 1922. The FER ceded Kamchatka to Soviet Russia in early 1921. See Pasvolsky 1922, pp. 105–6 and 123–4.

the toilers of the East in the face of a new danger. Our slogans are "Peace and Independence of the Country", "Land to Those Who Till It", "Factories to the Workers".[10]

The Washington Conference was one of what Trotsky called an 'interminable series of political, economic, financial, tariff, and monetary conferences' that took place in the aftermath of the World War.[11] As Zinoviev said in his opening address to the Far East Congress, the world was struggling 'like a bird imprisoned in trap' with the consequences of the war and the Versailles settlement. The agenda and outcome of the Washington meeting reflected the postwar balance of forces. While the European powers had bled each other dry, the United States and Japan were largely unscathed. The situation was aptly summed up by Zinoviev's Comintern colleague Georgy Safarov, who told the Far East Congress that the big winners were the two countries that had taken 'the least part, or a fictitious one, in the war'.

The United States had first profited as quartermaster to the Entente and then tipped the military balance at the cost of relatively few casualties.[12] US banks financed the allied war effort with loans that were spent inside the United States and fuelled an industrial boom. By the war's end the US fleet rivalled the Royal Navy. While not yet in the commanding position it would later occupy, the United States emerged from the war as *primus inter pares* among the powers. Japan had opportunistically joined the war to make gains while its rivals were preoccupied in Europe. In November 1914, backed by British forces, it captured the German concession of Qingdao on China's northern coast. The seven hundred soldiers killed in the operation were the heaviest Japanese losses of the war. The Japanese navy seized Germany's north Pacific island colonies, including the strategic Yap archipelago. In 1915, Tokyo forced China to accept most of a list of 21 demands that included the prolongation of leases on the Manchurian territories Japan had taken from Russia in the war of 1904–05.[13]

The US government's aims at the Washington Conference were to formalise its strategic parity with Great Britain and trim Japan's ambitions in the

---

10 Beckmann and Okubo 1969, pp. 38–9. Zhang Tailei did not attend the congress but travelled to Japan to persuade anarchists to attend. He was killed in a failed uprising in Canton in December 1927.

11 See Leon Trotsky, *Nationalism and Economic Life*, available at: https://www.marxists.org/archive/trotsky/1934/xx/nationalism.htm, retrieved 31 May 2015.

12 50,000 US soldiers were killed in action and a similar number died from disease and other causes. The casualty rate of US forces was seven percent compared to 70 percent in the case of France and Russia. Around 1.7 million French soldiers were killed. Across all the European armies more than 10 million were killed.

13 The Liaodong peninsula and the South Manchurian railway zone.

Pacific. Its principal target was the 20-year-old Anglo-Japanese alliance which allowed Japan to shelter under the protection of the Royal Navy. The alliance was replaced by a Four-Power Treaty by which the United States, Britain, France and Japan effectively agreed to respect the status quo in the Pacific. A Five-Power naval treaty fixed warship tonnage ratios of 5: 5: 3: 1.75: 1.75 for the United States, Great Britain, Japan, France and Italy.[14] The United States also prevailed on the other powers to sign a Nine-Power Treaty agreeing to the principle of the Open Door[15] – a move aimed at undermining Japan's claims to economic exclusivity in its Chinese concession areas. There was, of course, no question of giving China the keys to what was manifestly a Chinese door. China's request that it be allowed to increase its tariffs from 3½ percent to 12½ percent was dismissed.[16] While China's door was held wide open, America's was slammed shut. In September 1922, US import duties were raised to record levels of nearly 40 percent. However, the US government also brokered talks between China and Japan that resulted in Japan returning formal sovereignty over Qingdao (and its other concessions in Shandong) to China, albeit extracting a heavy economic price and retaining substantial control over the province.[17]

At the Far East Congress, of course, the Washington Conference was excoriated. Zinoviev ridiculed the disarmament agreement, in particular the exemption of submarine fleets which, he quipped, were presumably intended 'for the purpose of examining the bottom of the sea, collecting pebbles, etc.'. The Four-Power Treaty was no more than a truce concluded by four 'blood-suckers', for

---

14   The agreement applied to capital ships only, i.e. battleships and battle cruisers. Submarines and cruisers were excluded.
15   The Open Door policy was first formulated in diplomatic notes circulated in 1899 and 1900 by Secretary of State John Hay. It was intended to protect US commercial interests in China during the 'scramble for concessions' by the other powers while the United States was preoccupied with a counterinsurgency campaign in the Philippines which it had seized from Spain in 1898. See *The Philippine American War*, US Department of State, Office of the Historian, available at: https://history.state.gov/milestones/1899-1913/war, retrieved 6 July 2014.
16   'The Arms Conference', in *New York Times Current History*, Vol. 15, No. 4, January 1922. In 1925, faced by a wave of strikes and boycotts provoked by the 30 May Incident, the powers finally promised to grant China tariff autonomy by 1929.
17   The transfer of sovereignty was on paper only. In 1928, Japanese troops stationed in the provincial capital Jinan clashed with Chiang Kai-shek's advancing Nationalists. The Japanese bombarded the old walled city, killing thousands of civilians. China's protests were ignored by the other powers. As part of the 1922 agreement, China was obliged to take a loan from Japanese banks to purchase the Jinan-Qingdao railway while leaving Japanese railway officials in charge. See Fenby 2004, pp. 176–8 and Whitney Griswold 1938, p. 327.

the purpose of more efficiently exploiting the countries of the East, according to the formula 'I will help you in robbing such-and-such colonies, so that you may help me rob such-and-such others'. But no agreement could postpone an 'inevitable, grandiose war in the Pacific ... As sure as morning follows night, so will the first imperialist war which ended in 1918, be followed by a second war which will centre round the Far East'.

China, Japan, Korea and Mongolia

China, Japan, Korea and Mongolia, the four countries that accounted for the bulk of the delegates to the Far East Congress, had an intertwined history of war, colonisation and revolt. Following the Meiji reforms Japan had rapidly joined the imperial club, defeated first China in 1895, then Russia in 1905, and seized Korea as its prize. Having industrialised rapidly since the turn of the century, by the time of the Far East Congress, Japan had a working class of several millions. Zinoviev, in his opening address, expressed the Comintern's hopes for the Japanese proletariat:

'Marx said that without a revolution in England any European revolution would just amount to but a storm in a teacup. Well, *mutatis mutandis* the same may be said of the Japanese revolution ... The only thing that can really solve the Far Eastern question is the defeat of the Japanese bourgeois and the final victory of the revolution in Japan'.

One of the Comintern's principal aims at the congress was to create a Communist Party in Japan. The Japanese labour movement was divided between reformists, who favoured parliamentary action, and anarchists, who shunned 'politics', in favour of directly seizing power through mass strikes. The Comintern's best hope of short-term gains seemed to be to win over the anarchists. 'It goes without saying', Safarov told the Far East Congress, that 'anarcho-communists and syndicalists are rightful members of the Communist International, just as much as anyone is'. The initial signs were hopeful. Several anarchist-influenced organisations sent delegates, one of whom, Yoshima Hajide, announced his conversion to communism on the floor of the congress.

China had failed to construct a viable government since the Qing dynasty was overthrown by the Xinhai Revolution of 1911–12. The Opium Wars, the 14-year Christian-inspired Taiping Rebellion and Muslim-led rebellions in the north and southwest fatally weakened the dynasty. Following the Boxer Rebellion, a futile spasm of resistance to the scramble for concessions that followed defeat by Japan, Beijing was occupied by a concert of eight imperialist powers.

The Empire finally collapsed in the face of revolts by the New Armies it had created after the Sino-Japanese War. A national assembly in Nanjing chose the veteran anti-Qing revolutionary Sun Yat-sen as president, but he was obliged to resign in favour of the military strongman Yuan Shikai. Yuan's Beiyang Army had defeated the main uprising in Wuhan but he changed sides when the position of the dynasty became untenable.

After elections handed a majority to Sun's party, the Kuomintang, Yuan assassinated the party leader, Song Jiaoren, and dispersed the parliament. But Yuan was only first among equals of the military men. When he overreached by declaring himself emperor at the end of 1915 he was forced from office by another rebellion and the era of the warlords began. Nominally independent but hopelessly in debt, its territory dotted with foreign concession areas, the Chinese republic limped from crisis to crisis as competing cliques of militarists fought for control of the Beijing government. Sun Yat-sen and his supporters established a rival government in the southern city of Canton.[18]

Korea's Josŏn dynasty, a tributary state of the Chinese Empire, had ruled over a closed Confucian society for 500 years. France and the United States tried to break down the walls of the reclusive kingdom by force in the 1860s, but Japan was the first to sign a treaty, in 1876, that granted extraterritoriality to its citizens and challenged Korea's traditional relationship with China. Rivalry between China and Japan intensified in 1884 when the Kapsin putsch, carried out by Japanese-backed modernisers, was crushed by Chinese forces led by Yuan Shikai. In 1894, when Korea again called on China, this time to suppress a peasant rebellion inspired by the Tonghak religion, Japan sent troops to counter China's intervention. War broke out almost immediately. China's defeat left Russia as Japan's main competitor in Korea. The Sino-Japanese war had barely ended when Japanese agents murdered the Korean queen for supposedly promoting Russian influence. The rivalry culminated in the 1904–05 Russo-Japanese War, after which Japan first imposed a protectorate then annexed Korea in 1910. When Japan disbanded the Korean army in 1907, many of its former officers joined the insurgency of the so-called Righteous Armies. The rebellion was suppressed but insurgents fled to Manchuria and Siberia where they organised

---

18   A series of southern governments claimed legitimacy as successors to the national assembly dissolved by the Yuan Shikai in 1914. In 1917, Sun Yat-sen established the first Canton government with former members of the assembly. Forced out in 1918, Sun returned in 1921 with the support of the left-leaning warlord Chen Jiongming. Chen, in turn, expelled him from Canton in the summer of 1922, but by early 1923 Sun had returned to power.

resistance among the large Korean diaspora.[19] Inside Korea, religious leaders, including Christian pastors, were the backbone of the independence movement.

Mongolia had been incorporated into the Qing Empire in the seventeenth century. The rulers of the ethnically Manchu dynasty felt a cultural kinship with the Mongol elite, to whom they posed as successors to Genghis Khan. They ruled Mongolia on the same model as Tibet, as a local theocracy lightly supervised by resident Chinese officials known as *amban*. But in the last decade of the dynasty, fearing Tsarist expansion into the sparsely populated territory, the government began to encourage Han Chinese colonisation. The new policy was energetically promoted by the young *amban* Sando who, although born in Hangzhou and thoroughly Sinicized, was himself a Mongol. Sando provoked intense resentment and when the Qing dynasty collapsed, Mongolia's Tibetan-born theocratic ruler, the Jibzundamba Khutugtu, having first secured Russian support, declared independence and took the title of Bogda Khagan (Holy Emperor).[20]

In 1919, the Paris Peace Conference triggered two anti-Japanese mass movements. On 1 March, a group of religious leaders gathered in Seoul and ceremonially declared Korea's independence. Mass protests broke out and soon spread across the country. In six weeks of unrest, Japanese troops killed 7,500 protesters and arrested 40,000. Tens of thousands fled the country. The demonstrators had been inspired by Woodrow Wilson's fourteen-point peace plan that appeared to support the self-determination of subject peoples. In fact, Wilson's programme, drawn up in response to the Bolshevik's publication of secret treaties, merely called for an 'impartial adjustment' of colonial claims.[21] A Korean provisional government, set up in Shanghai shortly after the protests, appoin-

---

19   There were at least 200,000 Koreans in Siberia and over 400,000 in Manchuria this time. Many had emigrated for economic reasons during the nineteenth century. After the Japanese takeover they were joined by political exiles. Thousands of Koreans joined the Red Army during the Russian civil war. See Sooyoung Kim, 'The Rising of a Hegemonic Power in the East Asian Communist Movement', in *Guoji zhongguo xue yanjiu*, No. 12.
20   The Bogda Khagan was a reincarnation of the Bodhisattva Manjushri, a descendant of Genghis Khan through a previous incarnation, and a high lama of the Gelugpa school of Tibetan Buddhism headed by the Dalai Lama.
21   Wilson set out his peace programme in a January 1918 speech to Congress during the Brest-Litovsk negotiations between Soviet Russia and the central powers. He praised the Russian representatives for 'very justly, very wisely, and in the true spirit of modern democracy' insisting that the negotiations take place openly and in full view of the world. For the full text of Wilson's speech, see Finley and Sullivan 1919, pp. 207–15.

ted an American-educated Christian, Kim Kyu-sik, as its ambassador to the Paris talks, but he was not given a hearing.

Two months after the Korean upheaval, the decision of the peace conference to confirm Japan's possession of Qingdao caused violent protests in China. On 4 May, students from Beijing University and other colleges marched to Tiananmen, torched the house of the deputy foreign minister and badly beat the former ambassador to Japan. The demonstrations rapidly spread to Shanghai and other cities. Mass strikes and boycotts were directed at both Japanese interests and at the peculiar mix of authoritarianism and impotence that was the Beijing government. The students had correctly gauged that the government had secretly agreed to Japan's continued occupation of Qingdao in return for desperately needed loans. The result was a victory of sorts for the protesters, as the Chinese government found it impossible to sign the Versailles Treaty. The May Fourth Movement to a large extent shaped twentieth-century Chinese politics. The movement's 'commander-in-chief', Chen Duxiu, became the first leader of the Communist Party. The veteran nationalist revolutionary Sun Yat-sen took advantage of the mass radicalisation to re-launch the Kuomintang.[22]

Japan was not immune to unrest. The great rice riots of 1918 lasted three months and forced the resignation of the government of Count Terauchi Masatake. Strikers fought pitched battles with troops and police; miners used dynamite in the confrontations. More than 25,000 people were arrested. The doubling of the price of rice was partly caused by government purchases to supply Japanese troops being sent to Siberia as part of the allied intervention against the Bolsheviks. Japan's contingent, eventually 70,000 strong, was by far the largest of the 15-nation force. Even as the other interventionists quit Russia in 1920, Japanese troops were still landing in Vladivostok. Under the banner of anti-Bolshevism Japan was trying to carve out spheres of influence in Siberia and Mongolia, in league with its protégés, the White Cossack warlords Semenov and Kalmykov and their confederate, Roman von Ungern-Sternberg.[23]

The response of the Beijing government to the May Fourth Movement was to play the nationalist card by invading Mongolia. In October 1919, General 'Little Xu' Xu Shuzheng marched an army into Niislel Khuree.[24] The upper house of the Mongolian parliament was part-coerced, part-persuaded to renounce Mongolia's autonomous status.[25] But Chinese success turned into a debacle

---

22 Often referred to as the KMT or Nationalist Party.
23 Bisher 2005, p. xvi.
24 The Mongolian capital, often referred to as Urga, now Ulan Bator.
25 The 1919 revocation of autonomy by the Mongolian nobles was not entirely the result of Chinese coercion. Although extremely intelligent and able, the Bogda Khagan was also

when Xu lost his backers in Beijing and withdrew. Ungern-Sternberg moved his forces into the vacuum and began a reign of terror. Small groups of nationalists, enraged by the treason of the nobility, had formed the Mongolian People's Party (MPP). With the approval of the Bogda Khagan, they asked Soviet Russia to help restore Mongolia's independence. The Red Army supported MPP troops led by Damdin Sükhebaatur[26] (seen in Mongolia as the nation's Lenin) as they ousted Ungern-Sternberg's regime and, in July 1921, established a 'people's government'.[27]

The Dutch Indies (Indonesia)

Three hundred years of Dutch rule in Indonesia had seen only sporadic and localised resistance to the colonists, but around the beginning of the twentieth century several factors combined to give birth to a modern national movement. The development of modern industry and transport systems created a proletariat. The civil service grew and recruited Indonesians. In response to social change, the colonial government introduced the so-called 'Ethical Policy' that expanded education and created a local intelligentsia that was receptive to radical ideas. Nationalism was boosted when Japan's 1905 victory over Russia demonstrated that Asians could build a modern state and defeat Westerners on the battlefield. The indigenous petty bourgeoisie also resented the dominant role of Chinese businesses in some sectors of the economy.

The first organisation to appear, in 1908, was Boedi Oetomo, a mainly cultural-educational group. In 1912 a more radical group, the Indies Party, led by Ernest Douwes Dekker, declared itself 'revolutionary'. It was closed down by the Dutch, moderated its policies, and reappeared under the name Insulinde. Also in 1912, an organisation of Muslim businessmen, Sarekat Islam, was formed under the slogan 'Our homeland, our religion, our nation'. Its first leader was the batik trader, Hadji Samanhudi, and its initial aim was to protect local busi-

---

a notorious drunk and womaniser. There was widespread discontent with his rule, especially with the growing numbers of his privileged personal retinue, the Great Shabi.

26 General Damdin Sükhebaatur, the founder and commander-in-chief of the modern Mongolian army, was renowned for his courage and competence. As defence minister in the MPP government from 1921–22 he established a military academy and carried out other important reforms. He died of liver disease in 1923. The Mongolian dictator Choibalsan, Mongolia's Stalin, who had been Sükhebaatur's second-in-command, later created a cult that magnified Sükhebaatur's role to that of sole leader of the revolution. Atwood 2004, p. 522.

27 Mongolia was a constitutional monarchy from 1921 until the Bogda Khagan died in 1924.

ness from Chinese competition. It recruited 200,000 members in its first year but it had an ill-defined programme and as its activity mainly consisted of anti-Chinese riots, it was severely repressed. Samanhudi was soon replaced as leader by Omar Said Tjokroaminoto, mentor and father-in-law of future Indonesian President Sukarno. Tjokroaminoto, who was an impressive orator, broadened the appeal of Sarekat Islam and developed it into a mass anti-colonial movement.

In 1913, the prominent Dutch socialist and trade unionist Henk Sneevliet[28] emigrated to the Dutch Indies and established the Indies Social Democratic Association (ISDV). In conscious opposition to right wing socialists who saw colonialism as at least partly 'progressive', Sneevliet worked among the Indonesian population and sought allies among nationalists. Following a flirtation with Insulinde he switched his attention to Sarekat Islam. Sneevliet's aim, he later explained, was to turn Sarekat Islam 'into a communist organisation; an organisation which will be a member of the Third International'.[29] He sent Indonesian ISDV members into Sarekat Islam to form a 'bloc within' and win over its members.[30] Within a short time they achieved leading positions within the organisation. By 1917, under the influence of the Russian Revolution, Sarekat Islam had begun to denounce capitalism as 'sinful'. Tensions grew between the socialist wing and the leadership. But when they were expelled, the socialists, now reorganised as the Communist Union of the Indies (PKH),[31] took a major part of the membership into their new organisation, Red Sarekat Islam.

The Congress Agenda, Delegates and Speakers

The Far East Congress opened in Moscow on 21 January 1922, in the Kremlin's Sverdlov hall. After Zinoviev and the Soviet head of state Mikhail Kalinin welcomed the delegates, the meeting named Lenin, Trotsky, Zinoviev, Katayama and Stalin as honorary chairmen and elected a presidium. The main business of the congress was completed in ten sessions held over five days from 23 to 27 January, in a former church building. On 30 January, the delegates voted on

---

28   Hendricus 'Henk' Sneevliet is often referred to by his Comintern pseudonym Maring.
29   H. Sneevliet, 'De Wantoestanden in Indie' (Lecture for the Student Socialist Movement, Leiden), *De Tribune*, 21 April 1920, p. 4. Quoted in Bing 2009, p. 159.
30   The 'bloc within' tactic is also known as entrism or entryism.
31   Perserikatan Komunis di Hindia (Communist Union of the Indies). In 1924, the party changed its name to PKI Partai Komunis Indonesia.

the congress resolutions. They then travelled to Petrograd for a ceremonial closing session held on 2 February in the Uritsky Palace.

The agenda was structured around two main reports. On 23 January, Zinoviev spoke on the international situation and the Washington Conference. On 26 January, Georgi Safarov of the Comintern's Far East Bureau set out the Soviet view on the national and colonial revolution. In between, the delegations presented reports on the situation in their countries. The standing orders allowed for three speakers each from Japan, China and Korea, and one each from the Dutch Indies and Mongolia. In the event, China was allowed five speaking slots. These numbers can be taken as an accurate reflection of the importance the Comintern assigned to each country.

The congress credentials committee recorded 148 delegates, including 17 with consultative votes.[32] The largest contingent, of 54, was from Korea. There were 44 from China, 16 from Japan, 14 from Mongolia, one from the Dutch Indies, and two, with consultative votes only, from India. The remaining delegates represented Siberian national minorities, Buryats, Kalmyks and Yakuts, and the Far Eastern Republic. Among the 119 delegates from whom they collected information, the committee concluded there were 46 intellectuals, 46 peasants and 24 workers. Two thirds were members of Communist parties or affiliated youth organisations, four were counted as anarchist-communists, and 26 as non-party. Strangely, the ten classed as nationalists were all from the Mongolian People's Party.

Zinoviev's keynote address, in which he denounced the Washington Conference as an unstable 'alliance of bloodsuckers' and predicted war in the Pacific, was a rhetorical *tour de force*. The Chinese delegate Peng Shuzhi described how from his 'round face crowned with the already world-famous mop of tousled hair, he poured forth a torrent of words that surged over us in successive waves. What a magnificent agitator!'[33] Safarov, who was one of Russia's leading experts on Asia, delivered a more measured address in which he identified the Chinese peasants, the Korean 'bourgeois democratic' national movement, and the Japanese workers as the key revolutionary actors in East Asia.

---

32   The credentials committee reported that 144 delegates had travelled to the Congress. There were also four delegates from among foreign students in Moscow (two Korean and two Chinese), making a total of 148. At least 115 delegates filled in questionnaires, recording their age, occupation, political affiliations and so on. Some students (including the future top leaders of the Chinese Communist Party Liu Shaoqi and Qu Qiubai) attended as translators and facilitators.

33   Cadart and Yingxiang 1983, p. 297.

The Korean delegation was chaired by Kim Kyu-sik, former foreign minister of the Korean Provisional Government. He presented a long report on the Korean revolutionary movement. Kim was, in Soviet terms, a classic bourgeois democrat but disillusioned by repeated rebuffs from the United States he had thrown in his lot with Moscow. Another leading member of the Korean delegation was the moderate Communist Yŏ Unhyŏng.[34] At the end of World War Two, Yŏ was released from jail by the Japanese colonial authorities and asked to form a government. His short-lived Korean People's Republic was dismissed by the American military authorities. Yŏ and Kim campaigned for national unity in the period between the end of World War Two and the outbreak of the Korean War. Yŏ was assassinated by a right wing extremist in 1947. Kim died in North Korea in 1950, shortly after the outbreak of war, having left Seoul with, perhaps abducted by, retreating North Korean troops.

Katayama Sen, the grand old man of the Japanese labour movement, doubled as leader of the Japanese delegation and a platform speaker on behalf of the Comintern. Tokuda Kyuichi, was a founder member of the Japanese Communist Party and its general secretary from 1945 until his death in 1953. Two anarchist workers, the engineer Yoshida Hajime and the miner Wada Kiichiro embodied the Comintern's hopes of building a Communist party from among the most radical layers of the working class.

The leader of the Chinese Communist delegation, Zhang Guotao, later became a senior Red Army commander and challenged Mao for the leadership of the Communist Party. But his speech at the Congress made little impression, perhaps because his 'abominable' Jiangxi accent made it difficult even for the other Chinese delegates to understand him.[35] Sun Yat-sen sent an ambitious young politician, Zhang Qiubai, as his representative. Zhang made a rambling speech, for which he apologised, and clashed briefly with Zinoviev and Safarov. One of China's leading anarchists, Huang Lingshuang, delegated by the Machine Workers Union of Canton, wrote on his questionnaire that he had joined the Communist Party but a Russian hand added that he was only a sympathiser. Some working class members of the Chinese delegation, including the railway workers' leader Deng Pei, complained to the mandate commission that the 'gentleman' Huang, a former Peking University teacher, could not possibly

---

34 Several sources say that Yŏ never joined the Communist Party but in his delegate questionnaire he clearly states he was in the party and that his mandate to attend the congress was from its central committee. Russian State Archive of Socio-Political History, 495.154.179.025.

35 Cadart and Yingxiang 1983, p. 295.

represent trade unionists.[36] Among the few women delegates at the Congress was the prominent feminist and member of the Canton parliament, Huang Bihun, who made a powerful speech on the oppression of women in China.

The main speaker for the Mongolian delegation, Dendev, a founder member of Mongolian People's Party, gave an impressive survey of Mongolian history. The leader of the Mongolian delegation, Ajvaagiyn 'Japanese' Danzan, who was chairman of the MPP from 1923–24, spoke only briefly.

The two Indian delegates (who had consultative votes only since India was not in the 'Far East') were the co-founders of the Indian Communist Party, M.N. Roy and Abani Mukherji. They had recently followed up Zinoviev's call for a holy war by attempting to launch an invasion of the British Raj from Afghanistan.[37] They established a military school in Tashkent with money, guns and aeroplanes supplied by the Soviets and attempted to attract Muslim militants en route from India to Turkey to fight against the dismemberment of the Ottoman Empire, which they saw as the Caliphate. But Comintern plans for a revolutionary war in India were abandoned after Emir Amanullah of Afghanistan withdrew support. The military school closed in May 1921.

The sole Indonesian delegate, Semaun, first chairman of the Communist Union of the Indies (PKH), represented what was, at the time, the largest Communist organisation in Asia. But although he was elected to the presidium, Semaun seems to have been somewhat side-lined at the congress. His lengthy report, presented in writing because, as the chairman put it, he was the only delegate who could speak his language, was not included in the published minutes.[38] Semaun was a precocious activist, an official of the Indies Social Democratic Association at the age of 16 and a leader of Sarekat Islam at 19. At the time of the Congress of the Toilers of the Far East he was still only 23

---

36 The workers' letters and Huang Linshuang's replies are in the Russian State Archive of Socio-Political History, 495.154.175.

37 For more on the Tashkent military school, see Jacobson 1994, pp. 77–8. Abani Mukherji (1891–1937) was initially a nationalist (he was introduced to Rash Behari Bose in Japan during World War One by Sun Yat-sen) and was imprisoned by the British in Singapore in 1915 for trying to run guns to India. He attended the Third Comintern Congress in 1921. Mukherji later became Roy's factional rival in the Indian Communist Party. After returning to the Soviet Union to work as an academic he was executed during the Great Purges. His application to attend the Congress is in the Russian State Archive of Socio-Political History 495.154.175. On his meeting with Sun Yat-sen, see Chattopadhyaya 1976, p. 11.

38 Semaun's report is 54 pages long and covers anti-colonial political movements, the trade unions, peasants and co-operatives, the women's movement and youth movements, etc. A German language version is in the Russian State Archive of Socio-Political History, 495.154.174, but there is not even an extract from it in either the English or German versions of the minutes.

years old but, steered by Sneevliet,[39] he had played a major role in the 'bloc within' manoeuvre that attracted mass support to the Indonesian Communists.[40] Sneevliet and Semaun's success in the Dutch Indies was to significantly influence Comintern tactics in East Asia.

Béla Kun, leader of the short-lived Hungarian Soviet Republic and former Comintern celebrity, sat on the congress platform but did not say a single word, perhaps because his star had waned following the disastrous March 1921 Action in Germany.

Some others who were not present at the Far East Congress played significant roles off-stage. Sneevliet, now a Comintern agent, met with Sun Yat-sen while the congress was in session and went on to play a controversial role in cementing an alliance between the Chinese Communist Party and the Kuomintang. Yi Tong-hwi, a former Korean army officer turned anti-Japanese insurgent who founded the Korean Communist Party, was in Irkutsk at the time of the Congress, tasked with uniting the bitterly divided Korean Communists. Yi was the leader of the so-called 'Shanghai faction'. His rivals in the 'Irkutsk faction' dominated the delegation to the Congress. Japan's leading anarchist, Osugi Sakai, who had earlier been attracted to the Russian Revolution, was to play a decisive role in the Comintern's efforts to win Japan's anarchists to the Communist cause.

Unlike the Second Comintern Congress, the Far East Congress was not marked by significant political debate. The conference resolutions were carried unanimously. There was, however, some friction among the nationalities. The Mongolian delegate Dendev referred to 'the reactionary, bourgeois Chinese Republic, the so-called most democratic state of the East'. According to the Chinese delegate Ma Zhanglu, among the Chinese at the congress, including the Communists, only Zhang Guotao was reconciled to the idea of Mongolian independence. The Korean Yi Chaegon said 'the Japanese working class is one of the oppressors of the Korean working masses. Although they work side by side, they look upon their Korean brother workers with contempt', prompt-

---

39   Semaun addressed Sneevliet as 'my guru' in an August 1921 letter. See International Institute of Social History, Henk Sneevliet Papers, invoice no. 207, retrieved 20 September 2014.

40   The PKH was far bigger than the Chinese, Japanese or Korean parties at this stage. Within a few years, the party had attracted a mass following and had become the most popular and influential political group in the Dutch Indies. It is not clear how many actual members, as opposed to sympathisers, the party had. Ruth McVey, estimates it had around one thousand at this time, but at the Fourth Comintern Congress in November 1922, Tan Malaka claimed the party had 13,000 members. See McVey 2006, p. xiii; see also Abbie Bakan, *Tan Malaka* (short talk), available at: http://johnriddell.wordpress.com/2012/09/25/colonial-peoples-at-the-fourth-comintern-congress/, retrieved 15 October 2014.

ing Safarov to explain that the same charge could have been made in the past against some sections of the Russian working class but it had nevertheless carried out a revolution.

Most of the delegates were young; several dozen were in their teens to mid-twenties and their youth was reflected in the radicalism of their speeches. Yoshida Hajime declared 'we must use power, force and violence. Unless we use violence not only in revolutionary times but in all the workers' struggles, nothing will be accomplished'. Another Japanese delegate, noting the gap between the February and October revolutions in Russia, thought it was important in Japan to 'bring about these two revolutions at the same time'. Ch'ae Tongsun, delegated by a Korean brigade of the Red Army, said the Korean Communists would 'never unite' with groups that 'carry out a conciliatory policy' or extend 'even a finger' to imperialism. He also claimed, fantastically, that the party had 'under its influence' seven million farm workers, 300,000 industrial workers and a similar number of fishermen.

To Irkutsk, Then Moscow

The initial plan was to hold the Far East Congress in the Siberian city of Irkutsk and to open the proceedings on the same day as the Washington Conference – Armistice Day 1921.[41] Most of the delegates from China, Korea and Japan arrived in early November, crossing the Chinese border with the Far Eastern Republic at Manzhouli and then travelling onwards by train to Irkutsk. The Mongolian delegates arrived some time later.[42] The delegations then faced a wait of several weeks amid semi-famine conditions in the bleak Irkutsk winter before, to their relief, the Comintern decided to shift the venue to the relative comfort of Moscow.

Zhang Guotao left an account of his experiences in his memoirs.[43] The main topic of conversation in Irkutsk was the food shortage. Soldiers received a daily ration of two pounds of black bread, workers received one-and-a-half pounds, and party members three-quarters of a pound. But when Zhang was invited to eat with Boris Shumyatsky, head of the Comintern's Far Eastern Bureau, he was entertained in a house furnished like that of a 'Shanghai capitalist' and was treated to white bread, soup and a main course. Zhang depicted Shumyatsky as

---

41 In fact, the Washington Conference opened on 12 November, the day after the Armistice commemorations.
42 The delegates' arrival dates were recorded in questionnaires.
43 Zhang Guotao 1966, Vol. 1, Part 4, pp. 171–209.

a prototype of the bureaucrat that would later dominate the Soviet Union. As head of the regional party, government and military, he was, Zhang said, the 'King of Siberia'.

The streets of Irkutsk were deserted apart from a brief rush hour. Most shops were shut and barter had largely replaced cash transactions. When Zhang spoke to what was left of the local Chinese business community, they complained bitterly about the policy of War Communism. But the general population was still enthusiastic about the revolution. *Subbotniki*[44] were well attended and lively. A meeting of the local Soviet attracted 800 delegates, many of them women. The chairman, who made an impressive speech, was a worker who had only recently learned to read. But according to Zhang, behind this façade, Shumyatsky was pulling the strings.

On the train to Moscow, Zhang met the Mongolian delegation, men dressed in the red robes of lamas and women in traditional costume, like a scene, as he put it patronisingly, from an ethnographic museum.[45] As they travelled west, the effects of the New Economic Policy began to show. Stations had private stalls selling food. But they also saw people begging for food. When the delegates arrived in Moscow, a crowd greeted them with the Internationale. A group of young Chinese, including Liu Shaoqi and Qu Qiubai, had been studying in Moscow for some time and spoke a little Russian, but not enough to have meaningful conversations. The delegates, Zhang said, although physically present in Moscow, were unable to get a real understanding of the country.

Trotsky's picture hung everywhere alongside Lenin's and people usually mentioned their names together. Zhang heard Trotsky address several public meetings. In those days it was still permissible for the public to ask questions. At one meeting a 17-year-old Red Army soldier asked Trotsky why, despite having been wounded five times, he was homeless and hungry. Trotsky offered words of comfort but no practical solution. Zhang was unimpressed with the Bolsheviks' style of work. They were, in his eyes, dishevelled, disorganised and wasted time in interminable meetings.[46] But he was struck by their supreme confidence that, having overthrown the Tsarist Empire, they would overcome their current difficulties.

---

44 Voluntary Saturday work.
45 The Congress credentials committee noted that the intellectuals among the Mongolian delegation included 'lamas and princes'.
46 On the other hand, Zhang praised Georgi Safarov who, he said, had no bureaucratic pretentions, but rather the air of a professor who was mildly exasperated with his Asian pupils' poor understanding of Marxism.

Diplomatic Manoeuvres

It is possible that the two-month delay in opening the Congress was due to a debate among the Soviet leadership on how to proceed. By the end of 1921, the diplomatic situation had shifted in favour of Soviet Russia. British Prime Minister Lloyd George was proposing a world conference to promote economic recovery, to which both Germany and Soviet Russia would be invited. Chicherin had offered to honour Tsarist debts, with the exception of war loans, in return for diplomatic recognition and economic assistance. On 6 January 1922, the Supreme Allied Council met in Cannes and invited Germany and Russia to a conference to be held at Genoa. In a concession to Moscow, the allies agreed that 'nations can claim no right to dictate to each other regarding the principles on which they are to regulate their system of ownership, internal economy and government'. Chicherin immediately accepted the invitation.[47]

In the midst of these diplomatic developments the Congress of the Toilers of the Far East became a sensitive issue. On 21 December 1921, Chicherin wrote to Lenin: 'The idea of the congress of the peoples of the Far East arose at a moment of extreme aggravation in relations before the Washington Conference ... Now the situation is to the contrary. It is therefore, necessary, firstly, to avoid everything that might suggest the idea of a link between our government and the congress of the peoples of the East. Secondly, it is necessary to stop any noise rising up from this congress. This is extremely untimely right now. It is necessary therefore ... to arrange its sessions behind closed doors'.[48] Chicherin's advice was not accepted; the Far East Congress took place openly,[49] but it is perhaps significant that neither Lenin nor Trotsky attended. Zinoviev was the only full Politburo member to at the congress. In an interview with the New York Times in August 1921 Chicherin had emphasised that while the Comintern leader 'Mr. Zinoviev' was head of the Petrograd Soviet, he held no post in Russia's national government.[50]

By this time, the Soviets had almost completed their victory over the Whites in the civil war. Yudenich had fled Russia after failing to seize Petrograd in October 1919. Denikin fled after his simultaneous push on Moscow was defeated. His replacement, Wrangel, evacuated the remnants of his army from the Crimea

---

47 Fink 1993, pp. 39–41.
48 A.Iu. Sidorov 1997, *Vneshniaia politika sovetskoi Rossii na Dal'nem Vostoke (1917–1922)*, (Moscow), cited in Dukes 2012, p. 61.
49 The proceedings were reported in the Soviet press and the minutes published in English, German and Russian.
50 Dukes 2012, p. 62.

the following year. The Minsk government of the 'Supreme Ruler' Admiral Kolchak fell at the end of 1919. Strikes, partisan uprisings and mass desertions led to the virtual collapse of White forces throughout Siberia and the formation in April 1920 of the Far Eastern Republic. But the situation in Russia remained critical. Millions had died in the Volga famine. Elsewhere, the Russian people survived on meagre rations. The policy of War Communism had reached a dead end but the New Economic Policy adopted in March 1921 had hardly begun to take effect. Russia desperately needed to revive its international trade and attract foreign investment and expertise to assist in reconstruction.[51]

Russia's diplomats aimed to end the economic blockade and secure the withdrawal of Japanese forces. In pursuing the latter objective the Soviets exploited the United States' hostility to Japanese expansionism, and the Far Eastern Republic's democratic institutions had a key role to play. While the delegates to the Far East Congress were assembling in Moscow to denounce imperialism, an FER trade delegation was lobbying energetically in Washington. Although refused admission to the Washington Conference, the delegation carried on an effective campaign. At a critical moment, it revealed what it claimed was a secret Franco-Japanese agreement to transport Wrangel's troops to Siberia and guarantee Japan long-term concessions in the region. The revelation embarrassed the French and added to the pressure on Japan to withdraw its forces.[52]

Chicherin was no doubt right to be concerned about the possible impact of the Congress on Russia's diplomatic efforts. The Genoa conference was still in doubt. During the Cannes conference, the conciliatory French Prime Minister Aristide Briand was ousted in a parliamentary coup by the hard-line Poincaré. And the language used at the Far East Congress was anything but diplomatic. Zinoviev said the signing of the Four-Power Treaty in Washington was 'one of the blackest dates in the history of humanity'. But, in the end, the Genoa Conference went ahead. Soviet Russia and Germany attended, and although this early attempt at *détente* failed, mainly due to France's uncompromising stance, the Soviets and Germany mitigated their isolation by signing a bilateral treaty at the nearby seaside resort of Rapallo.[53]

---

51   The Anglo-Russian Trade Agreement of March 1921 was an early step towards normalising economic ties with the capitalist world.

52   The Siberian intervention was unpopular in Japan. In the summer of 1922, Japan announced its intention to withdraw. The bulk of its forces left in October but the last troops did not leave Vladivostok until April 1923, and Japan continued to occupy northern Sakhalin until 1925.

53   With talks on the point of collapse, Chicherin and the German foreign minister Wal-

Safarov Defines the Political Line of the Congress

Safarov's report *The National-Colonial Question and the Communist Attitude thereto* was the main policy address of the congress. It was intended as an authoritative guide to Comintern strategy in colonial and semi-colonial countries, and the conditions under which communists and nationalists should cooperate.

The success of the revolution in the East, Safarov said, depended on the mobilisation of the peasant masses, without which the 'small groups of workers and bourgeois-democratic radical elements' would achieve nothing. He also stressed the importance of creating soviets, as the 'best weapons in the hands of the toilers', even in a predominantly peasant country.

Communists should work with any national revolutionary movements, so long as they were sincerely committed to the struggle against imperialism and colonialism, irrespective of ideology. Even religious sects were welcome in the 'united national front'. But Safarov insisted on the need to preserve the independence of communist parties and the labour movement.

Safarov's speech, in its essentials, reiterated the *Theses on National and Colonial Questions* agreed at the Second Comintern Congress. According to the *Theses* the world was divided into oppressed and oppressor nations. The vast majority of the world's population was enslaved by a tiny minority of capitalists. Since they faced a common enemy, the working class, the Comintern and the Soviet Union should forge a strategic alliance with nationalists in the oppressed countries. In contrast with reformists, who were infected with imperialist ideas of a *mission civilatrice* in the colonies, Communists in advanced countries were obliged to offer active and practical support to liberation movements, even if they were led by bourgeois nationalists. Communists in oppressed nations should make alliances with revolutionary nationalists, but only on a temporary basis, and should not fuse with them. They should also guard against attempts to 'put a communist cloak' on nationalist parties.

---

ter Rathenau concluded the Treaty of Rapallo by which Germany and Russia agreed to renounce all financial and territorial claims on each other. They also agreed, secretly, to allow Germany to circumvent restrictions imposed at Versailles by training troops and developing weapons on Soviet territory. Rathenau was assassinated by right-wing extremists two months later.

Dispute with the Kuomintang Delegate Zhang Qiubai

Most delegates gave more or less unqualified support to the reports of the Comintern speakers. But there were a couple of fairly pointed exchanges between Zinoviev and Safarov and the Kuomintang delegate Zhang Qiubai.

In his opening address, Zinoviev had remarked that it would be the 'saddest mistake imaginable if among the representatives of Southern China ... there could be found any simpletons who would accept the catchword of the "open door" as the pure gold of real democracy', adding that he had been informed that there were some 'among the adherents of Sun Yat-Sen, among the important workers of his Party, who, at times, are looking not unhopefully towards America'. Zhang Qiubai countered that 'the ways of the Kuomintang do not coincide with those of imperialism, and we will rather follow the Communist International'. He said his party 'maintains a decidedly unsympathetic attitude to the Washington Conference'. But Zinoviev was nearer the truth. Sun Yat-sen had written several times to President Harding, albeit without receiving a reply. He had also attempted to raise money for the Canton government on the American bond market, a move that was blocked by the State Department. The United States had been hostile to Sun since he opposed China's entry into the war.[54] But had he received an invitation to Washington it is doubtful Sun would have preferred to send a representative to the Congress of the Toilers of the East. Zinoviev's remarks, it must be said, were rather hypocritical, since the Soviets, in the form of the Far Eastern Republic trade delegation, were busy lobbying the United States' representatives at the Washington Conference as he spoke.[55]

With both Chinese and Mongolian delegates at the congress, the issue of Mongolia, which Republican China had attempted to reconquer in 1919, was sensitive. When Zinoviev raised the Mongolian issue, he suggested that some leaders of the Kuomintang had raised the question of returning Mongolia to Chinese rule. Zhang Qiubai countered that he had 'never heard of such a thing'. Again Zinoviev was correct. Sun Yat-sen had initially focused on overthrowing the 'alien' Qing Dynasty and showed little interest in China's border territories. But he later adopted the new Republican vision of China as the union of five great peoples – Han, Manchu, Mongolian, Tibetan and Hui (Muslims), along with its implication that the Chinese Republic should inherit the entire

---

54 Bergère 1994, p. 300.
55 See Libbey 1977, p. 92.

territory of the Qing Empire. His 1920 book *The International Development of China* called for 'colonisation in Manchuria, Mongolia, Sinkiang, Kokonor and Thibet'.[56]

But the Soviet position on Mongolia was not clear-cut. Zinoviev had chosen his words carefully. He opposed Mongolia being *'immediately* given back to China'. Trotsky's close friend, the senior foreign ministry official Adolph Joffe, who later negotiated the Soviet-Kuomintang alliance with Sun Yat-sen, thought Soviet support for Mongolian independence was a serious mistake that would damage the cause of world revolution. Calling it a 'new edition of the Tsarist policy', he added 'it is not worthwhile, for the sake of two million Mongols who do not have any role to play in the world, to damage our entire policy and relationship with four hundred million Chinese who are having such a huge impact'.[57] The international status of Mongolia remained a sensitive issue in Sino-Soviet relations for decades. When Soviet Russia signed an agreement recognising Mongolia in November 1921, it was careful not to give the document the status of a treaty. In 1924, in return for recognition by the Beijing government, the Soviet Union acknowledged Chinese sovereignty over Outer Mongolia, albeit secure in the knowledge that the Chinese could not assert control. The Republic of China finally recognised Mongolian independence in the Sino-Soviet Treaty of 1945, but later repudiated the treaty. The People's Republic of China recognised Mongolia and established diplomatic relations in 1949 but the Republic of China government in Taiwan, which held China's Security Council seat until 1971, blocked Mongolian membership of the United Nations until the early 1960s.

Zhang Qiubai, answering Safarov's report, appeared to claim that the Kuomintang was a communist party in all but name. The Comintern's programme on taxation and land reform, he said, had been Kuomintang policy for twenty years, and the Kuomintang proposed a form of government that was, in its essentials, the same as the soviet system. The logic of his position was that there was no need for a separate Communist Party in China. Safarov was faced with what became a recurring Soviet dilemma of how to manage the relationship between communists and nationalists in China. He could scarcely agree with Zhang without denying the need for the Communist Party the Comintern had created the year before. He acknowledged the 'great revolutionary work' done by the Kuomintang and reaffirmed the Comintern's willingness to work side by side with it, but said it would be naïve to characterise it as a proletarian party. As

---

56   That is, Manchuria, Mongolia, Xinjiang, Qinghai and Tibet. See Sun Yat-sen 1920, p. iv.
57   See Joffe's telegrams quoted in Liu 2006, p. 60.

evidence, he pointed out that while the Kuomintang had a land reform policy on paper, it had not implemented it in the areas it controlled. In order for communists and nationalists to work together effectively, he said, it was necessary for both sides to understand each other.

Some accounts of the Congress see Zhang Qiubai's interventions as so embarrassing to the platform that 'a veritable storm broke around the head of the Kuomintang delegate'.[58] This seems to be an exaggeration, even if Zinoviev's remarks, in particular, were tactless. Zhang was, according to several accounts, a rather unimpressive figure. When asked to sing a revolutionary song at a reception in Irkutsk, he embarrassed his colleagues by performing a risqué ditty called 'Little sister plays dominoes'. Peng Shuzhi recalled that at the congress he 'fidgeted a lot and drew attention to himself but said nothing of interest'.[59] Nevertheless, as the representative of the Kuomintang he was elected to the congress presidium, appointed to the six-person committee charged with drafting the congress manifesto and taken to meet Lenin in the Kremlin. And whatever he reported to Sun Yat-sen on his return did not deter Sun from concluding an alliance with the Soviets the following year.

Women Delegates and Women's Rights

In her address to the closing ceremony of the Far East Congress, Klavdia Nikolaeva, editor of the Russian newspaper *Woman Worker*, pointedly remarked that only seven of the nearly 150 delegates were women.[60]

While women's rights were not a central concern of the congress, several delegates took up the theme. The Chinese trade unionist Deng Pei denounced the exploitation of female labour in China. In a meeting of the trade union caucus, Solomon Lozovsky, head of the Red International of Trades Unions, condemned reactionary trade unions that excluded women workers. 'While we say that women must work in industry the union lays down yet another slogan: equal pay for equal work. Whether it be a woman or a man, a wife or a black worker – it matters not: the pay for the same work must be the same

---

58   Whiting 1954, p. 83. See also Saich 1991, pp. 94–6.
59   Cadart and Yingxiang 1983, p. 296.
60   Four of the seven were from Korea, one was from China and two were in the joint Mongolian-Buryat delegation. It was perhaps indicative of the period that the congress credentials committee, while classifying delegates by age, occupation and educational background, did not report the number of women who attended. The delegate questionnaire forms had no box to record gender. The congress did, however, set up a women's caucus.

... [A]s soon as you base your activities on the just principle of equal pay for equal work ... it is not only the duty of justice that you are fulfilling, but also the chief conditions necessary for uniting and conquering the forces of the working class'.[61]

Katayama Sen prepared a report on 'Women's industrial condition in the Far East countries' at the request of Alexandra Kollontai. Women made up approximately half of Japan's industrial workforce and predominated in the textile industry where, Katayama wrote they were 'the most ill-treated and cruelly exploited workers in the country'. They began work 'usually very young say 13 or 14, often younger, and [are] placed in a spinning factory's dormitory ... and locked there to be exploited 12 hour per day or night'. Katayama also described how the rice riots of 1918, were started 'by fishermen's wives and daughters', and how, during the Ashio Copper mine strike, 'the wives and daughters of the striking miners made most effective demonstrations ... that made the deepest impressions on ... the wider public'. His report did not only touch on class issues. He described the enforced idleness of educated, middle class women as 'the most grave problem among women today'.[62]

Three of the seven women delegates spoke at the Congress. Kwon Aera of the Korean delegation said that the 'emancipation of the peoples of the Far East does not consist in the emancipation of the men only, but also of the women', and called for separate women's sections to be set up within the revolutionary movement. Her Korean colleague Kim Won'gyŏng emphasised the contribution women were making to the anti-Japanese struggle and claimed, somewhat improbably, that Korean women had 'long since shaken off oriental traditions which confined them to the hearth'.

The most prominent of the women speakers was the Chinese feminist Huang (Wong) Bihun, who was introduced warmly by Zinoviev as 'the famous Chinese authoress, the organiser of the women's movement in China, and member of the Canton Parliament, our comrade Wong'. Huang spoke about the subordinate position of women in China and the 'terrible oppression they suffer at the hands of men'. Confucian values, internalised by women over countless generations, prescribed 'three subjections', to father, husband, and eldest son, and 'four virtues' of home-keeping, modest speech, elegant dress, and skill at handicrafts. The Confucian cult 'completely subdued women's psychology'. Furthermore, women could not inherit property and were therefore entirely dependent upon men. Polygamy was still widespread, and upper-class

---

61   Russian State Archive of Socio-Political History, 495.154.169.
62   Katayama's report is in the Russian State Archive of Socio-Political History, 495.154.175.

women – Huang called them 'aristocratic' – faced the threat of being supplanted by second wives and concubines.

Huang was speaking from her own experience. The daughter of a businessman, she was married off to a manager in the family firm, but after her husband and father died in quick succession, her father-in-law stole her inheritance. When her in-laws began mistreating her she fled the household, leaving behind her two young sons. After working in Britain and Japan, Huang returned to Shanghai, where she defied convention by marrying a much younger man. She joined the group of activists around the magazine *New Youth* edited by Chen Duxiu. When Chen Duxiu was invited to take charge of the Canton education department by the left-leaning warlord Chen Jiongming, he offered Huang a job. In Canton, Huang established the Guangdong Women's Federation and set up reading rooms and training classes for working women. She played a leading role in a campaign for women's suffrage, during which she was beaten up by reactionary deputies of the southern government's legislative assembly.

Huang told the congress: 'When the call of Communism reached us in China, we, the oppressed women, received it as a sinking ship greets the sound of the siren of another vessel which is hastening to its rescue'. Since feminist ideas were largely confined to a few members of the Chinese upper classes, Huang wanted to establish a 'cadre of women propagandists' to campaign among proletarian women.

But when she returned to Canton, Huang Bihun became a victim of the factional politics of the southern government. In the summer of 1922, Chen Jiongming launched a coup against Sun Yat-sen. Chen was in favour of a federal China and therefore opposed Sun Yat-sen's plan for a northern expedition to reunify the country by force. Sun fled to Shanghai, but returned to power in Canton in February 1923. Shortly afterwards, Huang, who was a supporter of Chen Jiongming, was accused of plotting to assassinate Sun and executed. According to a relative who managed to visit her in prison, Huang blamed the Canton police chief, Wu Tiecheng for framing her. But a Soviet advisor to the Kuomintang later wrote that Sun Yat-sen had ordered her to be shot.[63]

63   See Xie Yanzhang, *Zhiliyu funu jiefang yundong de Huang Bihun* (*Huang Bihun, who devoted herself to the women's liberation movement*), available at: http://www.gzzxws.gov.cn/gzws/gzws/ml/46/200809/t20080917_8580.htm, retrieved 22 January 2014. See also Samuil Naumovich Naumov, *A Brief History of the Chinese Communist Party*, reproduced in Wilbur and How 1989, p. 456; Naumov, an advisor to the Huangpu (Whampoa) Military Academy, was contemptuous of Huang, saying she had 'behaved badly' while at the Far East Congress by asking Alexandra Kollontai for money. Wu Tiecheng was an old comrade of Sun Yat-sen from Sun's native place, but Sun's exact involvement is not clear. Whether Huang Bihun was involved in a plot against Sun is also questionable. She may well have been killed

Results and Legacy of the Congress

The ideas Zinoviev and Safarov expressed on the platform of the Far East Congress were undoubtedly influential: The Comintern, they said, was committed to world revolution of which the 'European revolution is only a fraction, a little corner on the map'. The revolution's main fighting forces would be peasants, without whom 'small groups of workers and bourgeois-democratic radical elements will not be able to do anything'. As Zinoviev put it, 'part of the European working class is being corrupted and bribed by imperialism' but

> the great masses, notably the four hundred million population of China, cannot be bought ... [T]hese, and many other hundreds of millions of the inhabitants of the countries of the Far East ... represent the main force that will overthrow imperialism. The better elements of the European workers have paved the way ... but the masses of infantry which will finally destroy imperialism, are you, the oppressed nations of the Far East.

It is interesting to compare Zinoviev's speech with Lin Biao's 1965 formulation of the doctrine of people's war:

> Taking the entire globe, if North America and Western Europe can be called 'the cities of the world', then Asia, Africa and Latin America constitute 'the rural areas of the world'. Since World War II, the proletarian revolutionary movement has for various reasons been temporarily held back in the North American and West European capitalist countries, while the people's revolutionary movement in Asia, Africa and Latin America has been growing vigorously. In a sense, the contemporary world revolution also presents a picture of the encirclement of cities by the rural areas.[64]

Lin's aim was to laud Mao Zedong as a great theoretical innovator. But Mao's views on the role of the peasants were anticipated at the Far East Congress. Zinoviev and Safarov were, in turn, drawing on Lenin's theory of imperialism

---

because of her political association with Chen Jiongming. The local branch of the Communist Party also supported Chen Jiongming – a decision the party leader Chen Duxiu characterised as a 'serious mistake'. See Pantsov 2013, p. 58. Peng Shuzhi accepted the story of Huang's attempted assassination of Sun. See Cadart and Yingxiang 1983, p. 296.

64   Lin Biao, *Long Live the Victory of People's War*, available at: https://www.marxists.org/reference/archive/lin-biao/1965/09/peoples_war/ch07.htm, retrieved 20 June 2015.

and adapting and extending his strategic view of the Russian revolution; that the working class should ally with the peasantry, rather than with the liberal bourgeoisie, as prescribed by Plekhanov.[65]

It could be argued that the consequences of the Far East Congress, and the Comintern's turn east, are still being played out in the rise of China to great power status under the rule of the Chinese Communist Party. But the Chinese Communists under Mao, and Communist parties in Southeast Asia, did not achieve major breakthroughs until after World War Two, decades after the Far East Congress, and after the Comintern had been disbanded. While recognising the echoes of the congress in the ideology of Maoism, its variants and successors, the following survey focuses on the fortunes of the parties that attended the Far East Congress during the interwar years, and especially in the decade following the congress, as they implemented or often, as we shall see, deviated from its political line.

Repression and Sectarianism in Japan

The Comintern made repeated attempts to launch a communist party in Japan during the interwar years but was frustrated by waves of arrests that broke up each embryo party within a short time. The first attempt was made in August 1921 when Takase Kyoshi and Kondo Eizo set up the Enlightened People's Communist Party using a Comintern donation of 6,500 yen. This tiny group of radical students distributed anti-militarist leaflets to soldiers and was immediately rounded up by the police, along with a Comintern agent who had arrived with additional funds.

When Takase and his fellow delegate, Tokuda Kyuichi returned to Japan from the Far East Congress they persuaded two older radicals, Takase's father-in-law Sakai Toshihiko, and the former anarchist Yamakawa Hitoshi, to form a new party. The Japanese Communist Party was officially launched at a meeting in Takase's house on 15 July 1922. Sakai was named party chairman. But on 5 June 1923, the entire party was arrested after the police found a membership list.

In September 1923, rightists within the state apparatus took advantage of the great Kanto earthquake to dispose of many radicals. Japan's leading anarchist, Osugi Sakae, was murdered along with his partner Ito Noe and his six-year-old

---

65 Mao's tactical originality was not his orientation towards the peasantry but his conclusion that only an armed party could survive KMT repression. Hence the creation of 'Soviet' bases in remote areas out of reach of the Nationalist army. On how innovative Mao was, see also Wittfogel 1960.

nephew. Vigilante groups went on the rampage against immigrants and their descendants; around six thousand Koreans and several hundred Chinese were killed. In the climate of reaction Yamakawa and Sakai decided, in March 1924, to dissolve the party. Yamakawa had been reluctant to launch the party in 1922 and believed the communists should work towards the creation of a broad-based, legal workers' party.

The Comintern ordered its agent in Shanghai Grigory Voitinsky to reconstitute the party. He managed to do so in December 1926, just over a year before Japan held its first national elections under manhood suffrage.[66] The Left conducted a vigorous election campaign and won seven parliamentary seats. One Communist was elected on the ticket of the Labour-Farmer Party. But the police had used the elections to gather intelligence and within weeks most of the Communists were jailed. In November 1928, another Communist organisation was set up in Tokyo, but in March 1929 the police found another party list and arrested the membership. In July 1930 and again in the autumn of 1932, further attempts to establish a party were frustrated by arrests.

It was not only repression that explained the weakness of the Communist Party. Having initially tried to win over the anarchists, the Comintern failed to convince their leader, Osugi Sakae. Osugi had initially been attracted to the Russian revolution. He had met with Chen Duxiu and Yŏ Unhyŏng in Shanghai, and had accepted Comintern funds to support his journal *Rodo Undo*. But he became disillusioned with the Bolsheviks after the Kronstadt uprising and the adoption of the New Economic Policy and declined an invitation to attend the Far East Congress.[67] In 1922 the split became definitive when Osugi led an anarchist walkout from a trade union conference in Osaka, calling the Communist leaders 'a bunch of crooks'.[68]

As well as failing to win over the anarchists, the party limited its appeal to reformist workers by failing to take a clear position on the movement for universal suffrage.[69] At the Far East Congress, Safarov said the task of the Japanese working class was to lead the 'petty-bourgeois, semi-proletarian masses' in the 'common revolutionary struggle for a completely democratic political

---

66   The election of February 1928 was the first since all men over 25 were given votes. The electorate had grown from three million to 13 million. Women did not get the vote until after the war.
67   Osugi said he was invited to attend the congress but declined. See Beckmann and Okubo 1969, p. 40.
68   Stanley 1982, pp. 79, 134, 138–40.
69   Yamakawa for some time continued to advocate a boycott of elections. See Beckmann and Okubo 1969, p. 66.

regime'.⁷⁰ But far from rallying broad support around a democratic programme, by the mid-1920s the Japanese Communists had retreated into the pursuit of theoretical purity under the leadership of the Fukumoto Kazuo. In the broader labour movement the activities of the Communists were often destructive. In May 1925, they engineered a split in the already weak Japan Federation of Labour (Nihon Rodo Sodomei) taking half of its 30,000 members into the left-wing breakaway the Japan Labour Union Council (Nihon Rodo Hyogikai). In July 1927, the Comintern deposed Fukumoto and appointed a new central committee. But the reorganisation did not save the party. By the mid-1930s Communist activity had been extinguished in Japan. In the interwar years, party membership had never reached one thousand.

Purges and Forced Collectivisation in Mongolia

In his address to the Congress, the Mongolian delegate Dendev said the Mongolian People's Party was 'by its programme neither Communistic nor socialistic'. The Comintern speaker Safarov added later that 'as long as the basic economy of Mongolia is cattle raising distinguished by patriarchal tribal features, to preach Communism and the proletarian revolution in Mongolia is ridiculous'. But just a few years later a full-scale leftist campaign was in progress. In 1928, alongside Stalin's collectivisation drive in the Soviet Union, herders were forced into collectives with disastrous results. Dendev had earlier fallen victim to faction fighting within the MPP which was intense from the outset. More than a decade before Stalin began to liquidate his rivals in the leadership of the Soviet party, the Mongolian leadership turned on itself in the first of a series of bloody purges. Six months after the Far East Congress, Dendev was shot on the orders the finance minister, Soliin Danzan,⁷¹ along with Danzan's personal rival, the

---

70 Trotsky defended a similar position at the Third Congress of the Comintern where he described Japan as a state where 'capitalist oppression blends with a feudal-caste, bureaucratic absolutism'. See 'Theses on the World Situation and the Tasks of the Comintern', in Trotsky, Wright and Campbell 1973, *First Five Years of the Communist International*, also available at: http://www.marxists.org/archive/trotsky/1924/ffyci-1/ch21.htm, retrieved 1 June 2014.

71 Soliin Danzan, not to be confused with Ajvaagiyn 'Japanese' Danzan, was the effective leader of Mongolia from 1922 until he was executed in 1924. He was born to an unmarried mother, raised in a monastery, and was a horse thief before finding a job in the Finance Ministry. When China reoccupied Mongolia in 1919, he formed the East Urga group, which merged with Bodoo's Consular Hill group to form the Mongolian People's Party. When Mongolia's new government was formed in 1921, Danzan became Finance Minister and

former Prime Minister Dogsomyn Bodoo.[72] Danzan was in turn ousted and executed in 1924, accused of profiteering. Among the evidence against him was his Harley Davidson motorcycle, a gift from an American businessman.

Warring Factions of Korean Communism

Conditions were extraordinarily favourable for the Comintern's revolutionary work among Korean nationalists. There were hundreds of thousands of Koreans in Siberia and sizable Korean communities in Moscow and other parts of European Russia. An earlier generation of economic migrants had been supplemented by political refugees from the Righteous Army rebellion and the uprising of March 1919. Dozens of anti-Japanese organisations, many of them armed militias, sprang up both in Russia and in the even larger Korean diaspora in Manchuria. With tens of thousands of Japanese intervention troops on Russian territory, allied with the Whites, the Soviets and the Koreans were natural allies. Thousands of Korean fighters enlisted in the Red Army, and independent militias were given training and weapons. The Koreans sent the largest, best organised and most representative delegation to the Far East Congress.

But despite these advantages, far from building a workable alliance between nationalists and communists, the Comintern was unable even to put together a viable Korean Communist Party. This was as much due to extreme factionalism as it was to the severe repression carried out by the Japanese. The Finnish Comintern official Otto Kuusinen, who was tasked with uniting the warring factions, wrote later: 'Over the years ... factional disputes have taken place in many Parties. There are parties which have achieved a certain amount of notoriety in this respect such as the American and Polish Parties, but the Korean factions hold the record'.[73]

The first step towards creating a Korean communist party was taken in June 1918 by the former army officer and Righteous Army insurgent, Yi Tong-hwi, who organised a Korean Socialist Party in Khabarovsk along with Alexandra

---

Bodoo Prime Minister. In August 1922, Danzan executed Bodoo and 14 of his supporters, including Dendev. Bodoo had been blamed, probably unjustly, for an ultra-left campaign to eliminate 'feudal forms of dress'. When Sükhebaatur died in 1923, Danzan replaced him as commander-in-chief of the army. In August 1924, during the Third Party Congress, Danzan was ousted by his former ally Rinchino and shot without trial.

72   See Batbayar and Kaplonski 1999, p. 233. Dendev's mandate to the congress is in the Russian State Archive of Socio-Political History 495.154.177.
73   Quoted in Martin 2013, p. 731.

Kim[74] and Pak Chin-sun. Pak, who was also known as Pak Din-shun, attended the Second Comintern Congress, was elected to the ECCI and became a semi-official Soviet spokesman on Korean affairs. The respected veteran Yi was named prime minister of the Shanghai-based Korean Provisional Government the following year.

The Provisional Government seemed to represent the sort of communist-nationalist co-operation advocated by the Second Comintern Congress, and Moscow donated a large sum to the government, to be delivered via Yi and his associates. But coexistence between the prime minister and the right-wing President Syngman Rhee proved impossible. Yi's strategy was to liberate Korea through armed struggle but Rhee placed his faith in diplomatic initiatives aimed at the democratic powers, principally the United States. Rhee's manoeuvres exasperated more radical nationalists. The last straw for many was a petition to Woodrow Wilson to have Korea placed under a League of Nations mandate. Yi, along with several other ministers, including Kim Kyu-sik, resigned from the government in May 1921.

Shortly afterwards, Yi and Pak Chin-sun diverted money Moscow had donated to the Provisional Government and re-launched their party as the Korean Communist Party. But simultaneously, in Irkutsk, a conference sponsored by Boris Shumyatsky launched another Korean Communist Party, made up largely of Korean members of the Russian Communist Party. The rival parties were known as the Shanghai faction and the Irkutsk faction[75] – slightly misleadingly, since not all Korean Communists in Shanghai supported Yi Tong-hwi. Yŏ Unhyŏng, for example, although based in Shanghai, was aligned with the Irkutsk faction.

In civil war conditions, where both sides had armed wings, the factional dispute rapidly escalated into violence. In June 1921, a bloody confrontation took place. Korean guerrillas retreating from a Japanese offensive had gathered in the Siberian garrison town of Alekseyevsk, where they had been promised training and supplies. But efforts by the Soviets to unite the guerrilla groups under a single command led to the so-called Free City Incident. Suspecting that the unified command would put them under the control of the Irkutsk group, Yi's Greater Korean Independence Corps resisted and battled with the

---

74 Alexandra Kim (1885–1918) is usually recognised as the first Korean Communist. She was born in Siberia to Korean parents. Her father fought against the Japanese in Manchuria. She joined the Bolsheviks in 1916 and was tasked with winning over Korean émigré community in Russia. She was captured and executed by White forces in September 1918.

75 Or the Shanghai Korean Communist Party (Sanghaep'a koryŏ kongsandang) and the Irkutsk Korean Communist Party (Irŭk'uch'ŭk'ŭp'a koryŏ kongsandang).

Irkutsk faction's Korean Revolutionary Military Congress. The latter, backed by Red Army troops prevailed. According to some accounts, hundreds of Koreans were killed or wounded.

The Comintern condemned both factions for the conflict. By the time the Korean delegation arrived in Irkutsk for the Far East Congress, Moscow had begun taking steps to resolve the dispute. Yi Tong-hwi and his Shanghai faction colleague Hong Do were sent to Irkutsk with instructions to unify the warring factions. Yi convened a joint meeting of a provisional central committee of the Korean Communist Party with the Korean delegation. According to Kim Kyu-sik, who was the chairman of the Korean delegation, Yi agreed to convene a broadly-based national congress, to be organised by the 'five main constituencies of the Korean revolutionary movement' – the delegation to the Far East Congress, the Korean Communist Party, the Organizing Committee in Shanghai, the Provisional Government, and the Korean National Council in Siberia.[76]

When the Korean delegation left for Moscow, Yi Tong-hwi remained in Irkutsk, supposedly to begin organising the national congress.[77] But, according to Kim Kyu-sik, instead of working towards a broad-based assembly, Yi decided that the 'congress should be convened by the Korean Communist Party alone' and sent an agent to Shanghai with a large sum of money to assemble a congress of some sort. In a letter to the Comintern, Kim charged that Yi was 'vainly hoping that he will become the head of a new government', and said that 'if the Korcom Ceco[78] convenes a congress alone ... the so-called national congress will be an insignificant affair and an absolute farce'. Yi, Kim said, had embezzled Soviet money donated to the Korean Provisional Government, and squandered it 'right and left together with Kim Rip, Pak Dzin-shun [Pak Chin-sun] and others to increase [his] staying power'.[79] Although Yi was considered a veteran leader by Moscow, he was only 'one of many leaders, and a very insignificant one at that'.

Kim and three other members of the Korean delegation remained in Moscow after the Far East Congress hoping to secure Soviet financial and military aid for the 'directing force' they hoped would issue from the Korean national congress. But Comintern efforts were focused on reconciling the Shanghai and Irkutsk factions within the Communist Party. Kuusinen organised a unity con-

---

76   See the Russian State Archive of Socio-Political History 495.154.175.
77   Some earlier accounts said that Yi Tong-hwi was a delegate to the Far East Congress and also that he had avoided going to Irkutsk for fear of being executed by Shumyatsky. See for example, Scalapino and Lee 1961, p. 155.
78   I.e. the Central Committee of the Korean Communist Party.
79   Kim Rip was assassinated in 1923, supposedly for misappropriating the Soviet funds.

gress in Verkhne Udinsk (now Ulan Ude) in October 1922 but failed to bring the two sides together. Kim's letter to the Comintern, written in April, expresses frustration at having waited 'nearly two months' and adds that 'it is not possible for us to spend too long a time here. Affairs in Korea and China among our revolutionary elements and undertakings may take such a turn … that we may find difficulty in making proper adjustments'. Kim was also clearly irritated that the People's Commissariat for Foreign Affairs had refused to deal with the delegation on the grounds that it did not represent a government.[80]

A fairly common perception is that the Shanghai faction was made up of nationalists who had only a thin coating of socialism, while the Irkutsk faction was supported by Russianised Koreans who were more or less indistinguishable from the Bolsheviks.[81] But Kim Kyu-sik, who was not a Communist but, in Soviet terms, an archetypal bourgeois-nationalist, was firmly allied with the Irkutsk camp. The moderate communist Yŏ Unhyŏng was also aligned with Irkutsk. Pak Chin-sun, by contrast, had made a radical speech to the Second Comintern Congress, declaring that 'the national liberation movement' was 'not only directed against Japanese imperialism but also against their own bourgeoisie'.[82] It is probable that the split between the two sides was as much a matter of personal loyalties as political differences. Yi soon lost his leadership position and worked for International Red Aid in Vladivostok until his death in 1935. Pak Chin-sun, whom Kim described as 'utterly ignorant of the Korean revolutionary movement and its history', seems to have played no further role in the movement. He was executed during the Great Purges.

After the withdrawal of Japanese troops from Siberia, Moscow's priorities changed. It was no longer in Russia's interests to support military operations that risked provoking Japan and would delay the return of Northern Sakhalin. Comintern emphasis shifted from supporting insurgents among the émigré community to organising a party inside Korea.[83] In the summer of 1923 a secret bureau and a legal front organisation, the Tuesday Society, were set up in Seoul by Kim Chaebong, Rim Wŏn-gŭn and Kim Tanya, all of whom had been delegates to the Far East Congress. On 17 April 1925, the first Korean Communist

---

80 Letter to the Executive Committee III Communist International, 5 April 1922, Russian State Archive of Socio-Political History 495.154.175.
81 See, for example, Kim 2005, p. 133.
82 Minutes of the Second Comintern Congress, Fifth Session, 28 July 1920, available at: https://www.marxists.org/history/international/comintern/2nd-congress/ch05.htm, retrieved 24 May 2015.
83 To avoid disputes with Japan, the Soviets deported some militants, and were accused of betrayal by both communists and nationalist.

Party to be officially recognised by the Comintern was established at a meeting in a Chinese restaurant. Kim Chaebong, a member of the Irkutsk faction, was elected general secretary. The executive committee included another Far East Congress delegate, Cho Tongho, also from the Irkutsk faction, and Yi Tonghwi's associate from the Shanghai faction Pak Hŏnyŏng.[84] But the Comintern's attempt to develop a party in Korea fared no better than its efforts in Japan. In November 1925 the police rounded up the party after discovering a list of names in the apartment of a youth league supporter they had fortuitously arrested over a drunken brawl. Attempts to revive the party over the next few years failed.

The Indonesian Putsch of 1926–27

When Semaun returned to Indonesia from the Far East Congress in May 1922, his successor as PKH chairman, Tan Malaka, one of the great leaders of the Indonesian movement, had already been deported after a strike by shop workers. In January 1923, the colonial government imposed wage cuts on railway workers. The rank and file demanded action and Semaun, who was the rail union leader, authorised a strike despite misgivings about its outcome. Before any action was taken, Semaun was interned – a move that was perhaps calculated by the government to provoke the walkout that followed. The strikers were dismissed, the railways put under military control and Semaun was deported. He returned to Russia and remained there for most of the next 30 years.[85]

On the political front, developments were more favourable to the party. The Sarekat Islam leader, Tjokroaminoto, decided to break with the Communists and Red Sarekat Islam. In February 1923, he forced through rule changes that made a split inevitable. But it was Tjokroaminoto's organisation that suffered. His 'White' Sarekat Islam quickly lost influence while Red Sarekat Islam, re-launched as Sarekat Rakjat (Union of the People), grew rapidly. By 1924, Sarekat Rakjat was indisputably the leading force in the anti-colonial movement. At the Fifth Comintern Congress, held that summer, the Indonesian party, now renamed the Partai Komunis Indonesia (PKI), was singled out for praise.

But within months, the PKI decided to downgrade its work in the nationalist movement in order to concentrate its efforts on the proletariat on the railways,

---

84　Scalapino and Lee 1972, pp. 52, 58–9. Pak Hŏnyŏng was executed in 1956 by Korea's mini-Stalin Kim Il-Sung.

85　Semaun eventually returned to Indonesia after independence. He worked as a government official and university teacher. He died in 1971.

mines and docks. Sarekat Rakjat was to be wound up and its local organisations turned into party branches. Semaun, now on the ECCI, urged the party to reconsider. But the leadership seemed determined to pursue what Semaun saw as an ultra-left course. Following the Fifth Enlarged Plenum of the ECCI in March–April 1925, Semaun wrote to the PKI urging it to revive Sarekat Rakjat and to renew relations with Sarekat Islam. The Comintern instructed the PKI Central Committee to form a bloc of all anti-imperialist parties. But the response of one of the PKI leaders was that 'a spirit of slackening, retrogression and dissension is prevailing in Moscow'.[86]

Labour unrest grew in the second half of 1925 and the authorities stepped up repression. The PKI response was to go underground and prepare an insurrection. In December 1925, at a conference in Prambanan, the party chairman Sardjono proposed working towards a general strike within six months. If successful, the strike would be followed by an insurrection. Tan Malaka, from exile in Manila, warned the party that it was planning a putsch not a revolution. The PKI could survive the current repression, he said, but if it attempted a premature revolt it would be destroyed. He called a conference in Singapore to readjust strategy. But when he arrived in Singapore two party leaders, Musso and Alimin, had already left for the Moscow to seek approval and material aid for the insurrection.[87]

In May 1926, to escape the government crackdown, the party moved its central headquarters to Bandung. Tan Malaka eventually persuaded the central committee to delay the planned revolt. But events were now out of control. The Bandung leadership was scarcely able to communicate with the party branches, some of which were, in any case, in no mood to listen. In the capital, Batavia,[88] and a number of smaller cities on Java's northern coast, party branches were determined to press ahead. The Batavia branch leader, Sukrawinata, established a revolutionary committee and set 12 November as the date for the uprising. He persuaded reluctant railway workers' leaders to call a general strike the following day – a sequence of events exactly opposite to that agreed at Prambanan.

The colonial police were aware of the plans and began arresting party leaders. The action in Batavia was defeated in hours. There was a scarcely more

---

86   McVey 2006, p. 289.
87   Musso and Alimin received neither approval nor aid for the planned insurrection. They remained in Moscow until October 1926 and did not return in time for the uprising. But when Stalin turned left, after the collapse of the alliance with the Kuomintang, they found themselves lionized as heroes by the Comintern.
88   Modern-day Jakarta.

serious effort in Banten (Bantam). Semarang, the former heart of party support, remained quiet during the revolt. Because of disagreements over the date among branch leaders, the uprising in Sumatra did not begin until 1 January 1927. Although the fighting was heavier than in Java, the rebels were defeated within days. In the aftermath, the Dutch authorities arrested 13,000 communist sympathisers. Some were executed, 4,500 were imprisoned and 1,308 were exiled to New Guinea. The party was destroyed. There was no further significant Communist activity in Indonesia until the end of Dutch rule.[89]

The First United Front: China's Failed Revolution of 1925–27

China was the main crucible in which the united front with nationalists was tested. But Comintern resolutions calling for communist parties to maintain their independence and enter into only temporary and conditional alliances with nationalists were comprehensively ignored. The Chinese Communists submerged themselves in the Kuomintang to the extent that their independent identity was almost completely effaced. The alliance with the nationalists was 'temporary' only insofar as it was eventually broken by Chiang Kai-shek, when he launched a white terror against the Communists and the labour movement.

To understand why the Comintern flouted its own decisions, we need to look at events elsewhere. While the Far East Congress was taking place in Moscow, Henk Sneevliet was meeting with Sun Yat-sen in Guilin. Hong Kong and Canton seafarers had just begun a major strike that ended in a big victory. Sneevliet was impressed by the links between the workers' movement and the nationalists. Although he had misgivings about Sun's militarist background, he decided the Kuomintang was a suitable host organisation within which he could repeat his 'bloc within' tactic.[90] And because of his success in the Dutch Indies, Sneevliet's views carried weight in the Comintern and with the Soviet government.

After Zhang Guotao returned from the Congress of the Toilers of the Far East, the Chinese Communist Party approved the idea of a united front with the Kuomintang and 'other revolutionary parties' at its Second Congress in July 1922. But in line with Comintern policy, the alliance was envisaged as a partnership of equals, and the party emphasised its intention to pursue independent

---

89   McVey 2006, p. 353.
90   Saich 1991, pp. 74–5, 78–81. Sneevliet had no illusions about Sun Yat-sen. He described Sun as one of three 'super warlords' (supper tuchun), along with Wu Peifu and Zhang Zuolin. See his *Notes on the existing parties in China*, in Henk Sneevliet Papers, invoice no. 214.

activities focused on the labour movement.⁹¹ Chen Duxiu later said that the positions adopted were explicitly based on the resolutions agreed at the Congress of the Toilers of the Far East.⁹² But in August, the congress decisions were overturned. Sneevliet, accompanied by Joffe, returned to China in July, carrying a Comintern mandate instructing the Chinese Communist Party to carry out 'all its work in close contact' with him. He convened an extraordinary plenum of the Central Committee in Hangzhou and forced through a resolution instructing party members to join the Kuomintang as individuals and downgrade independent party work.⁹³ Zhang Guotao opposed the new policy. In November, Chen Duxiu reiterated the orthodox line that 'if the Kuomintang party allied itself with reactionary and dark forces ... we must ruthlessly oppose it ... [We] must always show our true face to the masses [and] maintain our complete independence'.⁹⁴ Sneevliet brushed these objections aside. He had a low opinion of the leadership and would later say that the party 'was born too early (1920) or, better said, fabricated' and 'was supported too strongly by foreign means'.⁹⁵

The People's Commissariat for Foreign Affairs had, meanwhile, been searching for allies among the players in China's confusing political scene. As we have seen, one candidate was Wu Peifu, the power behind the throne in Beijing. To help win Wu over, the Communist Party ensured that railway workers on the Beijing-Hankou line gave crucial assistance to Wu in his 1922 conflict with the Manchurian warlord Zhang Zuolin. But Wu repaid the favour by shooting down the same workers when they went on strike in February 1923.⁹⁶ The other main candidate was Sun Yat-sen. The Soviets had hoped to persuade Sun and Wu to form a national unity government friendly to Russia. This plan failed because Sun was allied with Wu's enemy Zhang Zuolin. But Sun, who was in a weakened position after being ousted from Canton by Chen Jiongming, agreed to an alliance with the Soviet Union. In the Sun-Joffe Manifesto of 26 January 1923 the Soviet Union promised to assist Sun in his reunifying China, reaffirmed

---

91   See Tony Saich, *The Chinese Communist Party during the era of the Comintern (1919–1943)*, available at: http://www.hks.harvard.edu/fs/asaich/chinese-communisty-party-during-comintern.pdf, retrieved 13 July 2014.
92   Wilbur and How 1989, p. 46.
93   Sneevliet believed the publication of the party paper *Guide Weekly* provided enough independence.
94   Chen Duxiu, *The Immediate Tactics of the Communist Party of China*, in Henk Sneevliet Papers, invoice no. 271.
95   Letter to Zinoviev, Bukharin, Radek and Safarov, 20 June 1923, Sneevliet Archive No. 231, Document 0.9. Cited in Saich 1991, p. 99.
96   Saich 1991, pp. 122–3. Zhang Guotao was one of the strike leaders.

its renunciation of Tsarist-era treaties and recognised China's formal (but unenforceable) jurisdiction over Outer Mongolia. The agreement was extremely favourable to Sun. Not only did he receive a promise of substantial aid, and quasi-recognition of his status as a government leader, the manifesto included this key concession: 'Doctor Sun is of the opinion that, because of the non-existence of conditions favourable to their successful application in China, it is not possible to carry out either Communism or even the Soviet system in China. M. Ioffe agrees entirely with this view'.[97]

What had been a revolutionary tactic for Sneevliet became an alliance between a state and a quasi-state as, from autumn 1923, the Soviet Union began pouring money, arms and hundreds of political and military advisors into Canton to build up the Kuomintang and its National Revolutionary Army. Any scruples about preserving the independence of the Communist party were abandoned. The process was supervised by Mikhail Borodin who represented the Comintern to the Chinese Communists, but the Soviet government in his dealings with Sun Yat-sen.[98] With Sun's agreement, Borodin reorganised the Kuomintang on Soviet lines, with a central committee in Canton and branches throughout China. In January 1924, the Kuomintang held its first ever national congress. Since the existing membership was mainly based in Shanghai and Canton, the branches in other areas were set up by members of the Communist Party. The Trotskyist Zheng Chaolin later wrote: 'It was the experience, funds and firepower of the Soviet proletariat that fashioned a new political party, modelled on the organization of the Russian Bolsheviks, under the old and vacant sign-board of the Kuomintang'.[99]

Some in Sun's party were sceptical of his turn to Moscow and feared a Communist takeover by stealth. But Sun was confident he had the better side of the bargain. He reassured doubters that he had personally checked and approved Borodin's reorganisation plan. As for the Chinese Communists, he said: 'If the Communist Party enters the Kuomintang it must submit to discipline and not criticise the Kuomintang openly. If the Communists do not submit to the Kuo-

---

97 Brandt, Schwartz and Fairbank 1952, p. 70.
98 Sneevliet opposed Borodin's military-bureaucratic version of his 'bloc within' tactic. It was one thing to work alongside Kuomintang members involved in the labour and popular movements, quite another to lavish money, arms and advisors on its militarist and conspiratorial leadership. After returning to the Netherlands, Sneevliet sided with the opposition against Stalin in 1926 and in 1933 signed a manifesto supporting Trotsky's call for a new International (although in 1938 he parted ways with Trotsky). Sneevliet was active in the Dutch resistance and was executed by the Nazis in 1942. See Goodman 1990, p. 114. See also Williams 1980.
99 Benton (ed.) 1997, pp. 72–4.

mintang I shall expel them; and if Soviet Russia should give them secret protection, I shall oppose Soviet Russia'.[100]

On 1 May 1924, Sun presided over the opening ceremony of the Whampoa (Huangpu) Military Academy through which the Soviets organised and financed the National Revolutionary Army.[101] Dozens of Soviet military advisors, led by the civil war general Vasily Blyukher, provided military instruction. Zhou Enlai was appointed head of the department of political instruction. But these were posts that conferred only influence, not executive power. Control of the army was in the hands of the academy's commander, Chiang Kai-shek, and his clique of loyal officers.

During the two-year Second Revolution that followed the 30 May 1925 incident, the Chinese Communist Party grew rapidly but never asserted its independence from the Kuomintang.[102] An anti-leftist coup in Canton organised by Chiang Kai-shek in March 1926 was explained away as a 'misunderstanding'. After the Northern Expedition[103] placed him in a commanding position, Chiang turned on his Communist allies and massacred thousands in the Shanghai coup of 12 April 1927. Just days before the coup Stalin and Bukharin, who had replaced Zinoviev as Comintern chairman, described the Kuomintang as 'a cross between party and soviets', and a 'revolutionary parliament'.[104] The former Menshevik Martynov provided a theoretical framework for Stalin's policy, characterising the Kuomintang as not a bourgeois party, but a 'bloc of

---

100   Brandt 1958, pp. 32–3, cited in Tony Cliff, *Trotsky: Fighting the rising Stalinist bureaucracy 1923–1927*, available at: http://www.marxists.org/archive/cliff/works/1991/trotsky3/09-chirev.html#n36, retrieved 20 June 2014.
101   The Soviets provided 3 million Chinese dollars to set up the academy and a monthly subsidy of 100,000 dollars, as well as an initial shipment of arms. See Wilbur 1983, pp. 40–1.
102   On 30 May 1925, British police opened fire on a demonstration in Shanghai, killing nine students and provoking nationwide unrest. Chinese workers in Hong Kong and neighbouring Guangdong organised a year-long general strike and boycott of the British colony.
103   The Comintern and the Chinese Communists were initially opposed to the Northern Expedition but decided to back it when it became clear Chiang Kai-shek was determined to press ahead. The advance of the National Revolutionary Army during 1926 aroused great enthusiasm and was accompanied by uprisings directed against foreign concessions, a strike wave in cities and land seizures in the countryside. But Chiang Kai-shek used his troops to repress the popular movement. The repression was witnessed by Comintern delegation of Tom Mann, Jacques Doriot and Earl Browder. But the published account of their trip contained only praise for the Kuomintang.
104   Quoted in Zinoviev's *Theses on the Chinese Revolution*, presented to the Soviet Politburo on 15 April 1927. The Communist Party turned down an offer of military aid against Chiang. Xue Yue, a dissident army commander, warned the Communist leadership in Shanghai about Chiang's plans and offered to use his troops to defend the workers organisations. See Isaacs 1938, p. 152.

four classes' made up of the national bourgeoisie, urban middle class, workers and peasants.[105] Even after the massacre, the Comintern did not break with Kuomintang but switched support to the leader of its 'left wing' Wang Jingwei,[106] head of the Nationalist government in Wuhan. Wang, in due course, turned his guns on the Communists, whose rank and file members were by this time utterly demoralised and disorganised.

> The central leadership, evidently no longer able to control the situation, simply left comrades to their own devices. ... Since there was no longer any revolution in which to participate many of them were forced to beg for their living on the streets and await arrest and execution.[107]

The disaster in China was of such proportions that it threatened the position of the Stalin-Bukharin leadership in Moscow. The Chinese Communist Party was ordered to recover lost ground by staging urban insurrections, timed to coincide with important party meetings in Moscow, in the hope of producing 'good news' to bolster the campaign against the Opposition. In Nanchang and Canton, thousands were sacrificed in futile uprisings.[108]

Missteps and Defeats

Within a little over five years after the Far East Congress dispersed, the principal Communist parties represented – those of China, Indonesia, Korea and Japan – had been destroyed or crippled. Lenin's grand vision of a strategic alliance uniting workers in advanced countries, the exploited masses in the colonies and semi-colonies, and the Soviet Union, was not realised. Only in Mongolia did the People's Party continue to prosper, in the limited sense that it remained in power despite self-inflicted bloody purges. The defeats in China and Indonesia were the heaviest, since these represented the destruction of substantial

---

105   Alexander Martynov (1865–1935) was a member of Narodnaya Volya and later the Mensheviks. He joined the Communist Party in 1923. Sneevliet had earlier said the Kuomintang was made up of the intelligentsia, overseas Chinese, soldiers, and workers. His description at least had the merit of being based on observation. See Saich 1991, Vol. 1, p. 196.
106   Wang Jingwei remained Chiang Kai-shek's rival within the Kuomintang throughout the 1930s. He moved towards fascism and in 1940 accepted the post of head of state of a Japanese-controlled puppet government in Nanjing. He died in 1944.
107   Wang 1991, pp. 37, 42.
108   The Nanchang uprising coincided with a Central Committee plenum, the Canton commune with the Fifteenth Party Conference. See Elleman 2009, p. 2.

parties. In Japan it would be more accurate to say that the party did not progress beyond the embryo stage in the inter war years. Although the divided Korean party retained a substantial following in the diaspora, it was no more successful on home territory than the Japanese Communists.

Significantly, in none of these countries did the Communist Parties implement the policies defined at the Second Comintern Congress and reiterated by Safarov at the Congress of the Toilers of the East. These policies were, we may recall: To build alliances with nationalists who were genuinely committed to the struggle against imperialism. To guard and preserve the independence of the labour movement. And wherever and whenever the development of the mass movement permitted, to build soviets of workers, peasants and soldiers. In Indonesia, the Communists, deprived by arrest and exile of their most talented and experienced leaders, abandoned the work in the broader anti-colonial movement that had brought them so much success, and embarked on a suicidal course. In China, the Communists sacrificed their political and organisational independence and found themselves defenceless against their former allies. If the Chinese disaster can be seen as a negative confirmation of Trotsky's theory of Permanent Revolution, the Indonesian debacle was the refutation of a caricature.

Only in China did the Comintern, or more properly, representatives of the Soviet government, exercise effective control of the local Communist Party. Elsewhere the picture was rather one of impotence. The Comintern could only watch helplessly as the Indonesian party destroyed itself. It was unable to reconcile the Korean factions even on Soviet territory. And in Japan it could not prevent the capture of the party by sectarian purists. The overall picture was one of failure. It would take the long-predicted war in the Asia Pacific to revive the fortunes of Communism in the region.

Preface to the 1970 Hammersmith Reprint
Publisher's Note on This Reprint

Sam Carr[1] from Canada, Katayama from Japan, M.N. Roy from India, and Zinoviev representing the E.C. of the Comintern, were among the 119[2] revolutionaries from 40[3] countries who attended this Congress. A Manifesto was issued calling on 'the patient and resigned peoples of the Far East' to struggle against imperialism and achieve independence. This record of the proceedings has always been a scarce document and we hope our reprint will be welcomed by students of Asian history.

> The proposal to hold (the Washington Conference on the Limitation of Armaments on 11 November 1921) and to discuss at it Far Eastern affairs in general, came to Moscow's attention while the Third Comintern Congress was in session. Plans were immediately made to hold a counter-conference of Eastern revolutionaries which, after a preliminary canter in Irkutsk, opened in plenary session in Petrograd in January 1922,[4] as the First Congress of the Toilers of the Far East, attended by representatives from China, Japan, Korea, India, the Philippines and Indochina.[5] These two gatherings – the Washington Conference and the Congress of the Toilers of the Far East – set the stage for the world struggle between Russia and the West.
>
> – J.H. BRIMMELL, *Communism in South East Asia* (Oxford: OUP, 1959)

---

1 In fact, Carr was the pseudonym of L.E. Katterfeld, one of the early leaders of the US Communist movement. Sam Carr was a well-known Canadian Communist but he did not attend the Congress. He was born in July 1906 and was only 15 in early 1922.
2 The credentials committee recorded 148 delegates.
3 Another mistake. The 40 countries referred to here are those mentioned in the text. The delegates mainly came from four countries: China, Korea, Japan and Mongolia. There was one delegate from the Dutch East Indies. India, the Far Eastern Republic, Soviet Russia and Yakutia had delegates with consultative votes. There were also speakers from Soviet Russia, the United States, France and Germany.
4 The Congress took place in Moscow. Only the final session was held in Petrograd. It was originally planned to hold the Congress in Irkutsk, and most delegates travelled there initially, some spending two months there before moving on to Moscow.
5 There were no delegates from the Philippines or Indochina.

The First Congress of the Toilers of the Far East

Held in Moscow, 22 January–1 February 1922.
Closing Session in Petrograd, 2 February 1922.

HAMMERSMITH BOOKS, BARNES HIGH STREET · LONDON SW13
Originally published in Petrograd 1922.
Reprinted in the Hammersmith Reprints of Scarce Documents Series by The Hammersmith Bookshop Limited 1970.
NOTE: The original edition was badly printed on poor paper. Our reprint naturally reproduces the printing errors of the original but is otherwise superior and easier to read.

Opening Session of the Congress of the Toilers of the Far East

Saturday, 21 January 1922. Kremlin, Sverdlov Hall

Zinoviev.[1] Comrades, on behalf of the Executive Committee of the Communist International, I declare the Congress of the Toilers of the Far East open. (*Cheers, singing of the Internationale*).

Comrades, the Executive Committee of the Communist International attaches great importance to the present Congress. It instructed me to welcome all the comrades assembled here in the name of all Communist workers organised in the International brotherhood of Toilers, known as the Communist International. Our international brotherhood, since the first day of its existence, [has taken] clear account of the fact, that the complete victory of the proletariat over the bourgeoisie under the present circumstances is possible only on a worldwide scale. There is much that distinguishes us from the previous Internationals, but one of the most important features which distinguishes the Third International from the previous international organisations consists in the fact that we, not only in words, but in deeds, are trying to become the organisation not merely of the toilers of Europe, but also of the toilers of the entire world. The Communist International is all the time taking a clear account of the fact that the revolution of the toilers can be victorious under the present circumstances only as a world revolution. Too often has the idea of the world revolution been substituted by the idea of a European revolution. Of course, we know quite well what a tremendous sig-

---

1 Grigory Yevseevich Zinoviev (1883–1936) was chairman of the Petrograd Soviet from December 1917–26, and chairman of the Executive Committee of the Communist International (ECCI) from 1919–26. A Bolshevik since 1903, Zinoviev returned from exile with Lenin in the sealed train in April 1917 but opposed Lenin's left turn and denounced the October insurrection on its eve in a Menshevik newspaper. After Lenin fell ill, Zinoviev and his close comrade Kamenev joined Stalin in a triumvirate to prevent Trotsky inheriting the leadership. In 1926, he formed the United Opposition with Trotsky, but capitulated to Stalin the following year. In 1934 he was sentenced to 10 years imprisonment, accused of 'moral responsibility' for the murder of Kirov, his successor as leader of Petrograd. In August 1936, he was executed following the trial of the 'Trotskyite-Zinovievite Terrorist Centre'. Zinoviev was one of the Communist movement's great orators. A recent partial biography recounts his performance at the Halle Congress of the USPD (Independent Social Democratic Party of Germany) in 1920, when, debating Lenin's old rival Martov, he persuaded the delegates to vote for affiliation to the Communist International. See Lewis and Lih 2011, and https://www.marxists.org/glossary/people/z/i.htm#zinoviev, retrieved 29 January 2014.

nificance the labour movement and the general revolutionary movement in Europe possess in themselves. We do not by any means wish to underrate [them], but at the same time we know that the decisive victory will be assured only in the event of the struggle not being confined to the European continent alone, [but] when our struggle will rouse the hundreds of thousands, the hundreds of millions of the toiling and oppressed masses in the East. Everybody knows that the Communist International came into being and became a power only in conjunction with the victory of the workers' revolution in Russia. The revolution that took place in our country in 1905 caused considerable international consequences. That revolution aroused a revolutionary movement in Turkey and in Persia. Already our revolution in 1905 doubtlessly exercised considerable influence upon the revolutionary movement in China, which towards the years 1911–12 assumed more turbulent forms. But our revolution of 1905 met with the obstacle of the then existing international correlation of forces. It found an echo among the oppressed nations of other countries, including the oppressed nations of the East, but that echo was as yet far from adequate. The great workers' revolution in Russia, which we are now witnessing, has already found an incomparably greater echo among the toilers of the entire world, including those of the Far East. The Third International considers it its greatest task and will do everything possible to hasten the awakening of the toiling peoples of the Far East. At the beginning of our activity we were confronted with sharp criticism and even with the mockery of the heroes of the Second and Second-and-a-Half Internationals for trying to draw into the struggle of the most advanced workers of Europe, the toiling masses of the East as well. They tried to make fun of us because we wanted to form a union between the advanced proletariat of the West and the peoples of the East, which, in the opinions of some of the leaders of the Second and Second-and-a-Half Internationals,[2] are still in a trance from which they cannot by awakened, so that they are unable to become an active factor in the making of world history. We know perfectly well that these opponents of ours are merely socialist-opportunists, merely petty-bourgeois socialists; we know that they are the old, rusty, narrow-minded European petty-bourgeois, who see nothing beyond Europe, to whom anything outside of Europe is remote and obscure.

---

2   The two-and-a-half international, the International Working Union of Socialist Parties, was founded in Vienna in February 1921, by ten European socialist parties. Its political position was in between the old Second International that had fallen apart on the outbreak of war in 1914, and the Third, Communist International. It merged with the revived Second International in May 1923.

The Communist International understands with perfect [clarity] that the union of the advanced proletariat of Europe and America with the awakening toiling masses of the East is an absolutely necessary [factor] for our victory, Hence our attempt, a little over a year ago, to organise the famous Congress of Baku;[3] hence the present attempt on the part of the Communist International to come to an understanding with the toiling masses and their leading representatives who came from the Far East into the country where the Executive Committee of the Communist International resides. The E.C. of the Communist International and the entire Communist International, as you can judge from the decisions made by all our three Congresses, understand very well that you are compelled to work under conditions [very different] from those under which the proletarian parties of the West are labouring. The E.C. of the Communist International will listen with the greatest attention to the reports and information which will be given by you. We shall not hide from you that, hitherto, our connection with the countries where the delegates who have gathered here are working is very inadequate. We know very little of what is happening in such a country as Japan, and any report about an organisation such as, for instance, a trade union in Japan, deserves the greatest attention from the advanced proletarians organised in the Communist International. We know also very little of the revolutionary movement in China except for the information of the comrades who came here. We are absolutely certain that the present representatives of the Japanese proletariat, whom we are happy to meet in our own sphere, are sufficiently internationalised, in the true meaning of the word, in their relations with the Chinese, the Koreans, and all other nations who are oppressed by the Japanese bourgeoisie. We are convinced that our Japanese comrades keep alive the legacy of Karl Liebknecht, that the enemy is within [their own] country, that the principal enemies of the toilers are their own bourgeoisie. We are convinced that, at this Congress, the elementary idea that there can be no national antagonism among the toilers of Japan, China, Korea, Mongolia, etc. who are here represented, will be considered in the light of a self-evident truth. We are profoundly convinced that the present Congress will strengthen the growing brotherhood of the toilers of all countries in the form of organisation, too.

Comrades, I repeat, we attach the greatest importance to this Congress. The Communist International will fully accomplish its task only if it [succeeds] in

---

3   The Congress of the Peoples of the East was held in Baku in September 1920. There were 1,891 delegates from 37 nationalities, mainly from Soviet territory in the Caucasus and Central Asia, Iran, Turkey and Afghanistan.

translating into action the programme which it outlined, and which it elaborated in detail, at the Second Congress in 1920.

The Second International, now definitely becoming more and more an organisation that serves the bourgeoisie, failed for the principal reason that, [on] the question of the war, [on] the question of the attitude towards the colonial and semi-colonial nations, it had no clear line of conduct, and in the end it took up a clearly bourgeois line. The question of the attitude towards the colonial nations, far from being disposed of by the Versailles Peace and the Washington Conference,[4] will of course continue to exist even after the forthcoming Genoa Conference. [T]his question will stay on the order of the day until the time when the proletariat, [with] the Communist International, will consummate the final victory over the bourgeois system. It is upon this question more than any other that the Comintern has abruptly broken with the damnable tradition of the Second International which led to the victory of the bourgeoisie over the proletariat in the memorable days of the imperialist war. This is the question of all questions; this is the central knot of world politics and of the struggle of the toilers throughout the world.

At the Baku Conference, the E.C. of the Comintern issued the call *Communist Parties of all countries and toilers of all oppressed nations, unite!* It is this appeal that we now address to the representatives of the Far East whom it is our greatest joy to welcome today in our country. The Communist Parties of all countries and the toilers of the entire world, and of the Far East in particular, will unite under the banner of the Communist International and score the final victory over world imperialism. Long live the Congress of the Toilers of the Far East! (*Applause*).

---

4 The Washington Naval Conference (12 November 1921–6 February 1922) was convened by the United States to address a growing naval arms race among the victors of World War One and to forestall conflict in the Pacific. Britain, Japan, France, the Netherlands, Italy, Belgium, Portugal, and China were invited – all, apart from neutral Netherlands, having been on the allied side in the war. A Five-Power Treaty signed by the United States, Britain, Japan, France and Italy set limits on the size of each country's navy. A Four-Power Treaty, signed by the United States, Britain, Japan and France, replaced the Anglo-Japanese alliance and eased tensions between Britain and the United States. A treaty signed by all nine powers agreed to the Open Door policy on China, while recognising Japan's effective control of Manchuria. China's request for the right to set its own customs tariffs was rejected, but in a separate agreement with Japan, China regained sovereignty, if not effective control, over Shandong province. The fact that Soviet Russia was not invited was the motivation for convening the Congress of the Toilers of the Far East. But the Far Eastern Republic, which would soon merge with Soviet Russia, sent a delegation to Washington to lobby for the withdrawal of the Japanese intervention force from Siberia. Sun Yat-sen's request for representation of his Canton government was ignored, as was a Korean mission to the conference, led by Syngman Rhee.

Permit me now, comrades, to go over to the election of the Presidium of the present Congress. Comrade Kato has asked us for the floor for a motion on this question.

Kato [Yoshida Hajime] (*speaks in Japanese*).

Katayama[5] (*translates*). Comrade Kato wants to propose to the delegates to elect five honorary chairmen: Comrades Lenin, Trotsky, Zinoviev, Katayama and Stalin.

Zinoviev. Comrades, on behalf of the Presidium of the E.C. of the Communist International, I ask comrade Katayama to take his place in the Presidium, considering that he can certainly be considered to have been elected as a member of the Presidium. I hope there are no objections. (*Applause*).

Presidium Members: 1. Georgi Safarov. 2. Nogi [Taguchi Unzo]. 3. Kato [Yoshida Hajime]. 4. Li-Kieng [Zhang Guotao]. 5. Tao [Zhang Qiubai]. 6. Pak-Kieng [Kim Kyu-sik]. 7. Simpson [Semaun]. 8. Danzan [Ajvaagiyn Danzan]. 9. Kim. 10. Din-Dib [Dendev]. 11. Wong [Huang Bihun]. 12. Pak-Kop. 13. Béla Kun. 14. Carr [L.E. Katterfeld]. 15. M.N. Roy. 16. Shumyatsky.

Zinoviev. Are there any other motions? Apparently there are no more. I shall take a vote on this list which, we are informed, has been discussed by all the delegations. The above list is now to be voted on. I ask the delegates to vote.

I will ask one of the Comrades to translate into Chinese. (*A comrade translates*).

---

5 Katayama Sen (1860–1933) was one of the early leaders of the Japanese labour movement. He was a founder member of the Social Democratic Party in 1901, and authored the influential pamphlet *Waga shakaishugi* (*My Socialism*) in 1903. He became internationally known when he demonstratively shook hands with Plekhanov at the Sixth Congress of the Second International, held in Amsterdam in the midst of the Russo-Japanese war. Katayama attended college in the United States, where he became a Christian and was influenced by socialist ideas. After returning to Japan in 1896, he set up the newspaper *Rodo Sekai* (*Labour World*). He led the victorious 1911–12 Tokyo streetcar strike, but was imprisoned and after being released returned to the United States. In New York during World War One, he met Trotsky, Bukharin and Alexandra Kollontai and joined the communist movement. In 1921, he was sent by the Comintern to Mexico where he worked together with Mikhail Borodin who was later the Comintern representative in China. After the Congress of the Toilers of the East, Katayama remained in Russia until his death. He is buried in the Kremlin Wall. See Gale Research Inc. 1998, and Duus and Scheiner (eds) 1989, pp. 659–60.

The list is to be voted on. I ask the delegates who agree with this list to raise their cards. Is there any one against it? I ask the members of the Presidium to take their seats. Comrade Katayama, veteran of the Japanese revolutionary movement, will speak on behalf of the elected Presidium and the Communist International as a whole.

Katayama (*speaks in English*). Comrades of the Far East, we greet you on behalf of the Communist International. Although there is no enmity among you, yet you are fighting against each other, you are fighting on account of Japanese imperialism and Far Eastern imperialism and capitalism of the Western countries. You are compelled to fight, you are oppressed, you are despoiled, you are fighting each other, you are fighting against our race, but comrades, you are welcome here. We, the Communist International, have asked you to come here because here you are free, free from capitalism, free from imperialism. You have met here to discuss, open hearted[ly], Japan and the imperialists of Japan, to discuss capitalism, and the imperialism of the Western countries which are exploiting and oppressing all peoples. Now comrades, capitalist imperialist countries are holding a Conference at Washington – they call it a Conference on disarmament and the Far Eastern countries question. What is it in actual fact? Comrades, they are trying to find means of exploiting China and Korea, Siberia and the other Far Eastern countries. They want to exploit the Far East, but they cannot, for they are fighting each other. Therefore they come to the Conference. They compromise on how to exploit, how to oppress, how to subdue. Why? Simply because they cannot fight each other in the Far East just now. Therefore they compromise to jointly exploit, devastate, oppress and subdue the Far East without fighting each other. That is what they have done at Washington. Now, comrades, you have come here, we invited you to come here, open-heartedly, freely and in a friendly, comradely spirit, to discuss how to crush the imperialism of the Western countries which are devastating China. Siberia, and the Far East. We will commune here on this subject, and we will enjoy the kind hospitality of the Communist Party in whose name we welcome you, comrades.

Kalinin.[6] On behalf of the All-Russian Central Executive Committee of the Council of Workers' and Peasants' Deputies, I greet the delegates of the peoples of the Far East. Comrades, representatives of the toiling masses of the Far East,

---

6   Mikhail Ivanovich Kalinin (1875–1946) was an old Bolshevik who served as Soviet head of state (Chairman of the Presidium of the Supreme Soviet) from 1919 until his death. He was a candidate member of the Politburo. Kalinin joined the RSDLP in 1898 and was an early sup-

the toilers of the Soviet Republic greet you with the greatest joy, for the arrival of the representatives of these peoples increases the number of those who fight for the oppressed. Comrades, you are now in the capital of that country in whose boundaries the sun almost never sets. But it is not its size that characterises the difference from the other states. The chief peculiarity of the country in whose capital you now are, comrades, consists in the fact that this country considers it impossible, and does not desire, to enrich itself at the expense of the other border peoples. This is a substance and peculiarity of our country. It does not wish to exploit the toil of these peoples, for the toiling masses themselves are in power here. In accordance with that, all the relations of this State assume quite a different character from those of all other states.

Not long ago, only five years back, Russia was a country in which most of the products of labour were turned over to the large advanced capitalist states. Tsarist Russia, while giving away part of the labour of its workers to other countries, at the same time attempted to enslave other nations, by taking away and enjoying part of the labour of the peoples of the East as well, at any rate of those with which she came in contact.

Comrades, I see before me representatives of the countries of the Far East, the very countries who have not been [cosseted] by history, who have not been blessed with the opportunities of exploiting the labour of other peoples. On the contrary, the countries of the Far East, with the [sole] exception of Japan, are themselves being exploited by other states.

But, comrades, with regard to Japan this refers only to the smallest part of her population. I do not know what percentage, I think you know better than I do, but it is the most insignificant fraction of her population that benefits by exploitation. On the contrary, the major part of her toiling population, whose representatives we are welcoming here, are on our side and will doubtless fight against that part of their nation which desires to oppress the other nations of the East. This, comrades, represents the common ground whereupon we unite. For this common ground Soviet Russia has been fighting for four years now. What is she fighting for? For the right to dispose of her own labour. We are fighting for this end in the eyes of the whole world. It seems to me to be a just cause to fight for, the right of disposing of one's own labour and the products thereof, and I think that upon this ground our union will be complete and indestructible, the union of the Russian Federative Soviet Republic (as the Federative Alliance) with all the oppressed nations of the East, and also with that part

---

porter of its Bolshevik faction. In 1917, he initially opposed Lenin's call for insurrection against the Kerensky government. He consistently supported Stalin in later factional struggles. See Lazitch and Drachkovitch 1986, pp. 204–5; see also Trotsky 2009, p. 235.

of [the] population which is oppressed by its own exploiters if the country as a whole is not under oppression. Comrades, permit me to [express the wish that] the present Congress of the Nations of the East becomes the starting point of a speedy achievement [by] the Russian Soviet Republic and all the oppressed countries of the Far East of the sublime goal, when we shall be able to dispose of our labour without fear or hindrance.

Long live the nations of the Far East! Long live the closest friendship between the toiling nations of the Far East and the Russian Republic! Long live the toilers of the whole world!

Chairman. I will now call upon Comrade *Lozovsky* to greet the Congress on behalf of the E.C. of the Red Trade Union International.

Lozovsky.[7] Comrades, on behalf of the Red Trade Union International which unites nearly 17 million revolutionary workers throughout the world, we greet the Congress of the Toilers of the Far East. In the Far East, just as in Europe and America, capitalism is now developing, is assuming and has already assumed in some countries, particularly Japan, turbulent forms of development. Along with the development of capitalism, with the increasing numbers of the exploiters, quite inevitably rises the most primitive, the most elementary class form of the union of the proletariat; I mean the trade unions which are being formed also in the Far East. Your bourgeoisie throughout the Far East is doing the very same thing that the bourgeoisie of Europe and America has done. It wishes to lay its hands upon these trade union organisations, permeate them with the spirit of class [collaboration]. It carries to them the gospel of social peace; it aims to build them upon the [confused] principle of joint participation by workers and employers. It is trying to do the same thing that the workers of Western Europe and America have already gone through. For the labour

---

7 Solomon Abramovich Lozovsky (1878–1952) was General Secretary of the Red International of Trade Unions (Profintern) from 1921–37. Lozovsky joined the RSDLP in 1901, was exiled to Siberia in 1905, but escaped to France. He was elected secretary of the All-Russian Central Council of Trade Unions at its founding congress in June 1917. He was, along with Trotsky, Joffe, Lunacharsky and others, a member of the Mezhraiontsy (Inter-district organisation) that fused with the Bolsheviks at the end of July 1917. Shortly after the October revolution, Lozovsky was expelled from the Bolsheviks for (in Lenin's words) 'petty bourgeois negation of the dictatorship of the proletariat', but was readmitted in 1919. In 1939, Lozovsky was appointed deputy people's commissar for foreign affairs. During World War Two, as vice-chairman of the Soviet Information Bureau, he was popular among foreign correspondents as an accomplished and affable press spokesman. He also had responsibility for various Soviet anti-fascist organisations. He was arrested in 1949 and executed in 1952 following the anti-Semitic trial of the Jewish Anti-Fascist Committee. See Naumov, Kraiushkin and

movement of your countries, for those hundreds of thousands and millions of workers that are drawn into the big industries, for all exploited, there is a tremendous historical lesson in the many years' experience of these countries. From the experience of their long struggle for emancipation from class [collaboration] and from the theory of social peace, your workers must learn to create their own revolutionary class organisations, which together with the revolutionary class organisations of Europe and America will march towards the same common goal – Communism.

The Red Labour Union International, whose ranks are filled by the revolutionary workers of all countries, will greet with particular joy the revolutionary workers of your countries and accept into its ranks the workers who will carry on a determined struggle against the exploiters of their own countries, against their bourgeoisie, for the same purpose for which the workers of Europe and America carry on their struggles. Let this meeting between the workers of the Far East and the representatives of revolutionary Russia weld them together and develop among the representatives of the Far East the idea of the necessity of organising the great toiling masses of the East into mass unions. Let the millions of workers who are now engaged in your industries organise trade unions, but not in the way it is now being done by some representatives of Japan, who believe in reformist ideas and class harmony. Let them look to the Communist International, to the Red Labour Union International, which embraces all revolutionary workers, which is the expression of the revolutionary energy of the workers of all countries, and, side by side with it, fight for the same aims, for their emancipation. I greet you, representatives of the Far East, and I greet those hundreds of thousands and millions of the oppressed of your countries who, together with the toilers and workers of other countries, will achieve their emancipation. (*Applause*).

Chairman. On behalf of the Japanese delegation Comrade *Yoodzu* will address you.

Yoodzu [Mizutani Kenichi].[8] The Washington Conference is the centre of intrigue for English, French, American, and Japanese imperialism. They talk

---

Teptsov 2005, pp. 177–232; Carr 1952, Vol. II, pp. 62, 224; Lenin, *Concerning the Expulsion from the Party of S.A. Lozovsky*, http://www.marxists.org/archive/lenin/works/1917/dec/30a.htm#fwV42P049F01, retrieved 28 January 2014; Lozovksy biographical sketch, http://www.marxists.org/glossary/people/l/o.htm, retrieved 28 January 2014.

8 The list of speakers in the archive identifies the speaker in this slot as the Japanese Communist Party delegate Mizutani Kenichi. See Russian State Archive of Socio-Political History, 495.154.161.

about the limitation of armaments, they talk about universal peace, but their real aim is to grab as much as possible. After the world war, America and Japan remained the only big imperialist powers. Wide possibilities for exploitation are now open only in the Far East. A conflict of interests between Japan and America is therefore inevitable. This conflict will involve not only Japan and America, but also England and France. [T]hey have all suffered from the war. They naturally wish to avoid an armed conflict, and in order to achieve their aims easily and without dangerous complications, they are holding the Washington Conference and are organising a Quadruple Alliance. The victims of this intrigue are the toiling masses of Korea, China, Mongolia, and the young Far Eastern Republic. Also the Japanese proletariat is a victim of imperialism, and it must therefore be our aim to overthrow the Japanese militarists and imperialists. The Japanese proletariat finds itself in the same plight as the other nations of the Far East. The oppressed nations of the Far East must therefore unite with each other under the slogans of Soviet Russia.

Long live the Third Communist International! Long live the oppressed workers of the Far East!

Chairman. The Chinese delegate, comrade *Tao* has the floor.

Tao.[9] On behalf of the Communist and Revolutionary Parties of China, I greet the Congress. On 21 January 1922, the First Congress of the revolutionary parties of the Far East was opened. We, the delegates of the Chinese revolutionary Parties, on behalf of the toilers and the exploited of China [place] great hopes [in] this Congress. We believe that this Congress expresses by its very name the main task which is confronting the Far East, the task of revolution. We are certain that when all the revolutionary forces combine after the present Congress, the revolutionary movement in the Far East will become intensified and grow deeper roots than ever before. We know that, so far, the revolutionary movement in those countries has been weak, the revolutionary forces of the Far East [have been] divided, the revolutionary movement of the Far East [has] had no connection with the revolutionary movement of the rest of the world. And now we have the opportunity to [eliminate] this sad fact [through]

---

9 There is some uncertainty as to whether this is the Kuomintang delegate Zhang Qiubai or the leader of the Communist Party delegation Zhang Guotao. The lists of speakers in the Russian and Chinese versions of the minutes identify Tao as Zhang Qiubai but the Chinese minutes also appear to attribute the speech to Zhang Guotao (more precisely, and strangely, to Zhang Guoyao). Elsewhere in the minutes, the pseudonym Tao always refers to the Kuomintang delegate Zhang Qiubai. See Russian State Archive of Socio-Political History, 495.154.161, 495.154.166.

the present Congress. We hope that this Congress will give [birth to] a strong, powerful and united organisation, and will also work out a definite programme of action. There is a proverb among the European peoples that a revolution is the highest, most harmonious music produced by mankind, and we must now work out the same kind of firm and harmonious programme of action.

Comrades, we are certain that just as soon as our [powerful] union [begins] action in the Far East, the hour of doom will strike for the capitalists and the imperialists, and a day of true happiness and genuine freedom [will dawn] for the peoples of the Far East and of the world as a whole.

Comrades, I call upon you to unite and arise for the struggle. Long live the Congress of the Communist and Revolutionary Parties of the Far East!

Pak-Kieng [Kim Kyu-sik].[10] Comrades, fellow delegates from the revolutionary organisations of the Far East, in the name of the Korean delegation, on behalf of the revolutionary people of Korea, I bring most sincere and hearty greetings at the opening of this Congress of the toiling masses, the Communist movement, and the revolutionary peoples of the Far East.

Coming to this Congress and thinking for a moment of the place we are in – this great central historical city, Moscow – it brings back to us memories and associations of the past. Moscow in the past was associated with the idea of the Muscovite power. Very often we entertained the idea of that Muscovite power standing for imperial despotism and expansion. For many years past, we used to think that Washington was the centre of American so-called liberalism, democracy and prosperity – but the world is changing.

We have come to see that this has come to a practically vice versa condition. It is now just the opposite. Muscovite power is no longer represented here. Moscow stands here as the centre of the world proletarian revolutionary movement, and we realise that she is welcoming [with open arms] the oppressed

---

10   Kim Kyu-sik (1881–1950), one of Korea's most prominent liberal-nationalist politicians, served, at various times, as foreign minister, education minister, and vice-president of the Korean Provisional Government in exile. Kim was a Christian and studied English literature at Roanoke College in the United States. In 1919 the provisional government appointed him ambassador to the Paris peace talks but he failed to get a hearing. Kim remained in Moscow for several months after the Far East Congress hoping to enlist Soviet support in assembling a broad-based Korean national convention, an effort he claimed was being sabotaged by the leader of the Shanghai faction of Korean Communists Yi Tong-hwi. After Japan surrendered in 1945, Kim took part in a number of initiatives to avoid the division of Korea. He opposed the separate elections held in South Korea in 1948. He died in 1950 in North Korea after leaving Seoul with retreating North Korean troops. It is assumed he was abducted, but Kim no doubt had good reason to fear the South Korean forces.

peoples of the Far East in their revolutionary movement. [Meanwhile,] Washington stands as the centre of the world's capitalist exploitation and imperialist expansion. Now when we come here [to] this opening [ceremony], we realise that this opening is simply a [preparation] for our battle against world capitalism and imperialism. This is a moment when we are beginning to get together, and now is the time that we realise the necessity of getting together. We know the slogan that the workers of the world should unite, and our slogan here should be *Toilers of the Far East, unite*. In the past we have been struggling and toiling and fighting our battles separately, alone. Take for example the Korean movement; the Koreans, with their meagre strength and lack of preparation, have been carrying on their struggle against Japan – against Japan's imperialism and capitalism as well as the imperialism and capitalism of the world – and today we come to realise that we have only [just] begun fighting this battle of odds.

[Let us] think for a moment what Russia has gone through during the past four or five years. Soviet Russia – the great centre of proletarian revolution – what [has she had] to go through during these years? I want to say we have come together here in order to prepare for the battle against the world power of imperialism and capitalism. Let us think for a moment of all the frontiers of Russia – [with] Poland, Finland, in the Crimea, in the South along the Romanian frontier, in Central Asia, on the Mongolian frontier, in Siberia, everywhere – North, East, South and West. Yet, notwithstanding this, she has resisted the intrigues of the combined powers of the world. Kipling says that *East is East and West is West and ne'er the twain shall meet*. But I say here that [in] Moscow we are meeting; East and West have met. With us there is no East and there is no West. With us East is West and West is East, and now we have come to realise that there is a necessity to fight our battles together.

Comrades, we have an enormous battle before us. We, today, have come to realise that the oppressed peoples of the Far East and the revolutionary organisations must come together, we have come [together] to plan our movements for the future. What programme are we to [adopt]? It is my hope, and I am sure it is the hope of all, that we will obtain at this Congress the courage and energy that the Soviet Republic has shown in the past, notwithstanding all the tasks forced on her by the imperialists [from] all the points of the compass, and we want to carry that knowledge to the proletariat [throughout] the Far East so that the Eastern proletariat will stand as a mighty power in suppressing and crushing that so-called world capitalism and imperialism. And we want from this Congress to get that fire from the Russian movement which will burn to ashes the whole imperialistic and capitalistic system of the world. In the name of the whole delegation I wish to express [our greetings] to this Congress of the Far Eastern revolutionary peoples. Long live the Communist International, the stronghold and the directing power of this great movement, and long live Soviet Russia, the citadel of that great mighty force that is withstanding the world power of imperialism, and long live the combined efforts of the proletariat of the Far East, together with the proletariat of the West, of the whole world, in crushing to the ground world imperialism and world capitalism[!]

Zinoviev. Comrade Wong, representative of the women's delegation, member of the Canton Parliament, Chinese author, has the floor.

Wong [Huang Bihun].[11] Comrades, women are also human beings. Women need their freedom as well as men. Russia is the only country in which women have obtained full freedom, and this is the reason for the desire of Chinese women to help Russia. Inequality still prevails in China. Women are still oppressed in China. The women of China still work under extremely hard conditions, and it is therefore our task to unite the women, but our main task consists in relieving the situation in Russia. Russia is the only free country in the world, surrounded on all sides by capitalist states, blockaded. It is therefore

---

11   Huang Bihun (1886–1923) was a prominent feminist, anarchist, activist and educator. The daughter of a Guangdong businessman, as a child Huang regularly unbound her feet. She married a son of one of her father's employees and had two sons, but after her husband and father died her in-laws stole her inheritance and mistreated her. She abandoned the household and worked as a tutor in Britain and Japan. Back in China, she settled in Shanghai and defied convention by marrying a member of the Tongmenghui who was 13 years her junior. She joined the circle of activists around Chen Duxiu after he launched *New Youth* magazine. In 1920, the left-leaning warlord Chen Jiongming gave the Guangdong education portfolio to Chen Duxiu, who in turn employed Huang Bihun. Huang set up the Guangdong Women's Federation and organised a reading room and a school for working women. In 1921, she played a leading role in a campaign for women's suffrage and was beaten by conservative members of the southern government's Legislative Assembly. The following May, she led a protest movement in Macau after 40 Chinese protesters were shot dead by Portuguese colonial troops, and was one of ten delegates sent to negotiate the release of detainees. In January 1923, Sun Yat-sen returned to power in Guangzhou after being briefly ousted by his one-time ally, now adversary, Chen Jiongming. Shortly afterwards, Huang Bihun was arrested, accused of plotting with Chen Jiongming to assassinate Sun, and executed (on Sun's orders, according to a 1927 Soviet account). See: Naumov, *A Brief History of the Chinese Communist Party*, in Wilbur and How 1989, p. 456; Edwards 2008, p. 118; Huang Bihun delegate questionnaire, Russian State Archive of Socio-Political History, Moscow 495-154-181-020; Xie Yanzhang, *Zhiliyu funu jiefang yundong de Huang Bihun* (*Huang Bihun, who devoted herself to the women's liberation movement*), http://www.gzzxws.gov.cn/gzws/gzws/ml/46/200809/t20080917_8580.htm, retrieved 22 January 2014.

our duty to break the blockade between Russia and China in order to free Russia from all the [attacks] of the capitalists and imperialists. I came here to become acquainted with the situation of women in Soviet Russia, to study Communism and go back to China to carry on Communist propaganda among Chinese women for affiliation with the international organisation of women. But the main task is to free Russia from the sufferings which world capitalism is inflicting upon her.

(*Translation of greetings by the representative of the Mongolian delegation and member of the People's Revolutionary Party of Mongolia.*)

I greet the present Congress of the representatives of the Communist and Revolutionary Parties of the nations of the Far East for the first time gathered here in Moscow, the capital of the world revolution. I express my wish that the Congress, by its united and fruitful labours, may lay down a solid foundation for an alliance between the revolutionary nations of the Far East and the Russian Soviet Republic. Our situation in the suffocating atmosphere of the Far East was such that imperialist Japan brought its pressure to bear upon the weaker China, while the ruling classes of China, being the hired agents of Japanese imperialism, in their turn oppressed the toiling masses of Mongolia. Last year, in 1921, after the centuries of oppression, thanks to the aid of Soviet Russia and her heroic Red Army, Mongolia overthrew the yoke of the Japanese-Chinese oppressors. Liberated Mongolia has become convinced from experience, that Revolutionary Russia is the only [possible] liberator of the toiling nations of the East. The toiling masses of Mongolia therefore hope that the representatives of the countries of the Far East here assembled will create a united revolutionary front of the Communist and Revolutionary Parties of the toilers of the Far East against our common enemies, recently in conference at Washington.

Long live the militant organ of the toilers of the entire world – the Third, Communist International!

Long live the world's first Socialist Republic of Soviet Russia! Long live the union of the toiling masses of the Far East!

Chairman. Comrade *Simpson* of Java has the floor.

Simpson [Semaun].[12] On behalf of the toilers of Java and the Dutch Indies, countries with a population of 50 million suffering from the cruel exploita-

---

12   Simpson was the pseudonym of Semaun – alternatively spelt Semaoen – (1899–1971), one of the principal early leaders of Indonesian communism. A protégé of the Dutch revolu-

tion of the Japanese, American and Dutch imperialists, I heartily greet the First Congress of Communist and Revolutionary Parties of the Far East. The workers of Java and the Dutch Indies are toiling with the sweat on their brow for the benefit of the foreign god, and if the Washington Conference relegated the question of Java to the second place, it is due to the fact that the capitalists of the imperialist countries have long decided the question of how most advantageously to all of them to exploit the Dutch Indies. But this will not go on forever. The industrial proletariat [that has] sprung up due to the foreign capital invested in our country is already beginning to move on the road of the revolutionary struggle against the imperialists. In this struggle, the Java proletariat will not take the last place, and will play an important part in the great bout between capital and labour. The peoples of the Far East, and also the proletariat of Java and the Dutch Indies, will play, due to their geographical position, a decisive part, for that will be the chief base for the coming imperialist war. But this future war will be used by the proletariat of Java and the Dutch Indies, as well as by the proletariat of India, for the purpose of making a joint attack with the proletariat of the Far East upon world imperialism. At this Congress, I hope to find comrades from the Far East who will find means of uniting the proletariat of the entire world for the decisive struggle against imperialism, and for the achievement of the final victory of the proletariat.

On behalf of the Communist Party of the Dutch Indies, of the left wing of the Sarekat Islam[13] and the revolutionary Trade-Union Federation, I bring you my salaam.

---

tionary Henk Sneevliet, Semaun was elected chairman of the Communist Union of the Indies (PKH), forerunner of the Communist Party of Indonesia (PKI), at its founding congress in May 1920, and held the post until he left for Moscow towards the end of 1921. Semaun was a railway worker and became involved in trade union and political activities at an early age. He represented the Indies Social Democratic Association (ISDV) at the 1916 conference of the Islamic/nationalist organisation Sarekat Islam. He rose to a leading position in Sarekat Islam, and eventually much of its membership defected to the breakaway Sarekat Islam Merah (Red Islamic Association). In 1923, after a general strike called by the Union of Train and Tramway Personnel was defeated, Semaun was exiled by the Dutch colonial authorities and returned to the Soviet Union, where he remained for the next 30 years. See McVey 2006, pp. 22, 51, 154.

13   Sarekat Islam began as an association of Muslim traders directed against the dominant position of Chinese merchants in the Dutch East Indies, but was re-launched as a political party in 1912 and developed into a mass, anti-colonial movement. Its most prominent leader was Omar Said Tjokroaminoto, a mentor and sometime father-in-law of future Indonesian President Sukarno.

Schiller [Richard Schüller][14] (*Young Communist International*). Comrades, from the toiling youth I also bring the most enthusiastic greetings to you, the First Congress of the Revolutionary and Communist Parties of the Far East; to you, the representatives of the subjected and exploited toilers and peasants of the Far East. Comrades, there is a great call that goes over all the world, the call which stirs up the exploited, relieves and leads the subjected; the call of the workers' revolution, for the liberation from capitalism, for Communism. Comrades, this call has also stirred up the great masses of youth in Western Europe and America, and they have gathered together to fight on the front against capitalism and imperialism for the dictatorship of the proletariat, for the Soviets, and for Communism; and comrades, now there are more than 800,000 young workers and peasants organised in the Young Communist International movement, fighting under the flag of the Communist International. Communists, comrades, representatives of the revolutionary parties, I must especially greet the young representatives who are in great numbers among the delegates.

Comrades, I remember the great and mighty role and the great work the revolutionary youth in the countries of Asia and the Far East has done, and comrades, if there is a country, a continent, a workers' movement that needs the young workers, it is Asia, it is the revolutionary movement of the Far Eastern peoples, because to overthrow the old system, to liberate the exploited and subjected toilers and peasants of Asia, one needs the enthusiasm, the resolution and self-sacrifice of the youth. One needs the hundreds of thousands of young workers and peasants who are in Asia and the Far East. They are yet asleep. But comrades, great and large masses, the first front, [are] already in the battle, [are] already [taking] the first energetic steps. Comrades, [this] is an historic moment, for the representatives of the revolutionary and Communist parties of Asia have come together in Red Moscow, the heart of the world revolution, to build the front against capitalism and imperialism under the flag of the Communist International. Comrades, now the [powerful] forces of revolution of Asia are concentrated here [as in a crucible] and, after this Conference, they will go out again, they will go out, [to] all parts of Asia to stir up the subjected and exploited masses of toilers, workers and peasants, to lead them to their

---

14 Referred to as Shueller in the list of speakers in the Comintern archive. Richard Schüller (1901–57) was an Austrian who was in Moscow for the February 1922 extended plenum of the ECCI. After the Austrian civil war of 1934, Schüller fled to Czechoslovakia but was expelled to the Soviet Union. In 1945 he returned to Austria to work on the Communist daily *Volkssttimm*. See http://www.marxisthistory.org/history/usa/parties/ycl/1923/0410-ecyci-toywlaconv.pdf.

liberation from capitalism and imperialism, to lead them to unity with their brothers in all countries of the world, to lead them to Communism.

Long live the union of all the workers of the world! Long live the Communist Youth international! Long live the Communist International! Long live the world revolution!

Roy.[15] (*India*). Comrades, in the name of the workers masses of India, I give you the warmest greetings. This Congress is a very important and a very significant gathering because, while we are gathering here, we, the representatives of the exploited masses and of the exploited nationalities of the Far East, are meeting here in order to formulate the best means of fighting our common enemy, international capitalism and international imperialism are meeting in Washington in order to devise ways and means by which they can continue their domination in their respective countries as well as in our countries, a domination which has become unbearable, a domination which can no longer continue. Nevertheless, before collapsing, before meeting [their] inevitable downfall, they are trying to find ways and means by which they [can,] as long as possible, prevent this inevitable collapse. And, so we meet here, and we should try to go back with our weapons ready, making ourselves fit for this great struggle which is going on, a struggle that is rising all over the world, a struggle in which the exploited masses are going to take a very important part. This kind of international gathering of peoples of the Far East is very important also because,

---

15   Manabendra Nath Roy (Narendranath Bhattacharyya) (1887–1954) was an Indian revolutionary nationalist turned communist, who became a leading figure in the Comintern. During World War One, he travelled to Jakarta and Shanghai, seeking German arms and assistance to mount an uprising against British rule. Pursued by British agents, he fled first to the United States and then to Mexico, where he met the Comintern agent Borodin and helped found the Mexican Communist Party. He debated Lenin on the question of the colonial revolution at the Second Comintern Congress in July 1920. In October 1920, he travelled to Tashkent, where he founded the Indian Communist Party and, with the backing of Lenin and Trotsky, attempted to assemble a largely Muslim army to invade British India via Afghanistan. In 1927, while a Comintern advisor in Wuhan he inadvertently helped precipitate the break between the Communists and the Left Kuomintang by showing Wang Jingwei a Comintern telegram calling on Communists to take radical action after Chiang Kai-shek's Shanghai coup. He was recalled to Moscow after his indiscretion and expelled from the Comintern in 1929, after opposing the ultra-left 'Third Period' policy. He returned to India in the early 1930s and, after a failed attempt to form a left current inside the Congress Party, founded the Radical Democratic Party in 1940. In 1948 he retired from politics. See Chattopadhyay 2009, pp. 2874–6; Hopkirk 2001, Ch. 8; Elleman 2009, pp. 107–11; Roy biographical sketch, https://www.marxists.org/glossary/people/r/o.htm#roy-mn, retrieved 29 January 2014.

having been subjects of imperialism for a long time, we have never been accustomed to this kind of gathering. Imperialism – which has set all of us under its domination – has been able to do so by creating rivalry, distrust and animosity among us. It has been the policy of international capitalism all over the East to foment national jingoism among their own peoples, among their own countries, and so lead the working masses to war, as they led the working masses of Europe in 1914. They are conducting the same policy in the East, in order that we, the exploited people of the Asiatic countries, might serve as useful instruments for capitalism. The time has come that this imperialistic policy should not be carried on any longer. We cannot say that all of us, millions of people who live in these countries, are aware of this fact. We who have come here are aware of this fact and we must carry this idea, must carry this message, among those who do not yet understand that we must come together and not be the tool of imperialism any longer. The representatives of Japanese capitalism are trying to make us fight among ourselves. There is deadly rivalry between America and Asia, and they are trying to get and exploit Korea, Manchuria, Mongolia, and Siberia. Now there is a representation here of the exploited masses of Japan as well as of other countries suffering from the imperialism of Japan, and we have met here and we will undo the sinister motives and designs of our rulers. And so, we have a very important, tremendous, and broad task before us. We have met under the auspices of the revolutionary Communist International, which is directing the forces all over the world, and of the First Workers' Republic, which has kept the banner of revolution flying, and we hope that, under such auspices, we shall be able to carry on our work.

I give you greetings and let us say – Long live the Communist International! Long live Soviet Russia which has taken up the task of uniting and leading the exploited masses all over the world and the exploited masses of the East to liberation.

Carr [L.E. Katterfeld].[16] (*America*). Comrades, representatives of the revolutionary toilers of the East; it is my privilege to bring to you tonight the best wishes of the revolutionary workers of the Far West. From that land of the West

---

16   John Carr was the pseudonym of Ludwig Erwin Katterfeld (1881–1974) who was Executive Secretary of the Communist Party of America (CPA) in 1921 and 1922. Katterfeld was born in Strasbourg but emigrated to the United States, where he worked as a farm labourer. He joined the Socialist Party of America in 1905 and was elected to its national committee. He opposed US intervention in World War One and in 1919 he was elected to the leadership of the newly-formed Communist Labor Party which later merged with the CPA. In October 1921, the CPA sent him to Moscow as its representative on the ECCI. Katterfeld was expelled from the Communist Party in 1929. See Lazitch and Drachkovitch 1986, p. 212.

known as America; from the Communist Party of America. I say here tonight that although it was true at one time that east was east and west was west and that the two have nothing in common, that now it is no longer true, and east and west are one. And I agree with them, capitalism is making the whole world one and, today, the bourgeoisie of the West and East, no matter how much it may preach race hatred and national pride to the workers, it knows no patriotism itself but that of profit. Comrades, workers, since that time, a little over twenty years ago, when the American capitalist class carried Christian civilisation to the West and at the point of the bayonet to our little brown Philippine brothers, since that time, America has travelled along the way to world imperialism. At the Washington Conference recently held, America did her share for the future changing of our labour and sweat into profits. America has worked with the others and made her plans. You, comrades, have met here, and we have met with you to make other plans, so that the Washington plans may come to naught. We must have no illusions about the difference between the imperialism of a reactionary land like Japan, and the imperialism of the outpost of democracy – America. In essence the two are exactly the same; and the workers of [Puerto Rico] and [Santo Domingo], of Cuba and the Philippines can bear testimony to this fact. In America today, the bourgeoisie sits enthroned in power almost unquestioned. The press is at its disposal and in a few weeks it can stir up passions and prejudices so that the workers are willing to go and murder in other lands. And then another fact, comrades, let us remember that a few short years ago the power of the Russian Tsar here seemed unquestioned, it seemed inbuilt in the very rocks underneath this Russian soil, and, as the mists pass away before the sun in the morning, it passed away. Today, we are in this hall. Not one of you, ten short years ago, would have believed that in ten years' time he would be in this hall, in the Kremlin, in the very heart of what was black reactionary Russia, in order to help solve the problems of how to abolish imperialism from this earth – no one. Capitalism develops faster now than ever before. The same forces are still at work. The same forces that overthrew tsarism are still at work. No matter how firmly American capitalism seems to be entrenched, the same forces will overthrow it in your day and mine. Comrades, workers, although the American press can stir the American workers up to fight today, we of the Communist Party of America are firm in the conviction that, just as the great furnace fire burns off the dross from the metal, so, in the fires of the class war, these fires of national pride will be burnt away and will become a pure gold class solidarity. We are firm in that conviction. We want to make a pledge with you here to-night, and it is this; that we will do our very best, every one of us will put in every ounce of energy and every bit of his life, so that when the day comes when American capitalism puts guns into the hands of its workers and wants us to murder you for the benefit and glory of capitalism, the American workers will not obey for long, but will turn the guns on their masters. Out of that struggle will come the new. They will turn the guns against their masters who exploit them, secure that you will do the same. Out of the imperialist struggle will come the struggle of the workers, not against capitalism in one country, but against the capitalism of the world, to abolish this rotten thing from the face of the Earth. We hope to see the day, and we will put in every ounce of energy, [when] instead of meeting here to join hands, we shall be able to stretch hands in comradeship across the Pacific Ocean to you, and with you rebuild the world for the workers.

Chairman: Comrades, let us now close the official part of our Congress. The difficulties of language made themselves pretty much felt during the first session; nevertheless, I am certain that all our comrades understand each other quite well, for we speak a common language, the language of Communism and emancipation of the oppressed peoples. The Russian revolution will soon celebrate [its] fifth anniversary. This has been a long period in the life of each one of us, but it is only a minute on the dial of history. The world revolution has just begun; that which we have witnessed so far is only a small weak beginning of what we shall see when the hundreds of millions of the oppressed nations of the Far East rise. It will be then that the decisive page in the history of mankind will be turned; only then will come the true and complete liberation of the oppressed from the yoke of the oppressors. In closing the first session, we express that wish which is on the lips of every one of us: Long live the strong union of the toilers of the whole world under the banner of the Communist International! (*Applause*).

I declare the first session closed.

(*The meeting closes at 10:10 p.m.*).

Second Session
23 January 1922, 11 a.m.

Chairman: Comrade *Safarov*.

Chairman. The Second Session of the Congress of the Toilers of the Far East is hereby declared opened. We will now have to elect a Mandate Commission, and confirm the agenda and the rules of procedure.

Shumyatsky.[1] The representative of the Mongolian delegation has presented the following list of delegates for the Mandate Commission. The principle is as follows: Representation from every delegation and from the Executive Committee of the Comintern. Altogether, the following list has been presented:

1. Nogi [Taguchi Unzo]. 2. Roy [M.N. Roy] 3. Sun. 4. Won. 5. Tsoy [Cho'e].[2] 6. Zadbayev. 7. Kim. 8. Buyan-Namkhu [Sonombaljiryn Buyannemekh]. 9. Yurin.[3] 10. Trilisser.[4] 11. Voytinsky [Voitinsky].[5] 12. Dalin.[6] 13. Shumyatsky.

---

1 If Boris Zakharovich Shumyatsky (1886–1938) is remembered at all today, it is as the Soviet film industry head who persecuted Sergei Eisenstein. But in 1922, Shumyatsky was the most powerful man in Siberia, regional representative of the Party and the Soviet government, chairman of the Siberian military district, and director of the Far Eastern Bureau of the Comintern. He had previously served as prime minister of the Far Eastern Republic. Zhang Guotao regarded Shumyatsky as a high-handed, virtual dictator who lived a privileged lifestyle in the midst of mass hunger, and dubbed him the 'King of Siberia'. Shumyatsky was appointed rector of the Communist University of the Toilers of the East in 1926. In 1930, he was put in charge of Soyuz Kino. History has judged him harshly for his treatment of Eisenstein, Kuleshov, and other formalist directors. But avant-garde films were unpopular with Soviet audiences and signature techniques of formalism, such as montage, were losing their relevance with the onset of sound. Shumyatsky planned to build a Soviet Hollywood near Odessa and make films with mass appeal, but he was unable to meet production targets. After the expensive failure of *Bezhin Meadow* (ironically directed by Eisenstein), he was accused of sabotage and shot in June 1938. See Zhang Guotao 1971, Vol. 1, Part 4, pp. 171–209; see also Taylor 1991.
2 Probably Ch'oe Koryŏ who was a delegate from the First Korean Brigade of the Red Army and one of the leaders of the Irkutsk faction of Korean Communists.
3 M.I. Yurin undertook what was probably the first Soviet (more accurately, quasi-Soviet) diplomatic mission to China, on behalf of the Far Eastern Republic, in August 1920. See Wilbur and How 1989, p. 22.
4 Mikhail Trilisser (1883–1940) joined the RSDLP in 1901. He was exiled to Siberia and after the 1917 revolution was active in Irkutsk and helped establish the Far Eastern Republic in 1920. In

Chairman. As there are no other proposals, I will take the vote on the list of members for the Mandate Commission. Those in favour of the list of the Mandate Commission will kindly raise their delegate's card. Those against? The list is accepted.

Comrade *Katayama* has now a proposition to make concerning the order of the day.

Katayama. I propose the agenda as follows:

Agenda.
1. International situation and results of the Washington Conference. (Report by Zinoviev).
2. Reports from each country.
3. Position of the Communists in the national and colonial question and collaboration of Communists with national-revolutionary parties.
4. Manifesto.

Chairman. Are there any objections to the agenda as proposed? Are there any other propositions to the agenda? No? Then we will consider the agenda as proposed adopted.

We will now decide on the rules of procedure. The Presidium proposes the following rules:

Rules of procedure.
1. Time allowed for reports, 1 hour.
2. Time allowed for concluding words, 30 minutes.
3. Time allowed for general discussions, first time 15 minutes; second time, 10 minutes and third time 5 minutes.
4. Orators speaking for or against a motion, 10 minutes.
5. Questions on reports must be presented in writing and only while [the] report is being made.

  1921, he joined the Cheka and later rose to a leading position in the OGPU. He was arrested and executed in 1940.
5 Grigori Voitinsky (1893–1953) played a key role in establishing the Chinese Communist Party. As an emissary of the Far Eastern Bureau of the Comintern he met with Chen Duxiu and Li Dazhao in 1920. The party held its first congress in 1921.
6 Sergei Dalin (1902–85) was a Soviet expert on China. He was sent to China in 1922 and again in 1926. Dalin wrote several books, including *Sketches of the Chinese Revolution*, published in 1927. He was imprisoned in 1936 and released in 1956.

SECOND SESSION 67

6. Time for points of explanation allowed only at the close of discussion and no more than 5 minutes are given.
7. Time on points of personal explanation allowed at close of session and no more than 5 minutes.
8. All drafts of theses and of resolutions on points of agenda are to be submitted to the Presidium in writing on day prior to given discussion.
9. In voting upon theses and drafts one of the drafts is taken as the basis at the discretion of the Plenum of the Congress.
10. Voting is done by raising delegates' cards, while in counting attention is given only to the deciding votes. The counting of consultative votes is only optional.
11. On the second point of the agenda (Reports from each country) the following number of delegates will report:

    1. From Japanese Delegation .... 3 speakers.
    2.   "   Chinese   "   3   "
    3.   "   Korean   "   3   "
    4.   "   Java   "   1   "
    5.   "   Mongolian   "   1   "

Morning sessions take place from 11 a. m. to 3 p. m.; evening sessions from 6 to 10 p. m.

Are there any objections against the rules as proposed? Those in favour will please raise their hands. Accepted. I will now call upon comrade *Zinoviev* to speak upon the first point of the agenda.

Zinoviev. Comrades, my task will be, of course, to present to you in its fundamental features the international situation as our Congress finds it, to outline the general features of the tasks before our Congress as the E.C. of the Comintern conceives them.

Three years have already elapsed since the close of the imperialist war. But it is quite obvious that many a year will yet elapse before mankind will begin to forget the consequences of that war. The whole world is struggling, like a bird imprisoned in a trap, to effect the least possible mitigation of the evil consequences of the war which are felt upon every step. The main feature of the present post-bellum period, as I see it, consists of the fact that more and more urgently are coming to the front not European questions, but Asiatic and Far Eastern questions. By this I do not mean to say that, until now, these questions did not play an important part. Everybody knows that [for] decades the Asiatic problem has been playing an important part in questions of world politics. Everybody is well aware that even the first Revolution in Russia, in 1905, had the closest bearing upon the Russo-Japanese War,[7] which, in its turn, was intimately connected with the problems of the Far East. But, in the immediate future, the Asiatic and the Far Eastern problem is indeed going to take precedence before all other questions of world politics. We will realise this with particular [clarity] if we examine the struggle that is taking place around the peace that was concluded after the close of the imperialist war. If you take a glance even at the latest events, if you turn your attention to the recent resignation of the French Ministry of Briand,[8] which now makes even the proposed Genoa Conference questionable, you will at once see how European disputes are becoming more and more shallow and self-exhausting.

The victorious countries, and bourgeois France in the first place, [despite their best efforts,] have only managed to obtain an insignificant portion of what they expected to extract out of, and what France thinks herself entitled to get, from beaten Germany. You read yesterday the statement made by the French bourgeois minister Poincaré. He said: 'It is sought to represent us Frenchmen as crazy imperialists', – his actual expression – 'and yet we are only guilty of demanding that Germany should pay that which she has undertaken, that which she has signed'.[9] This sounds quite like a [reasonable] demand; yet we

---

7   The Russo-Japanese War (February 1904–September 1905) was the outcome of a long-running contest between the two countries for control of Manchuria and Korea. Japan surprised the world by defeating one of the established great powers. The Treaty of Portsmouth (New Hampshire) was facilitated by US President Theodore Roosevelt. It confirmed Japan's possession of Korea, and handed it the Liaodong Peninsula, the South Manchurian railway, and the southern half of the island of Sakhalin. Roosevelt, who favoured Japan over Russia, was awarded the 1906 Nobel Peace Prize for his efforts.

8   Aristide Briand (28 March 1862–7 March 1932) was a perennial figure in French governments in the early decades of the twentieth century, serving as Prime Minister 11 times. Initially a leftist, he was elected secretary general of the Socialist Party in 1901 and founded the newspaper *L'Humanité* together with Jean Jaures. He was expelled from the party in 1906, for accepting the post of education minister from Georges Clemenceau. Though he later acquired a reputation as a pacifist, Briand served as Prime Minister twice during World War One. He was Prime Minister on the eve of the Far East Congress – from 16 January 1921–15 January 1922. After the war, Briand took a relatively conciliatory stance towards Germany. In 1926 he was jointly awarded the Nobel Peace Prize with the German foreign minister Gustav Stresemann. Briand was an early advocate of the idea of a European Union. See *Nobelprize.org*. Nobel Media AB 2013. 'Aristide Briand – Biographical', http://www.nobelprize .org/nobel_prizes/peace/laureates/1926/briand-bio.html, retrieved 25 January 2014.

9   Raymond Poincaré (1860–1934) was a right-wing politician who was Prime Minister of France three times and President from 1913–20. France had achieved a supremely Pyrrhic victory in World War One, losing 1.7 million soldiers and incurring huge debts. Now militarily dominant in continental Europe but financially crippled, it was aggressively trying to extract the pun-

know that Germany is not in a position to pay; that whatever be the changes that take place in the French Cabinet, no serious change can be effected in the situation. This small insignificant fact furnishes an example of how strictly European questions are becoming shallow and self-exhausting. The desperate war, which has cost the most tremendous sacrifices, has resulted only in bringing about a stage of marking time.

The victorious bourgeoisie cannot obtain anything worth having from the vanquished country within the boundaries of Europe. These are quite extensive boundaries, and yet, in comparison with the entire globe, they are very small and within these boundaries no problems of any serious dimensions can be [solved]. It stands to reason that the Asiatic problems had also their share in the imperialist war of 1914–17, and played quite a significant part. Nevertheless, that war in many respects brought to the forefront strictly European problems: the Balkan question, the question of the Straits,[10] etc. Yet, after the close of the bloodiest and most desperate war which mankind has ever seen, we now see, more than at any other time, that the questions upon which the imperialists contend are being shifted into Asia. The Far Eastern problem is thereby becoming a million times more real than it has been hitherto, it is becoming the question of all questions, the pivot of world politics, and also the pivot of the entire liberation movement of the proletariat and the oppressed nations.

The history of the last few years can be told by naming a few important cities where the more important treaties between the imperialists and their victims have taken place. When we mention the names of Brest-Litovsk, Bucharest, Saint-Germain, Versailles,[11] we mention the greatest events in the politics of the imperialists in recent years. To the number of these cities another city has been added recently; that is Washington, which has become the centre of the Far Eastern problems which interest us here most. You can well recollect the noise that has been made by Washington. You remember how they promised at that Conference to solve the question of disarmament; how they promised at that Conference to heal the wounds of such countries as Korea; how they promised

---

       itive reparation payments imposed on Germany at Versailles. But Germany simply could not pay. In January 1923, Poincaré sent French troops into the Ruhr valley to collect reparations as coal shipments.

10   The straits question refers to the rights, or otherwise, of warships to pass between the Aegean/Mediterranean and the Black Sea via the Dardanelles and the Bosporus.

11   Zinoviev is referring to the Treaty of Brest-Litovsk (March 1918), imposed on Soviet Russia by the Central Powers (Germany, Austria Hungary, Bulgaria and Turkey), the Treaty of Versailles (June 1919), imposed on Germany by the Allied powers, the Treaty of Bucharest (May 1918) between Romania and the Central Powers, and the Treaty of St. Germain-en-Laye (September 1919) between the Allied powers and Austria.

there to solve the Chinese question; how they promised to make the Far Eastern nations happy. It is [self-evident] that the advanced representatives of the Far Eastern nations could have hardly any serious faith in Washington, could base upon it hardly any serious hopes. By tracing the course of events in recent years one cannot help becoming convinced that wherever imperialism assumes particularly hypocritical forms, one has to look for the authors of such hypocrisy to the representatives of the American bourgeoisie who combine the most arrogant imperialistic robbery with the most Pharisaical double-faced hypocrisy.

It suffices to recollect the memorable activities of Mr. Wilson,[12] who, as everybody knows, had also nearly solved all Far Eastern questions, who had also promised to make all oppressed nations happy. The same thing has been repeated [this time as] the more important imperialist predatory powers [tried] to create the illusion that the mighty ones of this world [want] to solve the most painful questions affecting the oppressed Far Eastern nations. The American bourgeoisie has again played first fiddle. A great miracle was to have happened at Washington. The martyred nations of the Far East and the oppressed nations in general, notwithstanding the many deceptions experienced in the past, nevertheless entertained some hopes of the Washington Conference, just as the Wilson promises had raised hopes among some oppressed nations. We are now already in a position to sum up the results of Washington. It seems to me that 10 December 1921, will [go down as] one of the blackest dates in the history of mankind. On 10 December 1921, Washington saw the conclusion of a treaty between four of the most powerful governments of the present day, four of the most oppressive and reactionary imperialist govern-

---

12 Woodrow Wilson (1856–1924) won his second term as President in 1916 by promising to keep America out of the European conflict, but five months later declared war and unleashed a domestic witch-hunt against socialists, pacifists and ethnic Germans. Socialist leader Eugene Debs was sentenced to ten years for opposing the war. When asked to pardon Debs in 1920, Wilson said the 'traitor' would never be released during his administration. Wilson appointed J. Edgar Hoover head of a General Intelligence Division established to target radicals. At the Versailles peace conference Wilson blocked a Japanese proposal to include a racial equality clause in the final treaty. Less well known is his imposition of racial segregation on some federal agencies, including the post office. His Fourteen Points, published in 1918, were the US's answer to the Bolsheviks' publication of secret treaties. Contrary to widespread belief, they did not include support for self-determination but only called for an 'impartial adjustment of all colonial claims' in which the 'the interests of the populations concerned' would be given equal weight with the claims of the colonising powers. In 1918, Wilson sent 5,000 troops to Archangel and 8,000 to Siberia as part of the Allied intervention in the Russian civil war. He was awarded the 1919 Nobel Peace Prize for promoting the League of Nations but the Senate refused to ratify the Versailles Treaty and the United States never joined the League.

ments: England, France, Japan and America. I think that this alliance, from its very beginning, will become known in history as the Alliance of the Four Bloodsuckers; the alliance of four of the most bloodthirsty imperialist powers which, before breaking with each other – and they must inevitably break with each other – have concluded between themselves an armistice for the purpose of more successfully oppressing the nations at the expense of whose blood these imperialist robbers have been living for many a year.

You know the principal promise made at Washington. It was to solve the problem of disarmament. In reality, and this is quite evident now, they solved the problem of armaments. Those of you who have followed the discussions of the enlightened gentlemen assembled at Washington, can well recollect the venomous altercation that took place between the now-resigned Briand and his opponents at that Conference, where wholesale bargaining was going on regarding the strength of submarine navies that were to be allowed to this or to that country. These gentlemen, unmindful of the fact that Europe is listening, that they are being followed by the eyes of the oppressed nations of Asia, and imagining for a moment that they were alone, were exchanging innocent sallies on the question of the submarine fleet, declaring that they needed such a fleet for the purpose of examining the bottom of the sea, collecting pebbles, etc. Of course, no disarmament was born at that Conference. That Conference has once more borne out the Communist contention that no disarmament is possible while capitalism exists, and that it will be possible seriously to speak of disarmament only when the oppressed nations [are] victorious over the imperialist governments.

This was how the question of disarmament was solved. Let us now see how the question of the various countries of the Far East has been solved. How was the Korean question solved? We have been informed that even some active members of the Korean liberation movement had some hopes in Washington, thinking that some miracle might happen, that some clarification of the Korean problem might follow afterwards. Now, what has happened? The word *Korea* was not even mentioned at the Washington Conference, as though Korea did not exist upon the globe, as though at Washington were assembled such powers that [had] never heard of the existence of Korea; nobody said a word about the Korean problem, at least, so far as official discussions at the Conference were concerned. This probably did not prevent these gentlemen from exchanging views behind the scenes as to who is to do the further crushing of Korea. If the Korean people needed any other lessons, then I think that they can get no more convincing lesson than the one furnished by the silence at Washington.

The Chinese problem, as you know, was solved wholly and entirely in the American spirit. More or less, agreement has been reached to recognise with regard to China the so-called 'open door' policy, advocated by American capitalism for selfish motives, because it thinks itself capable of beating all other capitalist competitors in the Chinese market by the free competition of the 'open door'. American trade with China, which amounted to 189 million dollars in 1916, reached in 1920 the sum of 385 million dollars, i.e. nearly double. This gives American capitalism all the more confidence of being able, by means of the 'open door', to extract even greater profits out of China. And it would have been the saddest mistake imaginable if among the representatives of Southern China, for instance, there could be found any simpletons who would accept the catchword of the 'open door' as the pure gold of real democracy and who would thus fall into the commonest capitalistic snare. Yet, it must be regretfully observed that, according to our information (and I must admit that we are very poorly and casually informed), there are some people among the active workers of the Southern Chinese revolutionary movement, among the adherents of Sun Yat-Sen,[13] among the important workers of his Party, who, at times, are looking not unhopefully towards America, i.e. towards American capitalism, expecting that, just from there, the benefits of democracy and progress will be showered upon revolutionary China. I hope that the Washington Conference will convince the more farsighted leaders in Southern China, the Chinese revolutionaries, all those who are struggling for real self-activity of their nation – even if they are not socialists – that the American capitalists are by no means their friends, but their most relentless enemies, who always approach their victims (this, as I have already shown, is the favoured method of American capitalism) with democratic catchwords and the most flagrant hypocrisy.

---

13 Sun Yat-sen (1866–1925) was China's leading nationalist politician. He was born in Guangdong province, attended mission school in Hawaii and studied medicine in Hong Kong. In 1894, while in Hawaii, he organised the Revive China Society (Xingzhonghui), his first revolutionary vehicle, which was succeeded by the Tongmenghui in 1905, and the Kuomintang in 1912. He organised a number of failed uprisings, but was in America when the Qing dynasty was overthrown in 1911. A revolutionary assembly in Nanjing appointed him provisional president of the republic but he was obliged to hand power to the military strongman Yuan Shikai, who forced him into exile. He revived the Kuomintang after the 1919 May Fourth movement. His political programme – the Three Principles of the People – roughly translate as nationalism, democracy, and people's welfare. At the time of the Far East Congress, Sun was head of the Canton-based southern government with the title 'extraordinary president of the Chinese Republic'. In early 1923, he negotiated a package of military and financial aid with the Soviet emissary Adolph Joffe. Sun presided over the inauguration of the Soviet-financed and staffed Huangpu (Whampoa) military academy on 1 May 1924, but less than a year later he died of liver cancer. His wife, Song Qingling, later became Honorary President of the PRC. Her sister, Song Meiling, married Chiang Kai-shek.

The Mongolian problem was also forgotten at the Washington Conference. Ever since Mongolia was liberated, thanks to some small support by the Soviet Government (the Soviet Government will, of course, always be proud of any possibility to lend even feeble assistance to Mongolia), the Mongolian problem has been thrown like a shuttlecock backward and forward between all the capitalists. The Japanese imperialists are now trying to make use of this problem, bribing a [section] of the mercenary Chinese politicians for the purpose of sowing discord between Mongolia and the Chinese revolutionaries under the pretence of patriotic democracy. They are advancing the question of restoring Mongolia to China. At the Washington Conference, there was nothing said openly about Mongolia, just as happened in the case of Korea. You know that the diplomatic talking-shop [in] Washington is going on even now, while no definite results have yet been achieved.

There has now come to the [forefront] the problem of a new Conference at Genoa,[14] which [is to some degree diverting] attention from the Washington negotiations. None of us can predict whether the Genoa Conference will take place, how it will end, to what extent Far Eastern as well as European problems will be discussed there. At any rate, one thing is certain: Washington confirmed that which was inevitable, namely that, while at the head of the now wealthiest countries – Japan, America, England, France – stands the imperialist bourgeoisie, the Far Eastern problem is bound to grow in acuteness, and in no case can a solution of the problem be expected. To put it plainly, Washington once more confirmed the sharing-out policy which the imperialist powers have been conducting for many years. Why, nine tenths of the aims of the war of 1914–17[15] centred round the distribution of the world. The world was parcelled out by the imperialists long before 1914. In this first imperialist world war, the question was merely one of a re-distribution of the world. Already before the outbreak of the imperialist war of 1914, it had been computed that one English merchant, on the average, exploits no less than 800 people among the natives of those colonies from which England sucks blood and profits. Further strife and contention arise out of the same cause. And now, Washington has, on the

---

14   The Genoa Conference 10 April–19 May 1922, attended by 29 nations (the United States did not participate but sent an observer), was the first postwar international conference to include Germany and Soviet Russia. The goal of Russian foreign minister Chicherin was to normalise economic relations and obtain loans, but France took a hard line on the repayment of Tsarist debt and the restitution of property seized since the revolution. Chicherin countered with a demand for compensation for damage caused by the allied intervention, and the conference ended in deadlock.

15   This should presumably read 1918, although Russia quit the war in 1917.

whole, confirmed the sharing out of the booty that [was] plundered in the year 1918, the year of the close of the imperialist war. Japan remains in possession of Korea, Yap,[16] Liaodong and Shandong; America retains the Philippines, England retains Egypt and India, France retains Indochina. How could they seriously tackle even one of these problems? It is quite clear that they were deliberating upon the formula: I will help you in robbing such-and-such colonies, so that you may help me rob such-and-such others. While following the discussions of the Washington Conference, one frequently has occasion to recollect a beautiful speech by the late Jaurès, uttered, one might say, a few hours before the outbreak of the imperialist war of 1914, when it was already evident that the war was inevitable, and when, examining the causes of the impending catastrophe, he declared at one of the meetings held in Paris: 'Tomorrow the war will break out, tomorrow they will tell you that this is a war for the liberation of the oppressed nations, but I tell you that this will be a war for the division of the spoils. I tell you that this will be a war for the sharing out of the oppressed nations'. And, further, he said: 'The representatives of the present-day governments act upon the following formula: I will rob this end of the street and will overlook your robbing of the other end'. The deliberations at Washington followed along the same lines. Japan said to America: I am going to close one eye while you [go about] plundering in some place or other, but I want you to close both while I rob Korea.[17]

The Washington Conference must have made it perfectly clear to all the leaders of the oppressed peoples of the Far East – and even those who do not share Communist views – that not a single conscious man could expect anything but new oppression and new exploitation from the imperialists of the strongest powers. More acutely than ever before, after the Washington Conference, all the members of the liberation movement of the Far Eastern peoples [face the question]: What will the next step be? Where is the issue, and where the solution,

---

16   Germany purchased Yap from Spain in 1899 after the Spanish-American War. Japan seized the islands in August 1914, and its possession was confirmed at Versailles under a League of Nations mandate. Yap was strategically located between the US possessions of Guam and the Philippines, and was the hub of a transpacific cable system that had been laid by the Germans. At the Washington Conference the United States wanted the Japanese mandate rescinded but settled for permission to land on the islands and install their own cables. Yap is now part of the Federated States of Micronesia.

17   There were precedents for this sort of agreement. In July 1905, US Secretary of War William Howard Taft agreed with Japanese Prime Minister Katsura Taro to recognise Japan's sphere of influence in Korea in return for Japan recognizing US control of the Philippines. President Theodore Roosevelt endorsed the agreement as 'correct in every respect'. Taft succeeded Roosevelt as US President in 1909.

of all questions of the national liberation of those peoples who are at present the objects of oppression of the imperialist powers?

Let us deal with [the] questions confronting the chief countries represented at this Congress.

The Chinese question. For the last decade, China has offered [a classic] example in all respects of what the bloodthirsty imperialists are capable of when they are faced by a defenceless country, or one, at least, that is not strong enough to resist them. Let us consider the events that took place at the outset of this century, to say nothing of what had happened before then. The unprecedented atrocities which have disgraced imperialists of all countries, including the Russian (R.I.P.), are the best example of imperialist cynicism and plunder. In no place were the savagery, the ferocity and barbarity of the so-called civilisation of the European powers so apparent as in China. A great people, with a population numbering hundreds of millions, [became] the prey of an imperialist gang. This gang is in itself quite small. The last figures I have seen show that there are but 20,000 foreigners as against one million and a half Chinamen in Shanghai. And we all know that these 20,000 hold the entire population in bonds of economic slavery and try to crush under their heel the cultural and national life of the local population. The imperialists do not shrink from inflicting unprecedented tortures on the Chinamen. Of course, comrades, it is not for me to tell you how American and English officers and merchants torture you, how they spit in the face of Chinamen, how their gardens are closed to the natives, and how they ill-treat women in your country. You could, of course, tell us, Europeans, much about all that. It is a great shame for the whole of mankind that such things should at all be possible in our day. If China has not as yet been torn to pieces, if she has sacrificed so much on the altar of civil war; if individuals like Zhang Zuolin,[18] a *hong-*

---

18   Zhang Zuolin (1875–1928), known as the 'Old Marshall', was a warlord who dominated Manchuria for nearly two decades until he was assassinated by his former Japanese backers in 1928. Zhang was a professional soldier who had fought in the 1894–95 Sino-Japanese war. He later set up a militia and fought a guerrilla campaign against the Russians during the Russo-Japanese war. He was appointed military governor of Fengtian Province (now Liaoning) in 1916, and inspector general of the three Manchurian provinces Fengtian, Jilin and Heilongjiang in 1918. With the support of the Japanese, he effectively ruled Manchuria as an independent statelet. He gained control of Beijing in 1924 after the second Zhili-Fengtian war. In April 1927, following Chiang Kai-shek's anti-communist coup in Shanghai, Zhang's troops stormed the Soviet embassy in Beijing and lynched the leading Communist Li Dazhao, along with 19 others who had been sheltering there. The following year, Zhang was forced to quit Beijing as the Nationalists prepared to take the city. Angered by

huzi[19] man who even now does not know how to write his name, could but recently rule over huge territories; if the notorious *dujun*[20] can plunder this richest country and draw it back into obscurity; if they want to keep the young Chinese Emperor, whose civil list [of] four million dollars a year is quite a big one for so young a monarch; if, at present, in connection with the capitalist offensive in China, we see there unheard of exploitation of the workers, it is all due, comrades, first of all to the insolent interference of foreign imperialism. And it is the task of the present Congress to show [a] guiding light to those active in the Chinese revolutionary movement. China's problem, and the problem of the present Congress in particular, is to bring unity [to] the scattered ranks of the Chinese revolutionists. The task of the workers organising the Communist International is to help the divided and oppressed Chinese people to carry out the most elementary, the simplest [task]: to drive out of China all its plunderers, to drive out all the oppressors of the Chinese people who cause you so much suffering.

We know well in what a difficult situation China is now. The imperialist plunderers piled up China's debts to such an extent that in 1920 they amounted to three billion dollars, two billion eight hundred and ninety-five million, to be exact. We know that, due to the intervention of the imperialists, due to the internal disputes, China maintains an army of nearly two million men, even although at the same time China seems, as it were, an entirely unarmed country; for due to imperialistic intervention, this army is divided, disunited, and is being used by the imperialists in their own interests.

We know that the European imperialists attempted to bestow upon you their missionaries, and they boast of the large amount of money which they have

---

his retreat, the Japanese blew up his train as it approached Shenyang. He was succeeded in Manchuria by his son, the 'Young Marshall', Zhang Xueliang who reconciled with the Nationalist government in Nanjing.

19 The *Honghuzi* (Red Beards – in Beijing Opera, a red beard indicates ferocity) were semi-bandit village militias operating in Manchuria. They carried out robberies and kidnappings, but also fought against the Russians and took part in the Boxer Uprising. In 1925, a Chinese scholar estimated that, in Jilin alone, there were 7,900 bandits, organised in 24 bands. The American surgeon Louis Livingston Seaman, who met Zhang Zuolin in 1905, estimated their number at around 10,000. The *honghuzi* were sometimes incorporated into Chinese regular forces; Zhang Zuolin had the rank of colonel when Seaman met him. The Japanese, Russians, and even Chinese revolutionaries, courted the *honghuzi*. In 1907, the future Kuomintang leader Song Jiaoren tried to involve them an uprising against the Qing dynasty. See Schimmelpenninck Van Der Oye 2005, p. 33; Billingsley 1988, pp. 29, 239; Seaman 1905, pp. 148–9.

20 *Dujun* is Chinese for military governor, usually of a province; here it is used pejoratively, carrying the additional sense of *junfa* or warlord.

spent upon them. Not long ago I read a book written by one of these imperialists who with great satisfaction quotes the following figures: the Catholic Church has 50 bishops, 1,500 foreign priests, 1,000 Chinese priests, etc. There are one and a half million Chinese converts to Christianity as a result of their work. The Protestant missions, according to his statement have 500 instructors, 383 missionaries, about 100 Chinese doctors, 1,092 ministers, etc., as a result of which there are about half a million converts to Protestantism. All these missionaries of yours, no doubt, spread many lies about the Washington Conference, but somehow, we [have] never heard of their raising a voice of protest; somehow, we have not heard of their descriptions of the sufferings and humiliations suffered by the Chinese people as a result of the intervention of the imperialist plunderers in its life.

Such is the mental picture that we paint of your struggles, of your sufferings, though unfortunately our actual information on conditions in China is very incomplete. We probably know much less than the actual facts; we see only a little corner of the sufferings, humiliations, and privations which the Chinese people are undergoing as a result of the brutal intervention of the imperialists. We know perfectly well that the protest which is growing in China against the imperialists is not a Communist protest; it is the elementary, natural desire of the people to be the master of its own fate. But we declare that the Comintern is entirely devoted to the support of the wishes of your heart, considering it indisputably just, and considers it its duty to throw all its power and moral authority on the side of the Chinese people striving to achieve [the] elementary freedom and independence naturally belonging to it. The Comintern will help to bring about the day when the Japanese, American and English bourgeoisie and officers will no [longer] be able to mock the masses of China, to behave there as if they were in a stable, will not be able to commit the atrocities which they committed with impunity during the suppression of the Boxer Rising,[21] the rising for which you paid not only with your blood and tears, but also with your gold.

---

21   The uprising of the Boxers (the Society United in Righteousness or *yihetuan*), which spread from Shandong in 1899, was provoked by Christian missionary activities and the imperialist scramble for concessions that followed Japan's defeat of China in 1895. (Germany took Qingdao, Britain took Weihaiwei, Russia took Liaodong, France took Guangzhouwan). The rising was at first repressed, but later supported, by the Qing government. It was finally crushed by the intervention of eight imperialist powers who occupied Beijing and imposed harsh conditions on China in the 1901 Boxer Protocol.

Korea. Korea's fate was at first closely connected with the competition between the Russian and Japanese imperialists, and during the last few years her fate was connected principally with the imperialism of Japan. We know very well that at present thousands of Korean revolutionaries are filling the dungeons; we have heard of hundreds and thousands who have fallen in the struggle against Japanese imperialism; we have heard of the insurrection of 1919, and we are following with undiminishing attention the struggle of the Korean people against its oppressors, which is just developing. Korea [is also] ruled by [a quite] insignificant number of Japanese imperialists. According to the data which I have read (perhaps they are not quite exact), in 1917 there were in Korea only 332,000 Japanese to about twenty million Koreans. Out of these 332,000, 144,000 lived in eight Korean cities, i.e. they did not go into the villages where the bulk of the Korean people live. Japan can boast of the fact that such an insignificant number of Japanese (one and a half percent of the total population), mainly capitalists and their hirelings and agents, rules and oppresses 98.5 percent of the Korean population. Of course, Japan is attracted to Korea mainly by her natural wealth – coal, graphite, iron and gold. In 1917, there was 38 million yen of Japanese capital invested in Korea. Japanese capital will become stronger and stronger every year in Korea, until the time, of course, when the Korean people will take its fate into its own hands. Korea plays in relation to Japan the part of, say, (of course there are some differences) Ireland in relation to England, with the only difference that, as is known, the nearer to the East, the baser, more bloodthirsty, more cynical, and shameless imperialism becomes. If English capitalists were strangling Ireland by comparatively civilised methods, so to speak; if the executioners from among the English imperialists treated Ireland with gloves on their hands, the Japanese imperialists treat Korea with the most unheard of barbarous methods, which ought to arouse the indignation not only of every Korean revolutionist, but of every honest man everywhere. The Communist International is watching the struggle of the Korean people for emancipation with the closest attention.

The Communist International followed with surprise and pain the turn in the course of the struggle of the Korean people for freedom, when some of the Korean leaders put their hopes on Versailles, figuring that they would succeed in ingratiating themselves with the European and Asiatic imperialists. The present Congress will have to tell all the Korean revolutionists, regardless of their particular beliefs, sincerely, and in a brotherly manner, that they must once and for all rid themselves and their people of any remnants of hope that the Korean national question can be solved in any way other than by a close union with the advanced revolutionary workers of Europe and America. They must, once and for all, drive away the thought that any compromise in the solution of the national question is possible by trying to come to an agreement with the imperialists.

Mongolian question. I said in passing that the question of Mongolia is expected by some to be solved by returning it under Chinese sovereignty, and that the imperialists play with this question as with a toy. The same imperialists mock any thought of autonomy in the case of those peoples they have in their clutches, as for instance in the case of Japan's rule in Korea. It seems to me that it would be a very sad situation if among the leaders of, say, Southern revolutionary China, men should be found who would be so doctrinaire on the Mongolian problem as to put forward the question of returning Mongolia [to] Chinese rule. It seems to me that the final solution of the Mongolian question will come at the time when China will free itself from the yoke under which it is groaning now, when China itself will drive out the imperialist soldiers of the foreign nations, when the revolution will be completely victorious in China, and when it will be sufficiently free to be able to say that the fate of China is in the hands of the Chinese themselves, when China will take the liberation from the yoke of oppression, under which she suffers today, in her own hands; when she will herself expel from her territory the soldiers of the foreign imperialist nations; when revolution will finally triumph in China, and the country will have reached the first stage of emancipation; when China will be able to say that her fate is at last in the hands of her people – then, and only then – can the Mongolian question be put in a new light. As for the present, we shall tell the Chinese revolutionists, who are themselves surrounded on all sides by foes and are busy enough with the imperialists; when they themselves can at any time fall victims to these imperialists, when the civil war is not over yet, and China is being torn and cleaved not only into a Northern and a Southern China, but a number of other territorial units; and when the country is still ruled by the will of foreign imperialists – we shall tell these Southern revolutionists that if any doctrinaire among them should demand that Mongolia be immediately given back to China (independently of the situation of the Chinese people) it would be the greatest mistake, nay, more than a mistake. This mistake would lie heavy not only upon Mongolia, but upon China also. A people trying ever so little to oppress [another] cannot itself be free. No people of the Far East should forget this truth. Indeed, we often see that an oppressed people understands perfectly well this [axiom] so long as it is itself concerned, but changes its mind directly its relations with other peoples dependent on it are involved. This same mistake we often noticed with regard to the peoples who had formerly constituted a part of the Russian Empire, and we now deem it our duty to give a word of warning to the Chinese revolutionists, so that they may not repeat it in respect to Mongolia. *As you give, so shall ye receive.* If you wish the emancipation of the Chinese people, if you wish [them] to be liberated from Japan and other oppressors, be mindful not to forget that your policy must be far-seeing when it comes to a people like the Mongolians whose fate is closely connected with yours.

This is the state of affairs with regard to the principal peoples which are most oppressed in the Far East and whose representatives we see here. But we have invited to this Congress, likewise, the representatives of the oppressing nation. We see here quite a large number of Japanese representatives, which, I think, is a correct indication and proof that the Communist International is on a fair way to solving the Far Eastern problem. There is no [solution] without Japan: the Japanese proletariat holds in [its] hands the key to the solution of the Far Eastern question, and the presence at this Congress of the representatives of the Japanese workers is our only serious guarantee that we are at least starting on our way to a true solution of this problem.

The Japanese are known as the Prussians of the East. A part of the Japanese bourgeoisie is proud of that name. They are trying to inoculate the Japanese workers with the venom of patriotism just in the same way as the British imperialists have partly succeeded in poisoning the British workers.

There can be nothing sadder than to see, for instance, the attitude of the British workers with regard to the Irish question, an attitude which is not always what it should be on the part of a worker; somehow you feel that they imbibed with their mother's milk the national prejudices with which the British bourgeoisie consciously imbued them. Well, let us say it openly, we sometimes find that even the British Communists have a wrong way of looking at the Irish question. It was Marx who 50 years ago had already pronounced that the British working class will not be able to emancipate itself unless it emancipates Ireland. Although they recognised it [in] principle, their attitude towards Ireland, towards the Irish workers and peasants, is still ignorant and contemptuous. There is no doubt at all, the Japanese bourgeois want to do exactly the same thing with their workers in respect to China and Korea, and are trying to inoculate the young working class of Japan with the disease known as jingoism. But we hope that the sense of self-preservation of the young Japanese proletariat will prevail against this danger of being inoculated with a serious disease. But at this Congress, when for the first time we see a considerable group of Japanese workers, we deem it our duty to say all we think on this subject fraternally, frankly and honestly. In view of all the experience gone through by the Communist International in all the other countries, we deem it necessary to warn them against the clever and subtle game that is being played upon them by the British capitalists and which the capitalists of Japan are also trying to play. The key to the solution of the Far Eastern question is in the hands of Japan. Marx said that without a revolution in England any European revolution would just amount to but a storm in a teacup. Well, *mutatis mutandis* the same may be said of the Japanese revolution, without which any other revolution in the Far East would be but a local event comparatively unimportant. The Japanese bourgeoisie rules over and oppresses many millions of men in the Far East, holding in its hands the fate of all that part of the world. The only thing that can really solve the Far Eastern question is the defeat of the Japanese bourgeois and the final victory of the revolution in Japan. Only after its victory in that country will the Far Eastern revolution cease to be 'a storm in a teacup'. The greater, then, is the responsibility of the young Japanese proletariat.

Our information is yet far from being complete (this is the first occasion we have for a friendly meeting with the Japanese workers), but even what we know goes to prove that the Japanese labour movement is beginning to awaken and to be organised. In many respects it is still passing through the stage of infantile sickness. Japan has almost three million workers (present-day investigators calculate it at much more). It has nearly five million propertyless peasants. Japan is experiencing a headlong development of capitalism and, at the same time, we nevertheless see that the labour movement in Japan is still very weak. The class-conscious Communists in the country can be counted only in hundreds. The number of revolutionaries, syndicalists, anarchists, also amount only to some hundreds. Since the rice riots in 1918,[22] (that great elemental mass movement) the Japanese bourgeoisie, it seems, has had no occasion to contend against any large revolutionary movement. If we examine the situation in Japan at the present moment, from a distance as it were, we will come to the conclusion that the Japanese bourgeoisie is under the impression that Japan is in the fortunate position of being able to gather in the fruits of an impetuous large-scale development of capitalism and is becoming fabulously rich. Up to the present, she has [had] no need to look on the reverse side of the [coin] and does not yet see the clenched fist of the Japanese labour movement.

---

22   The Japan rice riots of 1918 lasted from July–September, and forced the resignation of the Prime Minister Terauchi Masatake. The riots began in fishing villages in Toyoma prefecture on the northern coast of Honshu but soon spread to Japan's major cities, including Osaka, Kobe, Hiroshima and Tokyo. Major strikes involving tens of thousands of workers broke out in shipyards, factories and mines. Strikers fought battles with police and troops; the miners sometimes used dynamite. The cause of the rioting was general postwar inflation and the doubling of the price of rice in particular, the latter partly the result of government purchases to supply the troops of the Siberian intervention force. Around 25,000 people were arrested during the disturbances.

The fate of the Japanese labour movement is acquiring enormous international importance. I have already told you about the alliance of the four bloodsuckers, formed in Washington for the purpose of (for the time being, in close co-operation) crushing, torturing and partitioning the oppressed peoples of the Far East with even greater savagery than has been done hitherto. This quadruple alliance of bloodsuckers, however, cannot postpone the hour of the inevitable grandiose war in the Pacific Ocean. This war is inevitable. As sure as morning follows night, so will the first imperialist war which ended in 1918, be followed by a second war which will centre round the Far East and the problem of the Pacific. This war can be avoided only by a victory of the proletarian revolution. It is not possible to say whether this war will break out, in 1925 or 1928, a year earlier or later, but it is inevitable. It can no more be avoided than fate. It will be possible to avoid this war only if the young working class of Japan rapidly becomes sufficiently strong to seize the Japanese bourgeoisie by the throat, and if, parallel with that, there will be a victorious revolutionary movement in America.

If civil war breaks out in America, it will by far exceed anything we have seen until now. The civil war in America will be carried on with ruthless stubbornness. It seems to me, those American comrades are right who state that when the struggle between the bourgeoisie and the workers reaches the stage to which it has come in Russia, that whole cities will be blown up, that the American bourgeoisie will fight with such resoluteness that it will result in a terrible catastrophe, in comparison with which the struggle in Russia will appear as child's play. The resistance of the American bourgeoisie will be most determined. No less determined will be the resistance of the avaricious, adroit Japanese bourgeoisie, now still in its prime. Only rapid parallel growth and the strong organisation of the youthful labour movements of Japan and America will be able to save mankind from another war and prevent the tremendous ruin of industry which would result from the unprecedentedly destructive war between America and Japan.

Therefore we have the right to state that the fate of several hundred million people living in China, Korea and Mongolia is in the hands of the working class of Japan. And it is the task of the present Congress to co-ordinate the activities of the oppressed, the non-proletarian masses of the entire Far East with those of the industrial and village proletariat of Japan. You, a little group of advanced workers of your countries, voice the thoughts and aspirations of the hundreds of millions of oppressed of the Far East. You must find the happy solution which [will] really coordinate the movement of the young working class of Japan with that of the non-proletarian, but great masses of those countries which are being oppressed by Japan. The Communist International will attend to everything else. Co-ordination on a larger scale, that is co-ordination with the working class of America, England, France and the other nations who also participate in the exploitation and the division of spoils in the Far East, participate in the alliance of four bloodsuckers; the task of co-coordinating the movement on a world scale must be undertaken by the Comintern as a whole, which considers it the main reason for its existence. The Comintern [has] inscribed on its banner 'The World Revolution' and not merely the European revolution. The European revolution is only a fraction, a little corner on the map of the world revolution. We understand perfectly well that it is our business never to lose sight of these prospects, to do everything to attain the proper co-operation and co-ordination of the forces of the Far East with those of the working class of America and Europe. But the initiative is in your hands, and it will depend to a great extent upon you how far the proper co-ordination of the interests of the proletariat with those of the oppressed non-proletarian masses of the Far East, to whom national freedom and independence is of chief importance, will be attained. The sentiments expressed here are not Communist, but burgeoning nationalist revolutionary sentiments. Will you be able to effect the union of the nationalist-revolutionary movement with the mighty proletarian movement, whose aims are of a purely Communistic character? This union is necessary and inevitable. The Communist International understood the inevitability of this union from the very beginning of its existence. The Communist International considered the question of oppressed nationalities as a particularly important question during its Second Congress.

You will dwell on the policies of the various parties in the Far East in more detail. I need not speak of this question at very great length. I only want to outline in a general sort of way our attitude to the problems of your Congress in connection with the general international situation. I must remind you of the decisions of the Second Congress of the Communist International in 1920, which in the name of the Communist workers of the world declared that we cannot limit ourselves to the slogan of the equality of all nations. That the equality of all nations is necessary is a simple truth known to all of us. We must strive to bring about a situation in which the days when one nation ruled over another one should seem wild and barbarous. But we cannot stop there. Bourgeois very often smuggled their bourgeois contraband under the slogan of equality of all nations. The Communist International says plainly and clearly that the oppressed peoples should unite around a definite country, Soviet Russia.[23] This was pronounced not by some one party: 43 parties which were rep-

---

23   The *Theses on the national and colonial question*, adopted by the Second Comintern Con-

resented at the Second Congress, gathered from the entire world, declared this. They took the responsibility for Soviet Russia upon themselves, and called upon all the oppressed peoples to rally around the country where, for the first time in history, the national question found a happy solution. True, many other questions have not yet been solved by Soviet Russia; many questions particularly in the field of economics, have not yet been solved, there are still many open wounds causing much suffering to the Soviet Republic, but there is one question that exists no more in Russia – the national question. The national question has been solved by the Soviet Republic with unusual ease, quite painlessly, to the complete satisfaction of all the nationalities which made up the Russian Empire and are now living in the Soviet Republic.[24] Only the other day the All-Russian Central Executive Committee had to decide some national questions in the autonomous republics and districts in the Far East and Siberia, and they were solved just as easily and painlessly. You know that Russia is inhabited by tens of nationalities which were groaning under a troubled yoke; you know that during the tsarist rule, the rule of the bourgeoisie, they had many just grievances and hated and mistrusted everything Russian. That which the bourgeoisie and nobility in the course of many decades and centuries spoiled, the working class of Russia honourably and painlessly restored in a few months; it solved the national question in a fraternal manner to the complete satisfaction of all nationalities which have inhabited and which are inhabiting Soviet Russia. This is why we dare to think that, in this connection, we [have] a living, concrete example clothed in flesh and blood. There is no need now for us to discuss abstractions. We have an example of how a nation, [having conquered] its bourgeoisie, should solve its national problems.

This is why the Second Congress of the Comintern had, as it had to have, the courage to call upon all the oppressed peoples, including the oppressed peoples of the Far East, to rally round a definite country, which has had some

---

gress, stated: 'it is impermissible today to limit oneself to mere recognition or proclamation of sympathy with the toilers of various nations, but it is necessary to pursue a policy of bringing about the closest possible alliance between all the national and colonial liberation movements with Soviet Russia'. See Minutes of the Second Congress of the Communist International, http://www.marxists.org/history/international/comintern/2nd-congress/ch05.htm#v1-p177, retrieved 14 April 2014.

24 Zinoviev did not mention the Red Army invasion of Georgia, and the overthrow of its Menshevik government, in February–March 1921. In 1922, on the initiative of Stalin and Ordzhonikidze, Georgia was amalgamated into the Transcaucasian Soviet Republic, along with Armenia and Azerbaijan, despite opposition from the local Bolshevik leadership. Lenin opposed Stalin's bulldozing methods, but illness prevented him from taking effective action. The Transcaucasian republic was dissolved into its components in 1936.

experience in this connection, viz. Soviet Russia, in order that they, together with her, in the same way as she had, [may] solve the painful national problems which hang unsolved over many millions of people. This Second Congress, in the main, solved the very same questions which you have to solve – the problem of co-coordinating the forces of the awakening oppressed peoples who are conducting a struggle, as yet not for socialism, but for their own emancipation, with the fighting proletariat in those countries where a proletariat exists. China, Korea and Mongolia are not to blame because they [do not have] an industrial proletariat. They could not immediately skip several stages of development. There is no harm in this. But it will be a misfortune if we fail to combine this movement with the labour movement in Japan and America. We are not doctrinaires, nor [are we] sectarians. We do not abandon, nor will we abandon the [basis] of Communism. We will preach Communism wherever we meet even a small group of people, but at the same time, we will live and fight shoulder to shoulder with the many-millioned masses who are living and fighting in this sinful world, and take them as they are. We will advise our comrades, the Chinese, Korean and Japanese Communists who, for the time being, are a small group, not to stand aside and look down loftily upon the poor, sinful souls who have not yet become Communists, but to go right in among the tens of millions of people who are fighting in China, people who, for the time being, are fighting for their national independence and emancipation. They must go right in among them and become their leaders. This is essential because history has raised this question quite definitely. The solution of the national question lies not in Washington, but in the hands of the proletariat, and only in its hands.

To the leaders of the nationalist movement we say – give up your faith in Versailles and Washington. Do not believe these bourgeois intrigues. Remember that history has [posed] the question thus: you [will] either win your independence side by side with the proletariat, or you [will] not win it at all; either you receive your emancipation at the hands of the proletariat, in co-operation with it, under its guidance, or you are doomed to remain the slaves of an English, American and Japanese camarilla; either the hundreds and millions of toilers of China, Korea, Mongolia and other countries understand that their ally and leader is the world proletariat and once and for all give up all hope in any kind of bourgeois and imperialist intrigue, or their national movement must be doomed to failure and imperialists will always ride on their backs, sow civil war and crush and carve [up] their country. This question is presented in this manner, not by theoreticians, writers; it is not the fantasy of some leader, but has been so presented by the process of development of world history, by the process of development of world imperialism which [has pushed] forward the problem of the Far East to a place of first importance. This is what the Communist International says, addressing itself to both sections of the Congress; to that section which is composed of conscious Communists and whose function is to organise the working class for victory over the bourgeoisie, as well as to that section which is composed of non-proletarian elements, of the leaders of those toiling masses which are fighting against foreign oppression. An alliance between these two groups is essential, and we will be playing the game of the bourgeoisie if we by any means weaken this alliance. Our Congress will acquire universal historical importance if we manage to advance the solution of this problem of the co-ordination and co-operation between these two gigantic historical world forces.

Comrade Lenin has often said, [the] hundreds of millions of men in the Far East are, as he put it, the last reserves of humanity. Indeed, so they are. Today, after a struggle of many years, the Russian proletariat is still bleeding to death as the vanguard of the world proletarian revolution, unwilling to leave its post. Even if we achieve victory in Europe, ours will not be a final victory so long as the Far Eastern question remains unsolved, so long as the last reserves of humanity [have not been] called up and the many million masses in the countries whose representatives you are [have not been] roused. This Congress which is not so very strong numerically, but which is important for its quality, meeting as it does in most difficult conditions and while the canting chorus of the hypocrite plunderers assembled in Washington has not yet died away, has a worldwide and historical task before it. These imperialist plunderers are going to meet in Genoa very soon, and there they will try to stifle Soviet Russia and gamble for your clothes. For, do not forget that you, the many million people of the Far East, are today the only sweet morsel that has not yet been divided. Today, the bourgeois of the world are not aware themselves of what is happening, and of what the morrow has in store for them. They know not what awaits them when they awake, and they do not know whether they are on the eve of a new period of prosperity or on the verge of ruin; and at this moment you are [the ones] whose weight in the scale will be decisive. If this awakening of the Far Eastern peoples [proceeds] rapidly, in an organised manner and energetically, if you declare war [in] your slumbering East, if you who represent the most advanced elements of your peoples lead their struggle without any consideration for the inevitable sacrifices, and if you understand that your true leader is the Comintern, then many among you will live to see the real and final victory of the world revolution. (*Loud cheers*).

Chairman. The bureau proposes that the translation of Comrade Zinoviev's speech into Chinese, Mongolian, and Korean should be heard at the sessions of the national sections. The evening session will be opened at 6 o'clock, and the reports of the delegates will be heard. The debate on comrade Zinoviev's report will follow tomorrow. I now declare the full session of the toilers of the Far East closed, and I propose that the comrades should arrange for their translation of comrade Zinoviev's speech.

(*Closure of session*).

Third Session

23 January 1922. 6:20 p.m.

Chairman: Comrade *Safarov*.

Chairman. Comrades, the third session of the Congress of the Toilers of the Far East is hereby declared open. According to this morning's decision, we now have to receive the reports from the different countries. In the order of rotation I will now call upon comrade Li-Kieng of the Chinese delegation.

Li-Kieng [Zhang Guotao].[1] Dear comrades, I want to tell you about the sufferings of the many millions of our people, I also wish to explain to you the development of our revolutionary movement.

The most important and the most essential question in this respect is the question of the political position of China. You know that China is by its composition the most populous and most heterogeneous country. It has a popula-

---

1 Zhang Guotao (1897–1979) was a prominent leader of the Chinese Communist Party from 1921, when he chaired its founding congress, until 1938, when he defected to the Kuomintang following a clash with Mao Zedong. Zhang studied at Beijing University and played a leading role in the 1919 May Fourth movement. He then became a labour organiser, heading up the Chinese Labour Secretariat established on the initiative of the Communist Party in 1921. He helped organise the 1923 Beijing-Hankou railroad strike. Zhang was dropped from the Central Committee in 1923 for opposing entry into the Kuomintang, but was re-elected the following year after recanting. In 1927, he was elected to the Politburo. In 1928, he was a delegate to the Sixth Comintern Congress and stayed in Moscow to study at the International Lenin School where, despite campaigning against 'Trotskyism', he narrowly avoided being labelled a Trotskyist by the arch-Stalinist Wang Ming. After returning to China in 1931, he was elected deputy head of the Chinese Soviet Government. In 1935, during the Long March, he was appointed chief political commissar of the Red Army. He led a separate division and was seen as a rival to Mao. According to some, Zhang plotted to assassinate Mao after a disagreement over military tactics. Zhang's army was eventually routed and he arrived in Yan'an without troops and therefore at a disadvantage in the inner-party struggle. In 1948, he fled to Taiwan, later to Hong Kong, and finally to Canada, where he died in 1979, having recently converted to Christianity. When in Moscow for the Far East Congress, he met with Lenin, along with Deng Pei, Zhang Qiubai and Kim Kyu-sik. According to his own account of the meeting, he expressed minor reservations when Lenin urged the Communists and Kuomintang to co-operate. This angered Zhang Qiubai, who reported it back to Sun Yat-sen. Zhang Guotao's assessment of the Congress was that, by focusing on anti-imperialism, it defined a clear strategy for the Chinese revolution. See Zhang Guotao 1971, pp. 171–209; Pantsov 2009, pp. 3722–4; Yao and Su 2007, p. 51.

tion of nearly 350 million, but until some hundred years ago it was unknown to Europeans and to foreigners generally. Intercourse with Europeans was exceedingly weak. Nevertheless it was the belief of foreigners that China [was a] most abundant and affluent country. And as a matter of fact, China did enjoy comparative prosperity.

The first conflict with Europeans arose in 1839,[2] mainly with the English, on the question of the opium traffic. As a result of this conflict the English defeated the Chinese, and since then the foreigners began to invade China by force. That period may be considered as the beginning of the economic oppression of China, which kept on increasing by degrees until the very beginning of the twentieth century. The twentieth century found China already in the position of an enslaved country and since 1904 – that is since the beginning of the Russo-Japanese war – foreigners began already definitely to [reveal] their designs for dividing up China. In 1914, while the attention of the European Powers was occupied by the war in the West, [the] Japanese imperialists benefited [from] this very favourable opportunity to put the noose on China's neck, and in 1915[3] they presented to China the famous ultimatum consisting of 21 points.[4] This ultimatum was to bring about the complete economic and political enslavement of China; but even prior to that time, as I have said before, China was already a dependent country. Heavy taxation, railways, custom-house duties – all these, as a result of European influence, created an atmosphere of complete subjection and complete dependence. [The] big imperialist countries conducted in China the bitterest economic fight among themselves, trying to utilise and seize her natural wealth, and in order to achieve this aim, they resorted to all available means, particularly of [a] political nature. You know that the Japanese, like the English and Americans, at first tried to make use of the political

---

2   Britain started the First Opium War (1839–42) after China seized 20,000 casks of opium from British traders. In the Treaty of Nanking, China ceded Hong Kong Island to Britain, agreed to pay an indemnity, and opened five treaty ports.
3   The original text says 1916.
4   Taking advantage of the distraction of its imperialist rivals by the world war, Japan presented 21 demands to China on 18 January 1915. On 7 May, it presented an ultimatum, giving the Chinese two days to provide a satisfactory response. The demands, divided into five groups, affirmed Japanese predominance in Shandong, Southern Manchuria and Eastern Inner Mongolia, handed effective control of China's coal and steel industry to Japanese capitalists, barred China from granting coastal concessions to any other power, and required China to buy arms from Japan, appoint Japanese political and military advisors to senior positions, and hand over control of police forces to in certain areas. Japan also sought to use its control of Taiwan to demand economic privileges in the adjacent coastal province of Fujian. On 8 May, the Yuan Shikai government acceded to all the demands apart from those relating to arms sales, advisors, and Fujian province.

groups, and of the subsequently formed governments. We know that the English have definitely supported the Chinese general Wu Peifu.[5] We know that the Japanese have supported the Anfu Party.[6] All this has gradually brought about the disappearance of any government in China that could defend the country. Along with the development of economic competition, the Europeans invested in China huge sums of their capital. European enterprises in China began to grow, and along with this growth there has sprung up a Chinese working class. Now we may already speak of two million Chinese workers, whose position is an unenviable one. The working day consists of 12 hours, and sometimes more; we know that this involves the ruthless exploitation of female and juvenile labour. The Chinese workers are divided into general categories; there are categories of industrial workers known as skilled workers, and there are categories of unskilled workers whose position is much worse. A special category of workers, having no equal anywhere in the world, are the so-called coolies. They are people that toil from early morn till late at night, or even from dawn to dawn, without being assured a minimum subsistence. They are the most dispossessed workers in the world. There is yet another group of artisan-workers who, in connection with the present development of machinery and mechanical industries, are losing their independence and joining the ranks of the coolies.

There is also another group of the population, which experiences distress of a similar nature to that of the coolies. These are the peasants. The peasants in China represent 70 percent of the entire population and since time immemorial have developed a high [standard] of agriculture. In olden times, they possessed a sufficiency of land and could live in comparative ease. But since the foreigners began to invade the country, China began to be economically dependent upon Europeans. Industry began to develop, the condition of the peasants took a change for the worse, and towards 1911 we find the peasants in

---

5   Wu Peifu (1874–1939) was the leader of the Zhili Clique of warlords that was generally favoured by Western interests and fought several wars against the Japanese-backed Anfu and Fengtian Cliques. Wu was considered a talented military strategist and well placed to reunite China (he made the cover of *Time* magazine in 1924). He was courted by Soviet diplomats, who hoped to persuade him to ally with Sun Yat-sen to form a national unity government. Wu's political standing inside China suffered badly when his troops violently suppressed the 1923 Beijing-Hankou railway strike. In 1927, during the Northern Expedition, his army was destroyed by the Kuomintang's National Revolutionary Army and he retired from public life. See L.W. Pye and M.W. Pye 1984, p. 132; 'Zhili-Fengtian War (1922–24)', in Li Xiaobing 2012, p. 120; Saich 1991, pp. 123–4.

6   The *Anfu* (Peace and Happiness) Club was the political wing of the Japanese-backed Anhui clique of warlords.

a desperate position. This was the year of the first Chinese revolution, when the peasants, ruined by the hardships imposed through foreign domination, which found their chief expression in heavy taxation, both direct and indirect, and in a shrinking of the area [under] cultivation, were forced to look for light labour, thus creating a lumpenproletariat, or had to demand an improvement of their conditions. But no improvement came. Peasant farming was gradually shrinking. In 1920, they sustained a cruel blow from a natural calamity – drought – and it may be said that no trace was left of the former prosperity of the peasantry. The peasants that remain are suffering great hardships from the ceaseless civil war which is rending China. The war in the Lake provinces[7] of Hunan and Hubei undermined the existence of peasant farming in those regions, while the famine of 1920[8] had the same effect upon peasant farming in many Northern provinces. Conflicts with Europeans, millions [taken in] taxation [from] peasant properties, all these have accelerated the final economic ruin of the peasantry. The Chinese market is now [at the mercy of] of the foreigners. In the past the peasant could bring his produce and homemade goods to the cities and exchange them for the articles which he needed; now he cannot do so, because everything has been captured by the foreigners and the [city-dwellers] can purchase [better] and cheaper manufactured goods. Thus the peasant, as an economic unit, is losing his mainstay, and we [have seen] the gradual conquest of the market by foreigners and the decay of [the] peasant economy during the last decade. This has been accompanied by continuously rising prices, by [a high and ever growing] cost of living. During the last 15 years there has been an increase of 100 percent and even 150 percent in the price of food. It thus became extremely difficult for many Chinamen to gain the minimum of subsistence, [creating] tremendous hardships for the poorer population.

I will now touch upon yet another question which is of importance in China at the present moment. It is the religious question. We know that the foreign capitalists began their religious propaganda in Shandong and gradually spread over the whole of China a network of their religious communities of various shades but of similar character. Their religion by no means pursues that goal

---

7   This perhaps refers to the 1918 Constitutional Protection War between Duan Qirui's Beijing government and Sun Yat-sen's military government based in Canton. The war led to Duan's resignation. In February 1919, peace negotiations were convened in Shanghai to resolve the north-south divide, but the talks collapsed after the outbreak of the May Fourth Movement.
8   The North China famine of 1920–21 affected around 30 million people. The relatively low death toll of less than a million compared with the 9–13 million deaths in the Great Famine of 1876–79 was due to a well-publicised international relief effort led by Christian missionaries, as well as less well-known local initiatives by Buddhists and others. See Fuller 2013, pp. 820–50.

by which it is masked. The Chinese converts go to church on Sundays in order to indulge in flagrant robbery on weekdays. Thus, religion in China appears as something that protects robbery, and sometimes even [promotes] it. I also wish to say that Japan has sent her agents to buy up the land of the ruined peasants, expecting in this manner to become finally established upon the continent. This they achieve the more readily since the peasants, under the stress of economic oppression, quite willingly sell their land. Once the peasantry paid taxes which amounted only to one percent of their incomes, [but] now these taxes have gone up to one third of [the entire income] of the peasantry. It is this unbearable burden of taxation, along with the other hardships enumerated above, that drives the peasants into joining the [armies], looking for a means of easy earnings. It is [in this way] that the [armies] and robber bands [grow]. Bandits are one of the greatest evils in China and there is no possibility of getting rid of them as their ranks are always being replenished by new recruits from the peasantry. The only way of getting rid of this evil is to raise the peasants' [standard of living].

I will touch in brief on the question of education, of children's homes, which at one time were in existence in China. Owing to economic and also to political causes, namely, the absence of organs which could organise and support such institutions, the latter hardly exist at all at the present time. In connection with this question of education, another very important question in China remains unsolved.

The economic situation in China is becoming worse, and the position of China is becoming unbearable. This difficult situation has not only affected those groups of the population which I have enumerated, but also the small and middle employers who cannot [compete] against the foreign capitalists and cannot even succeed in holding their own in their home market. China's indebtedness to foreign capitalists has reached the enormous figure of several milliard dollars, and this indebtedness is the chief factor in the development of foreign capitalism in China. The more the indebtedness increases, the [tighter] becomes the capitalist hold over China and the more [pressing] becomes the question of revolution against the foreign yoke. We know that the first important movement against the foreigners [took] place in 1911. The revolution in China was fought out on the basis of the struggle against foreign penetration.[9]

---

9   In May 1911, the Qing government ordered the nationalisation of locally-owned railway projects in order to sell the operating rights to a consortium of foreign banks (the so-called First Banking Consortium). Poor compensation to shareholders led to mass protests, especially in Sichuan province, that sparked the 1911 Revolution.

In 1915, the well-known treaty with Japan consisting of 21 points was the cause of a powerful wave of risings against the Japanese – risings which convulsed the whole country.¹⁰

We well remember the [huge] students' movement in China in 1919,¹¹ which was of the same nature. This movement is continually growing in strength. Moreover, the [newly formed] proletariat in China is awakening. We know that in 1919 there has already been a rising against the foreigners. We know that there was a strike last year in Shanghai which was definitely directed against the English. The Beijing-Hankou Railway had a similar strike.¹² The attitude towards foreigners has been made clearer by a new circumstance – the Washington Conference – the secret intentions of which are now becoming apparent. This gives us an opportunity [to discuss] the question of our resistance to the world imperialists. We now have the opportunity to discuss the questions [facing] the revolutionary movement. We know that as life in China becomes more unbearable, the revolutionary movement grows in strength. We must follow the example of the Russian Revolution and we must find means of throwing off the foreign yoke of exploitation over China in order to emancipate the poorest [sections of the] population in China. In the first place, it is imperative to bring about unification among the poorest [proletarians]. And at this Congress, unification must be our chief concern. We know that no force is strong enough to resist us if we are united. The Third Communist International is the organ of world revolution. Let us unite under its banner. Let us confound the world imperialists. It is only [in this way] that we shall realise our aims.

I say: Long Live the Congress of the Revolutionary Parties of the Far East! Long Live the Third Communist International! Long live the world proletariat! (*Applause*).

---

10   In 1915, nationalists organised a boycott of Japanese goods to protest against the 21 demands.
11   That is, the May Fourth Movement. On 4 May 1919, thousands of students demonstrated in Beijing to protest against the award of Qingdao and other former German concessions in Shandong province to Japan by the treaty of Versailles. China joined the war in 1917 and sent 140,000 labourers to serve with the British army in France. The Chinese public had therefore expected to regain Shandong and were outraged at the betrayal of Chinese aspirations as well as the weak response of the Beijing government. Strikes and boycotts of foreign goods spread across the country. Many of those who took part went on to join the Communist Party. The most prominent May Fourth leader, Chen Duxiu, founded the party and became its first general secretary.
12   One of a series of strikes on the Beijing-Hankou (Beijing-Hankou) line. The most famous strike took place a year after the Congress in February 1923 and was bloodily suppressed by the warlord Wu Peifu.

Chairman. Comrades, we shall now proceed with the translation into the Korean, Japanese and Mongolian languages. To save time we shall do this in different halls, and while this is going on the plenum will go into recess.

Chairman. Comrades, the session is now resumed A proposal has just been made to limit the reports of the speakers to half an hour. Any objections?

We have two propositions – one to allow one hour for each report, to hear only one report today and the remainder tomorrow. The second proposition is to reduce time for discussion to half an hour. I call upon those who are in favour of the time being reduced to half an hour, to raise their hands.

Comrade *Wong-Kien-Ti* will now make his report – one hour.

Wong-Kien-Ti [Deng Pei].[13] It was only eighty years ago, when the world imperialists first came to China, that the Chinese workers came to be virtual slaves. From that time [on], Chinese industry developed day by day. It developed and expanded greatly until there were two million workers. These two million slaves of capital are new slaves, but real slaves. Their conditions are very hard and bad. The Chinese labouring masses exist in large numbers but there is not a single law to protect the Chinese workers, and therefore the foreign capitalists and foreign capital can exploit them and enslave them without any limitations. If a number of workers die from overwork or from starvation, capital [does not lose] by it. And, therefore, the Chinese worker may toil more than 12 hours a day – yes, even more, though mostly they work 12 hours. There are some who work nine or ten or eleven hours, but these are only 200,000 in number. The rest of them work more than 12 hours daily. And their [pay] is quite low, for it amounts to about thirty cents silver a day on average. [But] the cost of living

---

13   Deng Pei (1884–1927) was a workers' leader and trade unionist who joined the Communist Party in 1921. Born in Guangdong province, at the age of 14 Deng was apprenticed as a metal worker in a factory in Tangshan in northern China. He later became a mechanic in a workshop of the Jingfeng Railway. He attended the Congress as a delegate from the Tangshan railway workers union. While in Moscow he was received by Lenin in the Kremlin along with Zhang Guotao, Zhang Qiubai and Kim Kyu-sik. Deng Pei was an alternate member of the CPC Central Committee from 1923. In 1924, he was elected head of the All-China Federation of Railway Workers' Unions and was elected to the executive committee of the All-China Federation of Trade Unions on its foundation in 1925. In 1926, he moved to Canton and was elected chairman of the Guangdong Federation of Trade Unions. He was tortured and executed by the Kuomintang during the April 1927 counterrevolutionary coup in Canton. See Deng Pei's delegate questionnaire, 495-154-178-022, Russian State Archive of Socio-Political History, Moscow; http://www.baike.com/gwiki/邓培, retrieved 27 January 2014; http://baike.baidu.com/view/1806.htm, retrieved 27 January 2014; Yao and Su 2007, p. 51.

is at least 7 dollars a month and as a result,[14] if the worker lives only for himself and alone perhaps he may manage to exist, but when there is a family then he must suffer, and they must suffer, from hunger. Moreover, there is no labour legislation. There are no hospitals for the workers, especially workers in factories, and the workers are employed in [the kind of] factories which need such institutions. Most of the factories are [in poor condition]; there is a lack of air and lack of light, and yet [nobody cares]. The foremen [oppress] the workers, for as foreign capital [grows] in China, it wants to enslave the Chinese workers [even] more cruelly than native capital, and [employs] special foremen to that end. The workers are more enslaved than the soldiers. They are oppressed by the foremen, and now the foreign capitalists are using contractors. These foremen and contractors make the workers live under [still] harder conditions and so they suffer additionally.

Among the workers, only about 5 percent [can] read [at all]; the rest are quite illiterate and ignorant.

There are also ten million[15] women and children working in factories. The women workers are employed in [various] industries, [like] the men. The conditions under which they work are worse than those of the men. Children too [suffer harsh] conditions as they [work] even in dangerous industries. They work also 12 hours a day and often work in the night as do the men. Yet there are no laws or legislation by the State or in the different factories [to] protect them.

As regards the handicraft workers, before the coming of foreign capitalism they [survived, although with difficulty], yet they could exist by themselves as independent workers, they could work freely. But, after foreign capital came to China, of course, the handicraft workers were affected and could not compete with the foreign capitalists. Therefore their conditions became worse day by day. Day by day, conditions of life and work became harder. A large number of handicraft workers in the big cities and towns are now unemployed. They are all becoming the real slaves of the foreign capitalists or the interests of these capitalists, and there is no labour law to protect them. They also work 12 hours a day, or at least ten hours a day. They work from sunrise to sunset, and their wage is about 25 cents a day.

---

14   Chinese dollars. In 1914, Yuan Shikai silver dollars began to replace Mexican silver dollars and other foreign coins that had circulated in China since the seventeenth century, and the so-called Dragon dollars minted from the late nineteenth century onwards.
15   Ten million seems a little high given that Deng said earlier there were two million workers. Perhaps he meant ten million women and children in addition to male workers. Women were the majority of the working class in many cities since they predominated in the textile and other light industries which employed most workers. See Johnson 2009, pp. 42–3.

We now come to the question of the coolies. As the cost of living increases, the number of coolies also increases daily. In every big town one will find a great number of coolies waiting for work. Their wage is uncertain. Sometimes they can get work, but sometimes for a few days they are without work and they starve. As the new industries develop in China, the different factories attract a great number of coolies to them, but at the same time as the number of workers increases and as they join the army of slaves, so the army of coolies also increases daily. Even the worst factories attract a great number of coolies.

The workers [have] organised guilds. There [are] separate guilds for each [type] of worker. These guilds are not organisations to fight capital. They are organised to limit the [numbers] of workers in that particular trade. The guild is [an] organ concerned with the [internal] struggle[s] of the trade – for those already in the trade. And this means that it is not a fighting organ.[16] But now some of the guilds [have been] re-organised into unions and the remaining guilds are not many in number. Therefore they have no great influence on the labour movement. But the semi-proletariat still believes in the guilds and therefore they [continue to exist] as organs. Yet those that still [exist] have no important position. However, these guilds could be used to properly organise the handicraft workers.

In [the last] few years – [for practical purposes since 1919] – some labour unions have been formed. This, we can perhaps say, is influenced [on the one hand] by the Russian Revolution and [on the other] by the students' movement, by the movement of the intellectuals in China. Before 1919, there were some signs of a movement in China but not on any large scale. But [the factors] I mentioned above stimulated the workers to join the labour movement. After joining this movement their activities first began. Now the workers have some faith in their own organised [strength]. From 1919 [onwards], in [various] places labour unions began to be organised, for example in Tangshan, where a railway workers' union was organised. At first it was a kind of a patriotic union but now it is a fighting union. In Hunan there is now also a labour union. The labour union in Tangshan has 2,500 members. In Hunan there are 5,000. The Mechanical Workers' Union in Canton is the biggest union

---

16   Guilds sought to regulate prices and entry into the trade, and provided some welfare services to members. They included both workers and employers, with the latter occupying the leadership positions, although, from the nineteenth century on, separate worker sections were established in many guilds. Despite Deng Pei's statement that the guilds were on the decline, as late as 1925 there were still 175 occupational guilds in Shanghai. The defeat of the Communists in 1927 dealt a severe blow to the trades unions that were expected to supplant them. See Smith 2002, pp. 32–5.

in China. [A] Metal Workers' Union was organised in the last [few] years. These are the [major] labour unions in China. These unions, we can say, are the real fighting organs of the workers. The success of these unions, as we just mentioned, [was] influenced by the students' movement and the Russian Revolution. Of course, it is also [being] influenced by the activity of the Communists.

We now come to the activity of the Chinese workers – the movement of the Chinese workers. [Over the last] few years there have been several large and important strikes. In 1920, the metal workers struck in Canton; it was a [major] strike – about 14,000 workers took part. In May 1921, there was another strike of about 20,000 workers, and conditions improved as a result. Wages were increased and hours decreased. In Fula,[17] in 1921, the workers in the textile industry struck in order to get control of the factories. This strike did not result in a victory, yet it was a very important strike. There were 5,000 workers [involved]. In Shanghai recently, the tobacco workers struck and there was also a railway workers' strike. These are the important strikes which we know of in recent years. [They show] that the Chinese workers are beginning to awaken. And after these forces are organised and concentrated for the purpose of fighting with the imperialists, they will succeed.

China now has a very important position. The world imperialists consider China and the Far East as the most important place, and they are concentrating [their forces] to exploit it and enslave the Chinese working masses on a larger scale, more intensely than ever before. The Chinese toiling masses [number] 300 million. These masses, together with [China's] abundant raw materials, are of the greatest importance to imperialism, and as a large mass they are also very important for our revolutionary purpose. From our viewpoint, therefore, it is now our task to organise these large masses that are now beginning to awaken, to fight against imperialism.

This Congress is meeting here for the purpose of organising the toiling masses in the Far East. We hope that this Congress will bring the Far Eastern toiling masses together under the banner of the Third International, to fight against our common enemy – world imperialism.

Long live the union of the Far Eastern toiling masses with the world proletariat! Long live Soviet Russia! Long live the Red Trade Union International! Long live the Third Communist International!

---

17   There seems to be no place called Fula in China. There were many strikes in the Shanghai textile industry during this period.

Chairman. Now, comrades, we shall proceed to the translations. As, according to the standing orders, the session is to close at 10 p. m. and as it is now a quarter past nine, we shall have no time after the translations have been made, and so we shall now close the plenary session. I must ask all comrades not to leave for supper until after the translations are over, and same will be made into the Mongolian, Korean and Japanese languages. Any objections? The plenary session is closed and will open again tomorrow, at 11 o'clock.

(*Closure of session*).

Fourth Session

24 January 1922. 11:30 a.m.

Chairman: comrade *Safarov*.

Safarov. I declare the session opened. First on the agenda is the continuation of the report of the Chinese delegation. Comrade *Ping-Tong*, representative of the Young China Society, has the floor.

Ping-Tong [Yu Shude].[1] I am going to report on the economic situation of China which, as you know, is oppressed by the imperialists of [the whole] world. You know that the Chinese workers and peasants are exploited not only by foreign imperialists but are bearing the yoke of their own capitalists and military bureaucracy as well. The position of the Chinese masses is therefore extremely difficult, and it is therefore the first task of the revolutionists of China to bring about the economic emancipation of the Chinese people, for when this question is satisfactorily settled it will be easy to solve all other questions. If the Chinese people could now free themselves from their dependence upon foreign financial capital, all other questions connected with their existence would appear slight and unimportant. I shall therefore begin my report by dwelling upon economic questions and, first of all, upon their historic development.'

The year 1839 witnessed the birth of the first military collision between China and England. This collision was brought about by the contraband trade in opium which was carried on by the English plunderers. China suffered a

---

1 Yu Shude (1894–1982) joined the Tongmenghui (a forerunner of the Kuomintang) in his teens and took part in the 1911 Revolution. He studied at Kyoto University from 1918–21, where he was influenced by Marxist and Anarchist ideas. He attended the Far East Congress as a student union representative, but joined the Communist Party on his return to China and organised party branches in Tianjin and Hangzhou. Following the turn to working inside the Kuomintang, he attended the first Kuomintang national congress in 1924 and was elected to its executive committee. After the Kuomintang coup against the Communists, he dropped out of politics and devoted himself to research into agricultural co-operatives. During the war against Japan, he was appointed deputy general secretary of the China Industrial Cooperatives Association. After 1949, he was appointed to the standing committee of the Chinese People's Political Consultative Committee. See Yu Shude's delegate questionnaire, 495-154-181-035, Russian State Archive of Socio-Political History, Moscow; Yao and Su 2007, p. 51; http://baike.baidu.com/subview/288885/11518650.htm, retrieved 27 January 2014.

defeat, and since then, Chinese diplomacy has been unsuccessful in its relations with the foreign states which moved into China with constantly growing appetites. This conflict showed the foreigners that China was a peace-loving country; that she [could] be offended with impunity, and they thereupon began their attacks upon her.

Much has happened since then. I shall only touch upon the most important events. In 1895, war broke out between Japan and China,[2] [and] in 1900 the Boxer Rising took place. These two events prompted the Europeans, united in the so-called Eight-Nation Alliance, to send their troops to Beijing. After the Boxer Rising, various schemes were devised by them for the division of China. Foreigners obtained a number of concessions on Chinese territory; English concessions in Weihaiwei, Russian on the Liaodong Peninsula, German in Shandong, etc. In this division of China, American appetites had not yet asserted themselves. This country stood [aside] at the time the economic noose was tightening more and more around the neck of China. The war between China and Japan was the greatest stimulus for the development of spheres of influence in China. These spheres of influence act as a rope for the strangulation of China.

When the situation in China became unbearable, America apparently became envious at the successes of her competitors [and] began to carry out her own policy, ostensibly favourable to the interests of China, the so-called policy of the 'open door'. This policy was intended in reality to bring greater profits to the Americans who, being in a better economic position, could beat their competitors in China.

The events of 1914, which threw all Europe into the throes of the Great War, temporarily obscured the Far Eastern question, diverted the attention of Europe, and gave Japan a free hand in China. Japan [ramped] up her demands [on] China in the middle of the war, extended her influence and threatened to enslave and capture the whole of China. To counteract this attempt, a consor-

---

2   The 1894–95 Sino-Japanese War began as a contest for control of Korea between its traditional patron, Imperial China, and Japan, which had backed modernisers among the Korean political elite. In June 1894, Chinese troops were sent to help the Korean government put down a peasant rebellion inspired by the Tonghak (Eastern Learning) cult. Japan claimed that China's unilateral action broke an agreement concluded in 1884, after Chinese troops based in Seoul suppressed the Japanese-backed Kapsin coup. Japan sent 8,000 troops to Korea and fighting between the two sides began in late July 1894. Although, on paper, China had the more powerful armed forces, it was comprehensively defeated. In the 1895 Treaty of Shimonoseki, China relinquished all claims over Korea and ceded Taiwan, the Pescadores, and the Liaodong peninsula in Manchuria to Japan. Japan was, however, forced to hand back the Liaodong peninsula by the Triple Intervention of Russia, France and Germany.

tium of foreign States was [established] which, in taming the Japanese plunderers, intended to put China under their own economic and political control.

With the growth of foreign capital in China there [has begun] to develop a young working class which is awakening and becoming conscious of its own interests. This working class of China will soon be ready to take up open struggle against foreign oppression, against foreign intervention. This is the historic background of the present economic situation in China which I shall now describe.

I shall begin with the large industries. [Many] factories and mills in China belong to foreigners; the others, while ostensibly Chinese, in reality also belong to the foreigners. Of the concrete works, for instance, of which there are altogether 51, 30 belong to foreigners, the others being ostensibly Chinese. In the chemical and dye industry, 11 out of 20 works belong to foreigners. Of 33 fruit drying and egg powder factories, 16 are owned by foreigners. Shipbuilding yards, to the number of 13, are almost entirely owned by foreigners. Flour mills, textile factories, tobacco and other factories are either nominally or actually owned by foreigners. Thus all the big factories, all the industries of China, are closely connected with foreign capital and have no independent existence. With regard to the coal mining industry, I must say that, out of a total of 19 million tons brought to the surface, 9.38 million tons belonged directly to foreign companies. We observe the same thing in the iron industry. Out of an output of 400,000 tons of iron, 150,000 tons represented the foreigners' share. All these figures demonstrate quite clearly the condition of Chinese industry, which is totally dependent upon foreign capital. Out of about 7,000 miles of Chinese railways, 2,600 were built directly by Europeans, and the remainder [were financed by] foreign loans, i.e. on foreign capital. With regard to telegraphic, postal and telephonic services, these may be said to be directly subsidised and even managed by foreigners.[3]

With regard to the question of the financial condition and financial policy of China, I must say that China [runs] an unusually heavy deficit. The incomes obtained by direct taxation, to the sum of 3–4 billion taels, have been gradually shrinking, and in 1911, the year of the Chinese revolution, there ensued a rapid decrease of state revenues, which makes any [systematic] financial policy

---

3 China's Imperial Postal Service, established in 1897, was the successor to a mail service established for the Imperial Maritime Customs service by its Inspector General Sir Robert Hart in 1865. In 1878, the service was opened to the public and issued China's first postage stamps. Foreign control of the customs service was intended both to keep import duties low but also to ensure that taxes and duties were collected and, consequently, that the Chinese government had a stream of revenue with which to repay foreign loans.

a matter of impossibility. In order to ease the financial situation, the Chinese government, during the short period of 1912–18, contracted 23 foreign loans. But all these loans have brought no improvement. On the contrary, these loans have brought about the mortgaging of custom-house duties and many other internal revenues (e.g. duties on salt, tobacco, etc.) to foreign capitalist creditors who [assume] direct control over the revenues. This [leaves] China in hopeless financial bondage. Trade with foreigners is expressed by the following figures: from 1910–12, exports equalled 4.6 million yuan, which were exceeded by imports to the tune of 80–200 million yuan. Thus there was a colossal difference between insignificant exports and gigantic imports. This unhinged balance of trade caused tremendous losses to the population, particularly to the trading element, which was frequently brought to total ruin. Furthermore, this gave the foreign capitalists the possibility to control financial cost[s] and thus govern trade. Chinese exports consisted solely of raw materials, of those materials that were necessary to foreign factories and workshops. Such operations, whereby the foreign capitalists converted Chinese raw materials into manufactured goods and sold [them] back to the Chinese, were highly profitable to the foreigners. It must be added that Chinese merchants, afraid of distant voyages, preferred to stay at home and conduct trade within the country. This caused them colossal losses, and these losses were borne not only by the merchants, but also by the masses of the population, because the losses sustained by trade [directly affected] the entire country.

I also wish to say a few words about the peasantry. The peasants in China do not experience the same direct oppression as the rest of the population, but indirectly they do. It must be said that, since time immemorial, the Chinese peasants [have always engaged in] subsidiary employments. During the winter, they would work at some craft which gave them additional means of subsistence. In this manner, there developed a whole series of home industries which flourished extensively. I want to point out particularly the weaving industry, which employed many peasant women. [Since] the beginning of the new era, when China fell under the economic domination of foreigners who import their manufactures into China, the demand for homemade goods, which are of a lower quality and require more labour, [has been] continuously falling. All artisans, as well as peasants are beginning to give up these auxiliary occupations, as [they are] not worthwhile. This brings ruin to a great many peasants who are becoming dependent upon only one source of income – the land, of which they have very little.

Products which, when the country [depended on] its own production, were cheap, now that foreign industry supplies the articles of primary necessity, keep mounting in price. [As a result,] the position of the peasants is becoming ever worse. This is aggravated by political events such as insurrections within the country, and also by the droughts which affected five Northern provinces two years ago. This drought [threatened the lives] of many millions of Chinese and, to alleviate the situation, the government decided to put an embargo upon the export of corn. At this time relations between Japan and America [were] strained. Considering the necessity of preparing for war, Japan wanted to buy corn in China in the very places affected by the drought, that is, in Manchuria. China was so weakened by this time that she could not resist the demand[s] of the Japanese. Thus, Chinese corn was taken out of the country. The imperialists, interested only in retaining their power, did not, of course, bother about the fact that many millions of people might perish of starvation.[4] They were very little concerned about it, even though the sufferings of the people were enormous. Such, on the whole, is the present economic situation in China; a picture of cruel oppression and unparalleled exploitation by foreign imperialists. The present Congress should work out the means [to free] us from this yoke. All of us here are united by the fact that we represent countries in which imperialism [holds] full sway. Comrades, I hope all of you gathered here will consider this question and find effective means of ridding ourselves [of] imperialist oppression. (*Applause*).

Comrade Ping-Tong was asked to tell the history of the Consortium and its influence.

Ping-Tong [Yu Shude]. The Consortium[5] was organised in 1917 on the initiative of America, but so far it has not yet been applied in practice. There was a Conference in Paris in 1919 on the question of making the Consortium more

---

4 The North China famine of 1920–21 (see previous note).
5 A consortium established in 1909 by British, German and French banks (Hong Kong Shanghai Bank, Deutsche-Asiatische Bank and Banque de L'Indochine) to finance railway construction in China, was later joined by JP Morgan and other American banks. In 1911, the Qing government took out loans from the consortium to nationalise railway projects, but opposition from Chinese shareholders sparked the Xinhai Revolution that overthrew the dynasty. In 1913, the consortium, enlarged to include Russian and Japanese banks, made a £25 million loan to the Yuan Shikai government that allowed Yuan to destroy the Kuomintang despite its election victory. In 1918, American banks led by JP Morgan created a second consortium together with British, French and Japanese banks. But chaotic conditions in China meant that the second consortium made no loans, as the risk of default was too great. See Cain and Hopkins 2002, pp. 375–6; Louisa E. Kilgroe, *Banker as Diplomat, Thomas W. Lamont in Post-World-War I Japan (1999)*, available at: http://www.unc.edu/depts/diplomat/AD_Issues/amdipl_12/kilgroe_banker.html, retrieved 20 March 2014; Ji 2003, p. 96; Reinsch 1922, p. 62; see also: http://www.americanforeignrelations.com/A-D/Consortia-The-second-china-consortium.html, retrieved 28 March 2014.

effective, but it has not yet resulted in anything tangible. It has more a nominal existence than an actual one. The causes for the failure of this Consortium may be found in the diverging interests of the various groups of imperialists, particularly of those of America and Japan. The Washington Conference was called, partly, for the purpose of putting some life into this Consortium and making it work.

Chairman. The translators will now translate the speeches in the various sections into the national languages. Permit me to declare an intermission.

(*After the recess*).

Chairman. Comrades, the session is now resumed. I will read to you a telegram of greetings from the 17th Nizhny-Novgorod Division of the Red Army:

> The Second Non-party Conference of the 17th Nizhny-Novgorod Division sends greetings to the Congress of the Far Eastern-nations. The Soviet Government was the first to unequivocally recognize the right of every nationality to self-determination, and only in Soviet Russia can such a Congress be held. The Red Army, which guards the interests of all the toilers, and in particular the commanders and red soldiers of the 17th Division, declare that, on their part, they will remain at their posts of honour, and in unison with all the nationalities inhabiting the R.S.F.S.R., they will defend the Toilers' Republic against all the attacks of the world bourgeoisie. Signed: Vasilyevich, Chairman of the Conference.

Comrades, I have been requested to allow two more comrades of the Chinese delegation to address you; the representative of the Kuomintang Party,[6] and

---

6 Homindan Party in the original text. The Kuomintang was formed in 1912 by Sun Yat-sen and Song Jiaoren as the successor to the Tongmenghui. The party was dissolved following the assassination of Song Jiaoren in 1913, but reconstituted in 1919. It was the ruling party of the Republic of China (ROC) from 1928–49, and thereafter in the truncated ROC in Taiwan. In 1923, Sun Yat-sen concluded an alliance with the Soviet Union which provided large amounts of military and financial aid to support a plan to reunify China that was eventually realised under Sun's successor Chiang Kai-shek. On the instructions of the Comintern, CPC members joined the Kuomintang as individuals during this period until Chiang broke the alliance with the Soviets and massacred communist supporters in 1927. The party programme is based on the Three Principles of the People (Nationalism, People's Power, People's Welfare) devised by Sun in 1905.

the representative of the women's organisations. Comrades, in submitting this request for your approval, I wish to urge the importance of the Chinese question among the problems of the Far East, and I hope that the Congress will not decline their request to make their supplementary reports. Failing objections, I will consider the motion carried.

A motion is made from the floor to allow the delegates to speak after the delivery of all the other reports.

Chairman. A motion has been made, and I have to put it to the vote. In view of the fact that the Chinese delegation can be allowed to make supplementary reports only upon consent of Congress, I must take a vote. One comrade proposed to let them speak only after all the other reports; another comrade proposes that they be called immediately. I am putting it to the vote. Those in favour of calling upon them immediately, will kindly raise their hands; those against? A minority. The motion has been adopted to call upon them immediately. The representative of the Kuomintang Party, comrade *Tao*, has the floor.

Tao [Zhang Qiubai].[7] Our Congress, the Congress of the Communist and Revolutionary Parties of the Far East, has already heard the reports about the situation of the workers and peasants of China, as well as about its general

---

7   Zhang Qiubai (1887–1928) was a Kuomintang politician from Anhui Province. As the representative of China's southern government, Zhang Qiubai was elected to the Presidium of the Congress and was invited to meet Lenin along with Zhang Guotao, Deng Pei and the chairman of the Korean delegation, Kim Kyu-sik. Zhang had a reputation as a rather shallow opportunist. In Irkutsk, he embarrassed his fellow delegates by performing a risqué ditty when asked to sing a revolutionary song at a reception. He protested against Zinoviev's suggestion that Chinese nationalists were opposed to Mongolian independence. But according to another delegate, Ma Zhanglu, even the Communist delegation had to be whipped into line on the issue by Zhang Guotao. There are conflicting versions of how favourable a report of the Far East Congress Zhang Qiubai gave to Sun Yat-sen on his return. He was appointed head of the Kuomintang External Relations Department in 1923, but opposed the Soviet-style reorganisation of the party in 1924. In 1928, while construction minister in the Nationalist government, Zhang was assassinated in Nanjing by an Axe Gang team sent by Wang Yaqiao. The original target was General Chen Tiaoyuan, but when Chen failed to appear, Zhang was an unlucky second choice. See Yang Kuisong, 'Yuandong geguo gongchandang ji minzu geming tuanti daibiaodahui de zhongguo diabiao wenti' (The question of the Chinese delegation to the congress of far eastern communist parties and revolutionary organisations), *Jindaishi yanjiu*, no. 2 1994, 280; Saich 1991, pp. 94–6; Yao and Su 2007, p. 51; Zhang Qiao 2011, p. 68; Zhonggong Wuhu dangshi wang, *Wuhu shisheng fu fa qingongjianxue ji fu su fu de fu ri jiankuang* ('A brief introduction to Wuhu teachers' and students' work-study visits to France, and visits to the Soviet Union, Germany and Japan'), available at: http://wuhu.ahxf.gov.cn/Home/Content/1018511?ClassId=6639, retrieved 21 September 2018; Wilbur and How 1989, pp. 69–70.

economic situation. At this session I wish to report on the *political* situation of China, which has not yet been touched upon by the previous speakers. Up to 1840, China had not felt the political pressure of foreigners. And now, when the pressure exists, it is very painful to see that the country, which has a 5,000 years old history behind it, great stretches of land, and a population of hundreds of millions, is forced under the yoke of the foreign rulers. However, the country is not quite crushed, and this is due only to her very size and her large population. Had it not been for that, China would, perhaps, have been put out of existence altogether. The rule of the foreigners in China began after her bitter experience in 1840, when the Chinese people rose in protest against the poison which was being imported into China by the English. China then suffered defeat. One after the other the imperialists of all countries began to invade China and tear the country into pieces. The Chinese people were asleep in 1840, and when, in 1895, another war broke out with the new imperialist country, Japan, they were still dreaming. In this war, Japan had been aiming to get a strong foothold on the continent, to expand at the expense of China. She carried on this war very carefully, making sure of her ground and anticipating all eventualities. Her army is well trained and disciplined, and they paid the population for all products as they went along. China was unprepared. At the sight of the Japanese troops who treated the population in a humanitarian manner, the people treated them in many places as liberators, and did not expect the future developments. The Japanese plans to exploit China, to seize her territories, and use her wealth for her own purposes, were near to realisation when they were suddenly obstructed by other imperialists.[8]

In 1900, China began to wake up, having already felt some of the effects of foreign intervention. A political movement started aiming at the overthrow of the foreigners. This movement is known in history as the Boxer Rising. The rising was suppressed by the invasion of foreigners, but it had quite an important effect upon the future course of events in China. The result of this invasion, as has already been said, was the partition of China into spheres of influence. The Europeans, who obtained a strong footing in Beijing, began to think of various schemes of how to capture China. In 1900, the Chinese saw the light and understood that there can be no peace between the foreign invaders and China, and from that time, a revolutionary movement, as yet unconscious, began to develop in China. At the same time, two more or less definite political currents appeared in China; one of them was known as the Party of the Defence of the

---

8 The 1895 Triple Intervention by Russia, Germany and France forced Japan to hand back the Liaodong peninsula which had been ceded to her by the Treaty of Shimonoseki. Russia then occupied the peninsula and obtained a 25-year lease from China in 1898.

Emperor,⁹ and the other as the Party of the Revolution.¹⁰ These parties were strongly antagonistic to each other and began a relentless struggle. The Party of the Defence of the Emperor believed that all the evils and troubles were due to the imperfect system of government, to the insufficient power of the throne. It aimed at the strengthening of the throne and attempted to install a complete autocracy. On the other hand, the Revolutionary Party believed that all the sufferings of the Chinese people were due to the fact that China was governed by a foreign dynasty, alien to the Chinese people, which ruled it only for its own interests and purposes.

Bag-Wik-Wee,¹¹ who was a minister in the Cabinet of the Qing¹² dynasty, hoped to make a strong military state out of China, equal to any of the European states. With this aim in view he plotted, together with Yuan Shikai,¹³ against

---

9   The Society for the Defence of the Emperor (*Baohuanghui*) was formed in 1899 in Canada by the exiled Kang Youwei and Liang Qichao, following the defeat of the 1898 Hundred Days Reform. Its political programme envisaged a reformist constitutional monarchy and it competed quite successfully with Sun Yat-sen's more radical organisations for support and donations from overseas Chinese communities. By 1905, it had 37 branches in the United States. Following the death of the Dowager Empress Cixi in 1908, the party changed its name to the Constitutionalist Party (*Xianzhengdang*) and began to operate openly inside China. See Lai 2010 p. 12.

10 The Tongmenghui (United League) was a Han Chinese nationalist party formed in Tokyo on 20 August 1905 by Sun Yat-sen, Song Jiaoren and their associates. It was the successor to the Xingzhonghui (Revive China Society), formed by Sun in Honolulu in 1894, and the forerunner of the Kuomintang. The Tongmenghui called for the overthrow of the ethnically Manchu Qing dynasty and its propaganda was strongly anti-Manchu, and frankly racialist in tone. See Crane and Breslin 1986, p. 32; Zhao 1996, pp. 41, 69.

11 Steve McKinnon suggested this strange transliteration may refer to Wang Yingkai, who was a high official in the Ministry of War and a close associate of Yuan Shikai. Zhang Qiubai seems to be referring to the New Policies of the late Qing. In August 1908, the government adopted a document, 'Principles of the Constitution', which was largely drafted by Yuan Shikai. It advocated gradual reform along the lines of Meiji Japan. But in November, the Guangxu Emperor and the Dowager Empress Cixi died on successive days. The throne passed to the infant Puyi whose father, Zaifeng, the Guangxu Emperor's younger brother, was appointed regent. Zaifeng dismissed Yuan, but recalled him in 1911 in a failed attempt to stave off revolution.

12 Written as *Tzin* in the original text. The Qing dynasty (1644–1912) was the last dynasty of Imperial China, formed by the rulers of a former Chinese vassal state based in Manchuria. Under the Kangxi and Qianlong emperors, the Qing dynasty extended and consolidated the borders of the Chinese state, but as a non-native ruling house, it was resented by many Han Chinese. After a century of decline, faced with internal rebellions and European and Japanese encroachments, the dynasty was overthrown in 1911.

13 Yuan Shikai (1859–1916) emerged as China's strong man after the Qing dynasty fell. Yuan took command of China's most powerful military force, the Beiyang Army in 1901, when he was appointed viceroy of Zhili Province. He was dismissed from office in 1908, following

the existing court clique, hoping to turn the policy of the country in a different direction. However, as is well known, this plot was unsuccessful. Yuan Shikai was exiled; his accomplices shared the same fate. The Party of the Defence of the Emperor was still very powerful. It had in its ranks such able men as Kang Youwei and Liang Qichao.[14] The former was a frequent visitor to Europe, well educated in the political sense; the latter was also well educated, had been to America, and lived much in Japan. Thus these two men had shaped the entire foreign policies of China, and also undertook to protect the monarchy. The Party of the Kuomintang,[15] i.e. the Party of Revolution, carried on a determined struggle against these two men, exposing their secret schemes and hopes. This party carried on its campaign by means of its newspaper the *Ming Pao*.[16] The Party made its chief object of attack the fact that these men had calculated on the assistance of the Manchurians;[17] *Ming Pao*, the organ of the Party, pointed to the many defects of the government which was foreign to the people, always coming to the logical conclusion that the people could be well off only if they governed themselves. In this way the ground was gradually prepared for an explosion. The plot of a national revolution was being hatched. However, many of the population were still wavering; they were

---

the death of the Empress Dowager Cixi but the Imperial government recalled him when faced with revolution in 1911. Yuan took the opportunity to seize power. He enforced the abdication of the infant emperor Puyi, and was then handed the presidency by Sun Yat-sen who had been named Provisional President by a revolutionary assembly in Nanjing. After the Kuomintang won the December 2012 parliamentary elections, Yuan had the party leader Song Jiaoren assassinated, defeated a rebellion led by Sun Yat-sen, and dispersed the national assembly. But in 1915, Yuan overstretched himself when he attempted to found a new Imperial dynasty. He was defeated by a revolt of provincial leaders that began in far southwest Yunnan, and died a broken man. His death marked the end of effective central government and the opening of the warlord period.

14   Kun-U-Vai and Lan-Ci-Tzin in the original text – Kang Youwei (1858–1927) and Liang Qichao (1873–1929). Kang fled into exile after the failure of the 1898 Hundred Days Reform movement but remained a monarchist and supported Zhang Xun's attempt to restore the Qing dynasty in 1917. In a strange parallel with the English monarchist Thomas More, in the *Da Tong Shu* – the Book of Great Harmony – he described a utopian vision of a future in which private property and the family have been abolished. Liang Qichao, a renowned journalist, was Kang Youwei's protégé but adapted to the republican era after the fall of the monarchy. He established the Democratic Party and, later, the Progressive Party. Liang supported China's entry into World War One.

15   I.e. the forerunners of the Kuomintang established by Sun Yat-sen and others – the Revive China Society and the Tongmenghui.

16   *Ming Pao* (aka Ming Pao) was first published in Tokyo in 1905.

17   That is to say, of the Qing Dynasty. Sun's faction of Chinese nationalists regarded them as foreign conquerors.

liberally minded, but uncertain of the success of the revolution. Many, as for instance Sin-Min-Tzin, thought that a republic was an impossibility – that a revolution would bring nothing but great hardships and additional oppression.

Yet in connection with the economic oppression, in connection with the hardships that such oppression entails, the revolutionary movement develops to an ever increasing extent, and the notion of the impossibility of revolution begins to lose its sway. The causes that incite to revolution arise, properly speaking, from two sources. The first cause arose out of the foreign policies of the Qing dynasty, which introduced colossal disorder and chaos in the management of the country's affairs. A second cause was the invasion of foreign capital which undermined the organism of China. The end of the nineteenth century and the beginning of the twentieth present a clearly defined picture of an incipient revolutionary movement. After a long period of defeats, the revolutionary movement is at last assuming definite shape, and in 1911 scored its first big success – the establishment of a republican form of government.

But this success was more apparent than real, because there [had] only been a change of officials but very little change towards improvement in any other respect. Indeed, when Yuan Shikai, who by that time had identified himself with the Kuomintang Party,[18] was elected president, he concentrated in his own hands the control of the army and finances, and started a campaign for the maintenance of his power, proving even more autocratic than the deposed dynasty. This caused his own Kuomintang Party to turn against him, setting up a wave of indignation which extended in 1915 into a revolution.[19] But Yuan Shikai had foreseen the possibility of revolution and prepared accordingly, gathering those military forces by means of which he defeated the revolutionary masses and proclaimed himself emperor. Such a change on the part of Yuan Shikai had been foreseen by the Kuomintang Party already, at the time when considerable numbers of the population were paying homage to Yuan Shikai and allowing his ambitions full play. The Kuomintang Party tried to gain adherents and forestall these demands, to prevent Yuan Shikai from declaring himself emperor,

---

18   Presumably Zhang Qiubai means that Yuan Shikai had come out in favour of a republic. It can hardly be said that Yuan was a Kuomintang supporter since he crushed the party in 1913. Yuan was, in fact, associated with the Republican Party (Gonghedang), which later merged with Liang Qichao's Democratic Party to form the Progressive Party in opposition to the Kuomintang. Yuan was 'elected' only in the sense that the national assembly in Nanjing appointed him Provisional President on 15 February 1912, at the request of the first Provisional President, Sun Yat-sen.

19   The date seems wrong. The revolt against Yuan took place in 1913, after he organised the assassination of the Kuomintang leader Song Jiaoren.

but all in vain. Having become emperor (this was in 1915), Yuan Shikai sent his ministers to conclude the treaty with Japan, and the 21st article of the secret treaty between China and Japan was signed for the sole purpose of enhancing the influence of Yuan Shikai.[20] But this treachery could not go on any longer. A unanimous stand had to be made against the ministers and the emperor. The first to revolt was the province of Yunnan;[21] other provinces followed suit, and finally Yuan Shikai abdicated from the throne, but remained president, Eventually, however, as though unable to bear the humiliation of his deposition, Yuan Shikai committed suicide by poisoning on 7 July 1916.[22]

His closest follower was Duan Qirui[23] of the Beiyang Party.[24] Duan Qirui, being a general, was able to unite the military forces of the Northern provinces. This general was cherishing the hope of carrying out the plans which Yuan Shikai put into effect when he became emperor. He had connections with Japan, and in 1917 signed a treaty with her. The pretext for this treaty was his intention to carry on war against Germany. Japan gladly supplied China with both

---

20 This is also wrong. Yuan concluded the treaty with Japan in May 1915. He declared himself emperor in December 1915. It is not clear which demand Zhang is referring to. The final agreement did not include the 21st demand, which was for the right of Japanese Buddhist organisations to preach in China.

21 The original text says Hunan – another error. Yunnan province was the first to rebel. The provincial leaders Tang Jiyao and Cai E declared independence and led an armed revolt. Cai's forces occupied neighbouring Sichuan province. After Yuan's counterattack failed, Guangxi, Shandong, Guangdong, Zhejiang, Shaanxi, Sichuan and Hunan also declared independence. The episode is known in China as the National Protection War. The Chinese version of Zhang Qiubai's speech correctly refers to Yunnan – see Russian State Archive of Socio-Political History 495.154.166.

22 There are various theories about Yuan Shikai's death, including both murder and suicide, but the most widely accepted is that he died from the kidney disease uraemia. Oddly, the Chinese version of Zhang Qiubai's speech also says Yuan died of illness – see Russian State Archive of Socio-Political History 495.154.166.

23 Duan Tsi Jui in original text. Duan Qirui (1865–1936) was a general in the Beiyang Army and served as War minister in Yuan Shikai's government from 1912, but in 1915 he opposed Yuan's attempt to crown himself emperor. Duan was Prime Minister of China several times, and a largely ceremonial President from 1924–26. He was the leader of the Anhui Clique of warlords which relied on Japan for financial and military support, but his pro-Japanese stance was discredited when the allies handed Shandong province to the Japanese in 1919, provoking the May Fourth Movement. Duan lost power in 1920 when his army was defeated by forces of the Zhili Clique led by Wu Peifu. See Esherick and Wei (eds) 2013, p. xvii.

24 Bei Yan in original text. This refers to the clique of generals around Yuan Shikai, who commanded the Beiyang Army. After Yuan's death, the clique disintegrated into competing, and sometimes warring, factions. The term Beiyang refers to China's northeast coastal regions.

money and arms for the ostensible reason of fighting the Germans, in reality in order to suppress the Chinese revolutionists. When Japan proposed to start war upon Germany, Duan, knowing that America had become acquainted with these negotiations, sent a telegram in which he claimed that China being an oppressed country and completely ruined, would not be able to take upon herself much of the burden of carrying on the war, and asked to be freed from the necessity of declaring war upon Germany. However, Duan did not make the desired impression. Thereupon the entire Chinese press rose against war. Even some of the monarchist sympathizers raised their voice against it. Li Yuanhong,[25] who was then President, seeing that a strong campaign was developing against Duan which might have serious consequences, removed him from his post. This removal was so sudden that Duan felt offended and threateningly declared that he would not be responsible for any disorders that might take place within the country.

[And in fact,] soon afterwards, various rumours began to spread, and disorders occurred which were aimed at the overthrow of Li Yuanhong. All the strings in these disorders were apparently pulled by Duan. A number of war councils of generals began in Nanjing and Xuzhou.[26] The minority of the Chinese Parliament headed by Tan Huan Du Gi and Yan Tziz Ao,[27] former members of the Party of the Defence of the Emperor, joined these generals. These conferences passed resolutions with the slogans of the defence of the Constitution, the defence of the Republic, etc. Finally, on 7 June 1917, a conference

---

25   Lyan Hun in original text. Li Yuanhong (1864–1928) succeeded Yuan Shikai as President of the Republic of China in 1916, but was overthrown by Zhang Xun's monarchist coup in June–July 1917. He served another term as president in 1922–23. Li began his career as a naval officer during the Sino-Japanese War of 1894–95. He transferred to the army and was a senior officer in Hankou when the 1911 Revolution broke out in Wuhan. He became a reluctant figurehead for the revolution and was appointed vice-President to Sun Yat-sen when the latter was named Provisional President in Nanjing. He retained the post when Sun relinquished the presidency to Yuan Shikai. He supported Yuan against Sun after the assassination of Song Jiaoren and, with Liang Qichao, helped formed the Progressive Party as a rival to the Kuomintang.

26   The original text says Tzan Tzin and Su Jo Fu. It is possible that the names refer to Tianjin and Suzhou. Nanjing was the power base of Vice-President Feng Guozhang. Its garrison included a Manchu guards regiment. Zhang Xun held a series of inter-provincial conferences in Xuzhou as cover for a plan to restore the Qing dynasty. See Dickinson 1999, pp. 170–1.

27   It is unclear who Tan Huan Du Gi was. Yan Tziz Ao possibly refers to Zhang Shizhao (1881–1973), who was minister of justice and minister of education under Duan Qirui. After 1949, he became a member of the standing committee of the National People's Congress of the PRC.

of generals, together with the minority of the Parliament, took place in Beijing [and] put [a] demand to the President for the abrogation of Parliament, as not being in accord with the system of government of China, being opposed to the Constitution, and demanded a new election of Parliament. This demand was so unanimous, and written in such an ultimative form, that Li Yuanhong lost his head and agreed to it.[28] In reality this demand was based upon the hope of the united group of generals, and the parliamentary minority, to be able to let imperialism rule China. Their plans were realised, war was declared, and a loan was floated in Japan. A great army was recruited, Japanese officers were invited, Japanese arms were imported, the troops were disciplined, but instead of being sent to the front to fight the Germans, they were sent against revolutionary Southern China. The forces of Northern China were gradually increasing. Sun Yat-sen, seeing the danger of the situation, started an agitation for a quick decision of the relations with the Northern Government. He was able to convince the navy,[29] and win over many sympathizers, so that soon a split occurred between Southern and Northern China. In the meantime, Duan, supported by Japan, resorted to all means to exert pressure upon the Northern Government. He arranged various loans,[30] and finally signed an official secret treaty with Japan on the basis that the Russian Revolution, which at that time had already broken out and had assumed a socialist hue, was too dangerous for the Far East, as the Russian Communists might come to the East and try to

---

28 Public opinion was against entry into World War One. Duan Qirui attempted to force a declaration of war on Germany in May 1917, by strong-arming parliament with threats and demonstrations. Parliament responded by effectively paralysing his government. To break the political deadlock, President Li Yuanhong dismissed Duan. The crisis deepened when eight provincial governors, who were supporters of Duan, declared independence. Li Yuanhong called on General Zhang Xun, governor of Anhui, to mediate. But Zhang, who was a Qing loyalist, staged a coup, with German support, to restore the emperor Puyi. The Qing restoration lasted only 12 days before it was crushed by Duan's troops. Duan resumed his premiership and China duly declared war on Germany and Austria-Hungary on 14 August 1917. Zhang Qiubai seems to be implying that the entire sequence of events was orchestrated by Duan. See Gerwarth and Manela 2014, pp. 226–8.

29 Most of the navy defected to Sun Yat-sen's Guangzhou-based Constitutional Protection Movement in July 1917.

30 The Nishihara loans, named after Nishihara Kamezo, a businessman and Japanese envoy who advocated using financial means to dominate China. Japan made a series of loans to Duan Qirui's government in return for confirmation of Japanese interests in Shandong and Manchuria. Duan used the money to finance an army to fight his rivals inside China. When the loans were made public, they caused public outrage and helped spark the May Fourth movement. It seems that the Chinese delegation to the Paris peace talks was not told of the secret agreements with Japan. See Hunter 1984, p. 148; Elleman 2002, pp. 24–6; Dickinson 1999, pp. 162–4.

conquer it. In reality, in playing upon the danger of an invasion by the Russian Communists, [the Japanese] had in view something quite different; they meant to take China into their own hands.

When Feng Guozhang[31] became President, Xu Shichang,[32] an old official, well known and educated, felt offended for being neglected and made several treaties with Japan secretly in his own name. Japan paid him well to become President, the post which he is still holding. Jing[33] refused to recognise him, saying that he bought the Presidency at the price of Chinese blood. This refusal to recognise the President who won his place through foreign help, and the stormy indignation in the South, resulted in the calling of a congress in Shanghai in 1921,[34] which considered the question of the separation of Southern China from the North. The resolution stated that until Xu Shichang voluntarily resigns the Presidency, and until he will be able to find the means of annulling all agreements and treaties made by him with Japan, no compromise will be possible between the North and the South, so that the entire responsibility for the separation of the South from the North will be his. When peace was being made in Europe, and when the representatives of all the warring countries gathered at Versailles, China sent there, as its representatives, members of the Kuomintang party.[35] This peace gave Shandong to Japan, and severed other provinces from

31 Fun Go Chon in original text. Feng Guozhang (1859–1919) was a general in the Beiyang Army and a protégé of Yuan Shikai, but broke with Yuan when the latter proclaimed himself emperor. A leader of the Zhili clique, Feng served as vice-president to Li Yuanhong in 1916–17, while simultaneously holding the post of military governor of Jiangsu province (and residing in Nanjing, the capital of Jiangsu). After Zhang Xun's monarchist coup was thwarted by Duan Qirui, Feng succeeded to the Presidency on 1 August 1917. Feng completed his presidential term in October 1918, and died the following year. See Gray 2002, p. 169; Xu 2005, pp. 231, 242.
32 Su Shi Chan in original text. Xu Shichang (1855–1939) succeeded Feng Guozhang as President of China in October 1918 and served until June 1922, making him the longest serving president, and the only civilian to hold the post, during the warlord period. Xu was seen as a conciliator between the military factions, but was under the influence of Duan Qirui. At the end of 1918, he called a peace conference in Shanghai in an attempt to reconcile the southern and northern governments, but it was rendered irrelevant by news of the agreement to hand Qingdao/Shandong to Japan and the subsequent May Fourth protests. See Gray 2002, pp. 178–9; Saich 1991, p. 223.
33 It is not clear who or what Zhang meant by Jing. Perhaps a reference to Beijing.
34 This seems to be another mistake. According to newspaper reports, the Shanghai conference opened on 20 February 1919, see http://trove.nla.gov.au/ndp/del/article/75266685, retrieved 12 May 2015. The Chinese version of Zhang's speech says the conference took place in March and April 1919, see Russian State Archive of Socio-Political History 495.154.166.
35 Zhang Qiubai seems to be exaggerating the political reach of the Kuomintang. The Chinese delegation was headed by foreign minister Lou Tsieng-Tsiang (Lu Zhengxiang), a

China [that] opened the road to Central China. President Xu Shichang took this calmly, saying: 'What will you do if you do not agree to the arrangement? No matter how you excite yourself, you can do nothing with the European brigands'. Thus he exhibited his entire powerlessness, his entire inability to solve the question in any other way. All this worked so much against the President that a strong movement began, this time in Beijing itself, known as the boycott movement. It was based on the fear that Japan is plotting to swallow up all of China, [that since] Japan had obtained Shandong, she [would soon] get more. It [was] therefore necessary to counteract it by a real force. First came the economic boycott, but the movement developed further, putting out new demands.

A riot broke out in Beijing, in which some of the members of the Government were killed, including Cao Rulin, Zhang Zongxiang and Lu Zongyu.[36] Other traitors were assaulted and their houses burned. The government took strong oppressive measures against the students' movement – even more ruthless than those used against the South. These repressions were met by revolutionary resistance which spread throughout the country. Government officials and workers in government institutions went on strike in Shanghai; businessmen closed their places of business in protest against the government and in sympathy with the students. The movement expressed itself in various demonstrations where protest was raised against the government. Such were the

---

career diplomat who served the Qing dynasty, Yuan Shikai, and several northern governments before retiring to Belgium in 1927 to become a Benedictine monk. Its most prominent member was Wellington Koo (Gu Weijun). Hoping for the support of the United States, Koo made a powerful speech at the peace conference describing Shandong – the birthplace of Confucius – as a holy place for the Chinese people, but Woodrow Wilson backed Japan's continued control of the province. The Chinese delegation refused to sign the Treaty of Versailles and Koo's speech sealed his reputation as a patriot. But, while he later served in Chiang Kai-shek's governments, it seems an exaggeration to describe him as a Kuomintang supporter. In 1913, he remained loyal to Yuan Shikai despite the latter having organised the assassination of Song Jiaoren, the Kuomintang prime minister-elect. See Craft 2003, p. 30. The Chinese version of Zhang's speech says the southern government 'also sent two delegates'. See Russian State Archive of Socio-Political History 495.154.166.

36 Tkao-Ju-Lin, Jon-Kun-Syan and Lu-Sun-Ui in original text. This is another mistake, perhaps a translation error, since none of the three officials were killed, although Cao's house was burned down and Zhang Zongxiang was so badly beaten that some people thought he had died. Cao Rulin was deputy foreign minister and had agreed to Japan's 21 demands in 1915. He attended the Paris Peace Conference. Zhang Zongxiang was the Chinese ambassador to Japan. Lu Zongyu was a diplomat who attended the Peace Conference. See Mitter 2004, pp. 9–10.

events of 1919 and 1920. At that time, Duan Qirui was still quite influential. In his attempt to strengthen his influence, supported by the Japanese, he came into conflict with Wu Peifu,[37] who was dreaming of restoring China to its old glory and prosperity. Wu Peifu suffered defeat at the hands of Duan Qirui.[38] Xu Shichang, who had not yet come into power, was a friend of Wu Peifu, but when the latter rose against Duan Qirui, he did not support him. Wu Peifu then took money from Xu Shichang for arms and ammunition. This money was given by Japan. Thereupon a struggle ensued which requires more time than is at my disposal to describe. I shall therefore return to the political situation in China. The policy of the Chinese Government can be characterised as follows: to ride around in autos, organise assaults on the students and borrow money from foreigners. That is all there is to it. All the other questions connected with governing the country, with regulating the various branches of its life, are turned over to foreigners. I believe that not a day passes but that the Government contracts loans. Money was needed before the holidays for embellishments, presents, and gifts to the officials. The Government found it more convenient to [take out] a foreign loan than to borrow it in the country.[39] Thus, the entire policy of the Northern Government is based upon Japanese support. Such is our Government.

And what about the Southern Government? In order to form a government it was necessary to break down many obstacles. It is too long a story to dwell on it at great length. On 1 May 1921, the nucleus of the government was formed in Shandun.[40] This government adhered to the programme of the Kuomintang Party: the refusal to recognise the Northern Government which was a traitor to the country, and the creation of a government which expresses the will of the people and governs with its consent. In 1917, the Southern Government took upon itself the responsibility for uniting the South of China. The movement in Southern China began as far back as 1911 and was directed at the reorganisation of the government on democratic principles.

---

37   U-Pa-Fu in original text.
38   Van-Chi-Ju in the original text. In fact, thanks to a bold manoeuvre by Wu Peifu, which gave him the reputation of a great strategist, the Zhili clique defeated Duan Qirui's Anhui clique in the 1920 Zhili-Anhui war. Zhang Qiubai's meaning is not clear.
39   The Chinese version of Zhang's speech adds playing mahjong and dallying with concubines to the ministers' pastimes and relates how a government loan was provided by a concubine of the finance minister.
40   Sun Yat-sen was declared Extraordinary President of the Canton-based southern government on 5 May 1921. Presumably Shandun refers to Canton, i.e. Guangzhou.

In 1913, the Southern revolutionary forces were defeated and disorganised, and only in 1917 did they begin to organise and to reinforce their ranks. In 1921, a new active group of the revolutionary Kuomintang Government was formed. It set up the new Southern Government at Siang-Yan,[41] which fully shares the programme of the revolutionary government characterised by national aspirations. This party was organised by Sun Yat-sen in the period of 1911–13 when he was still compelled to lead the life of an exile, which greatly hindered the work of organis[ing] the Party.

This Party, in 1920, became the government party and has changed its name from Gemingdang[42] to Kuomintang, which means the National Party. With its principles and programme you are probably acquainted; they are national-socialistic and doubtlessly contain points that are directed against imperialism. The Party protests against the oppression of China. It maintains a decidedly unsympathetic attitude towards the Washington Conference.[43]

I regret that I only have five more minutes at my disposal, for I have a couple of important statements to make. Comrade Zinoviev has stated that the government of South China looks up to America as to a source of benevolent democracy and progress. What has been the case prior to 1911 we cannot tell, because we lack exact information, but speaking of the present situation I must say that the ways of the Kuomintang do not coincide with those of the imperialists, and we will rather follow the Communist International than the Chinese imperialists.[44] And one word more: comrade Zinoviev said that there are people who would wish to restore Mongolia to China. I do not think it possible. I know not the sources of comrade Zinoviev's information, but I wish to think that comrade Zinoviev was mistaken, for I never heard of such a thing.[45]

---

41 Presumably also refers to Canton. The Chinese version of the speech simply says the government was formed in Guangdong province.
42 Gemingdang means Revolutionary Party. It was the name of Sun Yat-sen's party from 1914–19.
43 The Chinese version of Zhang's speech says the Kuomintang 'time and again' opposed the Washington Conference as a gathering 'organised by imperialists to oppress China'.
44 Possibly Zhang Qiubai means those who would like China to develop into a great, imperialist power and, for example, reassert its control over Mongolia.
45 In fact, the Kuomintang-ruled Republic of China only recognised Outer Mongolia as an independent state in 1946, when it signed the Sino-Soviet Treaty of Friendship. After retreating to Taiwan, the ROC revoked the treaty. In 2002, the Taiwan government finally relinquished its claim to Mongolia and stopped including it in maps of its territory. The Chinese version of Zhang's speech simply says that he had not heard the Mongolian question raised by Kuomintang or Southern Government officials and that he 'doubted' there was an intention to retake Mongolia.

I am afraid that my report was somewhat fragmentary,[46] and I will ask the comrades to permit me to present my report in written form, so that they may examine it at their leisure. (*Applause*)

Chairman. I wish to announce that the delegates are going to their quarters for the purpose of translating the proceedings for the benefit of the various delegations, and the session is therefore adjourned until 6 o'clock.

(*The session closes*).

---

46 The Chinese version of Zhang Qiubai's speech is very different from, and somewhat more coherent than the version published in English. Possibly the Chinese version was based on speaking notes that Zhang departed from on the conference floor. Peng Shuzhi wrote in his memoirs that Zhang 'fidgeted a lot and drew attention to himself but said nothing of interest'. See the Russian State Archive of Socio-Political History 495.154.166 for the Chinese minutes.

Fifth Session

24 January 1922. 6 p.m.

Chairman: Comrade Pak-Kieng [Kim Kyu-sik]

Chairman. I declare the session open. The first speaker is comrade Wong.

Wong [Huang Bihun]. I must deliver my report today on the position of Chinese women, but, seeing that my time is limited, I cannot deal with the subject in detail. I must touch upon the most important items only.

There is an old Chinese proverb which says that woman must concentrate her attention upon the male and she must do what the man wishes. Since the earliest times in China, it has been impressed upon women that every wish of [men] was righteous and must be complied with. All this made a deep impression and greatly influenced the psychology of women. There is no equality of rights in Chinese society today. We could even say that the whole of society consists [only] of men; that all rights belong only to men, indeed, not to all men, but to a handful of officials, of bureaucrats, of capitalists and imperialists. They are all closely allied, with [a] view to concealing their crimes and plotting new ones. In this society they enjoy exclusive right of control, and prevent from coming into power, not only women, but also the men workers. These have no place in modern Chinese society. But it is not because the women cannot take up the burden of public duties that they are excluded from public life. The only reason is that the men will not let them. For a long time men have been depriving women of their individuality and have so thoroughly succeeded in this that now there are women who seem to think they are absolutely ignorant and could themselves in no way contribute to the management of public affairs. And yet, this conception is wrong.

Since the earliest times, the outlook of Chinese women on the social position of women has been that in China there are three objects of worship and four rules of life or four virtues.[1] The first three gods are the father, the husband, and, after his death, the eldest son. As for the four virtues, they are related to; firstly, family happiness and the creation of the family hearth; secondly, modesty in

---

1   Huang is referring to the *san cong si de* – the three subjections (to father, husband and eldest son) and four virtues (morality, proper speech, modest manner, and diligent work), of women, as laid down by traditional Confucian morality.

speech; thirdly, neatness and elegance in dress; fourthly, cleverness in handwork. All this amounted to a cult which completely subdued women's psychology and, tearing them away from the external world, made them patiently suffer all wrongs.

Now, is there any economic equality in the position of the Chinese women? Firstly, a woman cannot inherit her relations' estates and cannot seek work. Formerly, women were not admitted to factories, and women were thus obliged to rely entirely upon men. This gradually enhanced men's dominance and finally reduced women to a state of slavery. Women have never played any important political part in Chinese history. Palace revolutions, or the existence of an Empress on the throne, were rare exceptions; for, as a general rule, women wielded no influence and played no part in politics. But today, in modern China, women have partly succeeded, after a long struggle for emancipation and for the franchise, in obtaining their electoral rights, and there are now two women members of the South China Parliament.

The recent events which brought China and Europe more closely together, prompted many Chinese women to go abroad, to obtain a European education, to become acquainted with the women's question on a world scale, to rid themselves of their prejudices, and in this way views are spreading that the present state of the family is not as it should be, that more freedom is necessary, that reforms are needed. Nevertheless, all these reforms and hopes for the alteration of the family relations do not as yet give the key to the solution of the woman's question. The women who return from Europe [finally see] the terrible oppression they suffer at the hands of men, which they had not noticed before. I believe that there are very few women at present in China who do not feel themselves oppressed. Chinese women are becoming imbued with a great desire to free themselves from this yoke, to work in the social field, to lead the masses to emancipation, to participate in the movement for obtaining freedom. So far, they have achieved but little success. The women who [have] had the opportunity to visit Europe belong to the aristocracy. Chinese aristocratic women still take a very respectful attitude towards their husbands, flatter them, dress exquisitely; in short – retain the old habits and traditions in spite of the fact that many of them have become acquainted with European conditions. Why is this so? Because in the present state of family relations in China, which have been in existence since the beginning of the ages, women can only retain their husbands by these methods. You must remember that polygamy is still in vogue in China, so that an unattractive wife is in danger of repelling her husband forever. In their own sphere, Chinese aristocratic women conduct themselves in a proud, conceited manner, carry on eternal intrigues. They are envious, jealous, and continuously quarrelling. They like to dress well, to eat well. Another reason for their lack of inclination for public activity is the fact that they are representatives of the aristocracy, which has done very little for the people and which shudders at the mere word 'proletariat'. The women of the Chinese aristocracy not only entirely ignore the position of the proletariat, but do not even take an interest in such questions as the education of children and adolescents of the non-proletarian classes. As far as proletarian women are concerned, I mean working women, peasant women and servants, they completely lack education. They are not respected in society, they are never mentioned, as if they did not exist at all. Thus, when the call of Communism reached us in China, we, the oppressed women, received it as a sinking ship greets the sound of the siren of another vessel which is hastening to its rescue. The position of our women is an incentive for us to work for the unification of our proletariat with that of the whole world, in order to conduct a joint struggle against our common enemy. Our tasks are the same as yours, and our aim is your aim; the destruction of capitalism. Our aim is to create a society in China based on equal rights for all, men and women alike. We cannot as yet speak about the methods of propaganda which can be applied there, but some of them may be discussed here. In the first instance, we must strive for universal education and training. We must attract the proletarian masses to the co-operative movement in [factories and workshops]. This will bring about a change in the psychology of the proletarian masses in general, and of [women] in particular. This will give them an opportunity to take part in social activity. Owing to the lack of women organisers, in my opinion, a cadre of women propagandists should be established in China. It is also imperative to carry on [wide-ranging] propaganda in connection with the women's and the proletarian mass movements through the medium of the press, the publication of pamphlets, posters and leaflets, etc. In order to achieve speedy and complete success, we stand in need of energetic, active women workers, well-versed in feminist propaganda. It is only thus that we can hope to achieve the success of our great movement. (*Applause*).

Chairman. We shall now continue with our evening session. The report will now be from the Korean delegation. The first report will be 'The Washington Conference and its relations to Korea', which will be read by comrade *Wong-Kieng* and will be afterwards translated into Russian.

Wong-Kieng.[2] Chairman and comrades, before I read this report I want to come to an understanding with you. One hour is allowed for each report and

---

2   Wong-Kieng is referred to in the Russian version of the minutes as Pak Chen, in the Chinese

I want to know whether I can give my report within half an hour and so leave the remaining half hour to the following reports.

Chairman. There is an understanding that the remaining half hour will be allotted to the following reports. If there is no objection, this understanding will stand.

Report on the Washington Conference and its Relation to Korea.
Read by Comrade Wong-Kieng.

I. Korea's Position in the Far East

1. A glance at the map of Asia will impress even the most casual observer that the little peninsula of Korea, with an area of only about 220,000 square kilometres and a population of a little over 20 million, is the keystone to the arch of the Far Eastern problems, geographically as well as strategically. For this reason, Korea has played such an important role in the making of the history of Eastern Asia. Korea was, from time to time, compelled to repulse the imperialistic aggressions of some of the rulers of China, while along the southwestern archipelago of the peninsula Japanese pirates made repeated attacks. The object of the Chinese aggression was not only to conquer Korea, and thus complete their territorial acquisition on the Asiatic mainland, but also to have strategic control of the threshold against any possible invasion by Japan. On the other hand, from the beginning of the third century, Japanese piratical attempts at spasmodic plunder of the Korean coast gradually lead up to organised invasions, culminating in the notorious Hideyoshi Invasion by Japan in 1592–97, the object of which was to conquer Korea, the stepping-stone, and then invade the mainland of China.[3]

Thus we see that even from ancient times, Korea was not only the target of periodical attacks by the two rival nations – China and Japan – but also their vital concern in the defence of national [security], as well as in the struggle for the mastery of the Far East. In such a position, however, Korea not only maintained her continued independence for more than 4,200 years, but also acted

---

version as Piao Ren and in the German language list of speakers as Pak Tachen. None of these names appear on the list of Korean delegates or among the delegate mandates.
3 Toyotomi Hideyoshi, the former chancellor (*kampaku*) and chief minister of Japan, while formally in retirement but still effective ruler, launched two invasions of Korea, in 1592 and 1597, the ultimate aim being the conquest of Ming China. The invasions were defeated with the aid of Ming troops and the campaign came to an end with Hideyoshi's death in 1598.

as a buffer in checking the aggressions of [its more powerful neighbours against each other] and exerted an immense influence in keeping peace in [those] countries.

2. In the development of human affairs, however, we see that the Korean question could not long be confined to the nations of the East; and beginning with the last quarter of the nineteenth century, Korea for a while became the object of greedy aims on the part of the great capitalist countries of Europe and America as well. They came, one after another, to force open the country to foreign trade and exploitation, and American, Russian, French, German, and British war vessels consecutively appeared along the Korean coast and began a series of bombardments,[4] which were stubbornly resisted by the then existing handful of Korean [troops] and gave rise to the early diplomatic negotiations, finally leading to a general scramble for concessions in mines, railways, and commercial privileges, and the vying with one another for the exertion of political influence.

3. At the end of the nineteenth century, after her victorious outcome from the Sino-Japanese war, Japan began to play a dominating role in Korea and attempted to interfere even in the internal administration, which culminated in the assassination of the Korean queen in 1895 at the instigation of the Japanese minister to Seoul, Viscount Miura.[5] But with the inauguration of the twentieth century, Eastern Asia became the arena of [the] clashing interests of tsarist Russia and imperialistic Japan. The attention of Russia as well as of Japan was attracted by China with its great population, consisting of hundreds of millions,

---

4 In 1866, the American armed merchantman *General Sherman* sailed up the Taedong river to Pyongyang, seeking to trade. With talks leading nowhere, the crew took a Korean official hostage and opened fire into a crowd watching from the shore. Korean troops set the ship on fire and killed the few survivors who managed to swim ashore. Earlier the same year, thousands of Korean Catholics and nine French had been executed in a mass persecution organised by the conservative regent, the Taewon'gun. Shortly after the *General Sherman* incident, French warships sailed up the Han river to Seoul on a punitive expedition, but were forced to retreat. In 1871, a more destructive raid along the Han River by American marines killed hundreds of Korean troops. See Hwang 2010, ch. 13.

5 Korea asked for Chinese help to suppress the 1894 Tonghak rebellion, prompting Japan to send troops and provoking the 1894–95 Sino-Japanese war. Having defeated China, Japan installed a reformist government supported by King Kojong's father, the previously conservative Taewon'gun. Kojong's wife, Queen Min, enemy of the Taewon'gun, opposed the reforms and looked to Russia as a counterweight to Japan. On 7 October 1895, she was murdered by assassins sent by the Japanese ambassador Miura Goro. To assuage international opinion, Miura was put on trial but acquitted. See Kim 2005, ch. 6.

to which country Korea was the natural doorway. On the one hand, tsarist Russia was gradually penetrating into Manchuria and Korea, while on the other hand, the strengthening of Russia's position in Korea was an obstacle to the development of [Greater] Japan and compelled the latter to enter into war with Russia. Accompanying the coming of the imperialists, the palace *coups d'état*, the intrigues, briberies and murders of the noted revolutionary leaders of Korea, as well as the wars of 1894–95 and 1904–05, which took place on the territory of Korea, brought to the labouring masses of the country unspeakable sufferings. The Korean people are being deprived not only of their prosperous living, but also of their very properties and lives.

II. Forcible Annexation of Korea by Japan

4. The defeat of tsarist Russia in 1904–05 gave Japan the opportunity for complete freedom of action, the chance to seize Korea. The seizure took place with the consent of the Great Powers, including the United States of America, in spite of the fact that, according to the treaty of 1882, the United States was supposed to offer assistance to Korea in such cases.[6] Korea was valuable to Japan not only as the stepping-stone to the mainland of China, but also as a rich colony with a population of 20 million, with abundant agricultural and mineral resources. With chicanery and cruelty truly typical of imperialism, Japan began the forcible occupation of Korea as a conquered colony. She had not only made repeated treaties with Korean and other powers fully recognizing Korea as an independent state from the beginning of her national existence,[7] but had also proclaimed to the world that she would maintain peace in the Far East and that she was going to war with Russia for the express purpose of preserving Korea's political independence and territorial integrity. But as soon as the victories of her armies in Mukden[8] and Liaoning and the fall of Port

---

6 A footnote in the original text refers to the 1882 Treaty of Peace, Amity, Commerce and Navigation between the United States of America and the Kingdom of Chosen (Korea). The relevant text in the treaty is 'If other powers deal unjustly or oppressively with either Government, the other will exert their good offices on being informed of the case to bring about an amicable arrangement, thus showing their friendly feelings'. The United States, therefore, did not violate the letter, but disregarded the spirit, of the treaty. An earlier draft of the treaty had called for 'assistance and protection' in the case of unjust or oppressive treatment.

7 Footnote in the original text: See the Treaty of Amity and Commerce between Korea and Japan, 1876; Treaty of Shimonoseki between China and Japan, 1895; Anglo-Japanese Alliance, last agreement, 1902; Russo-Japanese Protocol, 1898; Treaty of Defensive and Offensive Alliance between Korea and Japan, 23 February 1904.

8 Now Shenyang.

Arthur[9] were reported, she began to throw off her mask and started to bring the old Korean government into further subjugation under Japan's control. In order to clear away any possible objection on the part of the western powers, she first obtained England's consent to a free hand in Korea by the revision of the Anglo-Japanese Alliance Treaty on 12 August 1905, by which instrument Japan's paramount political, military and economic interests in Korea and her right of full control and exploitation were recognised by Great Britain while, in return, Japan recognised the same privileges of England on her Indian frontier. This second Treaty of the Anglo-Japanese Alliance really paved the way for the terms of the Russo-Japanese Treaty at Portsmouth, which was concluded only three weeks later, by which Russia conceded to [Japan] control of Korea in exactly identical language.[10]

The United States of America not only gave silent acquiescence to all this, but also was the first Power to recall its Minister from Korea after Japan forced upon Korea the so-called Treaty of Protectorate at the point of the bayonet, on 17 November 1905.[11] There is neither time nor space here to narrate in detail as to how Japan, in exact contravention to the terms of the February 1904 Treaty of Defensive and Offensive Alliance with Korea, in which she had promised to evacuate her troops from Korean soil as soon as her Russian campaign was over, purposely concentrated her forces in Seoul, surrounded the palace with soldiers, patrolled the whole city, and put field artillery into position ready for action, while her special envoy, the late Prince Ito, intimidated the Korean Cabinet Ministers to surrender their 42 centuries of national existence to the realisation of Japan's imperialistic programme. Needless also to mention that neither the then Emperor of Korea, his Prime Minister, nor the Korean people consented to this red-handed robbery, but on the contrary, some of the ministers of state committed suicide and the Emperor dispatched secret envoys to Washington and to the European capitals, including the Hague Peace Conference in 1907,[12] to expose and protest against Japan's high-handedness. The people revolted and their Righteous Army[13] fought the Japanese forces year in

---

9   Now Lushunkou in Dalian.
10 Footnote in the original text: cf. Anglo-Japanese Alliance, 13 August 1905, with Russo-Japanese Treaty of Peace signed at Portsmouth, September 1905.
11 On 24 November 1905, the State Department instructed the American legation in Seoul to close. The closure was completed on 28 November. A footnote in original text refers to F.A. Mackenzie's *Tragedy of Korea* and *Korea's Fight for Freedom*.
12 The Korean delegation sent to the Hague in 1907 was not recognised, and the Japanese forced the emperor to abdicate shortly afterwards. See Edward A. Olsen, *Korea, the Divided Nation* (Westport, CT: Praeger Security International, 2005), 46.
13 The Righteous Armies (Ŭibyŏng) were Korean irregular forces that fought against the

FIFTH SESSION 125

and year out, even until the summer of 1918, although at overwhelming odds in numbers and means. Japan, however, had no hindrance or check from the outside world. She had obtained her necessary 'passport' from the Powers, by the above-mentioned alliances and treaties, to enter upon her road to political hegemony in Eastern Asia and monopoly of economic control in Korea and Manchuria. So no outside power could either know or interfere when Japan was robbing, in a most high-handed manner, the Korean people of their houses and agricultural lands under pretext of building railways and military roads, making summary arrests and murdering people right and left with the exercise of the so-called Peace Preservation Law,[14] burning villages and conducting wholesale massacres throughout the length and breadth of the entire peninsula in order to wipe out even a stain of any revolutionary spirit. The world calmly watched with a cynical smile as Japan disbanded the remnants of the Korean army in 1907 and finally, in 1910, annexed Korea as a colonial province.[15] The imperialist countries had previously reached an understanding among themselves (as they are doing with regard to China and Siberia, and as they always do when such necessity arises, whether it be for exploitation in Asia or Africa or anywhere else) and they had already decided to invest their capital in other lands and find larger fields of exploitation, such as China, Tibet and Mongolia, where there would be room for more than one imperialistic land-grabber. They saw, but pretended to be blind, they heard but played deaf, they knew, but feigned ignorance. Also, Japan saw to it that real facts and truths did not leak out from the land infested with soldiers, gendarmes, spies and police. On the contrary, by their cunning and systematic campaign of organised propaganda, the world

---

Japanese occupation, notably during the period of the protectorate from 1905–10. In Korean patriotic tradition, they traced their origin back to militias formed to fight the Japanese invasions of the late sixteenth century. The resistance reached a peak between 1908 and 1910 after the 1907 dissolution of the Korean army swelled the ranks of the rebels. In early 1908, a unified command of the Righteous Armies, headed by the Confucian scholar Yi Inyong (1867–1909), attempted to capture Seoul. The Japanese resident-general, Ito Hirobumi, waged a brutal counterinsurgency campaign. In 1908 alone, 11,562 Koreans were killed. But Ito was considered too moderate, and resigned in June 1909. Four months later, he was assassinated in Harbin by the Korean nationalist An Chunggŭn. Ito was replaced by the hard-line Terauchi Masatake and, in August 1910, Japan annexed Korea. Remnants of the Righteous Armies retreated to Manchuria and Siberia where many of their fighters joined exile guerrilla groups. See Lee (ed.) 1996, pp. 403–4.

14 Japan's Peace Preservation Laws were a series of catchall, repressive measures, passed between 1894 and 1925, directed against political dissent and the labour movement.
15 The Western powers accepted the conquest of Korea without protest. Great Britain was allied with Japan. Theodore Roosevelt, who was US President until 1909, had earlier made clear his support for Japan. See Buzo 2002, p. 17; Bradley 2009, p. 309; Shaw 2007.

was made to believe that the people of Korea were perfectly satisfied under the 'benevolent rule' of the Mikado, especially the peasants and labourers. But the real fact was that the country was being bled white politically, economically and morally, so that it may never raise its head again.

5. In order to facilitate the campaign for taking away the agricultural lands from the Korean population, a Japanese stock company was formed under the auspices of the Japanese government, called the Oriental Development Company,[16] with an annual subsidy of £500,000[17] from the Imperial Treasury. This concern, through a crafty system of entangling the peasants into debt, and by all sorts of acts and means, causes the land to be untenable by the Korean farmer and finally, for little or no price, buys off the land from the enslaved peasantry and hands it over to the Japanese landlords, thus making the Korean peasants not only serfs of the Japanese invader, but also driving them out altogether, so that they have had to emigrate by the hundreds and thousands into Manchuria and Siberia, where there are now nearly more than three million Koreans thus emigrated.[18] The Korean coolies are systematically forced to work for little or no pay, and thus being a cheaper kind of labour, some are even dumped to Japan in order to counteract the demand for higher wages on the part of the Japanese labourers. The Korean labourers dumped to Japan number more than 50,000. The Korean population is being levied with heavy taxes. The rural products are being mercilessly robbed; while in 1916 there was imported[19] approximately 42 million yen's worth of agricultural produce, in 1919 there was exported of the same kind to the value of 137 million yen. Korea is made a dumping place for the cheap low quality articles of Japanese manufacture. Japanese goods, which could not stand competition against those of other capitalist countries in territories free from Japanese gendarmerie, are being spread in Korea by force, sometimes through special law decrees, on an ever increasing scale – 52 million yen in 1915 and 17 million[20] in 1919.

---

16   The Oriental Development Company was a Japanese state-controlled company (the puppet Korean government nominally shared ownership) formed in 1908. The company was granted expropriated royal lands and purchased other land. Between 1910 and 1918, it settled around 6,500 Japanese farming households in Korea. But this was a small proportion of the total number of Japanese immigrants. Much of the company's land continued to be farmed by Korean tenants. See Conroy 1960, p. 483; Gragert 1994, p. 66.
17   Original text says 500,00 – it presumably means 500,000.
18   There are various estimates of the number of Korean emigrants in Manchuria and Siberia but certainly there were hundreds of thousands in each.
19   Presumably this should read exported, not imported.
20   Possibly this should read 170 million.

6. Besides having seized all the political and administrative power, and having taken control of the economic resources of the land, the Japanese have also started to assimilate the growing generation. Without granting an opportunity for education to the general masses of Korea, the Japanese government abolished nearly all the educational institutions established by Koreans and replaced them with an insignificant number of primary and secondary schools, where the pupils are forced to worship the Mikado's pictures, are taught the history of Japan, [exclusively] in Japanese, and are imbued with the Pan-Asiatic idea and the notion of the holy mission of Japan as the saviour of the yellow peoples from absorption by the whites, thus making the Korean youth a weapon for their imperialistic aims.

One only needs to stop a moment and realise that, up till the end of 1920 – in spite of their worldwide propaganda about reforms in the administration and educational system – Japan had established only 582 schools, of which all were of primary or elementary grade, excepting seven so-called higher common schools (grammar schools) and one each of Law, Medicine, Industrial Sciences, and Agriculture and Forestry, with a total attendance of 90,692 pupils among a population of 17,057,032 Koreans (according to Japanese statistics), while for a Japanese immigrant population of 336,872 there were 413 schools, including five middle schools, 11 girls' high schools, six commercial colleges and one technical school, attended by some 45,504 pupils. This shows that Japan realised that an educated Korean would ever be a unit of protest and resistance against Japanese tyranny and exploitation in Korea, since education – particularly modern education – breeds thoughts and ideals that deny the right of one nation [to hold] another nation in political and economic [serfdom]. This policy of limited education also explains why Korean young men are denied free access to the road to higher learning in [the] arts, sciences, law, politics, economics and [industry], and are also absolutely prohibited from going to Europe and America to seek a Western or modern education, even at their own expense.

7. The greedy Japanese capitalists, by their exceedingly cruel exploitations, have exhausted the patience of the Korean people. While struggling to prepare themselves with all possible means and utilising even the slightest opportunity, the Korean revolutionary leaders scattered themselves within and outside of Korea – some in Siberia and America – organising the different constituencies for the united revolt. On the other hand, armed revolts from time to time in the interior and remote districts continued, as mentioned above, even till the latter part 1918. In this seemingly almost hopeless struggle, every world event helped to give new inspiration and a faint ray of light even at the darkest

hours, [for example] the Chinese Revolution in 1911–12, the world war, and even the hypocritical declarations of the capitalist Powers, with Woodrow Wilson as their spokesman, regarding the rights of small nations and oppressed peoples. The cataclysm of the Russian Revolution of 1917 also gave new stimulus and showed [that the world was entering] a new era, signalling the eventual downfall of all imperialistic Powers.

III. The March Events of 1919

8. Obeying the will of the revolutionary masses of Korea, the leaders issued the famous Declaration of Independence and established a Provisional Government.[21] For the first time in Korea, the movement assumed gigantic proportions. The masses did not feel sure of the successful outcome of the struggle with Japanese imperialism, but in [front] of the Versailles Conference, they wanted to expose the real situation to the world and demonstrate their right to shape their own destiny. This was only the first step towards a real united effort, towards an armed struggle to the finish. But the cruel suppression of the peaceful demonstrations of the Korean working masses by the Japanese gendarmerie, with the silent consent of the Versailles Conference, only confirmed the belief of the real Korean revolutionary leaders, and disclosed before the masses the real nature of imperialism of any brand – whether British or French, Japanese or American.

IV. The Versailles Conference

9. The hypocritical declaration of Wilson about the self-determination of all peoples served its purpose for a while – it revived the attention of the pauperised and oppressed peoples of Europe and Asia to the Versailles Conference, but naturally the situation after the Conference was anything but favourable for the small nations.

---

21 On 1 March 1919, a declaration of independence signed by 33 Korean religious leaders – 15 Christians, 16 followers of Ch'ŏndogyo and two Buddhists – was read out in a public park in Seoul. After the signatories were arrested, millions took part in mass demonstrations across the country over a period of six weeks, despite facing brutal repression. The scale of the uprising, and the severity of the response, shocked world public opinion and forced the Japanese to moderate their colonial policies. Meanwhile, a Korean provisional government was formed in Shanghai, with the pro-US Christian Syngman Rhee as president and the Communist Yi Tong-hwi as prime minister. Yi Tong-hwi resigned from the government in May 1921. See Kim 2005, ch. 7.

Before the Conference, we had the Great Powers [competing] among themselves for the domination of one nation or another, or of a backward colony. This inner rivalry made their pressure upon their victims weaker, and it [gave] the oppressed peoples opportunities to appeal against the cruelties of their oppressors to the other powers hostile to the one complained of. At the Versailles Conference, where the small nations were being torn apart, where the map of Europe, Asia and Africa was being re-drawn and re-divided into new spheres of influence, the imperialists only succeeded in diminishing for the time being the enmity among themselves, [so that] each of them could start with full energy the robbing of other nations and peoples with the sanction of the Versailles Conference and the League of Nations.

10. The Versailles Conference silently sanctioned the strangling of Korea, thus giving and legalising the opportunity for the Japanese to continue the robbing of Korea and her people with [renewed energy]. For a while, Japan did not have to [cast a nervous glance] at America and Europe, for she knew that there [would] be no protest from that direction.

Japan [has] intensified the exploitation of the Korean masses since 1919. The vast profiteering [and] speculation [on] the rice crop, which was exported by the Japanese in 1917 to the value of 27 million yen, [and] in 1919, to the value of 113 million yen, and their further policy of depriving the peasants of the land by force, brings as its result starvation among the masses.

11. The unprecedented deprivation of the people, which came as the result of the greedy policy of Japan, as well as the slap in the face to Korea at the Versailles Conference, which has confirmed even to the masses the futility of expecting any fair and unbiased judgement from the capitalist Powers, compels the labouring masses to rebel. The rebellion has no illusions as to the possibility of any assistance from the imperialists and is not of the nature of peaceful demonstrations, but of persistent struggle, with the only hope [being] their own forces and help from Soviet Russia. The thunderbolts of the proletarian revolution and the heroic struggle of Soviet Russia with the imperialists of the world [have become] an inexhaustible source of energy for the Korean people in their struggle for freedom. The partisan movement (guerrilla warfare) [has] spread throughout the whole Korean population in Kando[22] and [has only been] temporarily stopped by cruel repression on the part of the

---

22 Jiandao in Chinese. More or less the same area is now the Yanbian Korean Autonomous Prefecture, in Jilin Province in the People's Republic of China.

Japanese, assisted by the Chinese arch-traitor Zhang Zuolin's men. The Hunchun affair is still fresh in our memory.[23]

v. The Washington Conference

12. While before the war of 1914–18, the object of contest among the capitalistic Powers had been Africa and the Near East, after four years of bloody butchery, after terrific devastation of Europe, the centre has moved to the Far East with its [population of] 800 million. The Pacific [has] become the focus of the entangled and clashing interests of the Great Powers – chiefly of America and Japan. All this must lead to a climax similar to the one of 1914–18.

The Conference at Washington called by the United States had as its aim to delay the moment of the bloody climax. The imperialistic statement that the chief aim of the Conference was their desire to lighten the burden of ever-growing militarism [on] the masses of the people has proven to be a black lie. It is sufficient to say that, at this very moment, the capitalist parliaments of America, England and Japan, as well as of other similar capitalist countries, [are voting] milliards of money [to build up] their navies and armies.

13. The Washington Conference has succeeded from their point of view. The imperialists have been able to establish [temporary] stability on the Pacific coast; they have come to terms among themselves and have created an international trust, under the ignominious quadruple agreement between America, Japan, England and France, for the exploitation of the Asiatic Continent. What does all this bring to the Korean labouring masses?

Undoubtedly, the United States of America attempted at the Washington Conference to secure most privileges for herself in China, giving Japan, as compensation, Korea for complete enslavement. And in this sense, the Korean revolutionary movement, with all its victims, is of value to America, not as a struggle that leads to the emancipation of the oppressed masses, but as a con-

---

23   Hunchun is a county in Kando/Jiandao that borders Russia and (North) Korea. The details of the Hunchun incident of October 1920 are disputed. One version is that Korean independence forces attacked the Japanese consulate in Hunchun city on 2 October 1920, and killed several Japanese officials. In response, the Japanese sent thousands of troops into the province, and a battle took place at Qingshanli on 21–26 October. Both sides claimed victory.

straint that has put Japan in a less favourable position [in] negotiations with America, and particularly during the negotiations at the Washington Conference.

At the same time, the Conference [has given an altogether] free hand to Japan. The tax burden in Korea will become even heavier, the [expropriation] of land will proceed at a faster rate, the dumping of starving Korean coolies, [like cattle], to Japan and other countries will increase, and the remnants of Korean culture will suffer destruction with even greater rapidity.

14. Korea, [like] China, [faces] an imperialist world which is deaf to the pains, tortures and groans of the masses crushed under the Japanese yoke. Although [in the past] American and European public opinion, often formally, reflected [instinctive] sympathy for Korea's sufferings and tortures from the imperialist machineries, such sympathy rose not on account of any moral motives but because of rivalry among the imperialists themselves.

15. The natural way out of this yoke, which has been [fastened] at Washington on the working masses of the Far East, is their union with the proletariat of the world, with the [other] revolutionary movements in Asia, and with the Third Communist International and Soviet Russia in the lead, for the overthrow of imperialism.

Chairman. Comrades, in order to economise time I propose not to have the sectional translations just now and to continue with the following report, and the sectional translations can be done after the regular session, at which time the typewritten copies may be furnished to the different delegations – English copies to the Chinese and Japanese delegations and Russian copies to the Mongolian delegations. So, if there is no objection, we will continue with the next report.

Carried.

We will now continue the report on the Korean revolutionary movement. The report will be read in English. The Russian translation will be read at tomorrow's session. Tonight we have time for only one reading. It has been suggested that the reading should take place in Russian only. But there are a good many comrades who understand English, and perhaps the percentage of these and of those who understand Russian is about the same. Perhaps there is even a higher percentage among the delegations that understand English. Therefore, we want your opinion as to whether both English and Russian should be used.

Agreed to have speeches both in Russian and in English.

Pak-Kieng [Kim Kyu-sik] then read the following report:

The Korean Revolutionary Movement

I. Causes, nature and development of the movement

1. The aspect of the Korean Revolutionary movement. The organised movement of the Korean revolution made its first worldwide echo [with] the Independence outbreak of 1 March 1919. From then onwards, the Korean people [began] to take an important place in the ranks of revolutionaries in the present epoch of world reconstruction, and have been recognised as a real revolutionary people.

But the real beginning of the revolutionary movement in Korea should not be looked for in the March events, but rather one should go back to the fundamental causes, motives and influences that gave rise thereto, in order to understand fully the true nature of the movement. In other words, [in] the historic progress of the class struggle of the Korean people, [it] is simply a landmark in the movement; and so, the event of the Manse[24] (Vive la Corée) demonstrations should only form an addition to the record of historic popular experiences.

Although in order not to create confusion in our minds we may take the March outbreak as the introduction to our revolutionary movement, we must nevertheless study the historical records which preceded and succeeded this landmark and must get a clear conception of the causes, i.e. the beneficial influence of the numerous activities and the effects therefrom, which gave the impetus to the sterner and more real undertaking. Therefore, the purpose of refreshing briefly the memories of the past is to show that we are not narrating an entirely new event.

2. The class struggle. Korea, boasting a continued historical existence of nearly 43 centuries, had long been struggling on the road of economic, political and social progress and development, the causes of which may be attributed to her geographical position, as well as to her political and religious institutions.

In the early days, Korea was a feudal empire, comprising the Manchurian plains and the present Korean peninsula, and passing through the period of

---

24 Manse – like Wansui in Chinese and Banzai in Japanese means long live – literally 10,000 years.

the three kingdoms and division into Northern and Southern realms – during which time her area and boundaries expanded or shrunk according to circumstances – towards the tenth century she had definitely limited herself within the peninsula, and, emerging from her feudal institutions, she became a really centralised state, divided into provinces and districts. However, during the thousand years of the consecutive rule of the Wang (Koryŏ) and Yi (Josŏn) dynasties, the political and religious relations of the nobility, with their idea of national seclusion, and the hereditary ruling class, with their special privileges, played havoc with the social equilibrium, which finally led the country into a state of decline from its height of long-standing [cultural] and economic development. Thus, some of the remaining ruins and [relics] of past glory gave food for some pathetic sentimentality which worked on the imagination of the labouring and peasant masses.[25] Korean society may be divided into two main classes – the yangban (nobles and gentry) and the Sangnom (commoners), and although there is a middle class between the two, they are really either attached to the ruling class or are a specially privileged sect among the ruled. Yangban originally [referred to] the civil and military officials but, later, it became a term designating [a] hereditary class, whether in or out of office, which ruled the common people and was endowed with special privileges, having in its hands the [power of] life and death [over] the lower class. Thus, not only their dwellings, clothing and social system, but also [their] food and daily

---

25   According to tradition, Korea was founded by Tan'gun in 2333 BCE, but it first appears in written history in 109 BCE, when the Chinese emperor Han Wudi conquered the protostate of Josŏn, located in northern Korea and southern Manchuria. After the Han Empire collapsed in 220 CE, the kingdoms of Koguryŏ and Paekche were established, bringing 400 years of Chinese rule to an end. From the fourth century CE, Korea was divided between Koguryŏ in the north, Paekche in the southwest, and Silla in the southeast. The Three Kingdoms period lasted until around 670, when Silla allied with the Tang Empire to defeat its rivals and unify the peninsula. Silla then fought the Chinese to preserve its independence, but remained a Buddhist kingdom modelled on the Tang. By the tenth century, Silla had fallen into decline, and following a period of civil strife, Wang Kon established the Koryŏ dynasty (935–1392). Like Silla, a Buddhist kingdom, Koryo introduced Chinese-style civil service examinations but, unlike in China, they did not undermine the power of the traditional aristocracy. In 1231, the Mongols began over a century of domination of the peninsula during which they introduced the ideas of Neo-Confucianism. Following the defeat of the Mongol Yuan dynasty by the Ming, Yi Songgye established the Josŏn dynasty (1392–1910). Neo-Confucianism replaced Buddhism as the state ideology. Invasions by Japan (1592–98) and the Qing (1636) in the late sixteenth and early seventeenth centuries caused deep-seated distrust of foreigners, but Josŏn still regarded itself as a tributary state of China. Unlike in China, Josŏn's scholar-officials were exclusively drawn from the yangban, a hereditary elite who were exempt from taxation and military service and lived segregated from the common people. See Seth 2011, chs. 1–6.

life, differed entirely from those of the common people. Although with the early abolition of feudal appropriation of the land, the peasants could carry on their toil without great hindrance, on account of the oppression by the yangban their life was turned into bitter serfdom, and, especially [towards] the close of the Yi dynasty, the record of the reign of terror could fill many blood-stained pages.

Although the history of the class struggle of the Korean people is [one] of slow growth, nevertheless, it was [one of] uninterrupted, continued strife. However, it was mostly of a local nature and scope and therefore did not make itself very much felt. Any clashes between the classes were generally [manipulated] to serve the interests of the political rivals of the workers. Thus, no remarkable results were obtained until the final [contest] in 1894, in the form of the so-called Tonghak Rebellion,[26] which has [become] the starting point for the pen of [all historians] of the Korean revolution, connecting past events with the subsequent happenings.

3. The first uprising of the revolutionary peasants – the Tonghak Rebellion.
The accumulated wrongs, especially towards the close of the 500-year rule of the Yi dynasty in the yangban country of Korea, came to an unusual climax in [a high tide] of the class struggle and the political revolution of the Korean peasants. During the latter half of the nineteenth century, with the gradual eastward advance of Western influence, the sudden and consecutive attacks on the part of the trade-cruisers of several countries of Europe and America caused the awakening of a fraction of the ruling class, which made desolate cries for reforms and [the] introduction of Western (capitalistic) ideals, [finally precipitating] the coup d'état of 1884. Afterwards, the intellectual class, taking upon [itself] to represent the desire of the masses, took to revolutionary ideas and ideals of all creeds and colours, which gave birth to a nationalist movement. On the other hand, the Korean revolutionary peasant masses, realising the unnatural state of the hereditary privileged class, finally, with the famine of 1893 as its

---

26   The peasant rebellion of 1894–95 was partly inspired by the Tonghak (Eastern Learning) religion, a faith established to counter Western ideas by the Confucian scholar Ch'oe Che-u. Although opposed to Christianity, Tonghak borrowed certain elements from it, including monotheism. The movement inspired peasant revolts in 1862, and Ch'oe was executed in 1864, accused, among other things, of being a Catholic. The 1894–95 rebellion began with demonstrations in Seoul calling for a posthumous pardon for Choe, but developed into an armed rebellion against corrupt officials in the southwest of the country. The government appealed to China for military aid to suppress the rebellion. Japan then sent troops without being invited, setting the scene for the Sino-Japanese war. See Kim 2005, ch. 7.

direct cause, started a general uprising in the following year in a concrete and violent manner. So came about the well-known Tonghak Rebellion. Although this movement of the masses took [the form of] the Tonghak (a religious sect), and outwardly seemed a fanatical uprising, it was, in reality, a united upheaval of the oppressed millions against centuries of wrong and injury, and, [proceeding] with deadly aim, it raised terror in the hearts of the [upper] classes [across the entire East].

Equalize the rich and the poor! Down with the privileged classes! These were the real [demands] in the hearts of the Tonghaks, although some of the conservative [sections of the] masses were [misled by] anti-Western, anti-Japanese ideas, and raised the slogan *Clear the palaces of rascally elements*, which was [mistakenly taken] as the slogan of this phenomenal upheaval. The reason lies in the fact that the political bandits, both within and outside the Government, tried to make this a weapon of propaganda in their [struggle] for power. Also, outside observers put the Korean Tonghak Rebellion in the same category as the Boxer Rising in China. This is because the [outcome] of the Tonghak revolt ultimately led to similar events as those of the Boxer Rebellion, which resulted in throwing open China's door to European and American capitalist exploitation.

However, this first uprising of the Korean revolutionary peasants and their united struggle created three historical phenomena in the annals of the Korean people:

a) It became the fuse that [detonated] the Sino-Japanese war of 1895, which [ushered in an] epoch of change in the whole [of the] Far East. On the one hand, with the defeat and retreat of the Chinese armies to the North, it precipitated the destruction of the hereditary idea of [Sinophilism, clung to by a section of] the ruling class and undermined completely the basis of the old conservative political thought, and on the other hand, it [stimulated] a plea for reforms along modern lines of capitalistic statecraft, which found far-reaching echoes.

b) The millennium of hereditary privilege of the ruling class of yangban suddenly lost its sublimity, and the whole system was shattered to pieces. Its foundation of support – the agricultural economic [system] – was shaken [and gave way] to the organisation of new commercial and industrial [methods that led to] the enrichment of the bourgeoisie.

c) The newly enriched bourgeoisie, having inherited the remnants of the old economic status [quo] and striving to expand along capitalist lines, were finally led to welcome foreign capitalistic enterprises and [were] absorbed by the accompanying exploitation.

4. The transition period of the revolutionary movement, 1895–1905. From the close of the China-Japan War (triggered by the Tonghak Rebellion), until the end of the Russo-Japanese War, which culminated in the [imposed] treaty [that created a] Japanese Protectorate over Korea (17 November 1905),[27] these ten years may be designated as [a] chaotic transition period [in] Korean revolutionary history.

A portion of the 'irreconcilables' [among] the Korean revolutionary peasants, [having failed to] attain the fullest aims in the Tonghak rebellion, on account of the combination of internal and external, old and new forces of oppression, were [forced into a] reactionary stand. They formed themselves into [bands] of [a] few scores [or] hundreds and entered upon a road of tangential activities, plundering and burning villages and towns, utterly destroying the existing status [quo] as their sole means of revenge, and thus became branded as bandits. The majority of the remaining moderates gradually [became] reconciled to the economic changes and some, fascinated by the [opportunities for] rapid profiteering [offered by] the new unhampered commercial and industrial enterprises, as compared with the slow results of the old agricultural economy, [abandoned] the revolutionary path and drifted with the concurrent waves of [their] old and new surroundings.

So the newly created bourgeoisie, which had taken advantage of the initial movement of the class struggle of the revolutionary peasants, and had inherited, without effort, the [remnants] of the ancient economic status [quo], allied themselves with the awakened portion of the former ruling class in advocating the introduction of modern ideas and methods – reforms, and thus extended and intensified the development of their own capitalistic strength. This reform movement, or rather capitalistic movement, as mentioned above, was the concrete [form taken by] their welcoming and [being absorbed by] foreign capitalistic exploitation. The question of [the apportioning of] spheres of exploitation [between] the imperialistic policy and capitalism of Tsarist Russia and Imperial Japan led to the war of 1904–05; Japan, with her geographical advantages, following up her victories, not only cast aside her greatest imperialistic competitor, but obtained also a free hand for her capitalistic monopoly in Korea.

Finance, transport, manufacturing, trade, every economic [resource], fell into the hands of the Japanese imperialists. Thus, the Korean peasants eventually became the victims of the colonisation policy of the empire of capitalistic exploitation – Japan. And yet, [temporarily], they could not help but follow the

---

27   Also known as the Eulsa Treaty, referring to the date it was signed according to the traditional Korean calendar.

[feeble] attitude of a portion of the moderates who advocated only the infusion of modern ideas and cultural [progress], among which the Christian elements became the nucleus.

11. Intense Nationalistic Tendencies and Growth of Patriotism

5. Rising tide of nationalism – the Ŭibyŏng[28] or Righteous Army. The Korean revolutionary peasants, [witnessing] the Russo-Japanese war of 1904–05, realised the menace from the imperialistic Powers. There was a recrudescence of patriotic nationalism after the forcible conclusion of the [Protectorate Treaty] (1905). So the revolutionary spirit, which seemed to have temporarily abated, appeared to have awakened anew with a strong anti-foreign tendency – particularly anti-Japan – which assumed alarming proportions. Thus, we see that the historical class struggle, which had [previously] entered upon its proper path, had met with the fate of being [diverted] into an intermediary stage of a popular nationalistic movement.

Again, a large number of revolutionary peasants answered the call of the revolutionary martyrs and raised anew their 'righteous' flags. The former 'irreconcilables' abandoned their [digression] and marched in unison with the Righteous Army. Numerous detachments of military units scattered throughout the land and carried on, with one aim and object, the heroic fight of the Righteous Army, as if under one general command. The remnants of the [disbanded] Korean army, [following] the second forcible treaty in 1907 which ceded to Japan Korea's military, judicial and administrative [powers], joined forces with the people's Righteous Army and augmented, to a considerable degree, their strength and organisation, making their activities widely known in and outside of Korea. Over five score detachments, [consisting of] over a hundred thousand men, [inflicted a death toll of more than twenty thousand soldiers on] the Japanese army and [greatly] hampered the progress of Japanese capitalistic exploitation. Therefore this stage of the movement is correctly designated as the Ŭibyŏng period in the history of the Korean revolution.

The Ŭibyŏng, or the people's Righteous Army of Korea traces its origin far back in the nation's history, [exemplifying] the outstanding characteristics of the Korean people, particularly their spirit of nationalism. Although, according to time and circumstances its appearance and activities may seem spasmodic, there is a remarkable tendency towards patriotic nationalism, as well as the

---

28   Uibyongin the original text.

idea of people's [self-defence]. The later Ŭibyŏng uprisings in Cheongju[29] in central Korea in 1895, and the other actions from 1905 down to the present day, constitute a chain of connect[ed] links.

Of course, [because of a] lack of systematic training, discipline, organisation, efficiency of command, arms, equipment, food and supplies, [perseverance, energy and fighting strength alone] were not equal to the occasion. Besides, [the fighters] received very little open and full-hearted support from the general public, while the [relentless] pressure of the enemy grew more and more intensive and extensive. Also, they came to realise that no effective results would be attained without a properly organised, up-to-date movement.

6. Movement for patriotic social culture. While the activities of the Righteous Army in the interior were at their height, in Seoul and other centres, the intellectuals of the different circles, in conjunction with the Christian community ([which] was more a political movement [hinging] on the co-operation and the initiative of compatriots who had been, and were still, abroad, particularly in Europe and America, and facilitated the introduction of Western culture) started a vigorous movement for a patriotic social culture.

The Korean Christians, having come early under the influence of Christian propaganda, in accordance with the policies of their respective missions, enjoyed to a certain extent what may be termed 'foreign protection', which [they often used] as a shield for holding gatherings and forming organisations. Thus Christianity came to exercise a great influence among Koreans who had been deprived of such liberties and in some cases it became a [leading] force. For instance, the Young Men's Christian Association in Seoul, and the 2,000 or more protestant Christian churches and affiliated organisations throughout the land, used their 300,000 Church members as a base and had a [dominant] influence on public sentiment for a time. Acting as a [conduit for the import] of European and American culture, it gradually became an unofficial executive force in the movement for democratic nationalism. Thus, all those who were aiming at the country's welfare in one way or another, whether they were Christians or non-believers, used this great shield [to temporarily ward off] the aggressors' harmful attacks.

In concert with the Christian churches, another great force which exerted a powerful influence in the nationalist movement was the [spontaneous growth] of educational associations. These were formed by the nationalist intellectuals and their respective provincial groups and were really active political organisa-

---

29   Choong-ju in the original text.

tions at a time when any and all such gatherings were forbidden in Korea. The Soh-Buk (north-western), Ki-Ho (central provinces), Ho-Nan (south-western), Kio-Nam (southern provinces) and Kwangiong (eastern provinces) were the five principal organisations, with some 100,000 members, and [had] the double aim of openly advancing modern education, directing some three thousand and more nationalist educational bodies, and [secretly] arousing anti-Japanese and popular nationalistic thought, while carrying on [clandestine] communication with the Righteous Army and thus abetting all [underground] revolutionary undertakings. All those who were known as progressives or reformers, [as well as] the moderate elements among the peasants, were included in their ranks.

Among the latter, the organisations of Koreans in America and Hawaii were the most influential because they were in a more advantageous position to [make] connections [inside Korea] and co-operate [with] Christian churches and educational associations [abroad]. Therefore, a secret society, affiliated to the Korean National Association in America, was founded in Korea under the name of *Sinminhoe*.[30] But on account of shortage in men and lack of preparation, no organised activities were concretely undertaken to any great extent, except a few cases of individual sacrifice, from time to time, when deadly blows were inflicted on the enemy.

Young men of Korea became the vanguard of these consecutive movements, and during the Japanese Protectorate there were the activities of the Korean Youth Associations and the Young Students' Federation, in which organisations the students who had returned from Japan were the leading lights. Thus, a vigorous patriotic national movement sprang up among the young men of Korea.

III. The Forcible Annexation and the Independence Movement

7. The forcible annexation. In [the situation] depicted above, the Korean people, particularly the revolutionary peasants, put aside their revolutionary attitude in the class struggle and joined in this historical nationalist movement with will and vigour.

---

30   Written as Sihn-Min-Whoi in the original text. The Sinminhoe (New People's Association) was a clandestine independence organisation established by the Christian patriot An Ch'ang-ho (1878–1938). Different sources give various dates for its formation – 1906, 1907 or 1909. The Sinminhoe advocated the formation of a democratic republic but believed a period of education and economic development was necessary before independence could be achieved. See Yi 1984, p. 339.

However, the nationalist movement, being by its very nature in line with the nationalism of the capitalistic European and American countries, naturally tended to help the prosperity of the wealthy, and seemed manifestly to succeed in Korea through the growing tendency toward capitalism, which in its turn attracted outside capitalistic forces and particularly Japanese capitalistic exploitation. Thus, parallel with the modern nationalist movement of the Koreans, regardless of its pro- or anti-Japanese tendencies and, in proportion to its expansion and growth, the colonial policy of imperialist and capitalist Japan became more and more aggressive, and its success was accelerated. Therefore the responsibility for the national extinction should not only be laid on the powerless ruler and his ministers, who had no other recourse but to tremble before the bayonet of the aggressor, but also on the hundred thousand peasant members of the Ilchinhoe[31] (a pro-Japanese society formed by Japanese agents in 1904), who became the victims of a few traitors who had sold themselves to Japan and had been designated as tools of the Japanese, an act which constitutes a blot on the record of Korea's national strangulation.

Thus, the Government of imperialist Japan, having taken control of all the economic resources of the country, and having completely seized all political power by the above mentioned successive treaties forced upon Korea in 1905 and 1907, found that it did not suit the insular mentality of capitalist Japan to leave [even] the empty shell of Korea's [nominal independence]. Finally, on August 1910, Japan proclaimed the annexation of Korea, a territory of more than 8,400 square miles with 20 million people who were made slaves, Korea becoming a monopolised colony.

8. The movement to restore independence. The Korean people, having been forcibly annexed to Japan and finding themselves a nationally extinct people, felt more than anything else the sudden tragic end of their history of over forty two and a half centuries of national existence. Therefore, the revolutionary peasants and people of all classes and creeds united in a general struggle against imperial Japan and, with extreme nationalism in their hearts, became vigorous agitators for independence. In their minds, they were the only really oppressed

---

31 Written Li-Jin-Whoi in the original text. Alternatively Iljinhoe. The Ilchinhoe (Advance in Unity Society) was a collaborationist organisation set up in August 1904 by a former Korean government official, Song Pyongjun, and Yi Yonggu, who was the leader of a group of Tonghak believers. It claimed to have a reformist and progressive agenda based on the belief that Japanese colonisation was Korea's best hope of modernisation. With Japanese backing, it recruited tens of thousands of members. It has been described as 'a collaborationist militia ... almost embarrassing in its enthusiasm to submit Korea to Japanese rule'. See Mitter 2000, p. 15; see also Kim 2005, ch. 7.

[nation] in the economic and political history of mankind; at the same time, they saw the Japanese as their sole oppressors. Thus, from the day of annexation (29 August 1910), the Korean people began to unite, morally and materially, in a universal movement for the restoration of Korea's independence.

But the Mikado's Governor General in Korea resorted to repressive [measures] against the Korean movement ten times more severe than during the Protectorate. The educational associations and [various other] organisations were [disbanded], nearly all private schools were closed, and an attempt was made to obliterate national history, language and culture. Of course, freedom of speech and of the press [was] not only prohibited but all newspapers [were] closed without exception and anyone infringing this legislation was severely punished. Anyone suspected as an agitator is closely shadowed, and often he is thrown into prison and tortured without charge. Thus one can imagine the fate which awaits any secret group or organisation which is suspected of having any political aims. In [pursuing] the Ŭibyŏng, the Japanese army made it their unfailing [practice] to massacre the people and to burn to the ground every village and town which was unfortunate enough to have been in the pathway of any passing Ŭibyŏng. Such villages and towns can be counted by the hundred.

When [a] secret movement [is] discovered, [passers-by], [even though they] may not have been in the least connected with it, and [are] entirely ignorant of the charge, [are] summarily killed [along] with the others. There [have been] tens of thousands of such victims, and those who are under suspicion are subjected to such economic limitations that they are deprived of their means of livelihood. Thus, [reports of] 'one kitchen knife to every ten houses' may not be a generally accepted fact, [but they] illustrate the nature of [Japanese] oppression in Korea.

Under such circumstances, a large number of those connected with the movement, [from] the Ŭibyŏng [and other] organisations were obliged to go into exile abroad – to China, Manchuria, Siberia and America. This exile [did not have] self-preservation for its object, but was the [only] means of continuing the struggle, and also of abating somewhat the sufferings of compatriots at home, and was actuated by the [most sincere and self-sacrificing] motives.

Yet, such organisations as the Sinminhoe carried on their secret activities and kept alive the efforts of the [Christians], together with the student leaders and energetic youths, mostly in the North; while the Kwangboktan[32] (Restoration Society) composed of the fiery young men of the South, who had been [inspired] by the Chinese Revolution of 1911, set out to harass the enemy

---

32   *Kwang-Pok-Tan* in the original text.

by destructive measures. However, the former groups received a severe blow [with] the wholesale arrests and imprisonment of Christian leaders and leading educationalists, under the pretext of the so-called conspiracy case of 1911–13,[33] while the latter's strength was greatly shattered by the premature disclosure of a plot in 1911, which [led to] the arrest and scattering of the majority of its most active members.

9. Political activities abroad. The Korean revolutionists who had exiled themselves abroad, in accordance with [their] geographical and other circumstances – whether in Siberia, Manchuria, China, or America – endeavoured to keep the movement [alive] at home, while, on the other hand, they secretly carried on the work of preparation for the inevitable day.

Nearly one million Koreans were scattered [across] Siberia,[34] [many of whom] had emigrated in the early days. [Because of] its geographical proximity to Korea, it had long been [a haven for] Korean political and other refugees, and with the influx of the Ŭibyŏng and numerous political workers and agitators, especially since the annexation, this area [became] one of the main bases of outside activities. Even before the annexation, several organisations of the nationalist movement [had been] formed in Vladivostok, [including] the Tonginhoe[35] (Cooperation Association) and others. In 1911, the Kwŏnŏp'oe[36] (Industrial Association) was formed, then appeared the Chŏnlo hanin hoe[37] (All-Russia Korean Association) which finally took the form of the Taehan kungmin ŭihoe[38] (Korean National Council), whose organised activities were

---

33   In 1911, the Japanese colonial authorities arrested around 700 Koreans, mainly Christians, including many members of the Sinminhoe, for supposedly conspiring to assassinate the Japanese governor-general Terauchi Masatake. Around 120 were charged, and 105 were convicted and sentenced to hard labour. The 'case of the 105' generated bad international publicity for the Japanese and the prisoners were later amnestied. See Seth 2011, p. 267.

34   Beginning in the 1860s, Koreans began emigrating to Manchuria and Siberia, at first for economic, later for political reasons. In Manchuria, they mainly settled in Kando (Jiandao in Chinese, now the Yanbian Korean Autonomous Prefecture of the PRC). In Siberia, they initially settled in the Maritime Province. Around 7,000 migrated to Hawaii to work on sugar plantations. Smaller numbers left for the United States and Shanghai. Today, there are more than two million ethnic Koreans in China and around half a million in the former Soviet Union. See Seth 2011, p. 267.

35   Tong-Ein-Whoi in the original text.

36   Kwern-Up-Whoi in the original text.

37   Chunlo-Hanin-Whoi in the original text.

38   Tai-Hahn Kookmin Eui-Whoi in the original text. The Korean National Council was proclaimed on 22 April 1919. MacKensie 1920, p. 168.

similar to those of a government. Though, on account of Russia's political changes and revolutionary events, as well as on account of the irregular coming and going of the Korean leaders themselves, the organisation and its work have been readjusted to meet requirements and conditions, still it continue[s] to be the central bulwark and one of the power stations of the Korean movement for independence.

Secondly, Manchuria, [or] rather northern and western Kando, also with an immigrant Korean population of nearly two million, became the nearest base of Ŭibyŏng and other activities outside of Korea. Although local conditions and economic means did not allow any [large-scale, organised actions], it became the breeding ground for a number of organisations of all colours and creeds such as the Pumindan[39] (Korean People's Association) and Kanminhoe[40] (Kando Korean Association) and others – and, while becoming a connecting link of the home constituencies with Siberia, it naturally became a comparatively direct base for military undertakings and managed to effect numerous armed attacks across the border in Korea, thus keeping the spark [of revolution] before the eyes of the people at home.

Thirdly, in America, Mexico and Hawaii, the 7,000 Koreans were united into one general organisation called the Korean National Association. Although few in numbers, they were advantageously placed to conduct their respective work and organisation in an effective way and became one of the directing forces connecting the churches and other constituencies at home with [overseas] activities. They have rendered considerable financial assistance since the March movement.

10. Activities of the religious sects at home. A number of men having been thus compelled to go abroad, the people at home resorted to a new method of activity in what may be called the movement of the churches or religious sects, where the leaders and agitators put on the guise of religion to carry on their real organisation, communication and propaganda.

First among the sectarian movement must be counted the Ch'ŏndogyo[41] or the Heavenly Way Doctrine. This is a modernised creed of Tonghakism,

---

39   Poo-Min-Tan in the original text.
40   Kan-Min-Whoi in the original text.
41   Chun-Do-Kyo in the original text. The Tonghak leader, Son Pyong-hui, changed the name of the religion to Ch'ŏndogyo (Religion of the Heavenly Way) in 1906. Ch'ŏndogyo played a major role in the March First movement. Son Pyong-hui was among 15 of the 33 signatories of the March First declaration of independence who were adherents. At present, there are over a million followers of Ch'ŏndogyo in South Korea and nearly three million in North Korea, where it has official status as an indigenous religion. See Seth 2011, p. 268.

which was the background of the Tonghak Rebellion. The Ch'ŏndogyo leaders, by wise utilisation of opportunities and tactful means, [marshalled] their million and more followers to take an active and leading part in the March movement; and during the period of repeated persecutions inflicted on the Christian churches it took into its folds leaders and men of the former educational associations and other organisations and became [an] underground citadel to which were gathered a large number of independent leaders and agitators.

Next in line are the Christian churches. Although they had sacrificed several thousand of their leading men and workers [for the cause] since 1911 and lost [much of] their former strength, they took advantage of their vicissitude[s] by causing the foreign missions to [bear] witness to [the suffering and persecution] they were enduring and, acting as an impregnable tower, not only sent forth their communications and serenely commanded the March movement throughout its different stages, but also, [through] their hundreds and thousands of martyred men and women became models of sacrifice in the front line of the cause.

[Third in line are] the Buddhists, who with their 1400 and more wealthy monasteries throughout the land, [exploiting the] protection of the anti-Christian and pro-Buddhist Japanese Government, gathered together young revolutionary elements as monks and priests and made use of their monasteries as [a refuge] for hiding the tracts of their compatriots. [They formed] the mighty rear-guard [of] the March outbreaks.

Fourthly, there is another sect called Taejonggyo[42] which worships Tan'gun, the founder of the Korean nation. The followers of this sect are imbued with the idea of historic nationalism and there are to be found in their [front] ranks some tens of thousands of patriotic young men, [determined to] regain the lost land of their great god and ancestor, who make up a [mighty] column in the great army of the Korean movement for independence.

Finally, one must not overlook all the remaining various religious sects, such as the Daoists, Confucians and [the] thousands and tens of thousands organised into [physical] units for the purpose of conducting the movement for independence.

---

42   Tai-Chong-Kyo in the original text. Taejonggyo was founded by Na Cheol in 1909. It worships the legendary founder of the Korean nation Tan'gun. After the annexation of Korea by Japan, it gathered followers among the Korean diaspora in Manchuria. Na Cheol committed suicide in 1916 to atone for what he saw as his failures.

FIFTH SESSION   145

11. Seizing the opportunity. As the Great War ended and plans for [a] World Peace Conference were being announced everywhere, among the [overseas] activities of the Korean revolutionary movement [there were] two groups that first voiced the sentiments of the March revolution, under unique conditions. [They] were the small Korean group in Shanghai and the Korean students in Japan. A few Korean political refugees had [already] formed connections [between] the Chinese revolutionists, and their small groups and organisations in Beijing, Canton, and other places, with Shanghai as the centre. In the winter of 1918, taking advantage of the opportune moment of the expected opening of the Peace Conference, the leaders [came] together in and [around] Shanghai and [decided] to send a delegation to Paris. At the same time, representatives were sent to Korea, Japan, Siberia, and Manchuria to communicate [these steps] and to effect the united co-operation of all groups and organisations into one concerted action, making use of [opportunities] inside and outside of Korea. During this time, the united body of 800 Korean students in Tokyo had been in close touch with their compatriots in America, and after forming the Youth Independent League[43] with the Japan Students' Association[44] as a nucleus, on February 8, 1919, authorising their Committee of ten to affix their signatures to the document, made the first Declaration of Independence,[45] voicing the sentiments of the Korean people and at the same time causing a great panic among the police authorities in Tokyo, while striking [a] chord in the hearts of the people at home.

Thus, the leaders and men of the different groups at home and abroad found that the plans that they had respectively laid for the great March movement within Korea coincided with those initial voices from without.

IV. The March Movement – its Nature and Scope

12. The March movement. [The] Chinese Revolution of 1911, the great war of 1914–18, the Russian revolution of 1917, and [reports of] the re-birth of minor Slav nations – regardless of the real motive of the Powers in creating and rein-

---

43   Probably the same organisation as the Korean Youth Independence Corps (Josŏn Ch'ongnyon Tongniptan). See Seth 2011, p. 268.
44   Japan Student's Association, an organisation of Korean students in Japan.
45   On 8 February 1919, several hundred Korean overseas students gathered in Tokyo to read a declaration of independence penned by the novelist Yi Kwang-su. Some of the students then travelled to Korea, where they played an important role in organising the March First Movement. See Seth 2011, p. 268.

stating these small Eurorean states – all tended to give added impetus to the Korean people, particularly the revolutionary peasants.

However, cut off by the regular Chinese Wall built around the whole peninsula by Japan, the Korean revolutionary peasants could only hear [occasional] distorted items of news through Japanese channels, and even in the case of the Russian revolution – although it was of such direct and vital concern to themselves as members of the great family of the revolutionary proletariat – having no way of learning the facts, they were unable to take full advantage of it by making a resounding echo. There was only a passive sympathy [and] the knowledge that it was different from an ordinary political upheaval.

Yet the entrance of America into the struggle of the capitalistic Powers of Europe and its outcome, and her role as the dictator of the peace negotiations, attracted the attention of the Korean masses, [mainly as a] result of long standing propaganda on the part of the Christian element. Although they realised that no peace would be concluded in actual accord with Wilson's Fourteen Points, on seeing the hypocritical approval of them [by] the Powers they hoped there might be a slight awakening of the conscience of nations after such a disastrous war, and that the imperialists of the world, while [devising] a scheme [to prevent] a recurrence of a like catastrophe, might see the necessity of trying to get rid of the possible causes of new conflicts.

Also, the Koreans knew that, given their own lack of preparation and strength, they could not obtain their freedom through [conventional] warfare and by driving away the Japanese oppressors, but finding their condition unbearable [even] for a single day, they waited keenly for the slightest possible opportunity. So when the reports of the rise of smaller nations began to be heard in Korea, the activities of the leaders outside found a ready response among their [long-suffering] compatriots at home, and without further deliberation [or] preparation, the initial steps were jointly undertaken in the first stage of their revolutionary experience, in the first peaceful movement. Thus the March outburst [opened a new chapter] in the Korean revolutionary movement.

13. Declaration of independence. After ten years preparation for the great day, 33 representatives of three religious constituencies, the Ch'ŏndogyo, the Christians and the Buddhists [together with other] revolutionary bodies, [expressing] the mandate of the entire Korean people, at one o'clock on 1 March 1919, [in the Pagoda Park in Seoul], solemnly and boldly declared the independence of Korea and the freedom of the Korean people. Immediately, the great mass of 100,000 people that had gathered to hear the declaration, with the young men and women [in the vanguard], marched in [a] great demonstration throughout the city, shouting *Taehan Tongnip Manse*[46] (Long Live Korean Independence). Thus began the March movement.

This declaration of the Korean people with [a glorious] 43 centuries [of] history, with the united loyalty of twenty million souls [determined] to perpetuate their liberty, and with [the] aim [of joining] in the movement for world reconstruction, expressing the true sentiments of the entire Korean people, was rather [self-critical] and did not try to lay the blame for the loss of their rights on the shoulders of others, [but rather] solemnly pledged to sacrifice themselves to the last man [and] to the last moment.

On the very same day, while the declaration was being adopted and the demonstration was in progress in Seoul, similar events took place in Pyongyang, Sinch'on,[47] Wŏnsan,[48] Taegu,[49] Chianju,[50] and another 300 centres, and the movement continued throughout the whole month, with over a million participants, which became a unique event in the record of Korean mass action.

14. A passive movement. The March demonstrations were a movement of non-resistance in the extremist sense of the word. Before the cold steel of the Japanese bayonet charges, suffering tens of thousands in dead and wounded, they [pressed] forward with increased zeal and yet did not commit the least act of violence against the enemy. Vengeance had been laid aside. Although the Japanese Governor General inaugurated a relentless slaughter and charged the crowds in a blind massacre under the pretext of retaliation for the death or minor injury of a few of their gendarmes and police [in fact caused by] the promiscuous shooting by their own men during the general scuffles, the Koreans rigidly [stuck to] their decision to do no violence, at whatever cost, and to demonstrate their demands with the cry of *Manse* only. The Koreans' sole purpose was to show to the world the [firmness] of their decision and their [steadfast] adherence to the idea of peace to all humanity. Their passive courage was tested to the extreme, [but] they looked upon their own life as a mere speck to be sacrificed for the great cause. This [spontaneous] movement of the motley crowd of peasants was orderly to the last point and devoid of any brutal violence.

---

46   Tai-Han Tok-Rip Mansei in the original text.
47   Sen Chun in the original text.
48   Wŏnsan is a port on the east coast of North Korea.
49   Taiku in the original text. Taegu is an industrial city in South Korea.
50   Presumably the city of Ch'inju in South Korea.

The demonstrations, led by the T'aegŭkki[51] (the Korean national flag), [advanced] undaunted in the face of the firing and butchering of the Japanese soldiers and gendarmes, and often the [flag-bearer] was shot or slashed down and replaced five [or] ten times in succession during the same advance until the enemy, armed to his teeth, dared not come further and [retreated] of his own accord, completely awestruck [as], with loads of bleeding and dying bodies on their shoulders as their war trophies, the demonstrators returned homeward in a din of tragic songs and lamentations for the lost. Po-Ghun in Kyng-Ka province [was] only one of many such places, while in many localities the demonstrators met and [faced down] the Japanese bayonet charges with bared chests. And if on occasions any of the fiery young men, unable to [hold themselves back any longer], attempted to show the least violence, the whole throng sternly reprimanded them for breaking their solemn [promises].

The motive [for] conducting the movement with such extreme non-resistance lies in the fact that the intellectuals and the religious leaders [wanted to use] the occasion of the Versailles Peace Conference, in the vague hope of rousing the sympathy and awakening the conscience of the 'civilised' world, and to obtain, if possible, their approval and [intervention]. This was the prevailing idea with which they led the masses to their supreme sacrifice within the country and carried on their propaganda [abroad].

15. The Provisional Government. The March movement gave birth to the Korean Provisional Government. The intellectuals gathered together a number of their leaders and [followers in] Shanghai, and [in the month following] the March outbreak, on 11 April 1919, in the name of the Korean National Council, [a] Provisional Constitution was adopted and immediately [afterwards a] Korean Provisional Government was [formed].

This Korean Provisional Government in Shanghai was at first [a] beacon [of] light for the Korean revolutionary masses. After having suffered the tyrannical rule of an alien power for nearly ten years, the Korean people of all classes and creeds welcomed even the name of a Provisional Government of their own. Though they did not know its real inner make-up, they saw in it a signal indicating the [road to] national restoration. So they were happy to obey and follow its directions and orders even [at the risk of] their own lives, and in spite of the rigid Japanese surveillance the peasants and labourers did their utmost to [offer it] material support – the men tightening their belts and the women cut-

---

51   Tai-Kou-Ka in the original text.

ting their hair.[52] The better part of the latter half of 1919 in the movement of the Korean people was thus spent mostly in making sacrifices towards its maintenance.

But the Provisional Government [became embroiled] in factional struggles and [busied itself with] successive changes in personnel even to the point of [making] several constitutional changes. It tried to maintain the pretence of a responsible cabinet with a provisional president at its head while making its one great policy to try and hold together a few so-called leaders of the different groups, and thus only added to the long list of their blunders and failures. This was due to the faults of the individuals as well as to [a] lack of basic strength.

The Korean Provisional Government in Shanghai was really a government of diplomatic [initiatives]. Although its internal [composition] and real aims did not [end there], they are the only outstanding efforts that can be found amongst its undertakings. So one sees that its greatest undertakings were its endeavours (together with a few related activities in propaganda etc.) to support its [delegation in making a pathetic appeal to the Powers at the Paris Peace Conference].

16. Diplomatic efforts in Europe and America. The greatest and most active undertaking of the Korean Provisional Government in its revolutionary efforts was the establishment and maintenance of Korean Commissions[53] to Europe and America. True, there were a few [other initiatives such as] the internal Administration and Communications Bureaus (operating secretly) called the Yŏnt'ongje,[54] the headquarters of the Northern and Western military units in Kando, and the Civil and Military Administrative Headquarters, also in Kando, but these establishments [exerted] less real influence than their names indicated.

The Korean Commission to Europe and America, with three members appointed by the Provisional President and [under] the personal direction of the latter, had its seat in Washington. It represented the Provisional Government, carrying on active official and public propaganda in the Occidental countries, with America as the [focus]. Its main object was to disclose to the Powers the atrocious repression by Japan and to show not only the real causes, proced-

---

52 Presumably to sell to raise funds.
53 Syngman Rhee set up the Washington-based Korean Commission as the diplomatic arm of the Korean Provisional Government, in August 1919. He came into conflict with the longer-established Korean National Association, based in San Francisco, over fund-raising issues. See Kim 2011, pp. 60, 67–71.
54 Yon-Tong-Che in the original text.

ure and aims of the Korean revolution, but also to testify [to] the fact that the Korean people were conducting a [peaceful] and orderly movement.

But the Powers of Europe and America paid no attention whatever. With the exception of a few people [who] were specially connected with the Korean movement, the Western public as well as [public figures] were absolutely cold and unresponsive, and so were the governments. [The supposedly] most friendly group, the Foreign Missions Board,[55] did nothing whatever in the way of any material or moral support except to [dash] off a few empty words of sympathy. The Wilsonian principles, such as self-determination of all peoples and the Fourteen Points, became mere bubbles in the air.

The Wilsonian principle of self-determination could not [deliver] full emancipation to the oppressed peoples and small nations. It absolutely could not be accomplished even in [theory]; not only because the imperialistic countries of Europe had to stand firm on their respective colonisation policies as their only means of national expansion, but it was also self-contradictory for the United States of America, one of the most typical capitalistic powers, to abolish her own institution of capitalism. In fact, American [talk of] a square deal, fair play, humanity and justice, are mere catchwords used in the extension of her gold market. America, soon [realising] that she could not [halt] the momentum [created] by the [outpouring of support for] that great idea of self-determination – [even if] in name only – abruptly changed her attitude and withdrew from the League of Nations[56] in a very ignominious [and] tricky manner, in order to escape from her responsibility.

But a large number of the members of the Korean Provisional Government still cling to [the idea of making progress through] European and American diplomacy. On the one hand they stirred up the people to make a great agitation, [while] on the other hand they wander round from place to place – Versailles, Geneva, and Washington – [seeking the payoff of the people's support]. However, all those conferences [officially gave Japan a free hand to continue her reign of terror in Korea] and [the Powers] decided [to observe] calmly how it will all work out for Japan and, from her experience, learn for themselves the art of effectively ruling the peoples of their respective colonies.

---

55 The Foreign Mission Board, now the International Mission Board, is a missionary organisation associated with the Southern Baptist Convention in the United States. Its most famous missionary was Lottie Moon, daughter of slave-owning tobacco planters, who worked in China for 39 years. An annual fund-raising event is held in her honour.

56 In fact, the United States never joined the League of Nations, because the Senate did not ratify the Versailles Treaty.

v. Japanese Repression and Korean Resistance

17. Japanese repression. The Japanese repression of the March movement culminated in such a degree of cruelty and high-handedness that no words can really describe it. The eyes of the outside world [were opened wide] by the reports of foreign missionaries regarding the persecution and sufferings of Christians, but secret assassinations and atrocities continued after the wholesale massacres (in April 1919, 38 men, women and children of Jeam-ri in Suwon district were thrown into a church building and set on fire without a word of explanation).[57]

Such methods of repression – that is, the [indiscriminate] arrests, imprisonments, torture, killing and wilful murder – might find the shadow of an excuse on the ground[s] that the movement was [intended as] an insurrection against the Japanese rule (even though of an absolutely passive nature), but the cold-blooded massacres of innocent women and children and the old and feeble, who had no direct contact with the movement except in the way of having some latent sympathy, find no parallel anywhere or at any time.

The statistics in connection with the March uprisings so far show 7,000 deaths, 46,000 wounded and 49,000 imprison[ed], a large number of [whom] were women, old men and weaklings, and the Japanese authorities tried to excel themselves in brutality and atrociousness. As to the method[s] of killing, some were boiled to death, some torn asunder, and some buried alive, but the outrages that they committed on the imprisoned women and the tortures they administered on the [young] cannot even be pictured in our normal minds. Because of lack of prison space, in devising means for the rapid disposal of the arrested mass, they instituted a system of flogging, whereby they administered thirty blows with split bamboo rods on the naked buttocks of the victim for three successive days, so that many a stalwart youth died, either while undergoing the torture, or in hospital after their release. And not being satisfied with this, they carried on a systematic campaign, as shown elsewhere, of depriving the Korean people of their means of livelihood.

18. Destructive undertakings. While the Japanese atrocities really find no equal in any country, in proportion to the extent of the exposure of such atrocities to

---

57 Chaiamni in the original text. Extracts from the journal of the Japanese general Utsunomiya Taro, confirming the Jeam-ri atrocity, and the steps taken to cover it up, were published in a Japanese newspaper in 2007. Utsunomiya sentenced the officer responsible for the massacre to 30 days detention. See http://english.donga.com/srv/service.php3?biid =2007030168648, retrieved 20 April 2014.

the outside world, the Japanese increased the intensity of their oppression [in] the vain expectation of intimidating the Korean people.

However, the Korean revolutionists have intensified their determination to carry on their movement to the limit. They realise that they can no longer continue to deal with their enemy in a pacific way, and so they have decided to [extend] their efforts as far as possible in the way of destructive and violent undertakings – assassinations, bombings, and the demolition of posts and telegraphs, railways, police quarters and government buildings – which has naturally [provoked a reaction from] the Japanese military and police authorities. But the Japanese, being sensitive [towards] their policy of iron rule, endeavoured most strenuously to conceal all these facts from the outside world.

The main bases for the above mentioned irregular activities are naturally found mostly in North and West Kando (Jiandao Districts in Northern Manchuria).[58] Small groups of young men with pistols and bombs incessantly cross the river boundary and leave no days of peace in P'yŏngan[59] and Hwanghae[60] Provinces, and often by carefully planned and placed attacks south of Seoul[61] – at Shin-Eve-Ju, Sinch'on,[62] Pyeno, Yanz, Seoul, Taegu, Miryang[63] and Jusan – on government establishments; and sometimes, by assassinating and killing Japanese officials and police, they have caused a great deal of unrest among the Japanese residing in Korea, quite a few thousands of whom have quit Korea altogether.

Of course, through lack of sufficient [training] and equipment the results are not at all [comparable to] the untold sacrifices made. Along the Yalu River regions alone the toll of lives given to the cause are numbered by the thousand.

19. Conflicts. While the partisans in the West Kando District were carrying on their armed undertakings in small detachments, the people in the North Kando District have been more intensively engaged in preparing themselves for future combats on a larger scale. Besides, on account of the geographical propinquity of this northern district to Siberia, the people here are in a somewhat more advantageous position to better equip themselves, comparatively speaking. There are such military groups as the Kunjŏngsŏ[64] (Bureau of milit-

---

58   Chientso in the original text.
59   Pyeng-Ahn in the original text.
60   Wheng-Hai in the original text.
61   Swul in the original text.
62   Senchun in the original text.
63   Milyanz in the original text.
64   Goon-Chung-Suh in the original text.

ary affairs) and the Kungmin'gun[65] (the National Army), Ch'onggunbu[66] (General Army Headquarters), Uigunbu[67] (Headquarters of the Righteous Army), Kwangbokkun[68] (the Independence Restoration Army), and the like. These different units are busily engaged in the training of officers, recruiting men, providing arms, and collecting funds.

But before all the above-mentioned minor detachments could be united under the command, which altogether numbered over 3,000 only, there occurred the Hunchun massacre (in the spring of 1920), when the base of their activities was exposed and destroyed by the Japanese army, and the partisans themselves were compelled to retreat into Siberia. These are really the so-called Kando conflicts. However, it is quite remarkable that in spite of the [overwhelmingly inadequate][69] strength of the different Korean partisan units – in the way of arms, fighting apparatus, supplies, as well as training and command – and in [the] face of the ever-increasing advance of the thoroughly equipped [and] powerful Japanese army, two divisions in all, the former have been able, not only to repulse and withstand the latter for quite a length of time, but also in nine cases out of ten whenever they were forced to an engagement, to completely rout the enemy. This shows that the Korean people [have] the advantage of detailed geographical knowledge of those regions, as well as the calibre of their fighting quality, even [against] immense odds. The phenomenal Korean victories at Wutso-Yang-Chang, Qingshanli,[70] Feng-Itung, etc. are a few of the most outstanding examples, where the vanguard of the Japanese army suffered overwhelming losses. But, of course, the Koreans could not hold out [for] long, and at the same time the general massacres and the burning and plundering of hundreds of Korean settlements only find their parallel in the organised savagery of the Japanese soldiers in Korea.

20. The base of the revolutionary army. The Kando affairs have undoubtedly caused a terrible setback to the expected advance on Korea, and [to] the Korean Independence Army, but if one observes it from a historical point of view, it was really a turn for the better in enlarging the scope and intensifying the preparations for more effective and [realistic] undertakings in the inevitable

---

65   Kook-Min-Goon in the original text.
66   Chong-Goon-Pu in the original text.
67   Eui-Goon-Pu in the original text.
68   Kwang-Pok-Goon in the original text.
69   The original text says *overwhelming and adequate*.
70   Chingsanli in the original text. For more details on the battle of Qingshanli of 21–28 October 1920 see earlier note.

struggle that is to come. The different units that had scattered into Siberia came to realise the necessity of firmly laying the foundation for future operations, first and foremost by complete unification of the different groups, and by thorough organisation. Also the Kando affairs have given occasion for the Ŭibyŏng (Righteous Army) in Siberia to [unite] with the incoming units under one united command, and at the same time to find ways and means of establishing a proper base for the training of men and for [their] efficient organisation into a real fighting [machine].

In Siberia the Taehan kungmin ŭihoe[71] (Korean National Council) was organised [early on] and [became] the focus [around] which the Northern Koreans gathered their efforts for military activities in connection with the Korean independence movement. Of course, in accordance with the changing times and local conditions, this organisation has gone through many vicissitudes; yet, in 1919, it chose the Amur region as its centre of military preparations, particularly [for the purpose of] building up an army. At the same time, it came into touch, directly and indirectly, with the Russian revolutionary army. With the influx of the different detachments from Kando, as mentioned above, all [groups] decided to combine the different units into one national military force and convened at Blagoveshchensk in order to accomplish this object, while linking themselves more closely with the Russian revolutionary army so that, with the latter's moral and material support, they commenced to constitute themselves into a properly organised, trained and armed force along modern lines.

Thus, formerly scattered and heterogeneous Korean independence forces, after going through some unavoidable controversies – [in particular] the Blagoveshchensk conflict[72] while in the process of unification – finally united themselves under one command and also have become closely affiliated with

---

71 Tai-Han Kookmin Eui-Whoi in the original text.
72 This is presumably a reference to the Free City Incident of June 1921, a battle between rival Korean factions at Alekseyevsk, 167 kilometres north of Blagoveshchensk. The Korean communists were divided between two rival centres. Yi Tong-hwi, a former army officer, founded a Korean Socialist Party in Khabarovsk in 1918, and was prime minister of the Shanghai-based Korean Provisional Government until May 1921, when he resigned after clashing with its president, Syngman Rhee. Yi's party, renamed the Korean Communist Party, was informally known as the Shanghai faction. A rival Communist Party formed in Irkutsk, was largely made up of Korean members of the Russian Communist Party and was sponsored by Boris Shumyatsky. A Soviet attempt to bring the Korean militias in Siberia under a unified command led to a clash between the pro-Irkutsk Korean Revolutionary Military Congress and the Yi loyalists of the Greater Korean Independence Corps. According to some sources, hundreds of Koreans were killed. See Kim 2011, pp. 84–5; see also Seth 2011, p. 276.

Soviet Russia and the Communist International in opening up a new and definite path for the revolutionary Korean people. At present, the nucleus of the Korean revolutionary army is the Korean brigade at Irkutsk, under the political supervision of the Korean Communist Party and attached to the Fifth Army of Soviet Russia, [and] has infantry and cavalry regiments and artillery regiment battalions, [as well as] an officers' training school connected with the same.

VI. The Awakening of the Masses [to] Revolutionary Ideals

21. The awakening of the Korean proletariat. The Korean people have gone through many stages of experiences and experiments in their revolutionary [struggle], viz. the March movement, the Provisional Government, European and American diplomatic propaganda, minor destructive undertakings, premature armed combats etc.; and the real result they have obtained after many untold sacrifices, is their awakening towards a genuine revolutionary movement and the entrance upon its only proper path.

This real awakening is all the more significant because it is an awakening of the Korean proletariat – that is the historic Korean revolutionary peasants and the newly conscious poor labouring masses – who had almost [lapsed] into passive indifference [but] are now [once more] becoming self-conscious and are [embracing] revolutionary ideals with eager and open minds. Having been themselves the real active [agents] in their revolutionary experiences, and having made such huge sacrifices to its cause, they were naturally led, in their present awakening and clear vision, to class consciousness. So the people [of] Korea, without waiting for any Communistic propaganda from without, have [heeded] the call of the world proletarian movement as [a clarion call] to the class struggle of the poor peasants and workers trying to unite with all oppressed peoples of the world – and of the Far East in particular.

22. The uniformity of the movement. [Given] the differences in conditions and circumstances within and outside of Korea, revolutionary activities naturally differ [in] their outward form and [their] real inward nature. For example, at home, the commercial and industrial enterprises, social undertakings, [cultural] movements, and so forth, are [outwardly the] religious tendencies of the past [but] are really camouflaged channels for bringing in [a] wave of social revolution from the outside. There [can] be observed, however, [a] unity of real aim and purpose of the different organisations such as the Peasants' Association, labour unions, Young Men's Federations, [the] Students' League, and women's societies. By taking advantage of the supposedly more lenient administrative policy of the Japanese Governor-General Admiral Saito[73] – implemented for the purpose of assimilating the Koreans into docile and law-abiding subjects of the Japanese Empire – [and so avoiding] a great deal of Japanese suspicion, even under such close surveillance, Koreans are able to organise themselves into a few corporate bodies.

The Peasants' Association [began] its first representative Congress in the spring of 1921, but the organisation of the General Assembly [was delayed] because of suspicion on the part of the Japanese authorities that it was really a red movement. [But] although as yet there is no central body, by using the names of former smaller gatherings [such] as Kyung-lank-Tan (Farmers' Union) and Poong-Mool-Ken[74] (Agricultural Guilds), local organisations [have sprung up] in nearly every town and village throughout the land, [and] keep the peasant masses bound together in the spirit of revolution, and act as the revolutionary nuclei of the entire Korean people.

There are two labour unions, one of which is a federation of trade unions and factory organisations called Chosŏn Nodong Taehoe[75] (General Labour Federation) with some 80,000 members. It is not only [becoming] an effective and influential body, directing the general labour movement, but is also [turning into] the real vanguard of the advanced revolutionary movement in Korea. The other organisation is on the [surface] more [engaged in] service and relief work, as the name Nodong Kongjehoe[76] (Labour Service and Relief Association) would indicate, but in reality it is a similar organisation to the General Labour Federation, with some 30,000 members.

The Young Men's Federation, called the Ch'ŏngnyŏndan yŏnhap'oe,[77] is a union of young men's organisation[s], free from any religious tendencies or control and simply [carrying out] revolutionary undertakings. It is a confederation of over 200 local organisations and is carrying on a very extensive and intensive movement – outwardly a cultur[al] movement. The Students' League is [made up of] matriculated students from middle school [and above] and, keeping in touch with the Japanese Students' Society in Tokyo and other student groups abroad, has come to be the vanguard of the [young Korean] revolutionaries. The women's movement is represented in the form of the

---

73   Admiral Saito Makoto (1858–1936) was governor of Korea from 1919–27, and 1929–31, and Prime Minister of Japan from 1932–34. He was assassinated in the 26 February 1936 Incident, a failed coup by junior army officers.
74   Possibly P'ungmuljang.
75   Lo-Tong-Tai-Whoi in original text.
76   Lo-Tong-Kong-Geh-Whoi in the original text.
77   Chung-Nyun-Ryan-Hap-Whoi in the original text. Also known as the Federation of Youth Corps.

Korean Women's Patriotic Society, and the Women's Educational Society, the former working secretly and the latter openly, which have opened the path [to] progress [for] Korean revolutionary women. The revolutionary organisations [inside and outside Korea] carry on their activities in [a dual mode of open activities] and secret undertakings.

23. Organisations of the Korean Communist Party. While the proletarian awakening was taking place in the homeland, the revolutionary elements [abroad grasped the] opportunity to definitely raise the Red Flag. The Koreans residing within and [around] the territory of Soviet Russia, having been in a position to come early into personal contact with revolutionary ideals and experiences, contributed no small share in connection with this first stage of [building a] real organised movement, [resulting in] the constitution of the Korean Communist Party and its admittance to the Third Communist International, [uniting] the Korean movement with the world proletarian revolution.

Therefore, the [various] groups of [conscious] Korean revolutionary elements are affiliating themselves with the Korean Communist Party and are trying to [join] hands with the Third Communist International, the directing [authority] of the world revolution. And, to a certain extent, the various Korean revolutionary organisations that have convened here to attend the Congress of the Communist and Revolutionary Parties of the Far East at the invitation of the Communist International, have come with this end in view. At present the Korean Communist Party is in fact becoming the real [centre] of the Korean revolutionary movement.

24. Definite revolutionary programme. It is an open secret that the Korean revolutionary groups are rapidly turning red, but we must also not forget the fact that, with the Provisional Government as their central organ, the pro-American element and the religious sects – particularly the Christians – still remain to a certain extent, and their strength will not wane [quickly] because of [support from] the Provisional Government with its short history, its [institutions] and personnel. But it is a fact that the more intelligent elements among them are also awakening to the necessity of changing their methods in connection with the independence movement. The policy of the Korean Communist Party is to rally the Korean masses in a united stand against the exploitation of the imperialistic Powers and to strive for the genuine emancipation of the Korean people, as the first and foremost steps to be taken. With these two main objects in view, the Korean Communist Party decided to help as far as possible in the unification of the whole Korean revolutionary movement, and as a means towards such an accomplishment, it is co-operating directly and indirectly with the present move on the part of the different groups to convene their respective representatives in a national constituent congress in order to bring all the various elements into a harmonious, united and comprehensive central revolutionary directing organ. There is at present in Shanghai an Organizing Committee formed by the delegates from the different localities in order to undertake the preparation for [convoking the Congress]. [Additionally, on this] occasion of the convening of the greatest Congress of the Communist and Revolutionary Parties of the Far East, the delegates from the various Korean revolutionary organisations will take it upon their shoulders to co-operate in effecting the above mentioned general unification, which fact will mark the opening of an important stage in the adoption of a definite general revolutionary programme.

VII. Conclusion

25. *The brightness of the future.* If we summarise the above outlined facts, the Korean revolutionary movement [found] its first concerted action in the early historic class struggle of the revolutionary peasants, passing through the stages of the national independence movement in reaction against the penetration of foreign exploitation. However, after numerous sacrifices, sufferings and setbacks it has finally entered upon the path of world social revolution. The Korean revolutionary proletariat [was at] first misguided by the [various] religious sects; then [it] relied upon the leadership of the intellectuals; but now [it is] really taking it into [its] own hands to lead the class that originally led them; to [a struggle for the revolutionary victory] of the whole of humanity.

The future path of the Korean Revolution is quite clear and certain, having [united with] the world revolutionary movement. The future is bright.

Sixth Session

25 January 1922 (Morning)

Chairman: Comrade *Shumyatsky*.

Chairman. Comrades, I declare the session open. The item of the agenda is the report of the Mongolian delegation by comrade *T. Din-Dib*.

Din-Dib [Dendev].[1] Before taking up the subject of the modern political and economic situation in Mongolia and of the struggle of the Mongolian people to overthrow the foreign aggressors' yoke, which is now being crowned with success, it is necessary to say a few words on the past history of the Mongolian people and relate a few facts about our country.

Mongolia occupies a vast territory running from east to west, commencing nearly at the Chinese Eastern and South Manchurian railway lines and proceeding to the mountain chains of Eastern Turkestan, and from north to south, starting from the Southern Siberian frontier of the Russian Socialist Federative Republic and the Far Eastern Republic, continuing to the foot of the mountains of Tibet.

Mongolia represents a mountainous prairie, interspersed here and there by wooded mountain chains and waterless and sterile sandy deserts, with scanty moisture on the whole, and with a typical continental climate, as if intended by Mother Nature for the raising of cattle, which indeed has been the [almost] exclusive form of agriculture until the present day.

Having been traversed in the remote past by numerous nomadic tribes, which in most instances have left no other trace except their names, e.g. the

---

1 Dendev (1882–1922). After China's reassertion of control in 1919, Dendev and other nationalists, including Soliin Danzan, established the East Urga group, which fused with the Consular Hill group of Dogsomyn Bodoo and Choibalsan to form the Mongolian People's Party (MPP) in June 1920. The party sent a delegation to request support from the Soviet government. Soon afterwards, the Russian civil war spilled over into Mongolia when the White forces of Baron von Ungern-Sternberg expelled Chinese troops from the capital. Red Army and MPP forces in turn defeated Ungern-Sternberg, and installed an MPP government in July 1921, with Bodoo as prime minister. But the government was divided by personal rivalries and over policy, in particular an unpopular campaign, blamed on Bodoo, to eliminate 'feudal' forms of dress. In August 1922, Soliin Danzan seized power and Dendev was executed along with Bodoo and a dozen others. Soliin Danzan was, in turn, ousted and executed in 1924, supposedly for profiteering and links with foreign business. See Batbayar 2005, p. 365; see also Atwood 2004, p. 473.

Oghuz,[2] the Uighurs,[3] Girgeni, etc. which were lost in the oblivion of the centuries or some very scanty records of their movements in the shape of tombstones, Mongolia in the twelfth century (European calendar) became the birthplace of a vast steppe kingdom under the lead[ership] of the famous conqueror Genghis Khan, with whose name is connected the original appearance of the Mongolian people upon the historical arena as a national entity, and who was the founder of the so-called Great Yuan dynasty (1280–1368),[4] which incorporated within the steppe monarchy the major part of Asia, including China and India and the Eastern half of Europe. In the course of time, with the decay of this enormous monarchy, which had been once united under Genghis Khan, the Mongolian people became broken up into several groups, scattered through Central Asia and Eastern Europe, gradually becoming merged among alien races, whereby many of the Mongolian tribes lost their natural features to a considerable degree and many even began to forget their tribal origin. Thus a part of the Torghuts (known under the name of Kalmyks)[5] found itself upon the lower banks of the Volga and Don, and, together with the Buryats[6] of eastern Siberia, fell under the yoke of the Russian tsars, while the major part of the Mongolian tribes (Urankhais, Derbeis, Alshus, Kuku, Korani, Olash, Khalkhas, in eastern and southern Mongolia), after a long struggle for independence, fell, towards the end of the seventeenth century, under the heel of the Manchu dynasty of China.[7]

---

2   Oghuz is a Turkic word meaning tribe. Descendants of the Oghuz are said to have created the Ottoman Empire. The epic poem *The Book of Dede Kortuk*, records their early history. See Nicolle 1990, p. 47.

3   Uygur in the original text. The Uighur Khaganate (Empire) ruled Mongolia from 744–840 CE. Bogu (Tengri Khagan, 759–79) adopted Manicheism as the state religion, but Uighurs gradually converted to Buddhism after the collapse of the empire. In the seventeenth century, the Uighurs converted to Islam. Their descendants are a national minority in Xinjiang, northwest China. See 'Uighur Empire' in Atwood 2004, pp. 560–1.

4   The Yuan Dynasty was proclaimed in 1271 by Kublai Khan, and comprised most of modern China as well as Mongolia. The Mongols had, in fact, begun their conquest of China decades earlier, and Ming historians dated the dynasty from the coronation of Genghis Khan in 1206. Following outbreaks of plague and hyperinflation of its paper money, the Yuan dynasty was overthrown by Zhu Yuanzhang, who proclaimed the Ming Dynasty in 1368. See 'Yuan Dynasty' in Atwood 2004, pp. 603–12.

5   The Torghuts and Kalmyks are related peoples of the Oirat group of western Mongols. The Republic of Kalmykia is now part of the Russian Federation.

6   Buryats are a northern branch of the Mongols, and speak a dialect of Mongolian (although the Buryat language is classified by UNESCO as endangered). About half a million Buryats live in the Russian Federation, mainly in the Republic of Buryatia, situated on the eastern shore of Lake Baikal. The capital of the republic is Ulan-Ude.

7   The Qing Dynasty, which originated in Manchuria, took effective control of Inner Mongolia,

As a result of the Mongolian loss of political independence and subjection to the Manchu dynasty beginning from the reign of Emporer Kangxi, China enter[ed] upon [a] road of active fortification of her political and economic domination in Mongolia, turning the country into her colony through the application of a whole series of well-thought-out and relentlessly enforced measures which gradually assumed the nature of a coordinated system of political, economic and spiritual oppression of the Mongolian masses.

Having deprived Mongolia of her independence, the Manchu not only preserved, but steadily strengthened and supported in the course of over two centuries, the old feudal system which they had found. They maintained the subdivision of Mongolia into dukedoms (Khoshun), and every one of these dukedoms was administered by special magistrates appointed by the Manchu, who either occupied military residences established by the Chinese government upon Mongolian territory, e.g. Khobdo and Ulasutai[8] in western Mongolia, or lived in adjacent centres of Manchuria and extra-mural[9] China. These dukedoms, at the moment of the fall of the Manchu dynasty in 1911, retained their conventional administrative and political subdivision into Outer or northwestern Mongolia, adjoining the Russian frontier and including the Khalkha and Khobdo districts, and Inner Mongolia, embracing the south-eastern dukedoms; only a few insignificant groups of these dukedoms were administratively included and now form part of the provinces of Turkestan, Isnduyan and Western China. Increasing [the number of] dukedoms by splitting up the large feudal possessions and distributing them among [their supporters], equalising the ruling Khans in their rights with the petty dukes, widely applying the system of bribing influential dukes by various bounties, decorations and marriages to princesses of the imperial Manchu house etc., the Manchu Government [in] Beijing, in the course of time, completely tamed the Mongolian dukes and found them a strong support and an obedient tool for the total enslavement of Mongolia.

Another mighty weapon for the strengthening of Chinese domination in Mongolia consisted in spreading the Buddhist religion, which [was encouraged by] the Manchu dynasty.[10] The pacifist dogmas of the Buddhist religious doc-

---

      mainly by forming alliances, before conquering China proper in 1644. Outer Mongolia became part of the Qing Empire in 1691.

8   Khobdo is in Mongolia. Ulasutai is now in the Xinjiang Uyghur Autonomous Region in China and is known as Shankou.

9   The original says extra-rural but should read extra-mural, meaning parts of China outside the Great Wall.

10   In fact, Buddhist influence dates back at least to the Great Mongol Empire and the Yuan

trine, denying war and bloodshed, preaching [high-minded] humanitarianism and non-resistance to evil, were made use of as an instrument for inculcating the once war-like Mongolian masses with the ideas of political submission. Securing the support of the higher priesthood by bestowing upon them the broken-up feudal possessions, the Chinese Emperors Kangxi, Yongzheng and Qianlong developed among the Buddhist priests a body of reliable adherents [who exercised] their influence upon the masses in the desired direction. The Buddhist church became in the course of time a particular institution, with an independent oriental administrative and legal regime, with tens of thousands of subject-slaves (the so-called Khutugtu administration[11]), a sort of *status in statu*.[12] This influence was widely utilised as an instrument of subjection of the people, despite the high principles preached by the Buddhist creed.

The third and strongest factor in the enslavement of the Mongolian people was the economic domination of Chinese mercantile capital. Being a country far ahead economically [compared with] Mongolia, [which was] an exclusively cattle raising country, China began [her] economic conquest much earlier than she became established politically. With the political conquest of Mongolia, the voracious mercantile capital of China, backed by Chinese officialdom in the person of the Manchu government in Mongolia, and particularly through the Mongolian dukes who are hopelessly in their debt, and partly by the higher lama order, created in the course of centuries a whole network of usurious chains whereby the Mongolian masses [were] crushed and forced to surrender the products of their cattle raising industry. The spendthrift dukes, in order to gratify their whims, contracted unredeemable debts with Chinese trading firms [and extracted] the enormous sums due from them to cover the usurious interest [from] the common people working upon their estates, assisting the Chinese merchants in every way in robbing these masses. Under such circumstances, there arose gradually a set of legal precepts, which for instance imposed upon the toiling population of the dukedoms, a system of mutual responsibility of all the toilers for the debts of any individual, not to [mention] the debts contracted by the princely owners of the estate or the obligation to pay the upkeep of merchants calling upon the estate for debt collection, etc.

---

dynasty. Genghis Khan sponsored both Buddhists and Taoists. Kublai Khan made Tibetan Buddhism the court religion and sponsored several other Buddhist schools. Altan Khan (1507–82) oversaw a Buddhist revival in Mongolia and created the title of Dalai Lama for the head of the Gelugpa school of Tibetan Buddhism. See Atwood 2004, pp. 48–50, 607.

11 Khutakhta in the original text.
12 I.e. state within a state.

Furthermore, with the development of Chinese agricultural colonisation of eastern Mongolia adjacent to extra-mural China, the private debts of the dukes were used by the Chinese trading firms during the last decade of the Manchu dynasty, and during the subsequent 'republican' government of Yuan Shikai, as a [pretext] for seizing Mongolian lands on behalf of the governmental colonisation fund. These were generally the methods of Manchu policy in Mongolia, which established Chinese political and economic domination and made the Mongolian masses the slaves of Chinese merchants and officials, and of their own spiritual and temporal dukes.

The middle of the nineteenth century saw the inauguration of a new period in Mongolia, marked by an increased interest on the part of Russian mercantile capital and the Russian tsarist government, which gradually brought Mongolia into the sphere of influence of international capital. Russian traders, hitherto interested in Mongolia only as a gateway for merchandise (mostly tea) proceeding from China into European Russia through Mongolia along the caravan route of Kalgan-Urga-Kyakhta,[13] in the 60s of the last century, began to penetrate first into Western Mongolia via the Altai and Uriankhai region, and then gradually extended their operations into other parts of Outer Mongolia, where they tried to establish themselves economically.

In its Mongolian activities, Russian mercantile capital adopted the same primitive predatory methods of exploitation of the Mongolian population [that] had been practiced by the Chinese merchants, including the famous mutual responsibility system, only with an even more arrogant and undisguised form of commercial usury compared with their competitors. [In this way they acquainted] the Mongolian masses with the seamy side of so-called European culture.

Japan's victory over autocratic Russia in the war of 1904–05, which gave her possession of Southern Manchuria adjacent to eastern Mongolia and opened [the] way for Japanese penetration [of] the Asiatic Continent, brought [onto] the stage a new pretender in the person of Japanese imperialism,[14] which coveted Mongolia for its raw materials and mineral wealth. Japanese political agencies made their appearance not only in parts of eastern Mongolia adjacent to the South Manchurian railway, where Japanese capital gradually established itself, but also began to penetrate into other regions of Mongolia. [Following] the Russo-Japanese War, the question of Mongolia gradually became one of the

---

13   Kalgan, in Hebei Province, China, is now known as Zhangjiakou. It was the starting point of the main caravan route from Beijing to Mongolia. Khyatkha is in the Russian Republic of Buryatia, on the border with Mongolia.
14   The original text says 'Chinese imperialism'.

leading questions in the Far Eastern policy of international imperialism, and attracted the attention of American capital.

During the entire period of subjection to the Manchu monarchy, Mongolia made almost no progress as regards cultural or economic development, while her social, administrative and political regime remained the same towards the beginning of the twentieth century as it had been at the moment when she lost her independence. At the beginning of the twentieth century, Mongolia [remained] the same old pastoral cattle raising country, with poorly developed agriculture owing to its unfavourable climate and soil conditions, devoid of any self-sustaining industries, with its population in bondage [to] Chinese and Russian mercantile capital, and serving as an apple of discord between the conflicting appetites of Russian and Japanese imperialists. The administrative apparatus of Mongolia at the time of the fall of the Manchu dynasty was in the hands of small hereditary groups, numbering, for instance on the territory of the four districts of Khalkha, [only one percent of the population]. The lama monks constituted a numerous and politically and economically influential group representing 40 percent of the entire population of Mongolia, while the remainder of the toiling masses of the population [lived completely outside the law], and continued to be the [semi-serfs] and subjects of the princely landowners, carrying upon their shoulders the entire burden of taxation and numerous [other] levies.

The fall of the Manchu dynasty, brought about by the revolutionary uprising of the Chinese people, seemed to open a [path for] the Mongolian people [to] a free existence. On 18 November 1911, at Urga – the present capital of Mongolia – the authority of the Manchu dynasty over Mongolia was declared abolished, the agents of the Manchu were driven out of Mongolia, and the country was declared independent. But the vacant place of the Manchu rulers was at once occupied by representatives of tsarist Russia, to whom the ruling princes and clergy of Mongolia resorted for aid. The tsarist Government utilized the Mongolian desire for freedom to further its own annexationist plans. The fate of Mongolia fell into the hands of the tsarist diplomats who hastened to establish their economic domination by [means of] the trade agreement concluded on 21 October 1912, with the Mongolian theocratic monarchy proclaimed with their assistance, and then concluded subsequent agreements, on 23 September 1913 and 25 May 1915,[15] with the Chinese diplomats, for the virtual division

---

15 Under the terms of the 1915 Treaty of Kyakhta signed by Russia, China and Mongolia, the Outer Mongolian government of the Bogda Khagan was obliged to recognise Chinese suzerainty and abandon its aspiration for unification with Inner Mongolia. See Sanders 2010, p. 403.

of Mongolia between Russia and China, contrary to the expressed wishes of the Mongolian people. Inner Mongolia, whose masses had suffered most from Chinese exploitation and colonial expansion, was declared a Russian dependency,[16] while Outer Mongolia was proclaimed an autonomy, and under Chinese sovereignty, but, in fact, became subject to autocratic Russia.

Eight years of Mongolian autonomy gave absolutely nothing to the Mongolian people. The state power was seized by [the reigning dukes, who had formerly been subservient to the Manchu, and] who, during this period, carried out no measure whatever [to ease] the burden of taxation or [improve] the education of the toiling masses. Acting upon the dictates of Russian diplomats resident in Mongolia, they began to hand over Mongolia, in concessions, to foreign capitalists for the exploitation of her rich natural resources, having wasted the loans obtained from tsarist Russia without accomplishing any improvement in the industrial situation [or] in the administration of the country, having attracted no new blood from the ranks of the people to direct the affairs of state, and finally, having made no attempt to liquidate the arbitrary rule of the feudal dukes and of the priests invested with temporal power. The masses of the people, [who] had been so hopeful of their emancipation from the Chinese yoke, remained as powerless and as voiceless as heretofore, dragging along the same chains of mercantile bondage which had, for the time being, become Russian instead of Chinese.

The world war and the Russian Revolution, affording a new opportunity for Japanese imperialism upon the Continent of Asia to continue preying upon dismembered and foreign-imperialist-ridden China while Russia was torn by civil strife, created a propitious moment for the attempt to seize Mongolia. For this purpose, Japan at first pounced upon the idea of the League of Nations announced by President Wilson, which in conjunction with the Versailles Conference, was supposed to assure the freedom of small oppressed nations. The nationalists of eastern Mongolia, thanks to that country having, by the Russo-Chinese Treaty of 1905,[17] again gone over to the rule of China, tried to organise [a] movement under the slogan of 'emancipating all the peoples of Mongolia', hoping to receive support for that movement from Versailles. Their strivings, at first it seemed, were supported by Japan, who gave them an opportunity to get up a conference in February of 1919 in the city

---

16 In 1912, Russia and Japan signed a secret agreement that divided Inner Mongolia into spheres of influence, the west being assigned to Russia, and the east to Japan. See Berton 2006, p. 81.

17 The date seems to be a misprint. This probably refers to the 1915 Treaty of Kyakhta that acknowledged Chinese sovereignty over Mongolia.

of Chita, thinking thereby to utilize the idea of uniting Mongolia [to spread] the political influence of Japan over that country. However, these nationalists [did not succeed in realising] their hopes because they received no response from the masses of Mongolia. [Their hopes of] aid from the Versailles Conference came to naught. The delegation [put together] by the government of the Chita Conference met with hindrances emanating from the Japanese authorities and Ataman Semenov,[18] so that it could not even leave for Versailles.

The Japanese imperialists decided to capture Mongolia in a quicker or better way with the aid of their loyal Chinese militarists from the Anfu Club,[19] who had at that time captured the power in Northern China. The latter, in the expectation of securing for itself the support of Chinese merchant circles interested in Mongolia and the support of the Chinese masses, to whom the liquidation of the [government] of Outer Mongolia was represented as a patriotic undertaking, organised a military expedition into Mongolia which was crowned with complete success. The part played by the then Mongolian government and ruling princes was an abominable one. Bribed by Beijing, the government gave its sanction to the Chinese occupation of Outer Mongolia while the princes were only concerned with the preservation of their class privileges, and after negotiations with the Chinese High Commissioner, Chen Yi,[20] adopted the Treaty of 64 Articles whereby the relations between Outer Mongolia and China were to be regulated, and in compensation for the renunciation of Mongolian autonomy, the dukes were guaranteed the maintenance of their feudal privileges [by the Chinese Government].

---

18 The conference was organised with Japanese support and hosted by their notorious ally, the Cossack Ataman and White warlord, Grigory Semenov, who was of Buryat descent. Semenov's activities were so brutal that he clashed with the American interventionists and he was briefly arrested when he visited the United States in 1922. The US commanding officer in Siberia, Brigadier General William S. Graves and his senior officer, Colonel Charles H. Morrow, told a Congressional Committee that Semenov was responsible for the 'wiping out of whole villages [in a] deliberate campaign of murder, rape and pillage, and the lives of 100,000 men, women and children were sacrificed as the result of his ravages'. Colonel Morrow told the committee: 'Had it not been for the influence of another power [meaning Japan], we would have disarmed all of Semenoff's forces'. Semenov was captured by Soviet forces when they conquered the Japanese puppet state of Manchuguo in 1945. He was hanged the following year. See Bisher 2005, p. 214; see also 'New Bail Bond or Jail for Semenoff', *New York Times*, 13 April 1922.

19 The Anfu (Peace and Happiness) Club was the political wing of the Anhui warlord clique led by Duan Qirui.

20 Written as Chien-Y in the original text.

In November 1919, the city of Urga was occupied by the troops of General Xu Shuzheng,[21] the leader of the Anfu Club, who compelled the Bogda Khagan and Jibzundamba Khutugtu[22] to sign a petition to the Beijing Government to incorporate Outer Mongolia within the Central Republic and to dismiss immediately the Mongolian troops and government institutions. General Xu Shuzheng recognised the treaty concluded between Chen Yi and the dukes as entirely superfluous. The treaty was annulled, and its author, the representative of the Chinese civilian authority, was arrested and expelled from Urga. Having decided to base his Mongolian policy entirely upon the military force of his troops, Xu introduced a military dictatorship in Outer Mongolia.

The Chinese occupation of Khalkha gave a great impetus to an awakening of the patriotic and revolutionary inclined elements of the Mongolian people, laying the foundation for the development of a Mongolian popular revolutionary party. The abominable rule of the landowning dukes in the liquidation of the autonomy completely discredited them in the eyes of the masses, which had hitherto still believed in their national sentiments. The Mongolian people, ignorant and cowed, gave up considering the dukes as the leaders of the social-political life of the country, and new leaders were soon found among the representatives of the Mongolian intellectuals that had sprung from the ranks of the people, from the lower orders of the priesthood and the officials, as well as some [landless] dukes who conceived the necessity of keeping in contact with the people by defending its interests. The Mongolian People's Party, coming into existence in the beginning of 1920, at the very moment when the Red

---

21   Sui-Si-Schin in the original text. Xu Shuzheng was a member of the Japanese-backed Anhui clique of warlords led by Duan Qirui. He commanded an expeditionary force that briefly re-established Chinese control of Outer Mongolia in 1919. He was killed in December 1925 when his train was hijacked by a rival warlord.

22   Bogdo-Cheband and Damba-Khushukhta in the original text. The two titles refer to the same person. The eighth incarnation of the Jibzundamba Khutugtu (1870–1924) was Mongolia's theocratic ruler from 1911–21, and constitutional monarch from 1921, under the revolutionary government, until his death in 1924. He was Tibetan, born in Lhasa, and a lama of the Gelugpa school of which the Dalai Lama is the head. As a reincarnation of the first Jibzundamba Khutugtu (1635–1723), he was also, supposedly, a direct descendant of Genghis Khan. Highly talented but eccentric, he was a heavy drinker, a tireless womaniser and chaser after boys, and contracted syphilis at an early age. When the Qing dynasty collapsed in 1911, the Jibzundamba Khutugtu was enthroned as the Bogda Khagan (Holy Emperor). By 1919, many nobles had tired of the extension of his personal power, and especially the privileged status granted to the growing number of his personal followers – members of the Great Shabi. After General Xu Shuzheng led 6,000 troops into Urga in October 1919, the upper house voted to ask China to revoke Mongolian autonomy. On 1 January 1920, the Jibzundamba Khutugtu acknowledged the restoration of Chinese rule. See Atwood 2004, pp. 269–71, 471.

Soviet Armies defeated the armies of Kolchak and the foreign interventionists in neighbouring Siberia, having discounted the lessons of seeking aid from tsarist Russia and from the Versailles Conference of the imperialists, began to look for a way towards the liberation of Mongolia among the very masses of Mongolian people among whom they started a national-revolutionary agitation, and also in the revolutionary experience and support of Soviet Russia, which had inscribed upon her banners the slogans of liberation from under the yoke of imperialism for all oppressed countries of the West and the East.

Meanwhile in China there was a new outbreak of civil war with the result that, in the middle of 1920, the militarist Anfu Party suffered defeat and lost its authority in Northern China. Deprived of a docile political tool thoroughly obedient to Japan, while the balance of forces struggling in Northern China was not yet quite determined, and the Japanese hireling general Zhang Zuolin had not yet [gained] the upper hand in the situation, the militarists admitted into Mongolia the Russian white guard bands under the command of Baron Ungern,[23] through whom they expected to recapture Mongolia and make her a base for attacks against Soviet Russia. [The Ungern bands, numbering several thousand men,] after entering Khalkha and defeating the Chinese troops, occupied Urga and began massacring and robbing the peaceful Chinese and Russian and Mongolian population. They burned entire villages and monasteries, carried off huge herds of cattle, and enforced compulsory mobilisation.

The Popular Mongolian Revolutionary Government organised in the northern parts of Khalkha by the Popular Mongolian Revolutionary Party in March 1921, having formed its own army, engaged in a battle against Ungern's bands and, together with the detachments of the [Soviet Red Army], inflicted a crushing defeat upon the Ungern bands at the moment when the latter were carrying on an offensive against the Soviet border.

Having liberated Khalkha from the Ungern bands, the Popular Mongolian Revolutionary Government began the liquidation of the white guard bands that infested Western Mongolia. Towards the end of June, Mongolian troops destroyed the Kazantsev[24] band at Ulasutai, and in December, after successful battles in the regions of Ulankosh and Kobde, captured several thousand

---

23   A great deal has been written on the egregious brutality of the White warlord Baron Roman von Ungern-Sternberg. For a recent biography, see Palmer 2009.
24   Captain I. Kazantsev was the commander of a battalion of Yenisei Cossacks in the army of Baron von Ungern-Sternberg. He was killed on 21 December 1921 during a failed attack on a Red village. See Tarasov 2008.

prisoners among the detachments of General Bakich and Karasoukhov,[25] after whose destruction the entire territory of Outer Mongolia could be considered cleared of white guards.

The Popular Revolutionary Party aims at the complete liberation of Mongolia from the economic and political yoke of the foreign oppressors, the emancipation of the masses from feudal and clerical bondage, the establishment of a popular government by the people, the development of the people, the development of the productive forces of the country, the protection of its resources against spoliation, and the spreading of universal education. Hence the Government that has been created by the Party, meeting with the wide sympathy and support of the masses, immediately after the occupation of Urga and the carrying out of urgent military tasks, began to carry out a whole series of measures directed towards the emancipation of the Mongolian people from the shackles of the feudal-theocratic regime and towards communion with the general culture of mankind. Thus the Government decreed and carried out reforms in local self-government upon an elective basis, abolished class inequalities before the law; has done away with corporal punishment and a whole variety of oppressive taxes that were weighing heavily upon the masses; annulled all the concessions granted by the old feudal government of autonomous Mongolia to sundry robbers and adventurers on terms extremely unfavourable to the state; liquidated all privileges that freed the dukes and priests from every kind of taxation; established a universal graduated income tax and a series of measures to encourage co-operation; and finally, adopted a system of administration which practically abolishes the theocratic principles, and a whole series of equally beneficent measures for the country which have been carried out with the sanction of periodic conferences of representatives from the constituencies.

In the domain of international relations, the Government of Free Mongolia concluded a treaty with Soviet Russia in November 1920,[26] which recognised the sovereign rights of the State of Mongolia. At the request of the Mongolian Popular Government, Soviet Russia consented to act as intermediary in adjusting the relations between Mongolia and China.

---

25   Bakitch in the original. According to an interview with the former White general Moltchanoff, Andrei Stepanovich Bakich (1878–1922) was a Serbian general who commanded an army that was, in theory, under the command of Admiral Kolchak, but in practice operated independently. A recent account says he was a Montenegrin who spent 20 years in the Russian army. See Moltchanoff and Raymond 1972, http://archive.org/stream/lastwhitegeneraloomoltrich/lastwhitegeneraloomoltrich_djvu.txt; see also Ganin 2004.
26   This is a mistake. The Soviet-Mongolian Treaty was signed on 5 November 1921.

These are the general features of the internal work of the Government during the first half year of the free existence of Outer Mongolia.

Summarising the past and present condition of the Mongolian people, we must make the following observations:

The Mongolian people through bitter and bloody experiences, through fire and water, as we put it, through the shattering of one illusion after another, is now gradually arriving to the understanding that while there exists upon the globe the present regime, which means the domination by the few over the enormous masses of toilers and backward nations and the absence of solidarity among the enslaved and oppressed, there is not and cannot be any freedom and happiness for the Mongolian people as a whole, nor for any other nation; that while there is no solidarity nor readiness for active co-operation among all the oppressed and exploited for the common interests of all, there is not and cannot be any assurance of maintaining the conquests that have been and are being achieved by the Mongolian people in the domain of free self-government and self-determination.

Before arriving at such conclusions, the Mongolian people passed through an extremely hard and highly instructive school.

The Manchu despotism which aimed at the destruction of the Mongolian people by means of impoverishing the people and subjecting it to feudalism and clericalism, compelled Mongolia to look for salvation in her own feudal [lords] and theocrats and in autocratic Russia. But nine years of government by [the] feudal [lords] and theocrats and by the officials of Russian autocracy had brought to Mongolia even greater misery and internal decay.

Imperialist Russia annexed from Mongolia the region of Uriankhai and was contemplating the annexation of the best part of Mongolia, along the line [from Manchuria through Urga to Lake Kosogol]. Nine years existence of autonomous Mongolia under the protectorate of tsarist Russia proved to Mongolia that there was no difference between Amban Sando[27] (the agent

---

27   Sando (1875–1940s), a Sinicised Mongol born in Hangzhou, was relatively young when appointed *Amban* (high official) of Urga (Ulan Bator) in 1910. He made himself unpopular by aggressively pursuing Han colonisation policies adopted by the Qing dynasty to counter Russian encroachment. In one of many setbacks to his authority, early in his administration he was stoned by rioting monks. Sando continued to work for the Chinese Republican government after Mongolia declared independence. In 1919, he was briefly left in charge of Urga after General Xu Shuzheng, who had led Republican China's 1919 re-conquest of Mongolia, quit his post following factional struggles in Beijing. See Lan 1999, pp. 39–58; see also Bisher 2005, p. 327.

of the Manchu despotism) and chinovnik Mueller (the diplomatic agent of tsarist Russia); that the reactionaries, whatever their nationality, are the same oppressors.

The subsequent seizure of Mongolia by the reactionary, bourgeois Chinese Republic – the so-called 'most democratic state of the East' – the cruel atrocities and violation of the best traditions of the Mongolian people, demonstrated to the Mongolians the identity between monarchies and bourgeois republics when it comes to a question of exploiting and oppressing small nations. On the other hand, under the influence of the pre-Versailles declarations of President Wilson regarding the rights of self-determination of small and oppressed nations, there arose in south eastern Mongolia a national liberation movement which had for its aim to unite the whole of ethnographical Mongolia into one federated democratic republic, but ended in complete failure under the pressure of Japanese, Chinese and Russian reactionaries and militarists, shattering one more illusion regarding the sincerity of bourgeois politicians and their high-falutin' [ideas of] liberty and democracy. And finally, the bloody adventure of Ungern by whom hundreds and thousands of men, women and children were tortured and burned alive at the stake, while robbery and violence were perpetrated upon the peaceful Mongolian population, was the last stroke that completed the hideous picture of the modern regime of violence and bloodshed. This is the tortuous and thorny path that led Mongolia and the Mongolian people, now guided by the Mongolian People's Party, to the Banner of the Third International and to the closest and sincerest friendship with Red Soviet Russia.

Our party is by its programme neither Communistic nor socialistic. It has for its aim the final liberation of Mongolia from the political and economic yoke of foreign oppressors and feudal and clerical exploitation and subjection, the establishment of [a] popular government, the development of industry and popular education etc.

Thus, [according to] our programme, we come under the category of the radical-democratic parties which exist in the so-called civilised countries. Nevertheless, our country does not go to the Washington Conference, but our party [sends] its delegates to Moscow. The objective conditions of our country, the survivals of medievalism, have made us into national democrats, while the sum-total of the historical political experience of our country and the substance of the modern political and economic regime of mankind drives us [relentlessly] into the channel of the international proletarian movement, into the channel of the closest contact with this great movement.

This movement attracts not only our conscious party-members but also the better elements of the privileged and prosperous classes, from whom our party obtains some measure of support, because their national instinct of self-preservation tells them that the merciless robbers from the imperialist countries, once they get hold of our country, will not spare them either. As to the problems before this Congress, our party considers them in the light of establishing permanent and active contact among all toiling and national-revolutionary forces of the Far Eastern nations, both among themselves and with the worldwide proletarian movement personified [by] the Third International [which is] organising a united centre of guidance for the purpose of self-defence against the aggression of world imperialism and of effecting internal cohesion within every one of the [participating] countries. Our party entertains no doubt with regard to the success of the movement in the near future, because the situation is a trying one for the toiling masses of all countries: China is torn by foreign imperialists into separate spheres of influence; Korea groans and is bleeding with the blood of [her] best sons under the iron heel of Japanese imperialism; a major portion of Mongolia is overrun by Japanese and Chinese military adventurers; and finally, Japan, having made enemies of all the Asiatic nations by her aggressive policy, and [encircled by] the competing great powers, finds herself sadly isolated, and with ever increasing insistence there come warning voices from among the Japanese public with regard to the dangers of such isolation. The only way for Japan to [avoid] national decay is the way of revolutionary reconstruction of her internal life upon new principles.

Thus, in our future struggle, the social aspect, the aspect of the struggle for a better future for the toilers, is everywhere intertwining with the national aspect, with the problems of the national emancipation and regeneration of the nations of the Far East, which naturally [increases] the force and depth of the movement.

Long live the Third International, the sole defender of all [the] oppressed and enslaved! Long live the union and the victory of the toiling nations of the East!

Chairman. The report of comrade Din-Dib will be distributed among you in English and Russian translations. Meanwhile I have received a request from the speaker to add a few remarks which have not been included in his report.

Din-Dib [Dendev]. In concluding my report on Mongolia and her struggle for freedom, I cannot let pass without comment the statement that has been made by the representative of the Kuomintang Party, comrade Tao.[28] You have

---

28   I.e. Zhang Qiubai.

all heard comrade Tao's declaration, in reference to that passage in comrade Zinoviev's report which dealt with the relations between China and Mongolia, that the Chinese revolutionaries have no desire and no intention to annex Mongolia. We, the representatives of the toiling Mongolian nation sincerely and joyfully welcome the declaration made by comrade Tao, the representative of the ruling party[29] of China, because we find therein the vindication of our hopes and aspirations. [For] many centuries Mongolia [was] cruelly exploited by tsarist Russia and reactionary-monarchist China, and toiling Mongolia could put no faith in them, nor expect from them any assistance or sympathy. Socialist Russia has restored to us our faith in Russia. This gives us strong grounds to hope that we, the Mongolians, will find a common language with the toiling democracy of China for mutual respect and collaboration. It is for this reason that the toilers of Mongolia look forward with faith and hope towards the final victory of the toilers of China over their enemies, fully confident that the Mongolian question will then be settled in the interests of both nations. (*Applause*).

Chairman. I will now call upon comrade *Kho* to read his report on the economic situation in Korea.

Kho [Cho Tongho].[30] This report was originally meant to be made in three separate reports. That is the Korean economic situation, the labour situation, and the peasant situation. So we had originally intended to make these three separate reports, and having to boil it down into one single report, we have not had time to [put] the report in proper shape, much less [complete] the translation either [to] English or Russian. Therefore this report will be [only] a preliminary report, and the full text will be translated later on and will appear in the minutes, we suppose.

The Korean Economic Situation. Korea was originally, and is even up till now, principally an agricultural country; therefore the economic life of the Korean people [has] its base in agriculture and even [taxation] finds its fundamental base in what may be termed land tax. Of course, in the Middle Ages, that is according to Korean history, during the thirteenth and fourteenth centuries, a great many industries developed and foreign trade [was] encouraged, particularly trade between China and Korea, as we see traces of it even now.

---

29   That is, of the southern government in Canton.
30   Cho Tongho (1893–1954) was a journalist. He was regional secretary of the Korean Communist Party in Shanghai.

But during the five hundred years of tyrannical rule of the Yi dynasty,[31] in accordance with the teachings of Confucianism [that the ruling class strictly adhered to], the idea was prevalent that agriculture was the most honourable occupation for any people, and the Government, as well as the ruling class, encouraged agriculture more than commerce or industry. They rather oppressed and discouraged [any attempts to establish] commerce and industry on a large scale which would be profitable. Not only that, the ruling class was very strongly imbued with the idea of national seclusion, which also explains the fact that Korean foreign trade [remained underdeveloped]. So as a result, the Korean people's [efforts were all channelled into agriculture]. [Agriculture was practically the sole] occupation of the Korean people, particularly during the [last] few hundred years, [and even this faced setbacks and was obstructed] and hindered in a great many ways, particularly by the ruling class, the so-called yangban class, and for this reason the farmers were not only discouraged from their peaceful occupation and means of livelihood but in many instances they were unable to continue their toil and were unable to save whatever products they had for any unforeseen disaster or emergency. Therefore whenever they [faced] famine or civil strife, the people [were] left at the threshold of starvation and misery. This explains the fact that in 1894 there arose the well-known, so-called Tonghak Rebellion. The Tonghak Rebellion, as mentioned in other reports, was an uprising of the oppressed peasants who [were driven] to revolt against the oppression [they were suffering and for their own self-protection and livelihood]. So [it] can be rightly termed a class struggle.

With the civil strife in the country, the historic occupation of the Korean people was shaken to [its] foundations, but then the Japanese capitalists came in right after the Russo-Japanese war. Of course there is a difference of opinion; some people [say] that Japanese capitalism [entered] Korea during the last quarter of the nineteenth century, but [it took on its particularly oppressive form] with the Russo-Japanese war. So the Korean people's [traditional] occupation faced [obstacles and hindrances] first from the yangban or ruling class, and then from the alien capitalist exploitation of Japan. [Regarding] this yangban or ruling class, their oppression and their policy can be rightly [compared with the oppression of] robbers or bandits, so that [a better] term for them might be the robber or cutthroat class. The Japanese came in and took complete control of the Korean economic situation, and one of the first things they undertook in carrying out their programme was to issue what [were] called

---

31 Written as Li in the original text. Also known as the Josŏn Dynasty (1392–1910).

military notes. They were bank notes, but bank notes used for military purposes. They were used first during the Russo-Japanese campaign. [The Japanese] forced the Korean people to accept these military notes [in return] for their produce. And [using] this monetary system they built the trunk line of the Korean railway from Pusan to Seoul[32] which is practically the whole length of the Korean trunk line. And, of course, these paper notes [were not backed by specie, silver or gold bullion], and the Korean people [were forced to use this paper currency which resembled that issued during the so-called Mississippi Bubble that preceded the French Revolution].[33] It goes without saying that this played havoc with [Korea's] economic equilibrium. It drove the prices of all articles [sky-high] and the Japanese capitalists found [a] great opportunity to reap profits in speculation. [Furthermore,] the Korean semi-bourgeoisie found an opportunity to preach the gospel of Mammon or the doctrine that money makes might. And this factor formed a link in the chain of causes of the Korean class struggle.

After imperialistic Japan had [destabilised] Korea's economic condition in this way, [following] the forced annexation, she oppressed the people [politically]. When the two states were combined after the annexation in 1910, the total amount [collected in taxation] was 11,953,000 yen, but after nine years of [Japanese rule, we can see from the Japanese statistics for 1919 that taxes had quadrupled] to 52,643,000 yen. Japan took control of all means of exchange as well as of all profit making enterprises. They issued laws, decrees, and regulations [governing corporations, banks and monetary organs]. They established their own corporations, banks, etc. and issued bank notes, principally what is known as the bank note of the Bank of Chosen,[34] in other words, the Bank of Korea. These bank notes were issued promiscuously without any species or bullion behind them. The outstanding example is the Oriental Trading Company – sometimes called the Oriental Development Company – which is a semi-governmental enterprise. This corporation took over all state land [without exception, and began buying up, confiscating and taking away by all sorts of devious means and overt acts] the lands of the Korean peasants. [In this way] they facilitated the influx of Japanese immigrant peasants and [by]

---

32   The original text says Fusan to Eviju. The Seoul to Pusan railway was built in 1905 by the Japanese.
33   The Mississippi Bubble was a speculative boom in the shares of the Compagnie D'Occident, which was established in 1717 by the Scottish economist John Law, and was granted exclusive rights to exploit the Mississippi valley by the French government. It ended in a Europe-wide financial crash in 1720.
34   Central bank established by the Japanese in 1910 and succeeded by the Bank of Korea in 1950. It was also known as the Bank of Joseon.

1912 Japanese farmers constituted one-ninth of the entire immigrant population, in other words over 40,000 people. [There followed] conditions which find no parallel in other oppressed or colonised regions. As mentioned before, agriculture was the fundamental occupation of the Korean people, [but] with the [arrival] of the 40,000 Japanese farmers there [was] one Japanese to every five Korean farmers, actively engaged in competition. [They took the land from several hundred thousand peasants, causing a huge emigration to Manchuria and Siberia]. [In order to supplement her own shortage of grain, in 1919, Japan, disregarding the famine that was taking place in Korea, exported one fourth of the entire produce of the land,] amounting to over 110 million yen. It was about 117 million to be exact, [well over half the total exports of Korea, which amounted to 222,200,000 yen]. These exports [consisted] of 20 million yen's worth of beans and eight million yen's worth of cotton and other [items – 80 percent of total exports]. What did the Japanese pay for these exports? They paid with low-grade articles which could not be dumped at other places without using force – mostly wine, tobacco, and cigarettes [and] other articles of general use. The trade and commerce of Korea were formerly in the hands of what [were] called traders' guilds, and these traders' guilds [controlled] Korean markets throughout the land, both in the cities and in the interior, but they [had been oppressed first by] the yangban ruling class and later [by] the Japanese in the same way as the peasants and workers. So the trader's guilds saw their influence [destroyed by] Japanese oppression.

After trade relations opened between Korea and Japan, the cities and ports began to be swarmed with Japanese merchants and traders, and so we find that in such places as Pusan and Chemul'po and other ports and cities, they control the [best] part of the commercial activities, [the means of communication] – railways, transport, posts and telegraphs – and [generally] have everything their own way. Then, [under the pretext of] building railways and roads and [other] communication facilities, they forced the peasants to work for them, and [as a result] Japanese shops and small traders are found [even in the most remote hamlets]. The old handicrafts and [small-scale] industries of the Korean people could not compete with the [large-scale industries] of the Japanese capitalists, and the Korean people were obliged to [buy] everything from the Japanese, [even down] to their clothing and articles of daily use. Therefore one can easily imagine that everything was completely in their hands, even in the hands of very small traders. These small traders and the larger merchants act as go-betweens in the [export] of Korean products and [the import of cheap Japanese] articles.

After the annexation, by means of discriminatory regulations, laws and ordinances, the Korean people were hindered in the organisation of commercial companies and enterprises, which was one of the causes that precipitated the March revolution of 1919. The purpose of these [discriminatory] regulations was to offer facilities to Japanese merchants and industrial undertakings [that] were in line with the capitalistic programme. According to the statistics [for] 1919, the total number of Japanese companies in Korea was 339, compared with only 63 Korean companies. With regard to capital, Japanese capital amounted to 552 million yen while Korean capital for all Korean enterprises amounted to only 23 million yen, in other words, just four percent of [the total]. From that, we can see how Korea's commerce and industry have been put under their control. [All] industries, excepting a few minor [ones], are under the control of the Japanese and according to the statistics [for] 1918 we find that in Korea there are 1,700 enterprises and factories, [large and small, employing between five to many hundreds or thousands of people]. These 1,700 undertakings are mostly Japanese, while there are a few Chinese numbering some 875.[35] The total capital of these undertakings amounts to 48 million yen, of which the Chinese and Japanese capital amount to about 40 million yen while Korean and [other] foreign capital amounts to something over 4 million yen.

The Korean Peninsula is, more or less, a maritime country and also a mountainous country. With the sea on three sides – South, East and West – it has over 9,300 miles of coastline, and maritime products constitute a large [part] of her national resources. Also, 73 percent of the land is hilly and mountainous, and constitutes one of the main reservoirs of Korean national resources. Then there are the unlimited mines and innumerable forests; so these three items, maritime products, mines, and forestry and agriculture, constitute the main resources, [all of] which are now under the absolute control of the Japanese. Taking the maritime produce of the fisheries in 1919, the total [value] of undertakings [owned] by Koreans in the fisheries, amounts to only 20 million yen, while the Japanese [control enterprises worth] 23 million yen. Of the mines, according to the statistics [for] 1919, Koreans operated only 621, while the Japanese operated 763. With regard to forestry, the Japanese control over 50 percent of [all forests, including former state forests]. The above gives merely an outline of the different means and channels of oppression, which show [the heinous methods of the imperialistic Japanese in their oppression] of Korea, economically, politically and morally.

The fundamental resources of the land are in the hands of the Japanese capitalists. Therefore one can imagine the condition [of] the Korean peasants and

---

35   The figures seem to be inconsistent; the 'few' Chinese enterprises amount to more than half of the total number.

labouring masses. It is really most pitiable, but [we have no time to describe it in detail here]. We can understand, however, that this is one of the main causes of the resistance that [Koreans] are putting up [to] this imperialistic and capitalistic exploitation.

The Situation of the Korean Peasants

85 percent of the population of Korea [is engaged in agriculture, amounting to] 3,980,000 men and 3,500,000 women, four fifths of [whom] are what you might call small tenant farmers. The masses having been oppressed by the ruling class, with most of the tillable lands in the latter's hands, the agricultural peasants are not, as a rule, landowners, and the overwhelming majority of them are tenant farmers, which also explains the early Tonghak uprising (although it did not succeed). We [know] that the Korean toiling masses suffered from the hereditary oppression of their ruling class, [but today] we have a situation which is more acute than that of the days of old. There is no rival to Japanese imperialism and its heinous methods. Japan, after establishing its Oriental Colonization Company,[36] encouraged the immigration into Korea of Japanese farmers, among whom are some of the worst elements and agents of the imperialistic and oppressive Japanese Government. In conjunction with the imperialistic suppression, they took away the few remaining acres of land that were left to the tenant farmers, to make room for the Japanese. With the change of landowners, the oppression to which the tenant farmers were subjected was multiplied. The former Korean landowners were more considerate [in times of] drought, famine or any unusual situation, but the Japanese, on the pretext of using modern methods, and [buttressed by] new regulations and ordinances from the Government, extracted from the people all and more than they could produce. The Japanese Government carried on propaganda to the outside world, saying that they were reforming the Korean agricultural methods; and, as a matter of fact, there were certain reforms instituted in the way of using modern methods and implements, particularly in the way of distributing [seed and fertiliser], and more especially in regard to irrigation. But this has profited, in the main, the Japanese immigrant population and not the Korean people. For example, they established irrigation plants under the control of the Japanese, but the working capital was paid by the Koreans. That is, the Korean farmers, as small landowners, were forced to [buy] shares [to provide] the working capital

---

36 The Oriental Development Company; see previous note.

[for] these irrigation plants, while the plants were put in the absolute control of the Japanese capitalists. All the land with irrigation dams and reservoirs [is] occupied by the Japanese, so that they have the best of the irrigation works and all the profits. In the matter of fertilisers, the peasants have even been forced to buy them whether they want them or not. As regards the land tax, it has multiplied many times, so that the Korean people have to give up more than fifty percent of their yearly earnings. In order to pay their taxes, these poor peasants, not having the cash in hand, have to borrow from Japanese speculators and money-lenders at enormously high rates of interest, and very often have to sell their products at very low rates. And then, finding themselves without provisions and grain to carry them through the year, they have to resort to selling the land still in their possession. Under government monopolies, the Japanese buy from them by force all their tobacco and ginseng (a tonic medicinal root used in the Orient), and the peasants are usually paid only about 50 percent of the market value. Even this payment is made sometimes [six months or even a year in arrears]. Then the Koreans have to pay exorbitant taxes for [growing] what they are, in turn, forced to sell at half price.

What the Korean peasants and the labouring masses fear and abhor more than anything else – even more than drought, famine [or any other disaster or natural calamity] – is forced labour. They are sent to [do] forced labour on the railways, roads, the building of government houses – even houses of Japanese officials and the police. In many cases they are [forced] to work on the private farms of Japanese officials. Sometimes this happens in the spring, when they find no time even to sleep or eat, because it may be sowing time or some other busy time. But regardless of this, they are forced to work without receiving a cent in payment. And those that fail to obey these orders are punished, imprisoned and fined. With regard to this I may add that Professor Yoshino of the Imperial University of Tokyo [has produced] several very interesting reports concerning [tenant farmers] who are obliged to make all [these] payments and do [the kind of] forced labour [described] above. Hereditary custom [was] that there was never any written contract between landlord and tenant, [which meant] the tenant farmers were at the absolute mercy of the landlords, who could take them on or discharge them at will. And of course, with the coming of the Japanese capitalists and bureaucracy, and the agents and brow-beaters that followed in their wake, the oppression increased. And the Korean people, [left] without any means of self-protection or redress, found themselves destitute and helpless. Nevertheless, in order to resist even in a feeble way and revolt against this oppression, they have formed themselves into what is called the Tenants' Cooperative Union. This union [is] prohibited by the Government. Nevertheless, [it carries on its] work. So the Korean peasants and the labouring masses [sacrifice] their blood and sweat to fill the mouths and bellies of the Japanese capitalists, and the historic class struggle of the Korean people is becoming more and more intense, not only as a national class struggle, but as a general class struggle against all imperialistic oppression, which [demonstrates] the class consciousness of the Korean toiling masses.

The Labour Situation

The labouring masses of Korea may be divided into four main groups: transport workers, builders, miners, and factory hands – a total of about 280,000. Besides these, there are the peasant workers and the workers [in] the fisheries, making up another 900,000. Thus the workers constitute [around one ninth] of the agricultural population, which again shows that Korea has been, and [remains], principally an agricultural country. The working time of these labourers is usually from 10 to 11 hours a day. Their wages vary from 50 sen to 1 yen a day. In Korea, as in all Far Eastern countries, the workers [are] looked down upon with utter contempt. The industrial plants and means of production, after the coming of the Japanese capitalists, all fell into their hands, so that the latter are now in fact the masters of the situation. In most cases the Korean labourer finds it difficult [to provide for himself and his family on his wages], even if he [has] a family of only three persons. So the Korean peasants, who prized their land, even though they were only leasing it for a few years, have had to give up their farming life and resort to labour in the cities, and face there the oppression of the labouring masses, and the difficulties they have to undergo. Unemployment among peasant farmers and labourers is a very acute [problem]. Also the Japanese labourers that [move to] Korea [go along with] the Japanese imperialistic exploitation and oppression. The minor Japanese bosses oppress their fellow workers – the Koreans – and look down on them with contempt, as if they were cattle. The Japanese authorities, regardless of the fact that the Korean labourer may do a better day's work with more skill, pay Japanese workmen [30 or 50 percent more]. We should remember here that the Japanese workers in Korea co-operate with their own oppressors, the Japanese capitalists. As a result the Korean labouring masses look upon the Japanese as their deadly enemies, whether they are labourers, farmers or anything else. They look upon them as a people who have taken away their means of livelihood and oppress them and on top of all [that], drive them [like] cattle.

After 1910, after Korea was robbed of her liberty by the Japanese, Korean people lost their right to form gatherings or to [take part in] any agitation in any way, so that they could have no organisation whatever. Besides, the Korean people, not having been trained, and not having had any [experience] of organisation and systematic co-operation, they of course found great difficulty in [organising] themselves into any co-operative bodies to withstand this oppression. Also, the repression from the Japanese Government, as just mentioned, made it practically impossible for them, and therefore the Korean people had no [means] of redress and self-protection. Such conditions brought [about] the [upsurge] of the March revolution in 1919. After the March movement, a decree was passed which made it possible for the Korean peasants and working masses to form themselves into many unions and bodies. [Since then labour organisations have mushroomed]. [Clubs and unions have appeared]. For example, economic clubs [have been] formed by the working people in the factories and different localities [to] manage their affairs and [co-operatively buy all their needs in the way of provisions and clothing, so as to save money]. They club together [to pay] for dormitories and evening schools. The largest among the labour organisations is the General Labour Confederation. There is another organisation called the Labour Co-operative Union which [pays] great attention to relief services. The Korean labour organisations have only started [up in] the last three years, [but] even in such a short time they have grown so fast that there are now 450 localities where these organisations exist, with more than 252,000 members. From this we can see that the Korean people have a capacity for [organising] themselves even under extreme difficulties, and there is a widespread class-consciousness among them.

The Korean labouring masses are now taking it in their own hands to form themselves into small corporations and companies whereby they can ease their situation and relieve their condition from the capitalistic oppression by carrying on certain enterprises for themselves. For example, in January 1921, about 100 shoe-makers organised a strike. They did not obtain what they had asked for, so they formed themselves into a company and established a factory of their own, the results of which have been very good. This fact alone throws some light upon the Korean labour movement and its consciousness and [its] feeling of solidarity. The increasing resistance of the Korean toiling masses found its greatest expression in the independence movement, because of the fact that they were unable to express themselves in direct action – that is in trying to [improve] their conditions of life when such things as strikes and labour movements were severely repressed. But even under such conditions, in 1921 alone, there were strikes in Seoul, Chanulo, Pusan, and many other places, which lasted for months. Most of these strikes were [in support of demands] for increased wages, which however failed. Not having had experience in the way of systematic organisation, and because of [a] lack of preparation, they also lacked perseverance in competing against the powerful odds they had to face.

[Furthermore, the Japanese capitalists are adopting the methods of compromise that the capitalists use in other countries]. That is, they [try to] hoodwink the Korean labouring masses [by] saying that they will better their conditions, but in reality that is never done.

The Movement of the Labouring and Peasant Masses

The much oppressed labouring and peasant masses are [longing] for the day when they will be free. The Tonghak Rebellion of 1894 was [the first stirring of a class struggle] which resulted from the historical oppression of the working class by the bourgeoisie in every [imaginable manner]. And in the same way, the toiling masses of Korea are today risking their lives to combat the oppression of the Japanese capitalists that provoked the March movement, in which hundreds and thousands of the toiling masses sacrificed their lives and blood for the cause of emancipation from the Japanese yoke.

They have [witnessed] the heroic stand that the Soviets have made [over] the past five years against such overwhelming odds, [and they have not only been inspired by this, but have realised that they are no longer fighting alone]. They realise that, with the proletariat of the whole world and the oppressed masses of the Far East united with them in a great struggle for world revolution, they are assured of final victory, and will go forward with determination.

Chairman. The Presidium proposes that the translation of the report we have just heard be made in the sections. If that is agreed, we can proceed to the next report. The next item is three reports from the Japanese delegation. Is that agreed? Carried. Comrade Katayama has the floor for a report on the political and economic problems of Japan.

Katayama. Comrades, the Japanese report is in a bad condition because the delegates came directly from Japan and are mostly workers. They have not been able to make a complete report in English, and unfortunately the secretary of the Japanese section fell sick and is now in hospital. Moreover, comrade Kuki is also sick in bed, and therefore I will have to present a short report to you. However, I have already made up a report on the labour, political, and economic conditions of Japan, and presented it to the Comintern, but this was compiled mostly from the materials which we brought from America, and what I am going to say now is mostly not in this report. You may see this report at some other time. The present report is on the political, economic and labour conditions. After I make my report the Japanese comrade Niz[37] will speak on the organisation of the Japanese Communist Party. Then comrade Yoodzu[38] will speak on his own organisations. We arranged it this way because this Congress has full faith in the Communist movement and the labour movement, and these comrades bring to you news about their movement. Especially comrade Yoodzu, who has been a revolutionary worker for many years, I believe for nine or ten years, and his organisation will be of great interest to you. I shall occupy about an hour and a half. I am not accustomed to speak with manuscript or material in hand. I am accustomed to speak with what I have in my mind. Moreover, with my broken English, it may be hard for you to understand, so will the stenographers kindly correct the English.

I begin with the political conditions of Japan. As you already know, Japanese imperialism exploits and oppresses the Korean people. I will not dwell on this point as you have already heard much on this subject.

Japan is a Constitutional Monarchy. The Mikado is divine, he is supposed to be a divine person, but his power is also executed by a minister. The statesman who controls the destiny of Japan at the present time is [one of the *genro*].[39] The constitution was adopted about thirty years ago, and we have a parliament, an upper house or house of peers, and a lower house representing the people. In the upper house there are chiefly representatives of the Emperor or Mikado who are appointed by the latter. These are usually people who were in the service of the government and have rendered some great service to the government. The lower house is elected by the people, but the suffrage laws are such that a very small percentage of the population is represented in this lower house. For instance, at the present time, out of a population of 68 million, only 2 million have votes. Lately the right to vote was extended to 3 million. Japanese legislation is quite capitalistic.

Now I will say a few words as to the political parties. There are three political parties: Seiyukai, Kenseikai and Kokuminto.[40] Seiyukai is the government party, the party of the big landlords and the high middle class farmers. Kenseikai is supposed to represent the big city merchants and the industrial mas-

---

37 The next speaker is later referred to by the pseudonym Yakiwa.
38 This is confusing. The anarchist worker Kato (Yoshida Hajime) speaks in the slot referred to by Katayama. But the list of speakers for the opening session names Yoodzu as Mizutani Kenichi, who was a lawyer and a member of the Communist Party. Perhaps this was a mistake by the stenographers or a slip of the tongue by Katayama.
39 One of the elder statesmen of the Meiji Restoration. The original text says 'is Geno'.
40 Written as Sai-Yu-Ki, Kenzu-Ki and Kokimento in the original text. Their full names were Rikken Seiyukai (Friends of Constitutional Government), Kenseikai (Constitutional Party), and Rikken Kokuminto (Constitutional Nationalist Party).

ters. Kokuminto is the centre party; its number of representatives has not changed in the past thirty years. It represents the sections of the country where its leaders come from and where they have [had] constituencies for many years.

The organisation of the government is bureaucratic. The bureaucracy has been growing steadily for the past fifty years. And everything possible has been done to build up a strong bureaucracy in Japan. Imperial universities have been established and we have now altogether, I think, five of these universities whose graduates are privileged. They can be judges, higher officers, and they can be in parliament. They can hold civil office without passing examinations. But all the other private school students, and even those in the other universities, have no such privileges at the present time. Thus, bureaucracy is well organised in Japan and although the Seiyukai is the present acting government, still the bureaucrats always control the real administration of the country.

Now as to the relations between the people and the government: The people are oppressed all the time. Imagine what the Japanese government has done to Korea. It has done the same thing in Japan. Of course, the Japanese have more patience because they are oppressed by the Japanese and they are accustomed to it. It is a condition to which they are used and they do not know how to be unsatisfied with such conditions. The government is always oppressive and puts the financial responsibility upon the workers. I can give you one or two illustrations. For instance, [if] we ride in a streetcar, one trip costs us one cent tax. If we buy a fifty trip ticket we pay [only] five cents tax. But the workers cannot buy a fifty trip ticket. And still more, if I buy a ticket for half a year for a three mile distance, I have what is called a season ticket in America, and I can ride any number of times all day long for six months and it costs only five cents tax. The government has issued about three million yen's worth of bonds, and bondholders [do] not pay income tax. The police system is in the hands of the Government and is very strong too. They have a well-established system of spies and gendarmerie so that the people are always oppressed. Then the government has a strong taxing power. Constitutionally, the Japanese are taxed only by passing laws in the parliament, but we have a monopoly on salt, tobacco, railways, telephones, telegraph, and so on. They are government monopolies, and the prices of salt, railway tickets and tobacco are controlled by the government; parliament has really nothing to do with it. It is the way they build up strong bureaucratism and taxing power. Thus are the people oppressed. The salt monopoly, for instance, is very heavy because the workers use a lot of salt. You do not realise how much salt is used. The poor people, especially, eat salty food. The rich people, who do no work, do not eat much salt. With all these direct and indirect taxes which fall most[ly] upon them, the poor are in a very bad condition. The socialist and radical movements are also very greatly oppressed. Of recent times I will speak more in detail. The government system is so organised that no liberal movement can exist or work openly, especially if its activity is directed against the government. Today, we have three political parties. Yet none of them has a platform; they simply represent certain sections of the people and the capitalists.[41]

Under the political heading, I will speak about armaments. Japan is an imperialistic country and is justly called the Prussia of the Far East. They are the disciples of Prussianism. Most of their military men were sent to Germany to study and learn how to oppress and how to shoot and fight. We have a standing army of about three or four hundred thousand, and nearly a million in the navy. The armament expenses require 48 percent of the entire national budget of Japan. This shows how the Japanese workers and peasants are oppressed by unproductive expenses of the government. The Japanese budget [has] increased from 280 million yen just before the Sino-Japanese war in 1894–95, to 1.5 billion yen today. In 1894, the farm or land tax was about 80 million yen, and today it is 178 million yen. During these twenty years, the national budget increased from 280 million to 1.5 billion yen, and as I have said, most of the expenses and taxes are paid by the peasants and workers, if not by direct taxes then by indirect taxes. There are taxes on cloth, and we pay more for sugar in our country than anywhere else in the world. I will speak more about the economic conditions, but I wish to give you an illustration as to how, by law and government machinations, the Japanese workers and poor are oppressed. Formerly China and Japan imported sugar from Java, but when Japan took Formosa, which is a sugar country although a poor one compared with Java, the Japanese capitalists wanted to get sugar [inside] Japan – that is, in Formosa.[42] Then the government started sugar production and established custom duties and sugar bounties. At one time about 80 to 90 percent of the sugar production was taken by the government. As I told you, twenty years ago we bought most of our sugar from outside, and cheaply too. But today we produce in Formosa over six hundred million pounds of sugar and we consume only about five hundred million pounds, and, as is seen, one hundred million pounds of sugar are dumped somewhere or sent to Canada or abroad. Yet when sugar was five cents abroad we were paying more, from 10 to 15 cents per pound, almost

---

41 The Mitsubishi *zaibatsu* financed Kenseikai, which was relatively liberal in opposition and protested against the Siberian intervention. But when in office in coalition with the Seiyukai, it passed the repressive 1925 Peace Preservation Law.
42 I.e. Taiwan.

twice as much as in America. It shows how the Japanese government is utilizing its political power to oppress the common people, and the workers and peasants especially.

Now I will speak about the economic conditions. If I were a capitalist employer, I should be very proud of Japan because, economically, she has been improving steadily for the past fifty years. Of course, the capitalist system was established just after the Sino-Japanese war.

There was a big revolution in 1868, and then all the old customs were abolished, almost everything was abolished. Monopoly taxes [and the] rice monopoly [were] abolished and so were the customary relations between men and women. Church property was abolished, and the priests were well disciplined, and their activities restricted.

The farmers until 1868 were all tenant farmers. They rented land from feudal lords.[43] But these tenant farmers had all the land, and their tenant rights were turned into real ownership of the land, and the making of whiskey or rice wine was not permitted in the provinces. Since this revolutionary change everybody can make rice wine or whiskey provided they pay two yen in komai, which is nearly ten bushels. The revolution of 1868 overturned nearly everything and the farmers were not paying very high taxes. At this time the [only] tax payers were farmers; 85 percent of the national expenses were borne by the farmers, i.e. the tenant farmers. They were taxed 3 percent of the land value, which was not very much. The revolution accomplished many things. At this time, however, Japan was purely an agricultural country. We had no factories, no steam engines. Steam was never applied to industry; one can imagine what kind of a country Japan was at that time. In 1860, England had 10,000 miles of railway, Europe had 31,000 miles of railway; America 30,000 miles. It was in 1785 that steam power was applied for the first time to industry, but we never had it. In 1860, England had 13 million spindles for the cotton industry, but we had none. America had five million spindles at that time, almost one year before Karl Marx's first volume of *Capital* was published in Japan. At that time, we Japanese had no railways, no factories, no steam engines – nothing – and even our smithies were of the old type. We were entirely different from Western countries, but we have learned, the Japanese workers learned in a little over 50 years how to produce. We have now more than 6,000 miles of railway in Japan proper, and we have over one million tons of steam boats, mostly built in Japan.

I will speak about labour conditions later; therefore I will now give you a few facts as to how economic conditions are in Japan today. In 1914, we had

---

43   English: "There were practically no landlords." Russian is clearer.

491 agricultural companies with a capital of 27 million. In 1919 there were 795 companies with an invested capital of 144 million.

My time has not progressed so far, so I can give you a few more figures. In 1914 there were 9,923 commercial companies with an invested capital of 974 million. In 1919 there were 13,137 companies with an invested capital of 3,768 million. In 1914 there were 1,178 trading companies with an invested capital of 1,100 million. In 1914 there were 5,266 industrial companies with an invested capital of 3,682 million. That shows the increase of industrial production.

Japan is a rice country. The Japanese cannot get along without rice. Japan produced in 1919 60 million koku[44] and in 1903 46 million koku (1 koku = 4.9629 bushels). We also eat quite a large amount of potatoes. I don't know whether Russians eat sweet potatoes or not, but we are great eaters of sweet potatoes. In 1919 we produced 75,170,000 kan (1 kan = 8.2673 lb). But in 1903 we produced 1,190,000 kan. That shows the increase of production. And such increases [were seen] not only in farm produce, but more so, especially, in manufactured produce, which shows the great increase which, you see, is earned by capital, and that is just what is wanted. We have poor peasants who cultivate little – less than two acres – there are 3,796,000 such farmer families. Altogether there are five million families who cultivate land, and 900,000 landowners who do not cultivate at all. Japan, during the last 55 years, [has become] one of the strongest capitalistic countries in the Far East. Of course, this means Japan [has become] an industrial country [and] consequently we have a large number of proletarians. You will see from the following tables the real economic and labour conditions.

Labour Statistics 1917 (From the Oriental Economist and Communist Year Book)

Industries	Males	Females	Totals
Raw Silk	20,010	285,291	305,301
Cotton Spinning	29,006	104,869	133,875
Silk spinning	4,100	9,460	13,560
Linen	2,364	5,035	7,361
Wool	1,009	3,639	4,648
Gloss Silk Thread	2,159	7,610	9,769
Floss Silk	382	682	1,060

---

44   3.5937 *koku* = one cubic metre. Traditionally, a koku was the amount of rice needed to feed one person for a year.

Labour Statistics 1917 (*cont.*)

Industries	Males	Females	Totals
Cotton Ginning	1,105	2,067	3,172
Silk Weaving	7,417	40,581	47,998
Cotton	22,747	106,488	129,235
Others	69,899	862,303	932,202
Sundry Industries	701,190	610,206	1,311,396
Miners	342,285	91,553	433,843
Fishermen	1,055,438	339,041	1,394,479
R. R.	112,550	4,703	117,250
Tokyo, Osaka, Street R. R. workers	25,351	–	25,351
Telephone, Telegraph workers	22,782	21,177	43,959
Others not classified above	2,028	222	2,250
Other workmen not employed	567,844	713,120	1,280,964
Coolies (included in the above workers)	58,236	17,315	75,551
Peasants (below 2.45 acres)	3,796,968 no. of families	–	3,796,968 (families) average family 5
Salt workers	45,155	–	49,155
Alluvial gold workers	21,972	–	1,972
Common seamen Sailing	254,113	–	254,113
Sailing ship sailors	144,637	–	144,637
Dockers approximate	299,150	–	299,150
Jinrikishaman[45] Government factories	50,345	–	50,345
Workers	125,907	32,166	158,073
Total	7,770,149	3,275,529	11,027,678

The above figures are old (from 'Peasant' to the end [the] figures [are] taken from the *Oriental Economist Year Book* 1916). It is estimated that there has been an average increase of 25 percent since the above census were taken, it would therefore be true to say that we now have 13,784,598 workers. With regard to the

---

45   Rickshaw pullers.

SIXTH SESSION

peasants it is estimated that there are five to a family, and if we calculate that two out of the five are at work, there must be at least 9,492,420 [rural] proletarian and poor peasant families.

Food

	1903	1906	1912
Rice in koku	46,473,298	46,302,530	50,222,509
Barley	7,468,220	9,445,153	9,790,709
Rye	4,207,497	6,957,932	7,900,112
Wheat	1,875,388	3,962,175	5,179,500
Total wheat and others in koku	13,545,104	20,365,260	–
Soy bean in koku	3,647,830	3,517,163	3,511,464
Red beans	918,219	896,534	947,145
Pea-nuts	–	342,282	391,225
Corn	–	611,007	742,648
Sweet potatoes in kan	75,117,766,171	798,664,238	980,502,214
Potatoes	71,296,171	135,650,090	186,202,338
Lily-bulbs	–	552,433	643,045
Cabbage	–	–	13,084,832
Pumpkin	–	–	68,815,636
Water Melons	–	–	23,233,258
Egg-plant	–	–	88,368,970

Note: 1 Koku = 4.9629 bushels
1 Kan = 8.28 pounds

Crops

1914	1915	1916	1918	1919
57,006,541	55,924,590	58,442,386	54,699,187	60,818,163
9,848,752	10,253,615	9,532,162	9,835,075	8,289,859
7,207,362	8,297,701	7,919,719	7,620,695	8,297,090
4,488,239	5,230,069	5,887,344	6,360,847	5,865,691
–	–	–	–	–
–	3,807,679	3,749,771	3,451,320	3,930,810
–	962,039	886,847	811,015	877,602
–	–	–	–	–

Crops (*cont.*)

1914	1915	1916	1918	1919
–	–	–	–	–
–	1,055,633,667	1,092,026,604	1,098,520,440	1,190,757,500
–	254,759,281	280,231,531	323,930,263	487,964,212
–	–	–	–	–
–	–	–	–	–
–	–	–	–	–
–	–	–	–	–
–	–	–	–	–

Development of Industry (in thousands of yen)

	1914		1915		1916	
	No. of companies	Capital	No. of companies	Capital	No. of companies	Capital
Agriculture	491	27,235	492	31,736	485	31,745
Commercial	9,923	974,020	9,943	1,010,939	10,551	1,071,44
Trade	1,178	233,961	1,225	245,563	1,241	273,794
Industries	5,266	833,569	5,489	879,540	5,942	1,057,18

General View of Industries

	1914		1915		1916	
	No. of cos.	Capital	No. of cos.	Capital	No. of cos.	Capital
Textile	1,080	135,623	1,071	141,241	1,110	160,975
Metal and machine	491	54,232	469	73,986	619	108,654
Mechanical	620	76,043	690	88,221	816	115,386
Foods	1,350	74,071	1,442	66,260	1,456	74,244
Electrical	427	274,634	463	317,654	479	339,454
Misc.	901	32,899	968	29,811	983	32,949

General View of Industries (*cont.*)

	1914		1915		1916	
	No. of cos.	Capital	No. of cos.	Capital	No. of cos.	Capital
Mining	197	165,545	190	139,429	234	207,988
Total	5,066	813,049	5,293	856,602	5,697	1,039,650

After the Great War

1917		1918		1919	
No. of cos.	Capital	No. of cos.	Capital	No. of cos.	Capital
587	76,170	624	77,723	795	144,607
10,714	1,918,170	12,132	2,934,145	13,137	3,768,469
1,430	511,262	1,694	858,121	1,833	1,100,605
6,677	1,826,960	8,221	2,757,183	10,112	3,682,850

For the Years

1917		1918		
No. of cos.	Capital	No of cos.	Capital	Increased percentage from 1914
1,302	224,508	1,609	296,943	118
746	166,486	1,129	340,848	520
1,197	192,644	1,650	325,491	220
1,577	69,076	1,737	118,766	90
581	433,499	599	449,370	90
1,254	69,795	1,497	86,875	175
288	301,810	357	468,210	195
6,945	1,457,818	8,578	2,086,503	Ave. %–201

As you see from the table of the labour statistics, we have something like 15 million workers. The workers in Japan live in awful conditions. I speak here of the conditions of the women workers.

As this table shows, we have 3,250,000 women industrial workers, mostly engaged in factory [work] and other industries; in the textile industries alone there are 425,000, [and] 91,000 women are engaged in the mines. We have then 339,000 workers in the fisheries. Women have to work 12 hours in the spinning industry and live in the company's dormitories. They are not allowed to go out even when not engaged at work. We have night work, and women work 12 hours at night and 12 hours a day [on alternate] weeks. In the dormitories conditions are very sad; girls who work in the night time sleep in the same rooms and on the same beds as the girls who work at day. Therefore girls who are occupied in the spinning industry very soon contract consumption and other diseases. The girls living near the factory work very little in the spinning industry. Most girls are from the country, and they work in the factory and live in the dormitory. They are given only two days rest [a] month, and those two days are for sewing and washing. And they are fed [with] the company's worst material. Therefore, statistics show that more than half of the spinners usually go back to their homes within a few months because they cannot stand the conditions.

I know workers from many Japanese factories and many working in government factories too. They tell me that when these government factories were first started, they worked only five days a week and eight hours a day, received good wages as government officials, and they were well treated. Of course the European managers [do] not work more than 8 hours and they receive a large salary, work Saturdays only half [a] day, and [on] Sunday, of course, they rest. In 1897, when I started the labour movement[46] Japanese workers usually worked 9 hours, including meal time, and [the] usual custom in the factories [was] to get fifteen minutes rest in the morning and afternoon smoking time. Now, three years ago, factory laws were inaugurated. These factory laws [allowed for] 12 hours legal work time and, by permission of the Minister for Agriculture, it can be increased to 14 hours a day. So [as] our capitalistic system

---

46   Perhaps he meant to say 'we'. But if not, Katayama's claim would not be entirely an exaggeration. The Japanese trade union movement grew out of the Association for the Formation of Trade Unions (Rodokumiai Kiseikal) which was formed in July 1897 by Katayama and the journalist Fusataro Takano. The same year, they formed the Metalworkers Union (Tekkokumiai) and Katayama launched and edited the journal *Rodo Sekai* (*Labour World*). Takano was influenced by Samuel Gompers and the AFL and tried unsuccessfully to develop Tekkokumiai into a craft-based union. See Nimura 1990, p. 686.

grows, industrial exploitation increases in severity, and Japanese workers are oppressed more and more.

Formerly the workers were free to strike, free to organise themselves into unions. Of course they did not know how to organise unions and what strikes meant, nor did they know about the labour movement and its advantages, ever growing in the Western countries. But our workers did organise and strike in the early stages of our industrial development. I know at least one labour organisation existed in Tokyo when we started the labour movement in 1897. There were no laws concerning the labour movement then, so we could speak freely about strikes and labour unions and so on. We could attack capitalism also. The labour movement of that time was reformist. By 1898 we had many unions – a printers' union with a membership of 3,000 and a railway union (engine men and firemen) with a membership of 1,500. [Within] a few years we had from 70,000 to 80,000 union members, so altogether there were nearly 100,000 organised workers. In 1900, a law was passed prohibiting strikes, saying that [striking] was a crime and [strikers] were criminals who could be arrested and put into prison for six months. [Nevertheless], the labour movement during the first few years was a success. But industrial conditions after the Sino-Japanese war became depressed [and] great distress prevailed, and finally the labour movement, by means of the police law, was suppressed. In February 1897, a strike broke out along some 500 miles of railroad.[47] Previously the workers had secretly organised the engineers and firemen [along] the entire line. A strike committee was set up. [On] February 14 the strike started. The workers in the railway workshops threatened to call a sympathy strike, and finally the demands were granted. By this practical demonstration, the workers learned that unity is strength. At the conclusion of the strike they formed [a] union. This union flourished, and they accumulated a strike fund which amounted to 70,000 [yen] at the end of 1901. But this union was dissolved in 1901 by the Government, acting in conjunction with the Railroad Company. This again shows how the capitalists and the Government suppress labour unions.

A comrade from Korea told me that the Japanese officials are extremely brutal. I believe it. We have heard of many cases of brutality on the part of the Japanese employers. In 1899 a fire broke out in a Bokoku mine; the mine was sealed up and 600 people perished in order to save the property. Another case: In a cotton spinning factory a fire broke out during the night in one of the dormitories. The doors were locked from the outside and so more than sixty

---

47   This should perhaps be 1898. In February that year, the engineers and stokers of the Japan Railway Company successfully struck for higher pay and resisted attempts by the company to victimise strike leaders. See Nimura 1990, p. 681.

girls were burnt. One of the delegates tells me that recently many thousands of miners were buried alive in one of the mines in Hokkaido. These are but a few of the many cases of the sacrifice of human lives for the sake of private property.

I will tell you something about the Japanese workers. Although inexperienced, they are capable of fighting against the capitalist employers. In 1906 a great strike broke out which ended in riots. This was in the copper mines of Ashio.[48] The company continued to oppress the workers until riots broke out and several million yen worth of property was destroyed. Soon after there was a similar case at the Bessi copper mines. The workers were so oppressed that they rose up in protest and went in a body to the house of one of the officials. There they found a great many guns and rifles. They thought that they would be killed in case of [a] strike and the miners became very angry. This news spread, and a general riot broke out. Much property was destroyed.

1918 will be remembered as the memorable year of the great rice riots.[49] On 3 September, these rice riots were started in one of the fishermen's' villages on the northern coast of the Sea of Japan. It was started by fishermen's wives and daughters because rice became so dear that they could not buy it. So the fishermen's wives and daughters went to the rice merchants and railway stations telling them not to send rice away but to keep it in the village. Of course this was suppressed. A merchant's wife said that if you have no money to buy rice you could starve. So began the rice riots; within a few days this had spread to the surrounding towns. Within a week or ten days they had spread as far as to the industrial centres of Japan, even to Osaka and Kobe, and soon all over Japan. The rice riots [were] compared to the Russian uprising of 1905. During these 45 days, 142 towns and cities were affected, covering two thirds of the entire area of the country. It is estimated that over 10 million people participated in them. In many places, much property was destroyed [and] the homes of the rice merchants and rich men were burned. The police protected the merchants and the rich fought against the rioters; many people were killed by them. In connection with these riots over 7,000 persons were severely punished. But this proved to

---

48 The riots at the Ashio copper mine took place over three days starting on 14 February 1907. After widespread destruction of mine property, the uprising was suppressed by the army. Two hundred miners were arrested and their union – the Shiseikai (the society of sincere persons) – was suppressed. Katayama describes how the miners were organised from 1903 onwards by two miner-activists, Nagaoka and Minami. The previously state-owned mine had been bought by the industrialist Furukawa Ichibei in 1877. See *The Labor Movement in Japan*, Chapter 5, available at: http://www.marxists.org/archive/katayama/1918/labor_movement/ch05.htm, retrieved 1 January 2014.

49 See previous note on the 1918 rice riots.

be the starting point of the awakening of the proletarians and the beginning of the labour movement in recent years. These riots gave hope to the Japanese workers and peasants and in fact 90 percent of the rioters were workers and peasants.

Of course, the Japanese police do their best to [suppress] the labour movement of the awakened masses. In the last four months of 1918 there were over 40 strikes and in 1919 there were 410. In 1920 many factories stopped [production] and many [workers] were without employment on account of the industrial and financial crisis. In 1920, a strike broke out in the biggest steel mill in Kyushu;[50] over 27,000 workers were engaged in the strike; 500 chimneys stopped belching forth smoke. The strike was suppressed by troops. We had many strikes in Hokkaido – miners' strikes. Since then there have been many strikes; in Kobe, in two big shipyards, some 30,000 workers [went on strike] and the strike lasted six weeks. During these strikes, there were many demonstrations and public meetings and the demands of the workers were distinctly radical. The workers have only on such occasions a chance to express their opinions on 'factory control', 'workers' industrial control', 'the eight hour day' [and so on]. The demands of the workers have been becoming more and more radical every day. They often hold mass meetings in which they demand industrial control by the labour unions. Last year, meetings [of the] unemployed were held [in] Osaka. They were organised by the Federated Unions and, in their resolutions, demanded the abolition of capitalism as the only remedy [for] unemployment. Thus you can see that the workers are making progress in every way.

I will finish this report with a reference to [another tactic] of the Japanese workers – that is sabotage.[51] Sabotage has existed [in Japan] for many years [but was] conducted secretly. Two years ago at the Kawasaki shipyards, the workers organised sabotage openly. The workers demanded a raise in wages, which the company did not grant. I think there were about 1700 workers employed in this shipyard. They [came to] the factory [on] time every morning, got together and talked and produced nothing. The company could not dismiss the entire 1700 [workforce]; it would have been a loss to them, and there was no single man

---

50   The strike at the Yawata Steelworks in Kyushu was led by Asahara Kenzo, who was described by *Life* magazine in 1952 as a 'former rabid socialist'. See Buckley (ed.) 2002, p. 545; http://www.gettyimages.com/detail/news-photo/portrait-of-kenzo-asahara-former-rabid-socialist-smoking-at-news-photo/50869354, retrieved 22 April 2014.

51   What Katayama describes is more like a sit-down strike or workplace occupation than sabotage as normally understood. Perhaps by 'secret sabotage' he meant unofficial 'go-slow' industrial action.

that they could dismiss without starting a protest, and without [the] possibility of trouble. This continued for ten days, and then at a meeting of the workers it was put to a vote whether to continue this sabotage or not, and it was unanimously voted to continue. The 800 managers in the shipyard voted to ask the Company to grant the workers' demands, and so did the 500 engineers. The company did not yield. Then 4000 workers of [a] branch factory declared [a] sympathy sabotage. The President of the Company yielded to the demands of the workers and paid [their] wages for [the] days they [had] sabotaged.

Well, I have explained a few things in the way of the Japanese labour movement. In the first place it is against the law to strike, and the police always break up the strike meetings. Therefore our workers find that sabotage is the strongest and safest means of fighting against the employers. Now I think that the Japanese worker has made as much progress in the last half century as the worker of Europe has made during the last two or three centuries, and so I am sure the Japanese proletariat will soon learn how to fight against the capitalist oppressors better and quicker than the workers of America or Europe, where the capitalistic system is fully developed and established. Our workers will be able to make revolutionary progress quicker in Japan where capitalism is still in its primitive stage. It is my hope and my desire that we shall make plans together with you to fight against capitalism and imperialism in the Far East.

Chairman. In view of the complexity of the report and the abundance of statistical data, the Presidium believes that for the sake of becoming better acquainted with it, it is necessary to make the translations into the various national languages only after the stenographic report is ready. If there are no objections we shall consider this order of translation of comrade Katayama's speech accepted.

Comrades, before giving the floor to the next speaker who will report on the work of the Communist Party of Japan, there is a motion to announce a five minute's recess. If there are no objections the Presidium will consider the motion passed and will ask all the members of the Congress and the guests to come back in five minutes.

No objections? The five minutes' recess is announced.

(*After the recess*).

Chairman. The session is continuing. The Presidium asks the delegates and guests to keep themselves in order, for during the previous speeches there was much walking in the hall which disturbed the speakers.

SIXTH SESSION											197

Comrade *Yakiwa* has the floor on the organisation and policies of the Japanese Communist Party.

Yakiwa [Mizutani Kenichi].[52] I wish to tell you how the Japanese Communist Party was organised, and what its position [is] at the present moment. First of all, I want to tell you of the events that occurred when our Party was formed. After the outbreak of the European war in 1914, Japan's economic influence greatly increased. On the other hand, the rise in the cost of living was enormous and wages were very low. This led to the great rice strike of the year 1918. This was an unorganised spontaneous uprising. It is true that the proletarians of Japan are not organised. They have no experience. At the same time, they have learned many things, and since this great strike, the workers of Japan [have] started to organise and [have] started to strike more frequently.

The socialist movement in Japan, which is still [at] a low level, was started in 1900 by Japanese intellectuals. They were academics and theoreticians. However, these leaders became more radical because of the oppression by the Government. The socialist movement [became more] extreme, but [had] little connection with the actual practical labour movement, which, [in any case], was not yet established. The workers were dissatisfied with this labour movement, so they started a new movement, the Syndicalist-Communist movement.[53] At the same time, [the need for a Communist Party] began to be felt. The movement was started by Communists conscious of the necessity of joining the masses together.

There were three kinds of Communist movements in Japan: one is petty-bourgeois, the second is a pure Communist movement started by Communists, the third is [a] Communist movement working in conjunction with the mass movement. The Communists of Japan took the third position to util-

---

52   Yakiwa was Mizutani Kenichi according to the Chinese version of the congress minutes. See Russian State Archive of Socio-Political History 495.154.166. Beckmann, however, identifies Yakiwa as Takase Kyoshi, who was the son-in-law of the Japanese Communist Party's first chairman, Sakai Toshihiko. See Beckmann and Okubo 1969, p. 41.

53   The labour movement in Japan was split between socialists and anarchists. Many anarchists were initially attracted by the Russian Revolution. The anarchist leader Osugi Sakae accepted money from the Communist International to publish the journal *Rodo undo* (*the Labour Movement*), but became disillusioned over the suppression of the Kronstadt revolt and the introduction of the New Economic Policy. The split between anarchists and communists developed into an open clash in September 1922, when Osugi led a walkout from a trade union conference in Osaka and denounced the communist leaders 'as a bunch of crooks'. See Stanley 1982, pp. 79, 138–40.

ise the socialist movement.[54] This is the reason why the Communists of 1920 succeeded. Of course, these parties contained all sorts of people – bourgeois, literary men and workers. The greatest number were intellectuals, a fact which dissatisfied the workers.

There is one strong movement – the Syndicalist movement – of which comrade Kato will speak. About this time, a group of Japanese in America, located in New York, sent Communist literature and resolutions of support to encourage the Japanese comrades. They also sent one comrade to Japan on an important mission for the Communist Party. That comrade was Kondo[55] and he is now in prison. He went to Kobe where he started work, and in April 1921, as a result of his activities and the activities of other comrades, the Communist Party was started there. Of course this was an underground movement. Although a Communist Party was formed, it was of a theoretical nature, as many of the members were of the intellectual class. Being a radical movement they were, of course, persecuted by the government; being intellectuals, they were somewhat timid and therefore the Communist Party was quite weak. But among them were younger men who were not satisfied with an academic Communist movement and who started [real] work among the masses. At the present time, 40 percent of the Communist Party (only 207)[56] are workers [and] 15 percent are intellectuals, [mainly] students.

As to work, they [have] published open legal pamphlets and underground pamphlets, and [have] also formed nuclei in the towns and big cities, in spite of the fact that they are all inexperienced, oppressed, and there is strict censorship. That is why the work is progressing very slowly, though the younger workers are very interested and are working among the factory workers and among the peasants.

Comrade Chow[57] came here for the purpose of acquainting himself with the Communist movement of Russia and also with the International Communist movement. He came in order to get experience and inspiration from the Russian comrades so that he might go back and work to make the Communist movement strong and successful.

---

54 Presumably this means to work alongside the socialists and recruit members from them.
55 Kondo Eizo was a protégé of Katayama, a member of a socialist study group in New York apartment in the years following the Russian Revolution. After returning to Japan, Kondo established the Association of Enlightened People in 1920, and the Enlightened People's Communist Party in August 1921. The mainly student party collapsed after a few months when most of its members were arrested for distributing anti-militarist leaflets. See Scalapino 1973, p. 322.
56 Not clear if this means total membership or no. of workers.
57 Perhaps this refers to Kato, who speaks next.

Here he met many comrades from Japan who are representatives of the Anarcho-Communists. After many consultations with them and with prominent leaders of the Comintern in Russia he came to realise that they must unite and form a strong Communist Party. The Communist representatives and the Syndicalist representatives came to understand the necessity of forming a unified Communist Party in Japan. With this agreement he goes back with inspiration and instructions and with the belief that the comrades all over the world will start a really strong movement in order to bring about the social revolution in Japan and all over the world.

Chairman. Comrade *Kato* has the floor for a report on one of the most influential labour organisations in Japan, the Rodosha.[58]

Kato [Yoshida Hajime].[59] What I am going to say is about my own labour movement. I want to tell you about the revolutionary workers' organisations of Japan. [At] present, Japan is under fire from Korea, Manchuria, China, and also Siberia, who are sending revolutionary representatives and trying to put fire into the Japanese movement. I therefore think that we must organise all the revolutionary workers into a union. But the socialist movement in Japan [was] created by intellectuals, whose leaders are comrade Sakai,[60] who is now [the] Communist leader [in] Japan, and comrade Osugi, who is an Anarcho-Communist, and whose influence is very strong because he does actual work in the movement [alongside] the workers. Although he is [an] intellectual, his work has always been among the workers.

However, among these leaders – Socialists, Communists, and Anarcho-Communists – there have been many conflicts. They have been fighting with each other. But comrade Osugi[61] is one of the strongest revolutionary leaders in

---

58 Rodosha means The Workers. See appendix on organisations attending the Congress for a note on Rodosha.
59 Kato was Yoshida Hajime (1895–1966) a working class anarchist who announced his conversion to communism at the Congress but reverted to anarchism on his return. In 1923 he was attacked by rightists and arrested. See Beckmann and Okubo 1969, pp. 41–5. Morton 2004, p. 45.
60 Sakai Toshihiko (1871–1933) was a schoolteacher and journalist imprisoned during the Russo-Japanese War for his pacifist beliefs. He was elected chairman of the newly-founded Japanese Communist Party in July 1922. He was arrested and imprisoned in 1923, and voted to dissolve the party in 1924.
61 Osugi Sakae (1885–1923) was a leading Japanese anarchist, translator, pamphleteer and Esperantist. He was imprisoned several times, and was murdered in the chaos following the great 1923 earthquake by a squad of soldiers led by the right-wing extremist Amakasu Masahiko. Osugi's partner, the anarchist and feminist Ito Noe, and his six-year-old nephew

Japan, who has done very able work among the masses, and wishes to advance the revolutionary movement in Japan.

In the Southern part of Japan there are unions like Yuaikai,[62] and Kajawas, but all these are moderate, petty-bourgeois, and reformist. Therefore, against these reformist leaders in the movement, we formed a revolutionary union which we called Rodosha. Its influence is very strong because it is really alive, active and practical in its work. We call ourselves Syndicalist-Communists and we have central organs in Tokyo, Osaka and Acuso.[63] These organs are really alliances of the workers and have a membership of 1500, of whom every one is actually a worker. There are no leaders among them, no intellectuals of course, and every member is also a member of some kind of union. The ultimate aim is to make of all the unions in Japan one revolutionary labour union.

Moreover, the movement I represent has openly published literature from three central places. We [also] publish underground literature and distribute it among the factory workers. I say again that our organisation has no intellectuals or leaders.

However, since I came to Russia to see the movement and the actual conditions of Soviet Russia for myself, and since I met many comrades who are all Communists, and moreover since my stay in Moscow, where I have met many prominent leaders, I have found out what was hampering the Japanese movement. I believed that leaders were not necessary; that a political party was superfluous. My only aim was to revolutionize the unions. But I have found out that this is not sufficient. Therefore I now declare myself to be a Communist. I give up the 'Anarcho' and leave the 'Communist'. As soon as I go back, I will work under the banner of the Communist Party of Japan, backed by the Communist International.

Our organisation extends from Tokyo to Osaka and Ukasa.[64] The next step is to extend our movement to Korea. It is of supreme importance to come here and meet the Korean revolutionary leaders, to shake hands with them, in the movement and for the movement, so that we can work together, not only for the Korean and Japanese proletarian cause, but also in the cause of all workers and peasants. (*Applause*).

---

were also murdered. Amakasu later became propaganda chief of the Japanese puppet state of Manchuguo. He committed suicide when Soviet forces took Manchuguo in 1945.

62   Uai-Kai in the original text. The Yuaikai (Friendly Society) established by the Christian socialist Suzuki Bunji in 1912. After World War One, in response to increased labour militancy, the union adopted a more radical stance and was renamed the Nihon Rodo Sodomei (Japan Federation of Labour).

63   Unclear where he means.

64   See previous note.

SIXTH SESSION

Chairman. The agenda of the morning session is [completed]. The Ballet in the Grand Opera has been put off. Therefore, the evening is free. Thus we shall open the evening session at the usual time. I ask you to be here at six o'clock sharp so as to continue the discussion upon the following items. This evening we propose to open the discussion on comrade Zinoviev's report and on the reports presented by the various delegations. In order that the discussions may be carried on smoothly, it is desirable that the delegations agree on the representative who is to appear in the general discussion, and present the list of speakers to the Presidium, remembering, at the same time, the standing orders of this Congress.

Seventh Session

25 January 1922. (Evening)

Chairman: Comrade *Safarov*.

Chairman. I declare [this] Session of the Congress of the Toilers of the Far East open. We shall now have to start on the discussion of Comrade Zinoviev's report on the international situation and on the results of the Washington Conference. In order to more efficiently use our time, [and] for the sake of achieving greater results at this Congress, the Presidium expresses [the] wish that this item on the agenda may be [completed] today, after hearing short speeches of the representatives of the various delegations. The comrades [should] try to speak briefly and without repeating themselves. Comrade Zinoviev will then have the final word. He cannot be present here tomorrow, [and] his presence during the discussion of his report is absolutely necessary. The comrades [should], of course, take that into consideration. Comrade *Yodoshu* has the floor.

Yodoshu [Yu Shude].[1] Comrades, the history of the oppression of the Far East by world imperialism, the history of the terrible sufferings caused to the Far East by the world imperialists united for its exploitation, dates back many decades. But that is not all. At present the capitalist states – England, America, France [and] Japan – are sitting at the Washington Conference discussing more cruel [methods of] oppression, of despoiling the Far East with greater efficiency. This, comrades, we know very well. We all understand it, and feel it on our backs. And to [avert] this danger, we must unite with the Western proletariat and, together with it, [begin] the struggle against our common enemy. We also believe that our emancipation cannot be accomplished by means of any compromise with the world imperialists, and that we cannot expect our salvation to come through their help. There is only one way out for us; we must unite under the banner of the Communist International; we must unite with Soviet Russia, and together with it and the world proletariat, create a single front. On behalf of the Chinese delegation I declare that we, one and all, approve of

---

1 Yodoshu is probably Yu Shude. The Chinese version of the minutes lists the speaker as Yang Yuguang, which may be a pseudonym.

comrade Zinoviev's report in its entirety and propose to accept it without any discussion or any reservations, as the guiding principle [of] our future work. (*Applause*).

Katayama *then spoke on the Four Powers' Pact and Far Eastern Situation.*

The Washington conference of capitalist robber countries [has] almost ended[2] with a policy of questionable compromise on the Far Eastern problems. They call this compromise the Four Power Pact. It contains four things, namely: 1) The four Powers (England, America, France and Japan) agree [among] themselves to respect [each other's] rights in relation to their insular possessions and dominions in the regions of the Pacific Ocean. Controversies among themselves will be dealt with in a conference with the help of those powers not in the controversy. 2) The nature of the pact is defensive against any other power or powers. 3) The pact is for ten years and after that, any one Power can withdraw from it at 12 months' notice. 4) When it is signed by the four Powers, the British-Japanese Alliance concluded on 13 July 1911 in London shall be terminated.

The pact is a compromise, at least for three powers, England, America and Japan. America wants the English-Japanese Alliance discontinued by all means. In order to get it done as America wished, she joined the pact, [contrary to] her traditional policy of non-interference with foreign country's affairs.[3] The New York Times, in its editorial on 9 December 1921, gives a rather laboured explanation that America's position on the pact is not opposed to her traditional policy. It says: 'President Harding and the American delegation are pleased with the result achieved. It has been their purpose to enter into no alliance, entangling or otherwise. The new arrangement is regarded by them as avoiding this complication'. America can now say to the American public that the pact is only [a series] of agreements with three Powers on [their] Pacific possessions and dominions, [and], at the same time, it [has] destroyed the obnoxious Alliance between England and Japan. Thus America gained her [objective while] giving [away] hardly anything. True, the pact is not [an] alliance, but its second article is a defensive agreement against [any] other Power or Powers. The signing of the pact puts an end to the British-Japanese Alliance, but that does not mean that the British and the Japanese [have broken off] off their relations in the Far East. They are still allies under the pact. And moreover, the pact of the present four Powers is nothing but the British proposal of a triple alliance presented

---

2   The Washington Conference ended on 6 February 1922. Katayama was speaking on 25 January.
3   Non-entanglement might be closer to Katayama's meaning.

by Lloyd George[4] to the Washington politicians, in a modified form, and also disguised as [a series of] agreements.

England's statesmen have accomplished their aims in concluding the Four Powers' Pact and can now pacify the British public as the American public has been pacified by the Washington politicians, because the pact puts an end to the very unpopular British-Japanese Alliance, and yet [Britain] retains Japan as her unpaid police for India, as before. Present British interests in China are too great for Britain to make Japan her possible enemy, while she does like to make American people consider that the British Government is not a friend of the American people. Thus England, in signing the Pacific Four Power Pact, killed two birds with one stone. There is a chance that England may manipulate America and Japan into some trouble with each other and [then] side with one or other of the two Powers. As to France, England can easily bend her to her own wishes.

French colonial interests in the Far East are in no way endangered by Japan or any of the other two Powers. But in case of war between America and Japan, France [will be] able to retain her colonial interests in the Far East by taking sides with either America or Japan, provided that England is on her side. So France thinks [it has] a very good card [to play] in the coming contest in the Far East. The latter half of the first clause of the pact is almost solely concerned with the very possible controversy between America and Japan, and hardly any other Power.

Apparently, Japan is also a [winner] in the Four Power Pact! Under this pact, there will be no immediate danger of going to war with America on the questions of the Far East. She has the tacit consent of [the other] three Powers [to] her activities in the Far Eastern regions. While America maintains her attitude toward China regarding the 'open door' and 'equal opportunity for all countries', she nevertheless changed her policy toward Japan on the return of the mission to the Far East in the Summer of 1920 headed by Frank Vanderlip and Lamont, the Wall Street magnate.[5] Among them, and the Japan-

---

4 In fact neither Lloyd George nor the Foreign Secretary Lord Curzon attended the Washington Conference as they were preoccupied with talks to end the Irish War of Independence. The British Empire was represented by the President of the Privy Council and former Conservative Prime Minister, Lord Balfour. Balfour proposed a triple alliance of Britain, Japan and the United States, as a way of preserving the essentials of the Anglo-Japanese alliance. The US Secretary of State, Charles Evans Hughes, rejected the proposal. See Lowe and Dockrill 1972, pp. 301–3.

5 Frank A. Vanderlip (1864–1937) was president of First National City Bank of New York – the forerunner of Citibank – from 1909–19, and also served as Assistant Secretary of the Treas-

ese capitalist clique headed by Shibusawa[6] and others, a definite agreement seems to have been arrived at on the Chinese markets, under the China Economic Consortium. After some strenuous propaganda conducted by the Wall Street magnates mentioned above, with the help of other small fries among financial circles, they succeeded in convincing the big capitalists of the country of the advisability of the *joint exploitation of China*. During the summer of 1921, the announcement of the change of American policy toward Japan appeared in the public press. It was sounded by the New York Times in the latter part of the summer on a very plausible [note]; it was somewhat in this tone: Japan has a teeming population which she must feed; she must either send her surplus population out of the country, or obtain materials for her growing industry from other countries. As the white countries, the American Pacific coast, Canada, Australia and other colonies held by the white races [have] shut their door to the Japanese, it is therefore fair and responsible to let Japan develop her influence in the Far Eastern regions. This kind of talk has been taken up by various dailies and periodicals all over the country.

Thus America prepared herself for the Washington Conference. The Japanese militarist Government at first had some suspicions with regard to the real motives of the Washington statesmen, but the government, having a certain understanding with the capitalists (Wall Street magnates), accepted the Harding invitation. For the first time, the Japanese became interested in the foreign politics of Japan, and they freely [discussed] the programmes of the Washington Conference among themselves. The disarmament question, in connection with the Washington Conference, was hotly discussed, and the best and the most intelligent classes of the people came to think, and openly declared, that Japan's best interest lies not in militarism, but in the peaceful pursuit of her national [livelihood]. This change of attitude on the part of the people toward militarism, made the military representatives [in] Washington yield readily to

---

ury. Thomas W. Lamont (1870–1948) was a leading American banker and diplomat. A senior partner at JP Morgan, he represented the US Treasury at the 1919 Paris peace negotiations. In 1920, Vanderlip and Lamont undertook a mission to Japan on behalf of the State Department, to overcome Japanese reluctance to join the International Banking Consortium for China. During the mission, Lamont tacitly acknowledged Japan's primacy in Manchuria and Mongolia.

Kilgroe 1999, available at: http://www.unc.edu/depts/diplomat/AD_Issues/amdipl_12/kilgroe_banker.html, retrieved 20 March 2014.

6   Shibusawa Eiichi was a prominent industrialist, sometimes referred to as the father of Japanese capitalism.

the proposals made by [the] American delegates, and Japan gave way to the demand of America in regard to the question of Yap.[7]

The Four Power Pact temporarily gives Japan [a somewhat freer] hand in the Far East, and tacit consent to help the [Russian reactionaries]. Japan had already [reinforced] her troops in Siberia and occupied other important places on the Amur. Thus Japan started to play the part of executioner for the imperialists of the world in the Far East under the Four Power Pact, and resolved to crush the workers' and peasants' power and influence in Siberia, and destroy the Workers' and Peasants' Republic of Russia. This gives Japan a still freer hand to exploit the fisheries and other industries [in] the Maritime Province and Kamchatka.

Thus, the Washington Conference has, at least temporarily, [defined] the imperialist policies of the capitalist powers of the world [on the joint] exploitation of China and Siberia. In the latter it tacitly gave Japan power to act freely with the reactionary elements of [the] old Russian tsarist and capitalist cliques. On the whole, the Washington Conference [has] succeeded in laying down a [compromise] imperialist policy of the Great Powers in the Far East, and yet the results of it show that they are preparing for the coming imperialist conflict in the Far East. America wanted the British-Japanese Alliance to be annulled simply because America cannot single-handedly fight against the combined power of England and Japan.

Politically, France is very much interested in the Far Eastern, and especially in the Siberian situation. The French Government took a lively interest in the Siberian intervention of the Allied Powers, including America, from the beginning. French statesmen have the idea that they can strike at Soviet Russia [via] the Siberian invasion and by helping the counter-revolutionary [armies] in Siberia. On the fall of Kolchak, however, they withdrew their army and [halted] their actual participation in Siberia, except for financial and other [material] support. They, along with the English and American Governments, left the task of giving actual support to the counter-revolutionary generals [in] the hands of the Japanese imperialist Government. Among the imperialist Powers, the French Government, next to the Japanese Government, has been the most interested in the Siberian invasion, and openly or secretly supported the reactionary leaders and Japan as its imperialist representative. The American and English Governments equally supported and acquiesced to the French and Japanese activities in Far Eastern Siberia. The American Government officially recognised, and declared that it had no objections to, Japan's

---

7 See previous note on the Yap issue.

Siberian activities. But when Japan occupied the northern half of Sakhalin Island, and also some important strategic points in Kamchatka, American statesmen, unable to make any protest against the Japanese audacious military and naval activities, feebly, and in a rather far-fetched manner made a declaration to the Russian people, [via] the Italian Foreign Office, about 'the integrity of Russian territory'. This was [intended] to deceive the Russian people on the one hand, and to enter an American protest against the Japanese occupation of Russian [territory], while [simultaneously] supporting the counter-revolutionary armies in the Near East, Ukraine, Poland and the border nations of Russia.

The much commented and criticized French-Japanese secret agreement[8] concerning Siberia played a quite important role in the diplomatic drama staged in Washington [over the New Year]. On 2 January, the Manchester Guardian devoted over two columns to the secret agreements between France and Japan on the policy against Siberia and Soviet Russia. French militarists are desperate and crazy about the Worker's and Peasant's Government.

They seem still to have [the] idea that they [will be] able to crush Soviet Russia by financing Poland and Romania or the Ukraine and by helping the counter-revolutionary leaders in Siberia [with] the aid of the imperialists of Japan. I do not think that the so-called secret agreement between Japan and France is such as is described in the Manchester Guardian in its last paragraph. That newspaper does not give any details of the conclusion of the treaty. But anyone can make it out by the conduct of the two Governments and the few

---

8   Far Eastern Republic representatives revealed what they claimed were secret agreements between France and Japan to the Guardian correspondent at the Washington Conference, HW Nevinson. A telegram from the French Foreign Office to Japan said: 'Our agreement with Japan on Siberian question forces us to be very careful, for our decisions are in conflict with policy of America, which is now playing important part in the East. America's intention to secure for herself place in Soviet Russia has been frustrated by our policy. Americans are therefore pushing Eastern question so as to gain supremacy in the East. We must resist such efforts by all means'. The French asked Japan not to withdraw from Siberia since 'well-disciplined and equipped armies are now stationed in Hungary and Jugo-Slavia ready to invade the country at any moment to restore order and give their assistance to the old monarchic regime'. The documents also revealed the terms of a March 1921 treaty between France and Japan, granting Japan control of Siberia after the defeat of the Bolsheviks, ownership of all concessions, the option to buy the Manchurian railway, and the right to maintain forces in strategic locations. In return, Japan was to transport Wrangel's armies from Crimea to Siberia. A wire to Tokyo from the Japanese commander in Siberia said a ship carrying White officers had arrived and five more ships were expected. See the Guardian and Observer Archives, *The Manchester Guardian* (1901–59), 2 January 1922, p. 7, retrieved 26 April 2014.

cables exchanged between them on the Siberian question. Whether [a] secret treaty between France and Japan has been entered into or not is a matter of mere conjecture, but it is a fact that Japan has been [transporting Wrangel's[9] officers from] the Crimea.[10]

Whether the French-Japanese treaty exists or not matters very little to the Far Eastern countries. The fact remains that Japan and France are enemies of the Far Eastern workers and peasants. They are trying to exploit them and their countries for imperialist purposes. But the exposure of the secret treaty will serve [a] propaganda purpose for England and America. It is natural that all the white capitalist countries cannot but regard Japan as a hindrance [to] their Far Eastern exploitation and [they] all want to crush Japanese imperialism in order to have free play in the Far Eastern regions. But the fact remains that Japan is the strongest power in the Far East, hence there arises the necessity of ousting Japanese imperialism, if only they could do so. England could crush Japan in conjunction with America even if France took sides with Japan.

As the result of the war of 1914–18 England crushed her then rival, Germany, but she now has a stronger rival in America than she had before in Germany. Lloyd George knows very well that if Japan [is] crushed with the aid of America the latter will become a greater rival to England than the rival she crushed in the last war. As we [can] see, all the imperialists [want] to crush each other in the Near East, while Japan wants to crush all the white rulers in the Far East. All this, of course, is not new in imperialist politics.

All the capitalist countries want the Chinese market for their goods and for their investments. But [they] cannot all get it. At least, no single one can get [it] for itself alone. There is only one way to get it alone for any country, namely, to fight for it and win in the fight. This is a plain fact that every capitalist country knows; but to fight for it is not an easy matter, and to win in the fight is not so sure a thing as to secure the 'open door' policy as a result of confabula-

---

9 Pyotr Nikolaevich Wrangel (1878–1928), nicknamed the 'Black Baron', commanded a Cossack regiment during World War One and rose to the rank of Major General. After the October Revolution, he joined Anton Denikin's White forces as a cavalry commander and captured Tsaritsyn (Volgograd). When Denikin resigned in April 1920 after failing to take Moscow, Wrangel took over as commander, but was forced to retreat. His flight from Crimea in November 1920 marked the end of White resistance in European Russia. Wrangel died suddenly in Brussels on 25 April 1928. His family claimed he was poisoned by a Soviet agent.

10 The original says 'to the Crimea'. This seems to be wrong. Wrangel's officers were to be evacuated from the Crimea and transported to fight the Bolsheviks in Siberia. The intention, apparently, was to place them under the command of Ataman Semenov. See *The Manchester Guardian* (1901–59), 2 January 1922, p. 7, retrieved 26 April 2014.

tion. Thus the Washington Conference [was] called in order to sound the sea of world public opinion.

The result is the Four Powers' Pact in the Far East. The pact apparently assures security in the Far East for ten years, but [in reality], the situation in the Far East [has become] much more dangerous and unstable than [it was] under the British-Japanese Alliance, because the pact is a mere agreement among four Powers, and the Pact Conference that might be held in the event of a controversy, say, of two Powers (America and Japan) may result in a tied vote [of] the two conferring Powers (England and France). The probable decision of the Pact Conference has no obligatory force for either of the two Powers. It has, therefore, no power, [just] like the Hague Peace Conference decisions [and] agreements. Thus the situation in the Far East has become more critical and dangerous than ever before. [Imperialist] war is unavoidable and it may come at any time; there is nothing now that guarantees the peace in the Far East. The Four Power Pact has, however, one good quality, in that it is a check on imperialist Japan in the coming Far Eastern capitalist [confrontation][11] because Japan's favourite tactic [in] foreign warfare is to steal a march on the enemy. Japan won its first fights by using these tactics in the Russo-Japanese war of 1904–05 and previously in the Sino-Japanese war of 1894–95. These [pre-emptive][12] tactics of Japanese imperialism [cannot] be used under the Four Power Pact. On the other hand, it will give a certain advantage to America, where [war fever] or jingoism can only be stirred [up] by [influencing] public opinion through the press and public meetings. The pact will give the American government the necessary time [to accomplish this]. This all means that America and France will have few[er] obstacles in their path in the next imperialist war in the Far East.

The world imperialist Powers, as I have shown above somewhat extensively, are [eager] to exploit the Far Eastern countries, and especially China. [Faced with] the aggressive, organised imperialist world Powers, and the ever-menacing Japanese imperialism in the Far East, the Far Eastern countries are in a deplorable and chaotic condition.

Korea is under the iron heel of Japanese imperialist rule; the people are oppressed; the poor peasants are exploited by the Japanese landowners who rob the land from the poor peasants. But the Oriental Colonization Company[13] [was] organised with the [express] purpose of exploiting the Korean agricultural industries. They are capitalising the best land in Korea and [turning] the

---

11   The original says 'Far Eastern capitalist country'.
12   The original says 'forestalling'.
13   Also known as the Oriental Development Company.

Koreans [into] tenant farmers to be enslaved under the Oriental Colonization Company's heel. Among the shareholders are Korean capitalists including [the] Korean royal family, but they have no power in the management of the Company. The railways, mines, and other industries are [also] monopolised by Japanese capitalists or the Japanese militarist Government.

The Korean independence movement and its nationwide uprising of 1919 were crushed by the bloody hands of Japanese militarism. The Koreans paid a terrible price with their lives and sufferings, and also many years of prison life, [but] the independence movement and the uprising gave the Koreans hope and impetus for future struggles. They showed to the entire world their capacity [for] revolt and national unity. The Korean uprisings of 1919 [reflected] the direct influence of the American missionaries, and without doubt the indirect influence of the Russian Bolshevik Revolution. The Korean people [have been] nationally awakened for their emancipation from the foreign imperialist yoke.

The uprisings of 1919, and the invasion of 5,000 Korean soldiers from Siberia[14] struck a severe blow at the imperialist army, but failed utterly, and must have taught the Korean Independence Union[15] the necessity for better and wider, as well as deeper, organisation among the Koreans outside as well as inside Korea, in order to strike the final blow against imperialistic Japan.

The Korean independence leaders outside Korea and inside Korea [need] firm organisations with strict discipline and well regulated [means of] communication. They must always keep in touch and act on a unified front, not only with Koreans alone, but they should act in co-operation with the workers' and peasants' organisations of China and Japan, as well as Siberia. They should realise that the independence of Korea cannot be accomplished without the [material] support of all the Far Eastern proletarians, acting in concert and simultaneously if possible.

China is [still] in the development stage of the political revolutions [that] started in the year 1911. [There is] no stable government that has power and influence over all China. The Beijing Government lives on the support of the foreign creditor governments. The Canton Government has little influence over the provincial governments and has been fighting for its [very] existence. Moreover, the provincial governors and different factions are all the time quarrelling among each other. The finances of the Beijing Government are in a bankrupt condition and it only exists by a policy of [constant] borrowing. The

---

14   Possibly a reference to the Hunchun incident. See previous note.
15   The Korean Independence Union/League was formed by Korean émigrés in Manchuria in 1919, had 8,600 members, and engaged in guerrilla warfare against the Japanese. It sent two delegates to the Congress.

Canton Government is in no better financial position than the Beijing Government. It has no relations with any foreign powers and is recognised by none of the governments. Thus China is living or going through [a] revolutionary period and has need of a strong government, whether that government be reactionary, liberal or democratic. China needs a strong government that can stand on its feet and fight against foreign aggression and imperialism. But such a hope is utterly impossible of realisation for China. China [has already been] divided economically among the capitalists of England, France, Japan and America [into] so-called spheres of influence and interests. China's only salvation is to become herself a Soviet republic like Russia and throw off the yoke of foreign imperialism and capitalism. The coming imperialist world war will not benefit China, no matter who [is] the victor, unless China takes advantage of the war to throw off the foreign yoke of the world capitalists and imperialists and join hands with the Soviet Republic of Workers and Peasants.

Chairman. Comrade *Flore* now has the floor.

Flore [Kim Won'gyŏng].[16] I welcome comrade Zinoviev's report in its entirety, and for the following reasons. Comrade Zinoviev in his speech has consistently developed the idea that we, the delegates of the toilers of the Far East here assembled, must unite; and he has shown us how to act in future against the union of the imperialists created at Washington in order to improve our position as toilers of the Far East. You, the delegates here assembled, can rest assured that the women of the East have been awakened, and they will march by your side with arms in their hands. During the March revolution of 1919,[17] the Korean women have already demonstrated their valour and devotion to the revolution.

The October Revolution in Russia was the impulse that called forth the revolutionary movement of the Koreans in 1919. The awakened Korean proletariat has adopted in their entirety the slogans raised by the October Revolution of 1917. The Korean women have long since shaken off [the] oriental traditions which confined them to the hearth and kept them in the bondage of their parents, husband and children.

Long live the union of the toilers of the Far East! Long live the rule of Soviets! Long live the Third Communist International!

---

16   Kim Won'gyŏng (born 1899) was delegated from the Shanghai branch (this does not necessarily imply she was in the Shanghai faction) of the Korean Communist Party. She was a member of the Korean Women's Patriotic League.
17   The original says 1918, an obvious misprint.

Tao [Zhang Qiubai]. The report made by comrade Zinoviev has been accepted by the Chinese delegation. On the whole I agree with the report of comrade Zinoviev, but I must take exception to two points. The first point is the statement that there are some elements in the Southern Revolutionary Party [that] are pro-American and welcome the American bourgeois democracy. This is not true. The Kuomintang Party was established twenty years ago, and from the very beginning this Party declared its intention to secure a free China.

The second step must be for [a] political revolution. The third step for [a] social revolution. With such a programme there can be no desire on the part of the Kuomintang Party to accept American bourgeois democracy.

The second point is the assertion in comrade Zinoviev's speech that the Kuomintang was against the independence of Mongolia. In China I met and discussed this question with important members of the Kuomintang and the government. They were not against the independence of Mongolia. I [do not] know whether the comrade has [received] some information that in the Southern Government or in the Kuomintang there is a view or inclination to oppose the independence of Mongolia. According to my information it is not so.

Kim-Khu [Rim Wŏn-gŭn].[18] Since the human race came into the world, it immediately divided into two classes, the oppressors and the oppressed. All wars mentioned in the history of mankind represent the struggle between these two irreconcilable classes.

The Washington Conference is of importance to us, the representatives of the Far Eastern toilers here assembled. That conference was a gathering of imperialists, of world robbers who, not content with their past exploits, are gathering their forces to further exploit us. Therefore, comrades, we must declare here with all emphasis that we will not allow them to exploit us any further. We must unite, in the literal sense of this word; otherwise we will not avoid being exploited by these imperialists. Comrade Zinoviev predicted in his speech that in the near future, in the year 1925 or 1928, war must inevitably break out in the Far East. If we [do] not prepare [together] for this war, we shall be defeated [separately]. Therefore we must begin preparing for this war from this very day. Perhaps by our union we shall repel this monster which menaces mankind. Maybe, thanks to our union, this war will not take place, for the saying goes: 'Unity is strength'.

---

18   Kim-Khu was Rim Wŏn-gŭn/Im Wŏn-gŭn (1900–63), a journalist for the Shanghai-based newspaper Independence News and a member of the Shanghai branch of the Korean Communist Party.

We will unite for the sake of unity, in order to work out common tactics, to coordinate the revolutionary forces of the Far East. We must accept comrade Zinoviev's report in its entirety as the basis of our programme. Long live unity! (*Applause*).

Chairman. Comrade *Booyan-Manhu*, representative of the People's Party of Mongolia, has the floor.

Booyan-Manhu [Sonombaljiryn Buyannemekh].[19] Comrades, the Mongolian section has discussed comrade Zinoviev's report and has found it, in the main, in accord with the interests and aspirations of the toiling masses of the peoples of the Far East. At the present time, the centre of gravity of world politics is moving to our countries; the attention of the world plunderers who destroyed, in the fratricidal war, the richest centre of world culture – Europe, is directed upon us. Therefore we, the toiling peoples of the Far East, for the sake of our national interests and of the ideals of all humanity, must shake hands with our natural ally – the world proletariat and its vanguard, the Communist International and Soviet Russia. If we do not do that, the great Asiatic continent and its richest, eastern part will become the arena for the struggle among the world imperialistic states, the arena of the greatest war in history, whose weight will fall upon us first of all. Our land and people, the entire world will be doomed to poverty, barbarism, and misery. European Socialism, during the peaceful pre-war days did not pay sufficient attention to our suffering, the suffering of the oppressed, coloured nations of the world. Only the Communist International, which was born in the womb of revolutionary Russia, took up our cause with [complete] sincerity and made it a part of the world movement for freedom.

The union of toiling Mongolia with Communist Soviet Russia, which has already existed for a year, [has] resulted in the liberation of Mongolia; the emancipation and autonomy granted to our related tribes – the Buryats, Kalmyks, and the other tribes which inhabit Russia, is [sufficient] proof of the fact that Soviet Russia and the Comintern are filled with genuine sympathy for the oppressed peoples and are able and willing to apply a policy to these peoples which is in complete accord with the national and historic wishes and

---

19   Sonombaljiryn Buyannemekh was a poet, playwright and journalist. He drafted the first MPP programme and wrote the Mongolian words to the Internationale. During the Far East Congress, he met Lenin together with "Japanese" Danzan. He was executed in 1937 on trumped up charges of being a Japanese spy. He was rehabilitated in 1962. See Sanders 2010, pp. 132–3.

peculiarities of these nations. On behalf of the Mongolian people, the Mongolian section reiterates and emphasises this before the present Congress.

Despite all the efforts and calumnies of the dark powers of world reaction, the sympathy and faith of the oppressed peoples of Asia in the Comintern and Soviet Russia is growing. Strengthening by its authority this growing sympathy, our Congress must create a strong union to counteract the four robber states which have recently agreed at Washington on the best way of exploiting us.

We, the Mongols, have long been most closely united with the Chinese people, both culturally and economically. As far back as last spring, our People's Party made a special appeal to the Chinese people, calling upon them to unite with us in the common struggle for the liberation of both peoples from the yoke of the world plunderers and exploiters.

On the question of the future relations between Mongolia and China, our party takes the same view as was expressed here by Comrade Zinoviev – that liberated China and free Mongolia will find a common language.

Chairman. I have received a number of notes pointing out that our time is up. I must say that since the session opened at 8.30, it will have to continue until we are through with the question. Comrade *Simpson* has the floor.

Simpson [Semaun]. Comrades, I speak very bad English because I have been learning that language only for the past two months, but I want to tell you that the speech of comrade Zinoviev is so good that I cannot make any propositions on it. But you know, comrades, that the European war resulted in very bad conditions for the people of Europe and also of America, and it is clear that [given] such conditions the next war [must be avoided].[20] The first war resulted in the Washington Conference, with the result that there is a great compromise among the world imperialists. But among the world imperialists, you have also a little boy of imperialism and that is Dutch imperialism. Dutch imperialism is very clever in diplomacy. At the Washington Conference that imperialism spoke very little about its attitude, but now it is preparing the Dutch Indies for a war. This past year Dutch imperialism has built more warships in preparation for a future war in the Indies.[21] The Java men are already being trained [as] military sailors. Already the Dutch Government in the Indies is preparing our country for the next war. It is the aim of the Dutch people to be neutral in the next war, but geography teaches us that the Dutch Indies cannot be neutral, and

---

20   The original says 'cannot be started'.
21   The original says India.

so the Dutch Indies are also of importance in the future.[22] And it is plain that the words of Comrade Zinoviev, calling you to fight against imperialism under the banner of the Third International, are also heard by us as words which are intended for us.

Chairman. I will now call upon comrade *Zinoviev* to reply to the discussion.

Zinoviev. First of all, comrades, I will deal with the objections made by the representative of the Chinese delegation, who declared that upon the question of their relations with Mongolia we are not well informed, and that among the Southern Chinese revolutionaries, among the adherents of the Kuomintang Party, no doubts are entertained on that score, that at present they must not aim to restore Mongolia to China. In my report I made the reservation that we indeed possess [only] very scanty information. I quite admit that, upon this point, we have been really insufficiently informed. At any rate, we note with the greatest pleasure the declaration made by the representatives of the Chinese delegation, in the sense that they recognise the necessity for the independent existence of revolutionary Mongolia at the present moment. It seems to me that, in the presence of such recognition, good neighbourly relations between these two peoples are really assured. If, at the present [transitional] stage – a very difficult one for the new-born revolutionary Mongolia and no less so for Southern China – if at this [transitional] stage there will prevail perfect unanimity among the principal political parties of the two countries, then it is, to my mind, the best guarantee that both countries will really be able to overcome all the difficulties that are confronting them.

I also think that the representative of the Kuomintang was correct in saying that they intend advancing northwards from the south only by degrees, that they see the necessity of first securing the revolutionary conquest in the south of China, and only then, after due strengthening of the main strongholds, continuing their advance forward. Of one thing only we would like to remind our friends, the revolutionaries of South China. It is, of course, easier first of all to become established in some centre and then gradually to spread out further. But this holds good only under favourable exterior circumstances; if we are so situated that the enemy does not wait, we may be often forced

---

22 Japan occupied the Dutch East Indies in March 1942 and held them until the surrender on 15 August 1945. Sukarno declared independence two days later. British forces employed former Japanese occupation troops to fight against the nationalists until Dutch troops arrived. The Netherlands fought a four-year war to try to retake its colony, before relinquishing control in December 1949.

into war and compelled to take the offensive and destroy the enemy, or otherwise he will destroy us. The same thing may happen between South and North China. North China would perhaps represent no menace to South China if behind North China and its present rulers were not the Entente and the hidden hand of foreign capitalism. Yet we know that such a 'perhaps' does not exist in reality. We know that, in consequence of the Washington Conference, the Entente will do everything possible to attack South China through the North, to weaken and divide her forces. It is for this reason that I think in this case, the tactics outlined by the Southern revolutionists – although correct in the main – underestimate the dangers lurking in the Quadruple Alliance, which will not allow any respite for the Southern Government to fortify itself [in] its centre. The questions are likely to be put in a far more acute form than hitherto, and our Southern comrades must be prepared for such a situation.

Most of the comrades have declared themselves in accord with our report. We can only regard this solidarity with the greatest satisfaction. I think that this solidarity, which of course is not mere ostentation but very real, is the best guarantee that we are on the right track.

Europeans, including [Europeans in the colonies],[23] frequently have only a [bookish] knowledge of imperialism, after all. They talk and read and write about imperialism at great length, but they do not see imperialism in its actual workings; at least they did not before the war. You, the nations of the Far East, have a great advantage over us Europeans. You know imperialism not only from books, not only in theory; you know imperialism as it actually is, in all its nakedness, with all its bloodthirsty features.

This is why we are firmly convinced, comrades, that the substance of imperialism is understood by the Far Eastern nations even better than by some elements of the European working class.

We cannot and must not conceal from you that a part of the European [working class is] being corrupted and bribed by imperialism, particularly in such countries as England and America. The same thing is now being attempted by the Japanese imperialists. The greatest danger of imperialism to mankind lies in the fact that, besides direct cruelty, it manages also to corrupt the soul of a [section] of the workers. We witnessed this during the imperialist war. It goes without saying that the better elements of the working class are quite aware of the bloodthirstiness of imperialism and see the depravity of its attitude towards the oppressed nationalities. But, alas, even among the enlightened workers of

---

23   The original says 'European colonies'.

the most cultured European countries, there are some who [have been] corrupted and demoralised by imperialism, saturated with the poison of nationalism, and [are] unable to serve as reliable allies in our struggle. This makes the role of the oppressed nations of the Far East of such great importance in the struggle for the final victory over imperialism. Attempts are still [being] made, and will continue to be made, by imperialism to bribe certain upper strata of the oppressed nations of the Far East, but the great masses, notably the four hundred million population of China, cannot be bought [out] by the imperialists. It is for this reason that these, and many other hundreds of millions of the inhabitants of the countries of the Far East, in historical perspective, represent the main force that will overthrow imperialism. The better elements of the European workers have paved the way. The better elements of the European workers will take the lead in this struggle, but the masses of infantry which will finally destroy imperialism, are you, the oppressed nations of the Far East. In your countries, with the exception of Japan, there is hardly any proletariat. Nevertheless we think that your countries also are ripe for the soviet system. We think that the real revolutionaries in China and Korea must even now raise the slogan of soviets.

The Comintern has pointed this out more than once in its resolutions: Soviets are possible even there where the proletariat is not numerous and where there is a preponderance of [peasants]. We are not speaking of soviets in the wide sense of the word,[24] but of the watchword of soviets. We are discussing the form of government which the revolutionists of China, Korea, Mongolia and Japan must propose to their peoples, when, after their return from Moscow, they [are] asked in the villages, what form of government the Comintern and the Far Eastern Congress have proposed for them. You may boldly state that we advocate the soviet system. This form of government is possible in the countries with no industrial proletariat.[25] Those Chinese parties which consider themselves the true followers of democracy must discard the old democratic watchwords which [have] been usurped and besmirched by the imperialists and must declare themselves in favour of true people's power, viz., the soviet system, even in such places where these soviets will be pre-eminently peasant soviets. It is only then that the leaders of the revolutionary movement in the countries which are represented at this Con-

---

24 Zinoviev's meaning is unclear here. Perhaps he means in the sense of introducing socialist measures.
25 This is a clear statement in favour of soviets, not simply as organisations involved in mass mobilisation, but as a form of government in peasant countries with no modern working class.

gress will be able, in the endeavour to free their countries from the foreign yoke, to identify the idea of independence with real and honest democracy. Then, they will awaken such enormous revolutionary forces in their countries, will kindle such enthusiasm and will arouse such [broad] masses of workers, that we shall feel assured that they will fulfil the tasks which are before them.

Comrades, if we had with us the representatives of India, we should be able to say that we had here the representatives of countries which constitute two thirds, if not three quarters of the universe. Comparatively, you are only a small group of people here. Your role is that of pioneers, of people who clear the path for others. But we have seen that during recent years small groups which, at first, represented small minorities were able to rouse enormous forces provided they employed the right methods and led [them] on to the right path. I am of the opinion that you have adopted the right path, and you have shown it at this, your first Congress. You have taken it for granted that the oppressed peoples must unite with the most advanced workers of the whole world. Having found this right path, you will succeed in rousing the [broad] masses which will turn the wheel of history in the direction most acceptable to the workers. At the present moment, some people might think that the world revolution [has been] considerably delayed. Yes, things have not progressed as quickly as many of us imagined they would, a few years ago. Nevertheless, things are progressing and are steadily moving forward. This Congress of yours is only another proof of it. The world revolution will be victorious. This is self-evident to anyone who can use his brains. And the victory of the world revolution is not so far distant. Of course, a few years are a considerable item in the life of the individual, but for the victory of such a great cause, it is only like a minute on the dial of history. We are convinced that the present Congress will not only awaken a few bold individuals, the vanguard and the leaders of the movement, but the vast masses of the oppressed peoples of the Far East. This Congress will seal the unification of the revolutionary Communist movement in Japan, and we have every reason to believe that all the revolutionary forces of Japan will [unite] under the banner of the Communist International. This will be a big event for the Japanese labour movement and for the entire Far East, for the victory of the Japanese labour movement is the key which will unlock the door of emancipation for the entire Far East. We shall not be able to do much at the Congress itself; let us unite all the advanced forces of the Japanese working class; let us consolidate the foremost revolutionary elements of the Far East. This, of course, is not much in itself but it is a step which, in a comparatively short time, will produce gigantic results.

The present Congress will show that there are no obstacles to the unification of [the] two world [forces],[26] which are determining the fate, not only of the European, but of the world revolution. Therefore, comrades, we shall go away from this Congress [fully convinced] that the revolution has reached the Far East, and that the vanguard of the foremost workers of Europe and America will fulfil their obligation to give comradely aid towards the unification of the foremost ranks of the oppressed workers of the Far East, in order, [through our] joint efforts, to overthrow the monster of world imperialism. (*Stormy applause*).

Djan moves to instruct the Presidium to draw up [a] manifesto on behalf of the congress and also to draw up a resolution on this question.

Chairman. Is there any one against this proposal? As no one is against it, I declare the motion carried. The translation of these speeches and also the concluding remarks of comrade Zinoviev will take place in the national sections. Tomorrow the session will open at 11 a.m. I declare the session closed.

(*Closure of session*).

---

26 The original text says *powers*. Zinoviev means the proletariat of the advanced capitalist countries and the peasantry and semi-proletarians of the colonial and semi-colonial world.

Eighth Session

26 January 1922 (Morning)

Chairman: comrade *Din-Dib* (Dendev).

Chairman. I declare the session open, and will call upon comrade *Safarov* to read his report *The National-Colonial Question and the Communist Attitude thereto.*

Safarov.[1] Comrades, never was the world capitalist system in such a precarious state as it is now. The imperialist war of 1914–18 brought victory to those nations that took the least part, [or] a fictitious one, in the war.

While this war ruined the greater part of Europe and [shook] the European capitalist system to its very foundations, in America and Japan it created, [at least] at first, on the basis of heavy war orders [from] Europe, [the appearance] of industrial prosperity. Upon an examination of the foreign trade statistics of America and Japan, you will see that during the period of war prosperity in these countries, [capitalist industry made great] progress, and it seemed as though those countries would be able to enjoy the fruits of victory, that they would really come out victorious from the imperialist war. [But] a crisis [broke out] in March 1920, [beginning with] a crisis of the entire capitalist

---

1 Georgi Ivanovich Safarov (1891–1942) was one of the Bolsheviks' leading experts on Central and East Asia. Among his works were *The Colonial Revolution (The case of Turkestan)* and *Essays on the History of China* (1933). Safarov was politically active from an early age and joined the RSDLP aged 17. While in exile in Switzerland, he became Lenin's secretary. In 1912, he accompanied Inessa Armand on a clandestine mission to Russia. He attended the Zimmerwald Conference in 1915 and in April 1917 he accompanied Lenin to Russia on the sealed train. He was chairman of the Urals regional Party committee when the former Tsar and his family were executed in Yekaterinburg in July 1918. From 1921, he headed the Eastern Department of the Comintern. A tireless organiser for the United Opposition, Safarov was sent to work in the Soviet embassy in Beijing in 1926 to remove him from the political scene. He was expelled from the Party in 1927, when the opposition was crushed following demonstrations on the tenth anniversary of the revolution. He capitulated and was re-admitted to the Party but returned to oppositional activities in 1932. He was arrested in 1934 following the assassination of Kirov. He testified against Zinoviev in the first Moscow trial and received a light sentence of two years. In 1936, at the second Moscow trial, he was sentenced to a further six years. According to different accounts, he either died from ill-treatment in prison or was executed in 1942. He was never rehabilitated. See Argenbright 2011, pp. 437–54. http://alter-vij.livejournal.com/117839.html, retrieved 27 April 2014. http://www.marxists.org/history/international/comintern/2nd-congress/delegates.htm, retrieved 31 January 2014.

industry in Japan. There was a [rapid] drop in foreign trade, [and] numerous bankruptcies of important banking establishments. The crisis, which originally started in the silk spinning industry in Japan, spread to the United States. America, the country of flourishing capitalism, the country of huge resources of raw materials and great reserves of productive forces accumulated in the past, has, for the first time, found itself with an enormous army of six million unemployed. Latest reports indicate no improvement in the economic situation of the United States.

The imperialist war undermined the European capitalist economy and subsequently [set] both Japanese and American imperialism on [a downward path]. The capitalist economy of the world has lost its equilibrium. On the one hand we see inflated production, while on the other hand, thanks to the ruination of Europe, there are not enough markets for America to dispose of her goods. Thus, the basis of the capitalist system has been narrowed. The Second Congress of the Comintern adopted a special resolution on the national and colonial question. This resolution laid [out] quite clearly that in as much as imperialist policy in Europe and America inevitably leads to the ruination, not only of the wide strata of the working class, but also of a considerable [section] of the rural and urban petty bourgeoisie, to that extent capitalism must maintain a predatory colonial policy, and seek to conquer new continents and fight for the seizure of new colonies. In as much as the imperialist war and the [postwar] crisis of capitalism have narrowed the basis of capitalist production, it is quite inevitable that the colonial question should now become the most important factor in the world politics of imperialism. In as much as the Far East has hitherto stood somewhat outside of imperialistic competition, of the general scramble among the individual Great Powers, it is natural that all eyes should now turn to the Far East, [in] the hope of utilising its enormous reserves of raw materials and cheap labour for the purpose of re-establishing [the] imperialist sway, both in the political and [the] economic field. Never has capitalism experienced so acute a crisis; never were the capitalists so imbued with spoliatory intentions.

The resolution of the Second Congress of the Comintern stated in direct and clear forms, that the [bourgeois-democratic slogan of] the formal equality of all nations, the idea that the people of all countries are all equal, whether of countries that have entered on the road of capitalist development or of backward countries, whether of free, or subjected, colonial countries, is an illusion. This illusion [was] dispelled by the resolution of the Comintern, which exposed the policy [hiding] behind pseudo-democratic phraseology.

During the reports of the different countries and the discussion on comrade Zinoviev's report, the comrades quite graphically depicted the meaning of the bourgeois-democratic slogan of the equality of all nations. The comrades have given a clear picture of what the slogan of the equality of nations really represents in a bourgeois society. Under the domination of the bourgeoisie, under the domination of capitalism, there can be no equality among nations, because the capital of the more powerful bourgeois countries always strives to subject the oppressed nations; because the capital of the stronger powers strives to exploit the backward nations as a [source] of cheap labour power, to exploit the natural wealth of these countries. And what is most important, what must be introduced and emphasised also in the resolution of this Congress, is [an] understanding of the fact that the road of conciliation with the world bourgeoisie, the road of conciliation with the great imperialist powers, offers no salvation for the oppressed colonial and semi-colonial countries. Many of those who only a year or eighteen months ago relied upon Versailles, who expected the aid of one group or another of the imperialist robbers, they have all come to us now, convinced of the futility of expecting anything from the great grasping Powers that would alleviate their condition. No nation can be free that oppresses other nations, and no capitalist and landlord government can give the oppressed that freedom which is as necessary to them as light, bread and air.

Comrades, in contradistinction to the bourgeois politicians, in contradistinction to the representatives of the great powers of the European and American bourgeoisie, the Communist International declares to the oppressed nations: 'Your liberation lies in your hands, but you can win your freedom only by standing shoulder to shoulder with the international proletariat, which is struggling for its own social liberation'. The international proletariat knows full well that it cannot destroy the capitalist yoke over the whole earth, that it cannot establish the proletarian dictatorship upon the entire globe, without attracting to this great struggle for freedom the most backward strata of humanity, the most backward proletarians – the very last human resources. World imperialism has bound together the fortunes of the toiling masses of Japan, China, Korea, Mongolia and Manchuria and now none of these countries can secure their freedom and unhindered national development without fighting shoulder to shoulder in the ranks of the international proletariat. In order to understand this, we must examine the conditions which prevail in those countries.

Most of the countries of the Far East are backward countries [that] are [taking] their first steps on the road of capitalist development. They are [taking] the first steps on the road to capitalist development under pressure [from] foreign Powers, under the whip of alien conquerors. In most of these countries, the prevalent form of agriculture is that of petty peasant proprietorship. The alien invaders [entered] these countries in order to exploit them. They did not upset the old, backward traditions; they did not destroy those traditions which were formed in the course of centuries, which bound all the toilers hand and foot, denying them all liberty, all possibility for independent development into a conscious force. Capitalism in the backward countries [makes] use of the medieval feudalism of China, Korea, and other Far Eastern countries [in order to] exploit their rich natural resources, their [massive] reserves of labour power and raw materials, for the purpose of extracting great profits for themselves. It is quite evident that under such conditions it is the bounden duty of every Communist, of every revolutionary, of every honest democrat, to form a clear conception of the stage of social and economic development of the oppressed nations of the Far East.

At first, the native Chinese bourgeoisie played only the part of an intermediary between European capital and the native market. The Chinese merchant was the commission agent through whom European capitalists conducted their operations among the natives, among the ignorant peasants, and helped to destroy the native industries which had [sustained] many millions of people. Foreign capital, as a sort of superstructure, established its power over the backward natives, over the backward toiling masses. The representative of South China, who participated in the discussion, has told us how foreign capital in China has gradually captured the fundamental sources of subsistence of the toiling masses. The comrade [gave us] details of every industry, and the extent to which it has been captured by foreign capital.[2] Foreign capital, in capturing a backward country and establishing its domination there, [creates] a [definite] classification of labour; it establishes a difference between the labour of the aristocratic Europeans and that of the backward, native toiling masses. The Chinaman must forever remain a peasant serf tied to the land, who gives away his last possessions to the village usurer, and through the latter he gives away his sweat and blood to foreign capitalism. The native artisan must discard his craft; his primitive tools cannot withstand the competition of European and American manufacturers in the open market, because such is the law of capitalist society. The artisan and the ruined peasant are thrown out of their economic element to eke out a miserable existence [among] the lumpenproletariat as paupers, powerless to improve [their] position under European imperialist domination.

European capital has captured into its hands the more important ports, the more important inland ways of communication, the more important political

---

2 In fact it was not the representative of South China, Zhang Qiubai, but Yu Shude, who gave these details.

centres, and has established its authority everywhere. As [a prime] example of bourgeois domination one might mention the various concessions [in China], based on the principle of extraterritoriality. Foreign imperialism has grabbed everything that could be grabbed; it has seized all the strategic points of [the] economy and politics. Foreign capital has gained control over the fate of the oppressed masses, and it forces the oppressed masses to work under its command. Capitalism, which accomplished a great revolutionary task in Europe by gathering the backward peasant masses into the factories, by teaching these masses collective labour, by organising them and imbuing them with the spirit of struggle and then making them fight for its own interests, this [same] capitalism does not develop industry in the backward countries, [but] everywhere aims to keep these countries in their backward [condition] as sources of raw materials. While in Europe capitalism converts [the] peasantry into [a] proletariat, here it converts the peasant into a tramp [who] is deprived of useful employment and is forced into joining the robber-bands in search of subsistence for himself and his family. The fate which has befallen China and Korea demonstrates the [utter] selfishness of European, American, [and generally speaking] international capitalism, whose aim is not to develop the industries of the backward countries, but on the contrary, to retard the industrial development of these countries in every possible way, in order to perpetuate its predatory interests at the expense of the vital interests of the large toiling masses. And therefore, when the naive representatives of the national-revolutionary organisations of bourgeois democracy expected aid from Versailles and similar broken reeds, they were met every time with the grossest misunderstanding of their interests, with hatred and spite. They could not be understood, because those conferences were [called] by representatives of the very class that [is] interested in the exploitation of these countries.

In China, there were several groups that supported feudal anarchy. This [has gone on] since the time of the revolution of 1911. Feudalism in China existed in the form of a military-bureaucratic organisation that reigned over a patriarchal petty peasant economic system. Foreign capitalism is trying to benefit [from] the war and its consequences, in order to tear the body of China into parts, in order to break up the integrity of Chinese territory, [by] deliberately giving encouragement to insurrection and civil war in that country in order to [secure] its predatory interests by means of disorder and anarchy.

Japanese policy is [a] policy of unashamed robbery, of open violation, well exemplified in a document issued by the Japanese black-hundred[3] patriotic

---

3 The Black Hundreds was a Russian ultra-nationalist, monarchist, anti-Semitic, proto-fascist organisation established in the first decade of the twentieth century.

party of the Black Dragon,[4] as far back as the beginning of the imperialist world war. In this document, prominent leaders of the Japanese imperialist policy wrote quite openly and unashamedly as follows: 'We must immediately take measures to induce the Chinese revolutionaries, imperialists,[5] and every kind of dissatisfied element in China to [create] disorder [ ]'.[6]

> At the same time, we must select, among the most influential and high circles of the population, a person whom we could assist in establishing a new form of government and pacifying the country. We can only do this with the assistance of our army, and if the latter protects the lives and the property of the Chinese population, [they] will have no objection [in recognizing] a government which will be ready to form a union with Japan.
>
> The present moment is opportune for the instigation of disorders. It is only financial means [that] are lacking. But if the Japanese Government [makes] use of the situation and [floats] a loan, risings will soon follow. Then we shall be able to proceed with our plans and will easily attain our aims. Nevertheless, in view of the trend of the European war, it is necessary to act quickly, for such favourable conditions as the present are not likely to repeat themselves.
>
> In studying the present form of government in China, we must consider how far a republican form of government suits the requirements of the people. Up till now, we have seen nothing but disappointment in every department from the very beginning of the establishment of the republican system. Even those who at first were in favour of the Republic are admitting that they [were] mistaken. Therefore, the maintenance, in the future, of the present form of government will render a rapprochement between China and Japan more and more difficult. The reasons for this are as follows: the basic principles [and] the moral and social aims of [a] republic clash with the basic principles and aims of [a] constitutional monarchy. The laws, and the whole system of administration, have a different character. Therefore, if Japan takes advantage, as it should, of

---

4   The Black Dragon Society, also known as the Amur Society or Kokuryukai, was an ultra-nationalist, far-right organisation founded in 1901 by Uchida Ryohei. Its pan-Asianist ideas meshed with those of some Chinese nationalists. The founding conference of Sun Yat-sen's Tongmenghui was held at Uchida Ryohei's home in 1905. See Jansen 1980, p. 370.
5   Presumably, this means supporters of restoration of the monarchy.
6   The original English text continues, obscurely, 'and this will bring about the overthrow of the Uana governments'. This line does not appear in the Russian minutes.

the present opportunity, China will have to alter its state system according to the Japanese model, and only then will it be possible to arrive at a satisfactory solution of the Far Eastern policy. Thus, it is in the interests of Japanese politics, which must aim at a permanent union with China, that together with the change of [the] Chinese government, there should also be a complete change of system and a transformation into a constitutional monarchy, which should correspond in every detail to the monarchical system existing in Japan.

Der Neue Orient, Vol. v, Nos. 7/8, pp. 234–5

These people [express] their opinions quite openly. Before embarking on their predatory policy, or rather before conducting [it] on a larger scale than they had hitherto, they expressed their aims and [presented] quite openly the programme of the Japanese Government and of Japanese imperialism; to create disorder in the country, to prevent [any] possibility [of] well-ordered economic development, and [in this way, to seize] the natural wealth of the oppressed country. What happened afterwards was the direct result of that plan. It consisted in supporting the dregs of the Chinese population, the robber elements – the *dujun*, fostering civil war, and bringing about the ruin of the Chinese nation. The representative of the Kuomintang Party has very aptly described the various Northern governments which succeeded each other during 1918. He said: 'These people drive about in motor cars, float foreign loans and do nothing. Their chief occupation consists in, firstly, selling their country, bit by bit, to foreign [predators], and, secondly, in selling themselves to these foreign [predators, by the day, by the hour, and by the minute]'.

It goes without saying that behind every militarist robber, every *dujun*, [who is carrying on civil war in China,] [stands] a foreign capitalist who makes clever moves, as on a chessboard. There is nothing surprising in the fact that Japanese imperialism expressed itself with such remarkable frankness and such remarkable cynicism in the document I quoted. It was driven to it by the interests of Japanese imperialism. Exports from Japan to China in 1908 amounted to 52 million tael, and in 1917 to 221 million tael. While in 1906 the Japanese exports to China amounted to 14 percent of [total exports], in 1917 [they] amounted to 42 percent of [total exports], a three-fold [increase]. After 1917, exports from Japan into China continued to increase. It was [precisely] because Japanese imperialism wanted to get rid of its rotten wares that it was necessary as quickly as possible to take advantage of the fact that the other imperialist robbers [were] occupied on other fronts, [to annex] a considerable part of Chinese territory, [to establish] Japanese rule in Southern Manchuria and in Northern China. The attempt of Japan to entangle China into the imperialist war of 1914 and later, due to the weakness of China, taking upon herself the noble mission of protecting Chinese interests against Germany, was nothing [more] than a diplomatic trick [to cover] imperialist aggression, well exemplified by her occupation of Shandong.

To the extent that foreign capitalism penetrates into such backward countries as China, it creates conditions of labour in the factories, and in all the industries, [that] are nothing short of [the] most brutal exploitation of the native working masses. Thus, for instance, in the two largest railway workshops, employing 6,000 people, three percent of the workers died of tuberculosis in 1920. The mortality from tuberculosis among miners has reached nine percent. One [would] have thought that Japanese capitalism which, [along] with the others, creates such inhuman conditions of labour in the backward countries, would treat its [own] workers better and provide them with better conditions of labour. But in reality we see the following conditions: [For] every thousand women in Japan in the cotton spinning industry, there are [annually] 266 cases of pulmonary tuberculosis and 217 of other forms of tuberculosis. In the silk weaving industry, there are 34 cases in every 1,000 of pulmonary tuberculosis and 47 of other forms of tuberculosis; in the weaving industry, there are 210 cases of pulmonary tuberculosis; of other forms, 280. In the hemp industry, [there are] 114 of pulmonary tuberculosis and 114 of other forms. Thus, the excess profit obtained [from] the life-blood of the working masses of China does not go to the Japanese workers and peasants, but goes entirely into the pockets of the Japanese capitalists and landowners, who [having increased] their profits by robbing another country, [are able] to exploit their own workers and peasants in a more brutal fashion. The mortality among the Japanese working class and among the Chinese workers is assuming alarming proportions. These figures remind us of those Marx quoted when describing the so-called period of primary capitalist accumulation.

It is only natural that, owing to the [current serious] shortage of raw materials, especially for the metal industries, [that] is [affecting] the whole world, that British, American, Japanese and French capitalism should turn their greedy eyes towards China. I shall read to you a list of the coal reserves of the whole world. In the United States of America, there are 3,838 milliard tons, in Canada 1,234, in China 996, in Germany 423, and in Great Britain 189 milliard tons.[7] Thus, we can see that the American Continent is the wealthiest, as far as coal is concerned. At the same time, you can see from this list that Europe is twice as poor in coal as China. Great Britain, which for many decades [was] the coal-

---

7   Billion, one thousand million.

mine for European industry, Germany, which was enabled, owing to her wealth in coal, to achieve enormous progress on the industrial field, these two countries together possess only half as much coal as China. In China, primitive methods are employed in the coal industry, which is only in its initial stages. In 1900, production reached 5 million tons; in 1917, 20 million tons.

Chinese industry is only beginning to establish itself. In 1913, the number of factories and workshops equipped according to modern technical standards [totalled] 1,913; the number of workers employed [was] 630,962. Of the 21,713 enterprises, 347 [are] equipped with mechanical motors, of which 298 were steam-driven; in addition, there were 141 electrical motors and 212 enterprises with various other types of motors. [Male workers number 478,000 and female workers number 212,000. Towards the end of 1913, there were 365 companies owning industrial enterprises, with total capital invested amounting to 69,857,000 dollars, and reserve capital of 1,857,000 dollars]. According to [the] latest statistics, factory and workshop enterprises were divided into the following branches:

Agricultural implements	6,030 employing	34,745 workers
Spinning and weaving	4,652	249,324
Food products	6,175	181,739
Paper and printing	2,134	64,352
Metallurgical	158	4,049

DER NEUE ORIENT, VOL. II, NO. 2, P. 10

The factories owned by native employers employ only hand workers. All the big industrial concerns are in the hands of foreign capitalists. If we consider China from the economic point of view, we must admit that, in the field of industrial development, it has a great future before it. No other country in the world possesses such natural wealth. No other country in the world is as thickly populated as China, and no other country in the world is so brutally exploited, excepting, perhaps, India. American and British capitalism are equally interested in the predatory exploitation of China's raw materials, but are not interested in the development of [industry in] China. For instance, the Washington Conference, together with the Quadruple Alliance which was formed there, shows that not only we Communists, but even the bourgeois democrats and the representatives of the Chinese bourgeoisie cannot have any hope in that direction. Chinese industry and Chinese capitalism cannot be developed with the assistance of foreign capitalism, with the support of American, British and

Japanese capitalism, because this is not in the interest of the great powers, because it is contrary to their colonial and capitalist interests.

Let us [now] consider the tasks [facing] the Chinese working masses. The chief task with which they are confronted is to achieve their emancipation from the foreign yoke. It is the duty not only of Communists, but of all honest Chinese democrats, to criticise most unsparingly the various Chinese politicians who are entering into any kind of understanding with any of the imperialist gangs. Comrade Zinoviev was quite right in saying (of course, not meaning the best representatives of the Kuomintang Party, [but] certain circles politically connected, more or less, with the Government of Southern China) that there are many American sympathisers in these circles. He was also quite right in saying that even the Chinese bourgeoisie has no hope that China will be able to enter the ranks of the Great Powers with the assistance of British, American and Japanese capitalism. Such hopes cannot exist, because American capitalism is, above all, interested in the exploitation of China as a labour reservoir and as a repository of raw materials. It is imperative to conduct an energetic struggle for the overthrow of the regime [that] supports feudal anarchy within the country. All Chinese democrats must fight for [a] federative Chinese Republic, and they must not rest content with working [among] the upper strata of society, the so-called intellectuals, but they must go right into the masses and must organise the peasant masses [around] the [slogan] of a democratic government which will bring down the cost of living. Every adventurer is robbing the Chinese peasant, for the latter is being robbed by the foreign capitalist, by the Japanese officer, by the Chinese *dujun* and by the native usurer. It is imperative to awaken the mass of Chinese people which forms the [backbone] of China and the chief portion of the Chinese population, [because] without the awakening of these peasant masses there is no hope of national emancipation. The small groups of workers and bourgeois-democratic radical elements will not be able to do anything without arousing the peasant masses, without telling them that in lieu of those taxes which are ruining the country and are digging the grave for future [generations of] Chinese people, that in lieu of all these taxes and requisitions, there will be established one uniform tax and an administration elected by the people and responsible to the people. Without bringing these [broad] peasant masses into the movement, it will be impossible to achieve any results. The Chinese peasant is being exploited on plantations belonging to Europeans, he is also being exploited by native usurers who, profiting [from] the rights of land-ownership, [exploit him] in his capacity of small tenant. We must raise the slogan of the nationalisation of the land, of heavier taxation of foreign concessions. [These are not only Communist slogans]; these slogans should be supported by any honest democrat who is really interested in the struggle of the [broad] masses and in drawing the great masses into the revolution. The bourgeois democrats must understand that they will not [achieve] a revolution, that they will not be able to overthrow the rule of the foreigners, without winning over the great masses. In this matter there should be no doubt, this must be understood fully. The first task confronting the Chinese labouring masses and their advanced elements, the Chinese Communists, consists in liberating China from the foreign yoke, in nationalising the land, in overthrowing the *dujun*, in establishing a single federative, democratic republic, in introducing a uniform income tax. They must establish a federative, united republic in the interests of the great peasant masses of China which, on the one hand, are the victims of the *dujun*, and on the other, are used as cannon fodder.

These peasant masses must be won over to the side of the revolution. The Chinese labour movement is just learning to walk. We are not building castles in the air. We do not expect the Chinese working class to take the commanding position which the Japanese workers [will be] able to [attain] in the near future. But the young Chinese labour movement is growing. The existing unions which were bound up [with] craft prejudices [and] which are still in many respects [old-style craft] organisations, must be reorganised as genuine proletarian unions. This is the first task. We must start a relentless struggle against the old forms of exploitation which are carried out by the help of foremen [and gang masters] in China, where the Chinese contractor [acts as a direct guide for the capitalist exploiters]. At the same time it must be definitely stated that the Chinese labour movement, the Chinese workers, must tread their own path, must not bind their fate to this or that democratic party or to bourgeois elements of one sort or another.[8] We do not intend to hide the truth. We know perfectly well that in the near future there can be no sharp conflicts between us and these bourgeois democratic elements organised in the national revolutionary organisation.[9] But at the same time we must tell these bourgeois democratic

---

8 The original English text is 'must not connect themselves with any democratic party or with any bourgeois elements'. This is a very misleading translation. The Russian text is 'не связывая свою судьбу с той или иное демократической партие, с теми или другими буржуазними элементами'. The meaning is clearly different. The original English text appears to rule out alliances with nationalists. Despite the fact that Safarov clearly speaks in favour of such alliances elsewhere in the same speech, this passage has been taken to mean Safarov was pursuing a 'leftist' agenda, out of step with Lenin. See, for example, Saich 1991, p. 95. Whiting, despite getting the translation correct, also said Safarov was opposing Lenin. See Whiting 1954, p. 82. But Safarov seems to have been faithfully repeating positions expressed in Lenin's theses on the national and colonial questions presented to the Second Comintern Congress. As it turned out, the Chinese Communists bound their fate to the Kuomintang with disastrous results.

9 Just over five years later, in April 1927, Chiang Kai-shek turned on his communist allies

elements that in as much as they endeavour to keep down the Chinese labour movement, in as much as they try to use the Chinese trade unions for their own petty political purposes and [preserve their] old craft spirit, preaching class harmony between labour and capital, to that extent will we keep up a determined fight against them. We support any national revolutionary movement, but we support it only in so far as it is not directed against the proletarian movement. We must say: he is a traitor to the cause of the Communist proletarian revolution who does not support the national revolutionary movement. But on the other hand we say: He is a traitor to the national cause who fights against the awakening of the proletarian movement, he is a traitor to his people and his national cause who hinders the Chinese working class in its efforts to stand on its own feet and speak its own language. I have before me the report of the Chinese Metal Workers Union of the city of Canton. The report ends thus: 'Bertrand Russell said: "If I were asked how China can develop her industries without capitalism, I should answer first of all through State Socialism". The writer of these lines, who is a delegate of this union, is of the same opinion as the famous English philosopher'. Bertrand Russell is the representative of corrupt, social-harmonising socialism. It [goes without saying] that the Chinese workers must reject the road pointed out by the leaders of this corrupt, compromising socialism of the European colonisers, and [must instead] follow the road taken by the great mass of the toilers of the entire world, the road of Communism. It is understood that any talk of state socialism in China without turning China into a Chinese republic, before the toiling masses of China are ripe for a soviet republic, is mere deceit. It is necessary that the working class should not isolate itself from the peasant masses of China. It is necessary that it join hands with the peasant masses and bring them light, culture, and Communist ideas. Of course China is not confronted with an impending Communist revolution, with immediate sovietisation, but at the same time the gospel of the idea of soviets, as [the] most suitable form of organisation for the revolutionary struggle of the masses and for the revolutionary control of these masses over the democratic organs of power,[10] must be preached. Soviets are the best

---

and slaughtered thousands of communists and trades unionists. Tens of thousands were killed across China in a year of purges of leftists and suspected leftists.

10   Safarov seems to be saying that soviets are not organs of state power (at any rate in the initial stage of the anti-imperialist revolution), but organs of struggle that, in due course, will become a means for the masses to exercise supervision over the institutions of a democratic republic. Zinoviev, on the other hand, in the 7th session, said 'You may boldly state that we advocate the soviet system. This form of government is possible in the countries with no industrial proletariat'. It is not clear whether these formulations are just rhetorical or indicate deeper differences.

weapons in the hands of the toilers of every country, whether it has a predominantly proletarian population or is a peasant country. The experience of the revolutionary movement in the Near East and in Central Asia most convincingly proves it, and this experience cannot pass the Far East without leaving a trace.

The problems confronting the toiling masses of Korea are [simpler]. There as well as in China we shall support any national revolutionary movement which stands against any compromise with imperialism and is ready to [head] persistently [towards] the goal of national emancipation. We shall not become confused and hesitate over the fact that some of these organisations are peasant societies, and others are religious sects, etc.

While fully realising that this movement is a bourgeois democratic movement, we nevertheless support it, as we support every nationalist movement for emancipation, because it is directed against imperialism and because it is in harmony with the interests of the international proletariat. And we demand this also from the Korean workers. There, it is Japanese imperialism which is the imperialist power [that] has destroyed the Korean aristocracy. Therefore, it is right to speak there of [a] united national front, but at the same time one must expose, in the most determined fashion, every attempt to achieve the emancipation of the country by compromise and pacifism. The March revolution in 1919 – the [great] event in the life of the Korean people – was a revolt of such down-trodden masses that it could not lead to victory. When the Korean people [advanced], full of enthusiasm, towards the serried ranks of Japanese bayonets and died heroic deaths, it was [clearly] a revolt which could not succeed. Every honest democrat must admit that it is only in an armed struggle, and by marching shoulder to shoulder with the Communist proletariat of the whole world, that the workers of the world can achieve victory over the foreign annexationists and coercionists and gain real freedom. The Washington Conference has done away with any illusions that Korea will be able, in some way or other, with the help of the imperialist countries of America and France, or any other country, to free itself from Japanese oppression. Korea is either doomed to complete extinction or it must emancipate itself on the revolutionary path. There can be no other [outcome]. The Japanese regime in Korea may be compared only with the British regime in India. Here are a few interesting figures concerning the expenditure for 1919–20.

According to the official account of the Japanese Governor General in Korea, the expenditure was as follows:

	1919 in yen.	1920 in yen.
For the household of the former Emperor of Korea	1,500,000	1,500,000
For the Japanese Governor General in Korea	3,192,000	7,202,000
For police and gendarmerie	19,826,000	41,940,000
For the construction of prisons	–	850,000
For schools	773,000	1,228,000
For public health	709,000	912,000
For Japanese garrisons in Korea	17,259,000	15,383,000

Thus, when the Japanese militarist, the Japanese officer, is counting up his expenses, he gives most of his income for the continuation of his predatory and coercive policy towards the Korean people. Korea has been plundered and conquered by Japan, and the struggle for the national emancipation of Korea as well as for the national emancipation of China is the foremost task of the Japanese working class. The Japanese working class must realise that [its] enemy is in its own country. It is the foremost revolutionary power in the Far East, and it must be the first to deal a decisive blow at Japanese imperialism, without which it will not [be able to] free itself from [the] chains which are fettering it, the fetters of Japanese imperialism. This cannot be achieved without breaking the fetters of China and Korea, without dealing this shattering blow at the policy of Japanese imperialism.

Comrades, my time is short, but I should like to speak quite briefly about the tasks with which we are confronted in Japan.

Japan is a country with a highly developed capitalism and a [large] working class which has a [great] future before it. Two-and-a-half million industrial workers, six million proletarians not connected with big industry, over 5 million small tenant farmers and semi-labourers – such are the figures which, if they [are] computed according to revolutionary arithmetic, must appear fatal for capitalism. Japan has [developed] on Prussian lines. Japanese officers have adapted themselves to bourgeois development and have absorbed in their midst the richer section of the Japanese bourgeoisie. At present the bloc between the *genro*[11] and the finance capitalists is the supreme [power]. It is a

---

11   Elder statesmen who had played a major role in the Meiji Restoration, including Ito Hirobumi, Yamagata Aritomo and Saionji Kimmochi.

plutocratic social order, masked by constitutional forms. In reality, the power belongs to the Mikado, to the old feudal families connected with various undertakings, which hold the fate of the Japanese people in their hands, as of yore. Thus, one section of these feudal families is connected with the army, [another] with the navy, and [a] third with various docks and shipyards. The Japanese landowners and nobility have become more bourgeois than the others, and even the Mikado who, as is well known, is of divine descent, is the proprietor of a smart hotel. It seems that in our times everything is possible, and even people of divine descent can own maisons tolerées,[12] big shipbuilding yards, and so on. Here, we witness the union of plutocracy with the remnants of feudal society. The Japanese bourgeoisie, which has been brought up in [a] spirit of servility, in [a] spirit of adulation of militarism and the monarchic social order, this bourgeoisie is not capable of solving the national problem.[13] The bourgeois parties of Japan are in the nature of groups and cliques and nothing else. One section of the Japanese bourgeoisie is principally connected with the big landowners and is a section of the Seiyukai, which is the party of militarist aggression. The other section, which [also] forms part of this party, and which, occasionally, indulges in liberalism, is the plutocratic, petty-bourgeois party which is oppressing the working masses. While Japanese imperialism has joined the ranks of the imperialist Powers and Japanese capitalism has become a [force in the world], the working class [has begun] to make its first timid steps on the path of the labour movement. The biggest trade union organisation in Japan, which comprises 50,000 people, is the organisation Yuakai, and has been organised by the typical trade union faker, Mr. Suzuki, the friend of Gompers.[14] The Federation was founded in 1911, and up to 1920, Suzuki together with intellectuals who are directly connected with the representatives of commerce and industry, dominated it, and even at the present moment, representatives of state socialism and retired generals, [hover around it and preach] co-operation between capital and labour under the yoke of an imperialist monarchy. But first

---

12   Brothels.
13   Presumably this means the problems of the nation, completion of the anti-feudal revolution and so on.
14   Suzuki Bunji (1885–1945) was a Christian social reformer and moderate labour leader who, in 1912, founded the Yuakai (Friendly Society) which was later renamed the Nihon Rodo Sodomei (Japan Federation of Labour). In 1926, Suzuki, with others, founded the centrist Social Democratic Party. In 1916 during a trip to America, Suzuki attacked Katayama, met with the right-wing AFL leader Samuel Gompers, and expressed understanding of the latter's exclusionary policies towards Japanese labour. He later invited Gompers to Japan and praised his 'constructive' approach to labour-management relations. See Scalapino 1983, pp. 70–1, 93.

the rice riots, which were a spontaneous outburst of unrest of the masses after the war crisis, on account of the capitalist state of affairs, and then the strike wave, led to the freeing of Japanese labour from the guardianship of the bourgeois intellectuals. Where there were 50 strikes in 1914, there were as many as 185 in 1920. In 1914, the average number of men involved in strikes was 158. In 1920 the number grew to 878. What does [this] mean? It means the awakening of the working class; it means that the workers are becoming a conscious power. [But] the great mass of Japanese labour [is not yet] imbued with the idea of the class struggle. During [some] strikes, the ruling classes terrorised the workers, who went into their temples and there prayed to God. In leaving these gatherings they would proclaim: Long live Labour and Bansai Mikado. That shows that the Japanese working class is not yet standing on solid ground. But Mr. Suzuki has already lost his influence. In 1920, a radical class wing was organised [in] the trade unions and this wing [is] represented at this Congress. These comrades who came here first called themselves anarcho-communists and syndicalists. After many talks with us, after they got their bearings [on] the Russian revolution and understood the international revolutionary movement, they came to the conclusion that they are adherents of the proletarian revolution, that they are Communists. And comrade Katayama declared that where there used to be anarcho-communists they now throw off the *anarcho* and are simply Communists.[15] This is a great victory. Really, when the better part of the Japanese working class formulate a definite attitude towards the intellectuals and their policies it is nothing more than a reaction against the social-compromising and autocratic spirit which was introduced into the trade unions by Mr. Suzuki. It [goes without saying] that these anarcho-communists and syndicalists are rightful members of the Communist International, just as [much as] anyone is.

Comrades, the union which is being welded here between the most influential elements of the labour movement is of great importance for the fate of the Far East. The Japanese proletariat is becoming a revolutionary power. It is living under worse conditions than those [we had to put up with], but still, it is organising [itself] into an independent power. The Japanese workers cannot expect to throw off the weight of oppression and make the proletarian social revolution directly. They must beat the adversary and use all means to defeat their class enemy and, first of all, they must defeat the bloc of plutocrats, the bloc of landlords. This bloc must be dealt the same decisive blow that was dealt by us, the Russian working class, first in 1917. The immediate demands must be: A

---

15   Actually it was Kato (Yoshida Hajime) who said this.

democratic republic, land nationalisation, the nationalisation of large industry with the provision of workers' control of production.

If we take a look at the data we will see that there is enough inflammable material in the Japanese village to do good service at the time of the democratic and proletarian social revolution.

According to the census of 1916–18, 219,859 families, or 4 percent of the farming population, possessed [more than] 7.85 acres of land, 1,449,340, or 26.5 percent, had over 4.90 acres, and 3,696,168, or 69 percent, had less than 2.45 acres. Large landowners holding more than 125.6 acres numbered only 3,495, or 0.07 percent. About 70 percent of the peasants have less than two acres of land. This is such a miserable lot that they are doomed to a state of continuous semi-starvation. Of course, these poor tenants and labourers are our natural allies in our struggle against the oppressors. The organisation of an independent union of semi-tenants, which was formed to unite their struggle for better leasing conditions, is the best proof of the fact that they are beginning to wake up. The fact that they are beginning to come in contact with the working class, that they are looking for its support, proves that the Japanese working class will follow the same line of union between the workers and the peasants [that] we Russian workers and peasants took up at the beginning of our revolution. They have a great future before them, and it must be stated quite definitely that, as young as this working class is, difficult as its position is, it will not shirk its duty of untying the Far Eastern knot. About 50 percent of Japanese labour consists of women, 25 percent of [the] proletariat joined the army of workers during the war. This variegated composition of the Japanese working class hinders it from using its own language, the language of the proletarian revolution, but on the other hand, when the vanguard does speak, it is quite clear that the union between the Japanese working masses and the petty-bourgeois, semi-proletarian masses will be a definite gain, and this union will secure for the working class the principal position in the common revolutionary struggle for a completely democratic political regime and give them the leading role in the social proletarian revolution. The slogan of soviets as the organ of revolutionary struggle and control of the masses of Japan must be very resolutely raised.

Comrades who call themselves anarcho-communists and syndicalists [have expressed] the fear that such a struggle using democratic institutions, in which we [never act alone and confront our opponents in isolation][16] may lead to [compromise] and the spread of democratic illusions. This is not so, and the

---

16   The original text is 'we never separate sections and meet our opponents singly'.

comrades have been convinced of this. At home, in Japan, they did not meet real Communists, Communist-revolutionists who use the political weapon in the interest of the proletarian struggle.

If we are now telling the working class that [it must march towards revolution via] the overthrow of the Mikado, of militarism and of hypocrisy, this does not mean that we are inviting it to compromise with the bourgeois parties, no matter what they call themselves. This does not mean that we are inviting the working class to give up playing an independent political role. It means that, by means of demonstrations, strikes and, if necessary, armed risings, it must conduct the struggle for the abolition of plutocratic and militarist [rule] in Japan. It means that it [must take] possession of all the means of production in order to get rid of the coercion of Japanese imperialism and capitalism.

The duty with which the Japanese working class is faced is an international duty, which demands that [it] shoulder the most responsible part of the struggle. The fate of the Far East, of Korea and of China depends upon the awakening of the Japanese working movement and upon its growing strength. This example should make it plain to every bourgeois that only the union with the proletarian movement, and only the assistance given to this proletarian movement, can lead the oppressed peoples to their emancipation.

Thus, the tasks with which the working masses of the Far East are confronted consist, above all, in the emancipation of the oppressed countries. We shall support every national movement directed against imperialist oppression, and we shall conduct a relentless struggle against all tendencies and organisations which will give the least assistance to the imperialists or to international imperialist diplomacy. The fundamental task consists in smashing up the edifice of Japanese imperialism from within. We trust that the Japanese working class will acquit itself of it with honour. I will now dwell on the separate paragraphs of the Congress [resolution] dealing with the national and colonial questions, and I will endeavour to adapt them to the situation now existing in the Far East.

It must be quite clear to everyone that only the Soviet Russian orientation, only the orientation of the Communist International and of the international labour force, as an international labour [movement], that only such [an] orientation can save the oppressed masses of Korea, China, Manchuria and Mongolia. It is only such an orientation [that] can free them from the imperialist yoke.

Comrades, the principal result of our Congress and of our discussion should be that all those who participated in the Congress should have a clear understanding of the [relations] between the national-revolutionary and the labour movements. We do not wish to impose our views upon anybody; we do not wish to force our programme upon anybody; we do not invite anyone that is [not ready] to enter the ranks of the Communist Party; we do not wish any forcible sovietisation; but on the other hand, we say that in as much as we support the national-democratic movement we demand a loyal attitude to the labour movement, to the Communist Party, to the working class. We call for a relentless struggle against imperialism. This Congress must create and [consolidate] the international solidarity of all the nations of the East. This Congress must bring about the union of the Japanese workers with the Chinese revolutionary workers and peasants and also with all those bourgeois-democratic elements that sincerely intend to fight. Proletarian revolutionaries cannot entertain the mistaken notion that we support only the proletarian movement in the colonies. It is not the fault, but rather the misfortune, of the backward countries that they do not possess a [large] proletarian class. Only in alliance with the proletarian movement will the oppressed nations obtain their freedom.

The result of our discussion must be a clear understanding, of course, that the chances of victory for the national-revolutionary movement will be [greatly] increased if the proletarian masses play an independent part in this movement, if the proletarian elements of the oppressed nations appear as leaders and standard bearers [of] this national-revolutionary struggle. The result of our discussion must be a clear understanding that the Japanese proletariat is the principal force which will solve the Far Eastern problem, that fraternal solidarity with the Japanese proletariat, with the Japanese Communists, with the Japanese proletarian revolutionaries, is the indispensable condition, not only for a successful struggle, but also for the real and final liberation of the oppressed masses of China and Korea from under the yoke of imperialism.

Long live the liberation of the toilers of the Far East! Long live the union of the workers and peasants of the Far East under the banner of the Communist International! (*Stormy applause*).

Chairman. Comrades, in view of the fact that comrade Safarov's report covers very important questions; the tactics of the Comintern as well as those of the national-revolutionary groups, which are at one with the Comintern upon this question; in view of the fact that this report contains a great deal of facts and statistics, it is proposed that it be translated into the various languages only after the completion of the two fundamental Russian and English stenograms. If there are no objections, the presidium will consider this proposal as carried.

A voice from the Floor: I wish to be permitted to speak on the motion. When will the discussion be opened on comrade Safarov's address? If the discussion is to be opened immediately, I would consider it necessary to translate the report now, so that all the delegates might take part in the discussion.

Chairman. In connection with the motion, if acceptable, there is yet another motion to adjourn until five o'clock, meanwhile the stenogram will be deciphered and translated, and the evening session will be devoted to discussions on the report.

From the Floor: That means to say that we have no other question on today's agenda besides the discussion?

Shumyatsky. That is so. Only the discussion on the report.

Chairman. There being no objections, the Presidium will consider the motion carried, and the session is hereby declared adjourned until 5 p.m.

(*The session closes at 1.05 p.m.*).

Ninth Session

27 January 1922, 11.25 a.m.

Comrade *Wong* (representative of the Korean Communist Women's Organisations) in the Chair.

Chairman. Comrades, the session is resumed. On the order of the day we have a discussion on comrade Safarov's report: *The Colonial Question and the Communist Attitude thereto*. Comrade *Din-Dib* will open the discussion.

Din-Dib [Dendev]. The Mongolian section, having fully acquainted itself with the details of comrade Safarov's report, fully endorses the line indicated by comrade Safarov with regard to the collaboration of the Communist Party with all the revolutionary-socialist parties of the Far East. Mongolia, a backward country both culturally and economically, at the present time has a democratic government and has an organised the People's Party, the party of democratic-revolutionary reforms. Mongolia will gladly join the union of the Communist Party with the revolutionary democratic parties of the Far East in order to march towards the chosen goal shoulder to shoulder with them.

Chairman. The next speaker will be comrade *Kor-Khan* of the Korean Delegation.

Kor-Khan [Ch'ae Tongsun].[1] Comrades, before speaking on the report of comrade Safarov, I wish to avail myself of the opportunity to emphasise the importance of our Congress of the Toilers and the Revolutionary Parties of the Far East. Our Congress, which has been called as a counter-balance to the various conferences and councils of the imperialist world-robbers, was to have opened contemporaneously with the Washington Conference, but unforeseen circum-

---

1 Kor-Khan was Ch'ae Tongsun (1892–?) Ch'ae moved to Russia as a child and worked as a teacher. He was conscripted into the Tsarist army in 1915 and was stationed in Turkestan. During the civil war, the Whites tried to conscript him but he escaped to Ekaterinburg where he joined the Russian Communist Party. He attended the founding congress of the Irkutsk faction of the Korean Communist Party. He was later elected to the executive committee of the Communist Party in Russia's Maritime Province. He attended the Far East Congress as a delegate of the First Korean Brigade of the Red Army.

stances caused us to postpone our Congress until 21 January 1922, i.e. until the moment when the Washington Conference as such had already achieved its purpose.

Comrades, I declare that this circumstance is of decided advantage to us. We have now obtained a clear view of the famous democratic America, which has so zealously preached the gospel of humanity and sympathy with the oppressed nations; we have also obtained a full view of the other imperialist Powers, England, France and Japan. Although we foresaw the consequences of the Washington Conference before it commenced, at that time it was only a subjective supposition, whereas now, as comrade Zinoviev has shown in his report, we are in possession of the facts and decisions of the Washington Conference. We will commit no errors in working out our common tactical line of struggle against the alliance created at Washington by the hateful world-robbers, who in the course of the imperialist war have piled up millions of corpses of the world proletariat. And now they are stretching out their blood-stained hands towards the toiling and oppressed nations of the Far East which have not yet had time to organise their resistance to the world-robbers. Comrades, the world imperialists have done their deed at the Washington Conference, creating an alliance of the four Mighty Robbers. What have we to do now? Our answer must be brief; our common road is as clear as daylight, and you, comrades, have conceived and outlined this road. Our common aim is to rally under the banner of the Communist International and around proletarian Soviet Russia. Comrades, I emphasize that this union of ours must not be rich in words and poor in deeds. [On] this union will depend the fate of the many millions of the nations of the Far East, because the insatiable world-robbers at Washington have gathered a dark cloud to suffocate us in the Far East.

Comrades, our Congress is not big [in] numbers, but as to revolutionary qualities it fully answers its purpose and its destiny. Here we have the representatives of the best forces of the vanguard of the toilers and the oppressed of the Far East. Our Congress has once more confirmed the fact that the world is divided into two irreconcilable camps. While the Japanese imperialists and the Japanese capitalists, through their representatives at Washington, have forged chains for us – the toilers and oppressed of the Far East – the Japanese proletariat has gained its class-consciousness and has sent its plenipotentiary representatives to us, their brothers by labour and by class. And this, comrades, lends tremendous importance to our Congress. Similar class-consciousness to that of the Japanese proletariat was shown also by the Chinese proletariat. The composition of our Congress is quite characteristic. It shows itself fully capable of shouldering the task of liberating the toilers of the Far East. Comrade Tao, the representative of South China, has taken exception to comrade Zinoviev's remark about some simple-minded South Chinese leaders who find it difficult to rid themselves of a sneaking regard for America. Comrade Tao, feeling offended, replied: 'Comrades, the ways of the imperialists are not our ways; we have long since buried our hopes in America, or Washington or Versailles; we have long since entered upon the path of Communism'. We cannot but welcome with the greatest joy this assurance by the representative of South China, comrade Tao. Comrade Zinoviev in his report also touched upon the revolutionary movement in Korea. He showed that among the Korean revolutionaries, there are certain leaders and organisations which cannot part with the illusion of Versailles or Washington. Comrades, what comrade Zinoviev has said is quite true. Among us there are indeed many such revolutionaries, many such leaders and such organisations that have not yet quite got rid of the American orientation. When the Communist International invited all the toilers of the Far East to a Congress of toilers at Irkutsk, our so-called Shanghai Provisional Government – that general without an army – sent its representatives to Washington instead. That [delegation] is now paying its humble respects at every door-step in Washington.[2] But this is no great loss. Why? Because the Shanghai Provisional Government never told us Communists that it had entered upon the road of Communism. Well may it blunder and hope for blessings from Washington, from America. Perhaps, as comrade Zinoviev said, they will deign to speak about Korea yet. But among us there are [also] 'Communists' who act like bats. It was these very persons, among whom there are some who call themselves members of some Party Central Committee, who supported the sending of a representative of the Shanghai Government to the Washington Conference.[3] They emphasised the necessity of it and even put obstacles in the way of our delegates who were leaving for the Congress of the Toilers of the Far East. They said: 'If the Washington imperialists find out that our representatives are going to Irkutsk in order to participate in the Congress of the Toilers of the East, they will perhaps refuse to admit our representatives to the Conference, they will

---

2 The Korean Mission to the Washington Conference consisted of the president of the Korean Provisional Government, Syngman Rhee, Philip Jaisohn (Sŏ Chaep'il) and Henry Chung. With the help of American advisors Fred A. Dolph and Charles S. Thomas, the mission sent a detailed appeal to the conference, but it was ignored. The lobbying effort cost $12,000, and was seen as a waste of money by many Korean exiles. See Korean Mission to the Conference on the Limitation of Armament 1922, pp. 3–7; see also Kim 2011, p. 86.

3 It is not clear which communists Ch'ae Tongsun is referring to. Ironically, the Far Eastern Republic, which was little more than a puppet of Moscow, sent delegations to both the Washington Conference and the Congress of the Toilers of the Far East.

ignore our representatives. Do not go to Irkutsk, Washington will solve our destinies. Our fate depends upon Washington where important, business-like men have gathered'. This is what they preached and, to some extent, they even subsidised this scheme. But, comrades, now that we are at this Congress to decide the future fate of the oppressed peoples of the Far East, I want to [speak] openly, and warn the comrades who have come here not to make any mistake in the decision of our question.

Comrades, on behalf of the Korean delegation I fully support, and consider it our duty to take as a basis of our work in the Far East, comrade Safarov's report. Nothing else is possible. Comrade Safarov's report states clearly that we Communists must work in nationalist and revolutionary organisations. As comrade Safarov emphasised yesterday, this policy was decided upon by the Second Congress of the Third Communist International. So I support it fully; I only want to repeat [it] in order to emphasise comrade Safarov's words: we shall unreservedly support all nationalist revolutionary and bourgeois organisations, but only in so far as these organisations [do] not follow the imperialists, have no connection with the imperialists, with these world plunderers, and [do] not extend to them even a finger. I declare that with elements [that] carry out a conciliatory policy, we, the Korean Communists, will never unite. Our Communist Party, which has for a long time had under its influence 7,126,000 farm labourers, 300,000 industrial workers and 292,127 fishermen,[4] [is] aimed at the union of all the proletarian elements of Korea and all possible co-operation with revolutionary and bourgeois organisations, but not with those which stand for a reconciliatory policy.

And so, I conclude [with] the cry: Long live the joint work of Communists and Nationalist Revolutionary Organisations in the Far East!

Chairman. Further translation of comrade *Pak Mu's* remarks will be done in the sectional meetings in the respective national languages. So we will continue with the discussion. The next speaker is comrade *Khwong* of the women's section.

Khwong [Kwon Aera].[5] We have been discussing the question of emancipation of the oppressed peoples of the Far East, and in that I want to remind the Congress that the true emancipation of the peoples of the Far East does not consist

---

4   This is clearly an exaggeration.
5   Kwon Aera (1899–1973) was imprisoned after taking part in the March First Movement. She was a junior school teacher delegated from the Shanghai branch of the Korean Communist Party.

in the emancipation of the men only, but also of the women. On that point I do not want to be misunderstood. I do not want the question of the emancipation of the women to become a separate question. The peoples of the Far East can be emancipated, men and women, together. The movement is one, and it is important that they should work together, that they should co-operate. Comrade Safarov [said] that in this emancipation movement we should aim towards the union of democratic principles and [the] union of democratic republican ideals. I want to remind the Congress in this connection that we should not forget the women; that they must always work hand in hand. In the labour movement, for example, the women must work together with the men. If all these movements are carried on by men only, without considering women, and also without co-operation on the part of women, they would become one-sided movements. I do not mean to say that women should be given a leading part, or that women should play the leading role, but that they should work hand-in-hand and shoulder-to-shoulder with men, and we say that we shall work together. But the first thing necessary is to give [women] their place, a separate place in the movement; they should have their proper work, separated into proper departments, so that they can carry on that work in co-operation and concretely.

In the matter of capitalistic oppression, women [suffer] the same amount of oppression as the men, and as far as oppression [in general] is considered, women [suffer] more oppression, at times, than men, though there is no time to go into detail. But in the class struggle, [as well as] in the oppression of the people by the capitalistic countries, women are the victims just as much as men, if not more [so].

Of course, very often people [say] that women must regain their lost liberty. I want to remind the Congress that women really have not lost their liberty. They [still] have it. It is their inalienable right; it is their natural right and what is due to them; [it] is born with them, and they have not lost it. But they have been hindered from exercising their rights, and it is this point that I want to make clear; that both men and women have the responsibility [to allow] women to exercise their full liberty and right [to work] with the men in this movement. Of course, women are weak. Maybe some will not agree with me, but it is a fact that they are physically weak. Nevertheless they have greater responsibility [for raising, protecting and training children, which] is also a great responsibility in the matter of building the future destiny of the nation. Nevertheless, women are also prepared to go [all the way] together and fight battles with their brothers against the oppression of the capitalists and imperialists. All you have to do is to put guns in the hands of the women and they will march side by side [with you] as they have done in many revolutions in Russia and other countries [like]

Korea and China. All that is necessary is to give them the opportunity and ask them for their co-operation and they will co-operate with all their strength and heart.

I want to impress upon the Congress that women should not be looked down upon with contempt, and that they should not be looked upon slightingly. They are not to be slighted [by] those that are gathered at this Congress, and it is of great importance that they should be given their proper place and channel to work in. They must be commissioned and delegated from their sections of work so that they can properly co-operate and work shoulder to shoulder with the men.

Kim-Chow [Yi Chaegon][6] (*Korean Youth Movement*). The main issue of comrade Safarov's report was developed along two lines. First he developed the point that the proletariat of the West must combine their strength with that of the workers of the East – the toiling masses of the East. The toiling masses of the East constitute a large majority of the whole population of the world. Let us say that taking China, India, Siberia, Japan, Korea and the other adjoining countries, including the East Indies, there are about 800 million. Unless the proletariat of the West really takes into consideration the fact that they must make use of this reserve force, it has already been shown that their present struggle may have a very acute crisis. In other words, if the proletariat of the West works alone against the combined forces of the capitalist nations of the world, they will continue to have uphill work. The point is to make use of this reserve force in the Far East, the teeming millions of the toiling masses. The toiling masses of the Eastern nations must also realise their position and they must realise that they must work hand in hand and in co-operation and become the real strength and bulwark of the proletarian movement. We must devise ways and means to effect this in a more positive way – to effect the joining of the proletarian movement of the Western countries with the toiling masses of the Eastern peoples.

The second point of which comrade Safarov makes an issue in his report is the fact that the Japanese toiling masses have a great responsibility in their relation to the revolutionary movement of the Far East, and the first step must be towards the emancipation of all oppressed peoples of the Far East. Now we must remember that this is not yet an accomplished fact but really far from it. In the same way, the Indian masses and the people of Ireland are

---

6 Yi Chaegon was the youngest Korean delegate, born in 1902. He was a law student and a candidate member of the Korean Communist Party.

oppressed, and yet, at the same time, the working masses of England are not conscious of the fact that they must oppose this oppression of the toiling masses of India and of their brethren in Ireland. The people [of] England, as has been shown in some of the reports, the working masses in England, have been brought up with the idea that their own conditions may be bettered, but the toiling masses of India and other colonies must be used to effect this improvement. In other words, the British toiling masses want to better themselves but they still want to keep the toiling masses of their [various] colonies under oppression and subjection in order to do this. Now the same thing is quite true of the Japanese working masses, in general, if not more so. As has been shown in one of the reports of the delegates, the Japanese working class is one of the oppressors of the Korean working masses. Although they work side by side, they look upon their Korean brother workers with contempt, and they also help the imperialist and capitalist Japanese Government to oppress them.

In other words, there is still a danger of the Japanese working masses clinging to their chauvinism, and there is also a danger of their clinging to the idea of the assimilation of the Korean people, [as well as] the exploitation of the Chinese people, and all the other Far Eastern peoples, in order to better their own conditions. This is a great mistake. So the main thing is that the Japanese working masses should realise that, to better their own conditions, they must first of all emancipate the other peoples of the Far East who are their brother sufferers and victims. [Therefore,] the question of internationalism must not be confused with the idea of chauvinism or assimilation. The Japanese toiling masses are [being] misled, as were the British toiling masses, and they must be awakened as to what the actual situation is. This cannot be effected in a day or two, or even in a year or two. It will take a long time. We must have no illusions on this point. We must not have illusions, as we had with regard to the capitalistic America and the capitalistic countries of Europe, particularly on the subject of the Versailles and Washington Conferences. In the same way, the Korean and Chinese working masses must also be awakened to the fact that they have responsibilities and must not regard the Japanese toiling masses as a separate element or unit. They must try to awaken the Japanese masses to such a consciousness, and the Japanese toiling masses must also awaken to the fact that they must help the Korean, Chinese, and other Far Eastern peoples. They must work reciprocally. They must help each other. There must be a mutual understanding and assistance. For this reason the Japanese delegates to this Congress have a very great responsibility in propagating this idea and principle: that we must all work together, and not work on the old basis of separate action, and we must work and try to destroy the idea of chauvinism.

Tao [Zhang Qiubai] (*of the Kuomintang Party*). I noticed that a regrettable misunderstanding crept into comrade Zinoviev's report with regard to the conduct of the South Chinese revolutionaries. Comrade Zinoviev stated that many of them were still flirting with America, expecting to obtain from that country the blessings of democratic progress. Comrade Safarov also spoke yesterday on the tactics which the Chinese revolutionaries are to pursue. I am fully in accord with comrade Safarov's report, but unfortunately I was absent while the Chinese delegates were discussing that report. I will therefore speak in my own name alone, not on behalf of the delegation. I think that there are still some points in the report which are not quite clear to me, and upon which I would like to be enlightened. Comrade Safarov said that the soviet system is quite suitable for China, and generally for all the countries where the proletariat is not in the majority. I fully agree with him.[7] I also agree that, with regard to China, it is necessary first of all to elucidate the more important questions, the question of authority, the question of taxation, the question of land nationalisation, and the question of the development of the proletarian movement. But I must say that these very ideas were laid down as a foundation by the Kuomintang Party twenty years ago. There are some differences, to be sure, but on the whole, all these points fully coincide. The question of the form of government was also discussed by the Kuomintang Party as a question of purely popular authority. Also, with regard to nationalisation, there are quite a number of points which coincide with comrade Safarov's theses. The question of taxation and all the other questions of state administration are put by comrade Safarov in a manner which is identical with that of the Kuomintang. The entire structure of the government, the entire administrative apparatus, is conceived by the Kuomintang Party in a manner which closely resembles the soviet form of organisation.[8] The Kuomintang programme contained some points which were substantially directed against the parliamentary system of Western Europe, proposing the creation of a great National Council, to include representatives from the local councils, while the franchise was to be extended to the entire population. The whole constitution of this National Council was [to be] more democratic than the existing constitution of Western European countries.

Comrade Safarov said further, that the land must be nationalised, i.e. put into the hands of the state. The government of South China had already intended to issue such a decree, but [it] was delayed by the fact that there has not been as

---

7   It is not clear that Safarov said exactly this, although Zinoviev appeared to. The 1923 Sun-Joffe agreement specifically excluded the soviet system for China.
8   Zhang Qiubai tries to paint the Kuomintang in reddish colours. Safarov later drew a clear line between Communists and nationalists.

yet a complete re-union of the whole of China. Such a decree therefore could not have been carried out universally, and its partial application might have been fraught with harmful consequences to the course of our further policy. A number of undertakings like railways, mines, etc. are already being handed over to the state by a series of legislative measures. The Canton Government has created a number of new institutions which deal with the agrarian and labour questions. Furthermore, it has established actual state control over administrative organs. In some places it has introduced a progressive income tax. The government relies entirely upon the support of the toiling masses. The members of the government are imbued with the consciousness that the working class alone is the basis of prosperity. This Southern Government, therefore, enjoys the wide support of the proletariat. The Kuomintang Party, [from the beginning], has managed to unite the workers, and even now, many thousands of the Party's members, scattered throughout North and South America and upon the islands of the Malay Archipelago, have come from the working class. With regard to the bourgeoisie, big and small, and to the bureaucracy, these elements were at first inclined to imperialism, but later on, after the revolution, a Progressive Party was formed,[9] which represents the bourgeois opposition to the Kuomintang.

Thus, everything that comrade Safarov has stated [approximates to] that which already exists in China in an embryonic stage, and we hope for gradual progressive development. One often hears grumbling voices about the state of affairs in China, particularly in the South. I must say that the cause of the revolution, as has been properly pointed out, advances at a slower pace than we would wish. For the corroboration of my statements with regard to my party, I refer you to the newspaper that we publish. You will find abundant material in them which demonstrates the internal structure of our party and characterises its activities. Besides, a book has been published by Su-Chusi-Seng-Di.[10] This

---

9   The Progressive Party (Jinbudang) was formed in May 1913 by a merger of Liang Qichao's Democratic Party, successor to the Society for the Defence of the Emperor (Baohuanghui), with Li Yuanhong's Republican Party (Gonghedang) and the Unification Party (Tongyidang). The merger was motivated by the need to form a viable opposition to the Kuomintang, which had won most seats in the National Assembly. In the event, the assembly was soon dispersed by Yuan Shikai. Within a few years, the Progressive Party had disintegrated due to clashes over Yuan Shikai's bid to crown himself emperor (Liang Qichao supported Cai E's revolt against Yuan), and China's entry into World War One. See Li, Teng and Ingalls 1967, pp. 294, 327.

10 This badly mangled Chinese name may refer to Sun Yat-sen. Sun wrote *The Vital Problem of China* (1917) and *The International Development of China* (Shanghai, 1920). A Chinese edition of the latter was published in October 1921. It may be the book Zhang is referring to.

book describes the whole substance of the national movement that is led by the Kuomintang Party in China. Comrade Zinoviev said that the Party is flirting with the American Democrats. While I cannot categorically refute this, still I do not think it is possible. I think that misunderstandings and errors may occur upon this point, yet I am firmly convinced that this has not been the case.

One more question. It has been stated here that Japan must play the most important part in the liberation of the Far East; that Japan must be the basis of the aspirations of the toiling masses. But I think that there should be no neglect of the Kuomintang Party, which has a record of twenty years behind it and enjoys the sympathy and support of the masses. I think, therefore, that in speaking of the development of the revolutionary movement in the Far East, we must connect it with the existence of the Kuomintang Party, which is of such great importance to China. With regard to comrade Safarov's report as a whole, I must reiterate that I am fully in agreement with it and am ready to accept it as a basis; but I regret that comrade Safarov did not make his report complete by the inclusion of the Mongolian question. He spoke of all countries, but did not say a word about Mongolia. (*Applause*).

Chairman. Several queries have been addressed to comrade *Tao*, and I will give him five minutes to reply.

Tao [Zhang Qiubai]. I have received two questions. The first question: how many proletarians are united through the Kuomintang Party? I will give the information that I possess. The Shanghai Industrial Workers' Union[11] has been in existence since 1920, but I do not recollect the exact date when it was founded. This union fully shares the programme of the Kuomintang Party. Besides, there exists the Amalgamated Maritime Transport Workers' Union[12]

---

11   It is not clear which union Zhang Qiubai is referring to. A Shanghai Machine Manufacturing Workers' union was established in 1920, but by communists rather than nationalists. See Saich 1991, p. 49.
12   Possibly Zhang Qiubai is referring to Chinese members of the Marine Transport Workers Union organised by the IWW in opposition to the right-wing, whites-only International Seamen's Union of America. A seafarers' strike that had just begun in Hong Kong throws light on the relative influence of the Kuomintang and Communists in the labour movement. The strike was called by the General Industrial Federation of Chinese Seamen (*Zhongguo haiyuan gongye lianhe zonghui*). The union president was Chen Pingsheng, a Kuomintang member, but the strike leader was Su Zhaozheng, who joined the Tongmenghui in 1908, but went on to join the Communist Party in 1925. The other main strike leader, Lin Weimin, joined the Communist Party in 1924. The Kuomintang donated money to the union and allowed the strike committee to operate in Canton. Harold Isaacs noted that 'in January, 1922, during the seamen's strike in Hong Kong, [Sneevliet] discovered that

with branches in a number of cities: Canton, Genoe,[13] Shanghai, and also in America. The headquarters of the union are in America. These workers also share the programme of the Kuomintang Party. Thus the Party enjoys the support of the organised workers. The exact number of workers in these unions I cannot state, because I lack exact information.

The second question was on what grounds the Southern Government [proposed] to carry out a levelling system of land nationalisation, which I am supposed to have mentioned. The comrades evidently misunderstood me. I said that the Government, in general, intended to nationalise the land. The Party was still in the process of formation and was composed of secret organisations which only subsequently became united. Until all the parts of China have been reunited, the question of land nationalisation cannot be pressed.

Chairman. Comrade Tao requests to be permitted to reply to a few more queries that have been handed in. The questioners will be able to obtain their replies at the sectional conferences. Therefore, in order to save time, I would propose to abstain from putting questions to comrade Tao just now. I have received, however, several contradictory motions on this point, and I will therefore take a vote on the question, whether comrade Tao shall reply now, or at the sectional conferences. (*The majority adopted the motion that comrade Tao answer the questions at the sectional conferences*).

Koo.[14] Comrades, we realise perfectly the harm done to us by the bourgeois. We know and feel it. We understand very well all its evil tricks and the malevolence of the union of the imperialists and capitalists of all countries. But how can these evils be removed, how can we escape the injuries inflicted on us by the bourgeoisie? There is only one answer, and that is through a revolution under the banner of Communism. This is the only way in which we can defeat our enemies. I believe that we all hold this opinion. But in order to be victorious

---

substantial connections already existed between the Kuomintang and the most active section of the young Chinese labour movement'. Seamen played a key organisational role for both nationalists and communists. Sun Yat-sen said of them 'Wherever they touched port, they spread the news to resident overseas Chinese, propagated our proposals, collected funds and performed meritorious deeds never to be obliterated'. See Isaacs 1938, p. 54; http://baike.baidu.com/subview/55002/9277104.htm; http://www.iww.org/history/library/iww/exposed; retrieved 1 May 2014. Chan Lau 1990, pp. 169–76; Benton 2007, pp. 11–12, 53. Chesneaux 1968, p. 181.

13　Presumably this means Genoa.
14　The Chinese version of the minutes lists this speaker as Guo Xuntai, which is probably a pseudonym.

it is necessary to know the relation between the forces; it is necessary to study well the situation under which the struggle is being carried on at the present moment, and make use only of those means which can be really effective. It is the task of the Third, Communist International to [continuously] study the situation and find ever new means of [struggling against] our enemies. While the Communist International's ultimate goal is the world revolution, the circumstances in which this revolution will be made are different in the various parts of the globe. We know how profoundly different the economic interests of the West [are] from those of the East. We also know that other conditions, particularly of a political character, are different in the various countries of the world. Even the economic situation of the countries of the Far East is not the same everywhere. Economically, Korea and Mongolia, China and Japan differ greatly from each other. China is both politically and economically dominated by England, France, America, and especially Japan. I think that the revolution in China will have to go through two fundamental stages: the first is the struggle for political independence, the throwing off of the foreign yoke. And the second is the overthrow of capitalism. Our tactics must be in accord with these facts. First we must expel the foreign capitalists. And in order that the foreign capitalists may be beaten thoroughly, it is necessary that the toilers of the entire Far East should [begin] the struggle simultaneously; they must start a national[15] struggle against the exploiters who oppress the Far East. We can draw into the struggle a part of the propertied classes, but this does not yet mean that we must compromise with them. We must first obtain our independence, and immediately after that the struggle for power will begin. We [have been] told here that a number of reforms are being made in China with regard to the land, etc. But all these reforms will give us no more [than] freedom in the European sense, and we [will] have to win the power for the proletariat after the first stage of the revolution is over. In this respect, I fully support comrade Safarov's report; I support it because I am a Communist. I call upon you, comrades, to accept this report and [be guided] by it in your activities in the Far East.

Kolokolov.[16] We have just received a note which informs us that the Shanghai Industrial Union of Chinese workers is in no way related to any party in China;

---

15   Presumably he means an international struggle.
16   The Soviet Sinologist Vsevolod Sergeevich Kolokolov (1896–1979) was one of the main interpreters at the Congress. In an indication of the language problems facing the delegates, Kolokolov admitted he found Zhang Guotao's speech in the third session 'very difficult to follow' because he was unfamiliar with southern Chinese dialects. See the Rus-

it is only a labour union. The claim that the union takes the standpoint of the Kuomintang Party is not in accord with the facts.

(*A comrade asks the Presidium why comrade Tao was given first 15 minutes, then five minutes, and refused the floor for the third time, whereas our standing orders are that the speaker is given 15 minutes for the first time, 10 minutes for the second time, and 5 minutes for the third time. The comrade wants the Presidium to explain this matter*).

Shumyatsky. Comrades, permit me in the name of the Presidium to clarify the misunderstanding which was shown by the question referred to the Presidium. The standing order is that [a] speaker who [has] asked for the floor in the order of discussion gets 15 minutes the first time, 10 minutes the second time, and five minutes for the third time. The second speaker speaking for a delegation is entitled to the same privilege.[17] The next speaker is comrade *U-An*.

U-An.[18] Comrades, at the last session Comrade Safarov dealt with the question of the colonial policy. This is a very important question. I should ask first of all, does everyone here understand the meaning of the colonial question and of the word *colony*? I think a colony is a territory inhabited, in most cases, by a people of a low cultural level, a territory extremely rich in natural resources which [is] mercilessly exploited by foreign plunderers. The worst of it is that these foreign marauders behave in any way it pleases them in these colonies. The rule of the foreigners is absolute. I am not the only one who thinks so, comrades. I believe this is the general opinion here. Let us take England. India is her colony, and she does there whatever she pleases. France has Annam,[19] Japan has Korea. These countries – India, Annam and Korea – were blessed by nature with rich natural resources. Is it right that they should be colonies? How do these countries like it? I [say] that there can be no prosperity in those countries, that it is the worst system possible. This is the system of colonial policy carried out by the Great Powers. I left out one country – China – and wish to ask: is China a colony or not? At first glance, China does not appear to be a colony, for she has an inde-

---

sian version of the Congress minutes, 495-154-161, Russian State Archive of Socio-Political History, Moscow.

17 Shumyatsky seems to evade the issue.
18 According to the Chinese version of the minutes, this speaker's name was Ju (or possibly Lü) Shizhen which is probably a pseudonym.
19 Vietnam, or more properly central Vietnam minus Tonkin in the north, and Cochinchina in the south. All were administrative divisions under French rule.

pendent government. However, economically and politically, China is without doubt in the position of a colonial country. [What] then is the way out of this situation? What must the colonial countries do? First of all, they must unite and rise up against the countries [that] rule them. If the rising is successful then the proletarians of the entire world [can] unite. Comrades, if we open our eyes, we shall see that with the exception of Siberia and Japan, the whole of the continent of Asia, a continent with a vast population and tremendous natural wealth, is a colony. This, comrades, is an impossible state of [affairs,] and we must therefore join the Communist movement; we must create an organised world movement out of the fragmentary movements of the separate countries. Not only the Chinese, but all the other peoples of the colonial countries must join in this movement. Long live the world proletariat! (*Applause*).

Nagano. I want to tell you how the Japanese imperialists oppress the Korean people so that in sizing up the situation in the Far East we [can draw] corresponding conclusions.

As you know, the Japanese imperialists annexed Korea in 1910, turning it immediately into a [market stall] for Japanese traders. At first only cheap, [readily] saleable goods were exported to Korea. But this was not enough for the conquerors, and in 1911, the Japanese Governor General of Korea, being an obedient servant of the Japanese imperialists, passed a law prohibiting the Koreans themselves, the native bourgeoisie, from organising business concerns.[20] By such draconian means, the avaricious Japanese capitalists developed, within [a few] years, a flourishing industry and trade in Korea.

Japan is [determined] to take hold of the Korean people and squeeze the life out of them by handing them over into the grasping clutches of her large capitalist concerns. [Monopoly rights to] enormous forests near Yaluchan[21] [have been] given over to the Japanese firm Mitsui.[22] The same firm was given the special privilege of selling [the] much-used medical product, ginseng.[23]

Toyo Takushoku, the Eastern Colonizing Company,[24] organised by Japanese capital, has been robbing and seizing the land from the toiling Korean peasantry for the last several years.

---

20 The Corporation Law of 1911.
21 This perhaps means the Yalu jiang, i.e. the Yalu river, on the border between Korea and China.
22 The original says Mizui.
23 The original text says *Jenschena*.
24 The Oriental Development Company.

Brought down to a state of semi-starvation by Japanese capital, ill-treated and beaten at every step by the Japanese gendarmes, the Korean toiling population is deprived of any opportunity of taking part in the political life of the country, of raising [any] voice of protest against the economic and political exploitation of the Korean people carried on by Japanese capital.

Under these intolerable conditions, the Korean Communist Party and a number of national-revolutionary organisations [were organised] in Korea.

We, the Japanese Communists, [greeted] the news of the organisation of the Communist Party in Korea with joy and watched the heroic struggle of the Korean toilers with the Japanese brutes with the greatest attention. We only wish that all the truly national-revolutionary organisations of Korea would take the road of active revolutionary struggle against the Japanese plunderer.

The awakening of the Japanese proletariat brings nearer the day of the coming social revolution in Japan [and] the [complete] liberation of Korea from the yoke of Japanese capital. The hopes of some elements of the Korean people, that Korea may obtain its salvation from the hands of the imperialists, have vanished completely after the Washington Conference exposed the rapacious character of international capital. The Washington Conference was called under the slogan of limitation of armaments and the solution of the Far Eastern problem. But the negotiations of the Great Powers [in Washington,] in reality, dealt with the question of how [to exploit the toiling masses of the Far East] more efficiently and intensively.

To prevent the international bourgeoisie from realising its rapacious hopes in the countries of the Far East and enslaving their population, we [have] decided here, in Red Moscow, at the Congress of the Toilers of the Far East, to seal our union with the Korean comrades, so that hand in hand with them, we [can] carry on a determined struggle with our common enemy, Japanese imperialism, and establish the rule of the toilers in the Far East.

Yakova. Comrades, I have the honour to say a few words in approval of the speech of comrade Safarov. The Japanese proletariat [occupies] a very important position in the Far East, but the Japanese workers are still weak and disorganised. They have, as yet, no strong unions but they are also rapidly awakening to the [necessity of revolution]. Yet they [remain] very weak. On the other hand, the capitalists of Japan are very strong. They [exploit] the workers not only in Japan but also in Korea and Manchuria, and are trying to exploit more in China. Moreover, the Japanese petty bourgeoisie is quite strong. So to fight against [the] capitalists and petty bourgeois is very difficult and therefore it is almost impossible to bring about a social revolution at one stroke. Comrade Safarov says that it is necessary for Japan to have a political revolution first in order to nationalise the land and the [major] industries, and secure workers' control of production.[25] In this way the Japanese workers will [secure] more freedom to organise. The first revolution, the political revolution, is not, of course, our final aim. Our aim should be, and must be, the second revolution – the social revolution to establish the dictatorship of the proletariat and a Soviet government. That is why two revolutions are [needed]. The Japanese workers must [direct] the political revolution and become leaders of that political revolution in order to make the social revolution easier. In Russia they had two revolutions – a political and a social one. The political revolution in Russia occurred in March,[26] the social revolution in October, and between these two revolutions seven months passed. But in Japan, the workers must endeavour to shorten this duration to two or three months. If possible, we must bring both the political and the social revolution about at the same time. In order to shorten the time, or bring about these two revolutions at the same time, the Communists and [the] workers must prepare for these revolutions. The Japanese workers must co-operate with the Koreans and the Chinese. The Japanese workers are very weak and the Japanese capitalists and petty bourgeoisie have learnt how to oppress the Japanese workers [and have passed laws to ensure] that the workers [cannot] learn European [methods] of fighting against the capitalists. But [the workers] are awakening. The combined imperialism and capitalism of the Japanese Government compels these poor workers to fight against the weaker nations in the Far East – Korea and China. The Japanese Government [compels] the Japanese workers to oppress and exploit these people. We are very sorry. We want to [put an end to] this. We have no enmity against the Koreans [or] the Chinese and we are trying to prevent the Japanese [workers] doing what the Government forces them to do. We want to turn upon the Japanese imperialists and capitalists so [as to] free ourselves and, at the same time, free the Far Eastern proletariat. We must work together to bring about these results. As comrade Safarov says, we, the Japanese, must help the Chinese to free themselves. We ask the Chinese workers to help the Japanese workers destroy the imperialism of Japan. Comrade Safarov [said] in his theses that in the war of 1914–18, the Japanese Government asked the Chinese Government to join the European war, but I want to ask comrade Safarov to think about that, because I [have] read the theses of the Comintern and the manifesto of the Comintern [on] China's joining the war of 1914. The theses say that Japan wanted to capture and [gain] possession of all German rights and possessions in the Pacific

---

25   This sounds very like a social revolution already.
26   23–27 February, according to the old-style Julian calendar, 8–12 March, according to the Gregorian calendar.

Ocean and China, [and that], therefore, Japan was against the Chinese joining the Allies. As a matter of fact, the greedy Japanese capitalists thought that if China joined the Allies to fight against Germany, Japan must get Germany's possessions. When America asked China to join the Allies, Japan agreed as if they had been asking China to join the Allies to fight against Germany.[27] These two differences of opinion are what I would like comrade Safarov to keep in mind.

China also had two revolutions – [they also had] a second revolution. But that revolution destroyed the Beijing Government – the emperor – and [handed] power to the *dujun* – the provincial governors.[28] Now the provincial governors have [enormous] power in the provinces. They [fight] each other and exploit the people – the workers. Not only that, these provincial governors [work] together with the Japanese imperialists to oppress and exploit the Chinese workers. So, first of all, the Chinese workers must destroy the power of the provincial governors and in that way bring about the social revolution. We must [create] a revolutionary movement and unite together in it.

Kato [Yoshida Hajime]. I approve of Comrade Safarov's speech. The Japanese workers [must] destroy capitalism and imperialism. We, the Japanese workers, must recognise the necessity for a social revolution and the dictatorship of the proletariat. Revolution is not theory; it is practice, action. In order to accomplish the Communist revolution we must use power, force and violence. Unless we use violence, not only in revolutionary times but in [all] the workers struggles, nothing will be accomplished. We must use strikes, sabotage and riots. We must use violent force and [the methods of] class struggle – [in] the struggle against the employers, [and] against the government. We must strike against everything [that oppresses] the workers. Comrade Safarov spoke about [workers shouting] 'Mikado Banzai'. Of course there are many imperialistic or jingoistic workers in Japan. Our workers are not all awakened, but intelligent workers do not [shout] such nonsense. Sometimes in meetings organised by the labour unions 'Banzai' is called out. But [these shouts are] started by the bourgeois intellectual labour leaders, especially by jingoistic labour leaders who [do not shout] 'Mikado Banzai' themselves but bribe coolies to do it. Just [as in] China, we have many [irresponsible, ignorant and poor] coolies in the city of Tokyo. The leaders arrange [for] one or two of the coolies [to shout]

---

27 This is all rather unclear. Is Yakova agreeing or disagreeing with Safarov?
28 Dujun is written Thoo-Goon in the original. Yakova is presumably referring to the National Protection War initiated by Yunnan provincial leaders after Yuan Shikai declared himself Emperor on 12 December 1915.

'Mikado Banzai'. [For every] shout they get five yen. This is the price the bourgeois leaders pay for [shouting] Banzai. But the [conscious] workers do not shout this. This shout cannot be interpreted as an indication that the workers are reactionary.

On the first of May last year there was a big parade, a [huge] mass meeting. It passed by the Imperial Palace of Tokyo. [As they passed the palace] the workers cried out that the Japanese worker's enemy was in the Kyujo[29] (Kyujo means Imperial Palace), meaning that our enemy is in the Imperial Palace, and then they began to sing revolutionary songs. Perhaps you do not know that revolutionary songs – of which we have a great many – are prohibited. One is allowed to sing alone, and [you] will not be arrested, but in company, or in a meeting, the singing of revolutionary songs [such as the Internationale or the Marseillaise] results in arrest. But on this occasion there were tens of thousands of workers in the procession, and therefore they were not stopped. Afterwards, the Government, and especially the Prefecture of Police, were surprised and amazed at the boldness of the Japanese workers. So you see, the Japanese workers are led by bourgeois leaders, and yet on occasions [such as] 1 May 1921, they not only [shout, but also act], and so they will bring about the social revolution.

Chairman. A comrade asks comrade Nagano how the Communist Parties of Japan and Korea can coordinate their [activities].

Nagano. Considering the importance of the question of coordinating the actions of the Japanese and Korean Communist Parties, I believe it necessary for the Japanese and Korean delegations to consider this question [together], making use of the fact that we are both present here in Russia. I cannot give my opinion now because it is [difficult] to do so in five minutes. I hope the Korean delegation will find time to talk [this] over with us, [so that] various ideas and thoughts [can] be expressed [on] how to coordinate the activity of both Communist Parties.

Chairman. Before closing the session, in answer to a question received from the floor, I want to state that all the reports of the delegations have already been made, with the exception of that of the representative [from] Java, who presented his report in writing. He is the only one who can speak and understand his language here, so there is no sense in having him present it orally. I suppose there will be no objection to having his report presented in writing, which will

---

29 Written as Tiodo in the original text.

be published [later]. [Also,] the Women's Section announces that their session has been postponed [until] tomorrow, in view of the fact that there is going to be an evening session of the Congress at 6*p.m.* today.

(*Session closes at 3.55 p.m.*).

Tenth Session

27 January 1922. (Evening)

Comrade *Zhang Guotao*[1] in the Chair.

Chairman. I declare the session open and call upon comrade *Safarov*.

Safarov. Comrades, the fundamental question which is before our Congress is the question of the interrelations, and the right understanding of these interrelations, between the national-revolutionary movement on the one hand, and the revolutionary proletarian movement on the other hand, in the countries of the Far East. The discussions which [have taken] place on my report have led me to believe that some of the comrades have arrived at a wrong conception of these interrelations. Thus, for instance, the representative of the Kuomintang Party, comrade Tao, asserted that the principles of the Soviet system and the basic demands [of] the Soviet revolution are nothing new in China. He said, if I am not mistaken, that the Kuomintang Party has been propagating these ideas for the last twenty years. Of course I do not in the least wish to question the revolutionary development of that Party, but I am convinced that in order to come to an understanding between the Communists on the one hand, and the revolutionary nationalists on the other, it is absolutely necessary for both sides to know each other well. We know that the party [that stands] at the head of the South China Government is a revolutionary-democratic party and we do not wish to question this fact. We are convinced that this Party has done great revolutionary work [that] was absolutely necessary in China, and we hope to fight side by side with this party in the future. But, on the other hand, we are not so naive as to imagine that this party is a revolutionary Communist party. We are not so naïve as to be mistaken as to the origins of that party, and to picture it to ourselves as [a] proletarian Communist party. Such a conception would not correspond with reality, and would put the wrong complexion on [our] relations with that party.

From this platform, which is an authoritative one, we have the courage to say, quite openly and definitely, that we shall support, have supported, and are supporting, every bourgeois-democratic movement in the colonial and semi-colonial countries, to the extent that these bourgeois-democratic move-

---

1   Tjan-Go-Tao in the original text.

ments [really aim] at the national emancipation of the oppressed peoples. I believe that this statement [expresses] our position in a nutshell. By this statement, which was officially made at the Second Congress of the Comintern, and which was already contained in the Manifesto of its first congress, we have clearly stated our point of view. We say: In colonial and semi-colonial countries the first phase of the revolutionary movement must inevitably be a national-democratic movement. We give our support to this movement, to the extent that it is directed against imperialism. We are supporting it, have always supported it, and will do so in the future, but on the other hand, we cannot recognise this struggle as our struggle, as the struggle for the proletarian revolution. If we made such a statement we should be wrong, it would be doing a [disservice] to the workers and peasants of China and Korea, [because] the peasant masses, the proletarian and semi-proletarian masses of China and Korea have a greater task to fulfil than that of national emancipation. They are confronted with the task of the *complete* liberation of their countries. Insofar as these masses, that is the proletarian and semi-proletarian elements of the city and village, take upon themselves the task of the social emancipation of the toiling masses of the oppressed countries, it is wrong, and fatal, to [create] any illusions on this matter. If we, the Communists of China or Korea, raise the slogan of a democratic government, of a uniform income tax, of land nationalisation, that is [to say] the slogans of the democratic revolution, we thereby show that we are ready to co-operate with all honest nationalist, democratic organisations, if they have the interests of the toiling majority of their country at heart. But on the other hand, the proletarian and semi-proletarian elements must organise independently in their class unions. The unions [that] are now being formed as guild and craft organisations directly connected with the Kuomintang Party cannot be recognised by us as class unions. They do not understand the class principle; they are not organs of the class struggle of the proletariat for its emancipation. Therefore, in dealing with you, [the] followers of the Kuomintang Party, as allies, friends and comrades, we at the same time tell you openly and frankly: We [support] and will continue to support your struggle in so far as it is a matter of a nationalistic and democratic uprising for national emancipation. But at the same time, we shall independently carry on our Communist work of organising the proletarian and semi-proletarian masses of China. This is the cause of the proletarian masses themselves and must be [carried out] by the Chinese workers, the Chinese proletariat. In this sphere, the Chinese labour movement must develop quite independently of the radically-minded [bourgeois-democratic] organisations and parties. I think all this is quite clear to all those present at this Congress. A number of protests against comrade Tao's statements [that] came to the Presidium fully affirmed this. For a definite historical period, we can arrange for a division of labour between us, the representatives of the proletarian revolution, i.e. the proletarian class and the semi-proletarian elements among the peasantry on the one hand, and the representatives of the nationalistic radical and democratic elements of awakening China on the other. However, both sides must understand that this division of labour must be based upon a voluntary agreement. The proletarian masses need not reject their own views; they need not refrain from organising their own class party. Only under these conditions are co-operation and a voluntary agreement possible.

I do not know who could profit by the statement that the Chinese masses are already ripe for a Soviet revolution, for the establishment of the Soviet system. If comrade Tao claims that the Kuomintang Party has been preaching this principle for the last twenty years, it can be explained only by the fact that he is not well acquainted with the principles of the Soviet system. The principle of the Soviet system consists in the self-organisation of the toiling masses, in their organisation into an independent class revolutionary power. In China, the working class is just learning to walk; it is just beginning to develop. The peasant masses are brow-beaten and ignorant, and therefore do not put forward their own demands and views. Comrade Tao's statement on the question of the land nationalisation is the best proof of it. According to what he said, the Southern Government was considering the nationalisation of land, and this project was not carried out only because this important revolutionary measure requires uniformity, it is necessary that it be carried out throughout the Chinese Republic. Therefore, according to the Kuomintang Party, it is necessary first to clear the Chinese territory of imperialists, and the marauding *dujun*; it is necessary first to establish democracy in China. This is not a correct way of looking [at] this question. As long as we want to organise the masses under our banner, and [bring] the majority of the people [to] our side, we must [address] the vital interests of the masses, in order that these masses may follow us to the end; that they be ready to die for our, and their, cause. For the Chinese peasants of Southern China, the question of land nationalisation is not one that can be settled from above by administrative reforms – for them it is a vital necessity. We must therefore carry out this revolutionary measure even in a small section of the country, in order to [demonstrate] to the Chinese peasants living on the territory occupied by the hostile forces, that where [a] democratic regime has been established, the peasants live a thousand times better, that their interests are a thousand times more secure. Without a clear understanding of this, without a correct attitude on the land question, the great masses cannot be drawn into the struggle on our side.

It is not enough to work out a good programme; it is not enough to advocate this programme in a small circle of so-called educated society; it is necessary to make it the burning demand of the toiling masses. Only then will this programme become a real live programme, a programme of revolutionary action. Therefore, I contradict comrade Tao's statement and claim that in order to arouse the Chinese toiling masses it is necessary to do much preparatory organisational and agitational work. In order that the Chinese toiling masses should organise the state system which best [suits] the interests of the toilers of all countries – the soviet system – it is necessary to do much preliminary work; it is necessary to carry on a relentless struggle not only against the foreign imperialists, not only [against] the *dujun* marauders, but also [against] the native usurers in the village and the native bourgeoisie in the city. It is not a question of the direct capture of power, but of the protection of the peasant in his everyday life from those who oppress and exploit him by charging enormous rents [that] leave him a mere pittance.

Comrade Tao [mentioned] the Mongolian question. I did not touch upon this question in my report because the fundamental question before us is that of the relations between the national-revolutionary and the Communist movement, and it is natural, therefore, that the Mongolian question was put aside. As long as the basic economy of Mongolia is cattle raising distinguished by patriarchal tribal features, to preach Communism and the proletarian revolution in Mongolia is ridiculous,[2] for it is quite clear that it is no use putting the cart before the horse; [that is to say] it is impossible to skip over a number of inevitable historical stages. Our programme, i.e. the programme of the Comintern with regard to Mongolia, consists in supporting the elements striving for national emancipation, those elements which are now in power and whose representatives are present at this Congress on behalf of the People's Revolutionary Party.[3] On the question of the relations between Mongolia and China,

---

2   But just a few years later, during the 'leftist' Third Period initiated by the Comintern in 1928, and coinciding with Stalin's collectivization drive in the Soviet Union, religion came under attack, property was confiscated from nobles and high lamas, the party was purged of 'class enemies' and tens of thousands of poor herders were recruited to replace them. Non-Soviet foreigners were expelled, devastating foreign trade. In 1930, herders were forced into collectives, with disastrous results. Livestock numbers fell from 24 million to 16.2 million within two years, reversing the period of strong economic growth that followed the 1921 revolution, during which herds had nearly tripled in size. With a Buddhist-inspired armed revolt in the northwest threatening the existence of the government, Stalin ordered an about-turn. In June 1932, the Mongolian party's central committee announced the New Turn, dropped the campaign against religion, and disbanded hundreds of collectives. See Atwood 2004, pp. 329–30, 405, 474.
3   There seems to have been general confusion about the name of the Mongolian party. It was

comrade Zinoviev gave an adequate answer. In fact, the experience of the Russian revolution and of Soviet construction in the former border states of Russia is in itself a complete answer in this respect.

I am going to deal now with another question. The comrades have not quite [correctly] interpreted comrade Zinoviev's and my statements about Japan occupying a leading position in the revolutionary movement in the Far East. This must not be interpreted in a narrow nationalist sense, as this would bring confusion into our movement. But on the other hand, comrades, we must not be too utopian, and we must not shut our eyes to real facts. It is quite true that Japanese imperialism is as reprehensible as tsarist imperialism, and that it is hated in the entire Far East. But surely, comrades, you will admit that tsarist imperialism was also hated the world over. Yes, tsarist imperialism was the international executioner and the international gendarme. Nevertheless it is because tsarist Russia coerced the peoples living on its territory, because it was one of the worst oppressor states, that the influence of the social revolution, of the workers' and peasants' revolution, was so great at the time of the November upheaval. It was so great because these peoples were drawn into the revolutionary whirlpool and were able, with their own forces and with the assistance of the Russian proletariat, to establish the soviet system and to achieve not only their national, but their social emancipation. You must admit that the destruction of this most important stronghold of imperialism in the Near East and in Eastern Europe – Russian tsarism – had a [decisive] influence on the fate of all the peoples living in the Near East and in Eastern Europe. One must be blind not to see this.

Let us now consider the position of Japan. Japan is as predatory a power as was tsarist Russia. Japan is as great a robber and as brutal a gendarme as tsarist Russia [was]. If this imperialist monster [is] overthrown by the united forces of the Japanese working class, if it [is] destroyed by the forces of the Japanese proletariat, will this not constitute a great revolutionary upheaval for the entire Far East? If the Russian revolution [was] really the beginning of the international proletarian revolution and of the struggle of the oppressed peoples of the East for their emancipation, would not the overthrow of Japanese imperialism be the beginning of the national and international emancipating revolu-

---

founded as the Mongolian People's Party in June 1920. Although it was referred to informally by Russians as the People's Revolutionary Party, the term 'revolutionary' was not included in its title until 1925, following the death of the Bogda Khan and the proclamation of the Mongolian People's Republic, when it was renamed the Mongolian People's Revolutionary Party. See Atwood 2004, p. 380.

tion in the Far East? In this question we must discard the narrow nationalistic point of view and must [accept] the position as it really is. Not only the worker and the peasant, but every honest democrat and defender of his people, must understand that there are two Japans. There is the Japan of the Mikado and of plutocracy, militarism and imperialism and coercion. But there is also another Japan – the proletarian and working class Japan to which belongs the future, and which will solve the Far Eastern problem. It is imperative to distinguish between these two irreconcilable camps and not shut one's eyes to existing facts. Emancipation in the Far East and in the whole world can only be achieved by international solidarity.

One of the Korean representatives has pointed out that the Japanese worker in Korea treats the Korean proletariat with contempt, that he is a chauvinist and a nationalist in Korea. Here again, we must go back to the Russian example. Before the revolution of 1917, revolutionary organisation among the Russian workers was very weak in our border states, as for instance in Turkestan, Kyrgyzstan and in part of the Caucasus, where no strong Bolshevist parties existed. The European section of the population in these border states had hardly any revolutionary [tradition]. And the reason for this [was] that tsarism drove the most backward sections of the proletariat, the poorest sections of the Russian population, into these border states. The dregs of the Russian population were driven by tsarism into these colonies. Japanese imperialism is doing exactly the same. But it would be ruination for the proletarian cause, and for the revolutionary movement, to consider the Japanese proletariat as so much ballast on the scales of the international revolution, simply because Japanese imperialism sends its agents into Korea [to] bribe and corrupt the lower classes among the labourers.

Without a proletarian movement in Japan, none of the Far Eastern countries can achieve their emancipation. But it would be petty-bourgeois and foolish to imagine that the Japanese proletariat will be able to do it all on its own. No, the Japanese proletarian movement is significant in the sense that the first, decisive blow against foreign and predatory imperialism and imperialist coercion must be dealt by the Japanese proletariat, as the best organised and strongest force. Organisation is an outcome of industrial development and of factory life. If we were to take the armies of occupation and add to them the mercenary troops of the *dujun* and the *honghuzi* bands, all these together would form a negligible quantity compared [to] the 400 million Chinese peasants. This handful of robbers and annexationists is only able to exploit 400 million people because the latter are not organised. It is much more difficult, however, to exploit the Japanese workers and to [put] them in a similar position. It is not a question of giving certain people privileges or of giving them a more prominent position than others. On the contrary, we say to the Japanese workers: Much has been given to you, and therefore more will be demanded of you.

The reason why we are appealing to the Japanese working class is because, when it was unorganised, it disgraced itself by innumerable sanguinary acts in the Far East. For that reason, it must be the first to break the sword of the Japanese imperialists. Therefore, we do not mean to give any preference to anyone by this appeal. We spoke precisely in the same way to the Russian proletariat. The Russian Bolshevik Communists spoke thus to the Russian workers because the Russians, including the Russian working class, had become the curse of the East, and of Europe. And this is why they had to be the first to make the revolution, and set [an] example of revolutionary heroism to all the other peoples. It behoved the Russian workers to deal the first decisive blow [to] the imperialists.

I do not agree with comrade Kato, who paints too rosy a picture and represents the Japanese working masses as fully awakened. We must not forget the power that is exercised by petty-bourgeois chauvinist prejudices. The petty-bourgeois influence is still very strong among the Japanese working class and the Japanese proletariat must struggle energetically against it. It was very good to hear that Japanese workers demonstrating in front of the Imperial Palace on 1 May 1921, shouted that their enemy was inside the palace, and to hear comrades from this platform declare that, very soon, they will not limit themselves to mere shouting, but will actually settle accounts with their enemies in the palace. But revolutionaries should never paint the situation in too bright colours. They must [comprehend] the task confronting them in its real proportions.

In summing up, we may say that, in colonial and semi-colonial countries like China and Korea, which are actually colonies of foreign capital, the Communist International and the Communist Parties are obliged to support the national-democratic movement. In these countries, the Communist Party must [call for] the overthrow of imperialist oppression, and support democratic demands like the nationalisation of the land, self-government, etc. At the same time however, the Communist Parties must not abandon their [own] Communist programme, just as they must not abstain from organising the working class in trade unions independent of bourgeois influence. Neither must they abstain from organising the working class in an independent Communist Party.

In Japan, the fundamental task of the working class is to deliver smashing blows against Japanese imperialism, to shake its position in the Far East, in order to give the oppressed nations of China and Korea national freedom for their revolutionary movement, in order to guarantee the freedom to labour to these countries, and finally, in order to [create the conditions] for the Japanese proletariat itself [to emancipate] itself from wage slavery.

Thus, we explain our point of view with regard to the relations between ourselves – the Communists – and the representatives of the bourgeois-democratic and national-democratic elements quite clearly and without any reservations. We wish to prevent any confusion of views [or] ideas on this question. We definitely [want] to avoid all unnecessary and useless attempts at painting all nationalists in Communist colours, even such nationalists who are fighting for the equality of Chinese and Japanese capitalism. We say, quite frankly that we support such bourgeois nationalists, [who are] bourgeois to the very marrow, because Japanese, American and English imperialism is the most reactionary force. We are not afraid to say frankly that we will support the nationalist bourgeoisie who are striving to emancipate the productive forces of China and Korea from the yoke of foreign capitalism. On the other hand however, we [unreservedly] demand from these bourgeois-democratic and radical-democratic elements that they make no attempt to [dominate] the young labour movements of China and Korea, and that they make no attempt to divert it from its true path [or supplant] its ideals [with] radical democratic ideals painted in Soviet colours. We will more easily come to an understanding if we tell each other [who] we really are. We have every opportunity of coming to a frank understanding, and we must take advantage of this opportunity in order that our [respective] tasks [are] quite clear. Realising these tasks, we may accomplish the great revolutionary aim towards which we are all striving – the great aim of the national emancipation of the colonial peoples and the emancipation of labour from the oppression of imperialism. (*Loud applause*).

Chairman. In view of the fact that comrade Safarov's speech is very important and that all the delegates should acquaint themselves with it in detail, the translation of it into all the Far Eastern languages, will be made in the sections.

I call on comrade *Zand-Bei* to address you on the report of the Credentials Committee.

Zand-Bei. Comrades, before giving you the number of representatives from the various countries, I will read to you the regulations which guided the Credentials Committee. They consist of four paragraphs.

The Credentials Committee has not received enough information from the delegates about their party, social position and education, but nevertheless the Credentials Committee elucidated the position from the information which was at its disposal. In all there are 127 delegates with deciding votes and 17 with consultative votes, making a total of 144.

By country: the Korean section has 52 deciding votes, the Chinese 37, the Japanese 13, the Mongolians 14, the Buryats 8, Java 1, and the Kalmyks 2. The Mongols and Buryats form one section.

The following countries have consultative votes: India 2, Japan 3, Yakutia 3,[4] China 5, and the Buryats 4.

The ages of the delegates range from 17 to 63 years.

(*After this report comrade Zand-Bei gave information on the social position of the delegates, on their standard of education, and also stated to what Parties they belonged.*)

In addition we have here two representatives with deciding votes from [among] the Chinese students from the Communist University, [as well as] two from among the Korean students in Moscow.

Chairman. Tomorrow there will be no session of the plenum, but there will be a session of the trade union section, and the resolutions of comrades Safarov and Zinoviev on the Washington Conference will be elaborated. Comrades will be able to acquaint themselves with the reports through the translations in the various delegations. The closing session and adoption of the manifesto will take place in Petrograd, where the delegates will go on Wednesday. But we shall nominate a committee here for the elaboration of [the] manifesto. I declare the session closed.

(*The session closed at 8.30 p.m.*).

---

4 Jakutia in the original. Now the Sakha Republic of the Russian Federation. In 1921, in one of the last acts of the civil war, Yakutia was the scene of a White revolt. In 1922, it was constituted as the Yakut Autonomous Soviet Socialist Republic.

Eleventh Session

30 January 1922, 6.20 p.m.

Chairman: Comrade *Shumyatsky*.

Shumyatsky. Comrades, the session is now open. We have in our midst the representatives of two of the most prominent Communist Parties of Europe – comrade Ker, the representative of the French Communist Party, and comrade Walter, a member of the Executive Committee and a delegate of the German Communist Party. I call upon comrade *Ker* to greet you on behalf of the French Communist Party.

Ker.[1] On behalf of the French Communist Party, I greet the first Congress of the Communist and Revolutionary Parties of the Far East. I regret that I have little time at my disposal. I was not expecting the honour [of being] called upon to greet the Congress of the Toilers of the Far East on behalf of the French proletariat. I left France on 12 January, when no news had yet been received about the imminence of this Congress. It is for this reason that, to my regret, I am not in a position to deliver to you the sympathies which the French proletariat entertains for this Congress.

We used to speak of the Chinese wall [that] separates China from the rest of the world. But this can rather be said of France, because France is indeed surrounded by a Chinese wall and isolated from the rest of the world, so that [hardly any] news from the East reaches France. The first Congress of the Eastern Nations at Baku gave the French proletariat the first inkling of the movement of the oppressed nations of the East.

Now when the workers of France learn that in China, with her 400 million people, a serious movement of the toiling masses has begun; that in Japan labour organisations are rapidly growing; that there is a determined movement

---

1 Antoine Ker (1886–1923) was a leading French Communist and a member of the Executive Committee of the Comintern. A teacher by profession, he was conscripted in World War One and was awarded the Croix de Guerre. He joined the Socialist Party in 1919, and supported its affiliation to the Comintern at the 1920 Tours Congress. He was detained in 1921 and charged with subversion, but acquitted. On his release, he became editor of L'Humanité. While in Moscow for the Fourth Congress of the Comintern, he was confronted by Trotsky about his membership of the Freemasons and agreed to relinquish it. Ker died suddenly in 1923. See Wohl 1966, p. 298; see also Boris Souvarine, *Comrade Ker*, available at: https://www.marxists.org/history/etol/writers/souvar/works/1923/08/ker.htm, retrieved 2 February 2014.

against the imperialists in Korea where there are also apparently strong labour organisations, the French proletariat will become more and more imbued with the idea that it must go [forward] hand in hand with its Far Eastern comrades. The French proletariat will look forward with great interest [to] the results of the present Congress.

An obstinate, relentless struggle for national emancipation is [being] carried on by the toiling masses of the Far East. Led by the Third, Communist International, this struggle will result in a triumphant victory of the oppressed masses of the Far East. I greet this Congress on behalf of the French proletarians, and if I am permitted to [submit] a motion, I move to send an appeal to the proletariat of France reminding it of its duty. The French proletariat has duties and obligations towards the Eastern peoples, [because] imperialist France has colonies in the East, whose people she exploits and oppresses. I [hope] the present Congress [will] send such an appeal to the French workers reminding them of their obligations. For there are no proletarians of [different] countries, but [only] one single world proletariat. We must strive to unite with the workers and toilers of the Far East and [advance] together with them [in a] determined struggle against capitalism. (*Applause*).

Chairman. The applause with which comrade Ker's speech was met seems to be an approval of his motion to send a special appeal to the French proletariat on behalf of this Congress. If the delegates of the Congress approve of this, the Presidium will draft the appeal in the proper form. (*Applause*).

We shall consider comrade Ker's motion first. Comrade *Walter* of the German Communist Party has the floor.

Walter [Jacob Walcher].[2] Comrades, I am very happy to be able to greet the present Congress which has gathered in Moscow – the heart of the world

---

2 Walter is referred to as Walcher in the German language list of speakers. He was probably Jakob Walcher (1887–1970), an SPD metal worker who joined the Spartacists, chaired the founding conference of the KPD, and was later elected to its central committee. In 1923, he met with Trotsky to discuss the possibility of an uprising in Germany. He was expelled from the KPD in 1929 for opposing Stalin and became a leader of the Sozialische Arbeterpartei. After Hitler came to power, he lived in exile first in France, where he again met with Trotsky, and later in the United States. He moved to East Germany in 1947 and joined the ruling Socialist Unity Party. He was expelled from the party for a four-year period in the 1950s because of his previous association with Trotsky. See Lazitch and Drachkovitch 1986, pp. 501–2. See also Ernst Stock 1997, 'Why Jacob Walter was a non-person', translated from *Neues Deutschland*, 10–11, May, by Mike Jones, available at: https://www.marxists.org/history/etol/revhist/supplem/walcher.htm, retrieved 8 June 2015.

revolution – on behalf of the German Communist Party. The working masses of the Far East are under a double yoke. They bring their sacrifices [to] the altar of their native capitalism, and at the same time they are oppressed by the foreign capitalists. Such is the situation all over the East, and in the Far East in particular, where the capitalists are ever digging a grave for the toiling masses of the [teeming] population of the various countries. [But] in the end they will find that they have dug these graves for themselves. The revolutionary movement in the East [is growing and spreading], and when it unites with that of the West, capitalism will be doomed forever.

It may sound like a paradox, but the German proletariat finds itself in a similar situation to the proletariat of the colonial countries. Germany is now in the position of a colony just as much as China and Korea. [The] German proletariat is also under a double yoke, just like the proletariat of the Far East. The German workers are oppressed by their own capitalists, and these same German workers are forced to pay heavily to the imperialists of the Entente.

How did it happen that the German proletariat with its history of a 60-year-old struggle for its interests, numbering 13 million organised workers of whom eight million declare that they stand on the platform of the class struggle – how did it happen that this mighty working class has not been able to change its conditions? The answer is simple. It did not have at its head a single, strong revolutionary centre. The German proletariat is headed by reformists who have been, [and remain], opponents of the revolutionary struggle. Thus the German proletariat has enemies, not only in the hostile camp, but among its own ranks as well. The German proletariat is forced to carry on a struggle not only against the capitalists and imperialists but also against the reformists in its own ranks. The German Communist Party was organised not so very long ago, in November 1918 when the German revolution broke out. It was formed [during] the storm of the revolution and was quite weak at first. Our best fighters and leaders were killed. Rosa Luxemburg and Karl Liebknecht, together with 20,000 other comrades, fell in battle. Many more thousands of comrades are sitting in German dungeons, which are filled with the leaders [of] the workers of Germany. The German proletariat was left without capable leaders and therefore could not develop its power as rapidly as the Communists and its vanguard would have wished. The Menshevist and reformist parties are doing their best to spread their demoralising influence over the German workers. Eight million papers are [distributed] by them to the workers throughout Germany [in an attempt] to shape their views along reformist lines, but they are not very successful. Communist influence is growing [by the] hour. The Communists of Germany now number 300,000. The Communists [publish] 35 papers and [are struggling] successfully against the [propaganda] of the social compromisers and reformists. The growth of Communist influence can be judged from the fact that the largest trade union of metal workers [comprising] 6 million members gave 35 percent of its votes to the Communists during the last elections [for] the [leadership] of the union.

Slow but sure is the progress of the German Communist Party, [the] vanguard of the German workers, though accompanied by many sacrifices. This vanguard is [preparing] for revolution, and its influence on the German working class is growing rapidly. The German proletariat realises that the proletariat of each separate country cannot achieve victory by itself. Neither the French nor the American, [nor the] Russian proletariat, nor that of any other country [can] conquer [alone]. They must unite with [their] brother proletarians in the other countries to form a united front against capitalism.

Long live the Communist International! Long live the revolutionary movement in the Far East! Long live the world revolution! (*Applause*).

Katayama. I move that comrades Ker and Walter be elected as members of the Presidium of our Congress. (*Applause*).

Chairman. The delegations having expressed their unanimous consent to comrade Katayama's motion, it rests with the Presidium to invite comrades Ker and Walter to become honorary members. We can now proceed with the business of the day. Today, we have on the agenda the discussion of the resolutions on the reports of comrade Zinoviev and comrade Safarov. I wish to remind the comrades that according to the decision of the Plenum, the elaboration of the resolutions has been left to the Presidium. The latter has put, through the Executive Bureau, its proposals for discussion before every delegation. You have discussed them and today we shall be able to [see] the conclusions arrived at by each separate delegation, and [make our judgments]. We must now arrange our procedure. I do not think that it is necessary to read the draft proposals of the resolutions elaborated by the Presidium. According to the preliminary negotiations with the various Executive Bureaux, each delegation will put forward one representative who will speak on behalf of the delegation and will express his attitude towards the proposals. There will be four speakers: the representative of the Chinese delegation, comrade Sun, of the Japanese, Katayama, of the Korean, Kho-Syl-Mon and of the Mongolian, Din-Dib.[3] After the speeches, [a] vote will be taken on the resolutions. There are no other questions on the agenda, and as no one is against it, we shall at once proceed

---

3 I.e. Dendev.

with our work. (*Translation*). As there is no opposition we shall proceed with the business part of our session.

Comrade *Sun* will speak on the attitude of the Chinese delegation to the draft resolutions on the reports of comrades Zinoviev and Safarov.

Sun (*on behalf of the Chinese Delegation*). The purpose of our Congress is to bring the oppressed peoples and the revolutionary forces of the Far East together to unite and to carry on the work towards the revolution. It has been made clear by[4] comrades Zinoviev and Safarov that this is our purpose and our delegation is in accord with their reports. The Washington Conference has clearly shown that the peoples of China, Mongolia, Japan and Korea cannot expect anything [from that quarter], and this [has made] us realise [fully] that we must unite the toiling masses of the Far Eastern peoples with the proletariat of the more advanced Western countries. We have shown many times that we all agree with this and we all want to fight under one banner. We know that we must carry on our revolutionary movement in a united form. Therefore the Chinese delegation agrees completely with the theses of comrade Zinoviev and those of comrade Safarov.

Katayama (*on behalf of the Japanese Delegation*). Comrades, I will speak on behalf of the Japanese delegation. We of the Japanese delegation concur with the resolutions proposed by comrades Zinoviev and Safarov. I have [long advocated] an understanding and co-operation of the workers of the Far East to form a revolutionary army in order to attack Japanese imperialism and capitalism, as well as the imperialism and capitalism of the Western countries which are devastating, exploiting and destroying the lives and happiness and the wealth of the peoples of the Far East. The Washington Conference shows the uselessness of expecting emancipation for the Eastern peoples from the Western capitalists. The Washington Conference made a clear-cut issue of the fact that they are not for the Far Eastern peoples but wish to exploit them, to rob the Far Eastern peoples and their countries.

We especially agree with comrade Zinoviev and also with comrade Safarov, because they point out that we, the workers of the Far East, must unite and combine our forces to attack, first of all, Japanese capitalism and imperialism. This has been very often advocated by many sections of the Far Eastern countries, especially Korea and China. We must all jointly attack Japanese militarism, [but] together with the Japanese workers and peasants. But these res-

---

4   English text says "made clear to".

olutions point out that we, the workers of all the countries of the Far East, must come together, combine and attack not only Japanese imperialism, but also that of the other Western countries, in order to establish workers' governments. So we, the Japanese delegation, are very glad to support the resolution that the Japanese, Chinese, Korean and Mongolian workers must now fight together. Though there may be Japanese soldiers murdering you and your people, they are compelled to do so by the Japanese militarist system and the Japanese imperialist Government. So the Far Eastern workers achieved a great thing when they [came] here to organise their fight for emancipation, liberation, and freedom of the workers; when they realised that they must come together to attack Japanese imperialism and capitalism and also the exploiters of all countries in the West.

Kho-Syl-Mon (*on behalf of the Korean Delegation*). The world imperialists have already divided amongst themselves all the parts of the world at the Versailles Conference. The only countries which have [not] been portioned out are the countries of the East. The Washington Conference is nothing but an assembly of sharks who have decided to divide amongst themselves the countries of the Far East. We were [well] aware of this. Nevertheless many leaders of the bourgeois classes were hoping once more to obtain emancipation with the assistance of the world imperialists, and have once more [sent] their delegates to the Washington Conference. But now the results of this conference have shown us what the world imperialists were aiming at. Their only aim is the enslavement of the peoples of the Far East. Therefore we, the oppressed peoples of the Far East, must unite among ourselves, in the first instance in our [own] countries, and subsequently we must [join] the Third Communist International and unite with the Russian proletariat. The fact that the alliance brought about by the world imperialists will not last long makes our task considerably easier. We must rally round Soviet Russia in order to overcome the imperialists who are [already] beginning to quarrel among themselves.

I fully endorse the resolution presented by comrades Zinoviev and Safarov.

Din-Dib [Dendev]. The Mongolian Section, having studied the two resolutions proposed by comrades Zinoviev and Safarov finds nothing objectionable or unacceptable in them.

We believe that Mongolia, which has just begun its independent political life, and has begun it under the most elementary bourgeois-democratic conditions, will find in these resolutions a clear and definite road for further cultural and revolutionary development. On behalf of the Mongolian Section, I declare their belief that all the representatives of the Far East, as well as the more cultured peoples, will establish [united] and fraternal relations among themselves.

Chairman. Comrades, the resolutions which are now being discussed by the plenary session have already been discussed by the various delegations and accepted by them. At this session it has been declared that, in its fundamentals, the delegations agree with the contents of the resolutions of both comrades Zinoviev and Safarov. The Presidium therefore finds it advisable to put both resolutions to the vote together. Please prepare your mandates for we shall vote immediately. All those for the resolutions of comrades Zinoviev and Safarov please raise mandates.

Both resolutions are accepted unanimously. (*Applause*).

Comrades, the Chairman of the Executive Committee of the Communist International[5] invites the Congress of the toilers of the Far East, on behalf of the Petrograd workers, to the city of Petrograd, the capital in which the revolutionary movement of the Russian workers and peasants began; to the city in which the revolution over the dark powers which were oppressing the Russian workers and peasants was crowned with victory. Comrade Zinoviev believes that the unfinished work of the Congress [can] be successfully finished within a few days within the walls of the heroic city of the struggle of the Russian workers and peasants, and he also supposes that this [proposal] will be accepted unanimously.

Since there are no objections, we shall consider the invitation of comrade Zinoviev and of the Petrograd proletariat as having been accepted unanimously. Thus we finish the business part of our session. We still have to elect a committee to revise the draft of the manifesto, which is a special item on the agenda. The Presidium believes it necessary to elect [to] this Committee the following comrades: Safarov, Katayama, Pak-Yeng, Din-Dib. Tao, and Li-Kieng.[6] Any more motions? None. We shall then consider it accepted. Permit me to close the session.

(*The session closes at 8.30 p.m.*).

---

5 Zinoviev, who was also chairman of the Petrograd Soviet and Chairman of the Council of Commissars of the Union of Communes of the Northern Region.
6 Safarov, Katayama, Kim-Kyu-sik, Dendev, Zhang Qiubai and Zhang Guotao.

The Results of the Washington Conference and the Situation in the Far East

Resolution on Comrade Zinoviev's Report.

1. The Washington Conference, which has brought about the formation of the extremely unstable Quadruple Alliance (America, Japan, England and France), has concretely proven that the Far Eastern question is at the present time the most important problem of world imperialist politics. The colossal wealth of raw material, the reserves of cheap labour power of over-populated China, the natural resources of Korea, Mongolia, the Far Eastern Republic, and Soviet Siberia – all this is whetting the appetite of world imperialism, which is vainly striving to regain its former equilibrium and is trying to make the Far East a dumping ground for its surplus products and capital.

The Washington Conference has temporarily postponed the outbreak of a new imperialist war for the domination of the Pacific.[1] But this conditional postponement was obtained by still further enslaving the already oppressed peoples of the Far East. There was no word said at the Washington Conference with regard to long-suffering Korea. British imperialism, which holds India and Egypt in subjection, as early as 1911 struck out the word *Korea* from the Anglo-Japanese Treaty in exchange for the assurance of Japan to support England in her colonial policy. American imperialism which forcibly seized the Philippines and is directly participating in the plunder of China, has also demonstrated its total indifference to the fate of the Korean people. As for the French militarists and capitalists, since the fall of tsarism, they have invariably acted as the allies of the Japanese aggressors in the struggle with Soviet Russia, thereby protecting their 'special interests' in the region of the Chinese Eastern Railroad which is dominated by the French 'Russian Asiatic Bank'. It is evident that the recent advance of the Japanese [within] the Far Eastern Republic is nothing more than the carrying out of the decisions on that matter at the Washington Conference.

---

1   There are competing dates for when World War Two broke out in East Asia. In 1937, Japan launched a full-scale invasion of China, having previously completed its occupation of Manchuria in 1931, and established the puppet state of Manchuguo in 1932. In December 1941, Japan attacked Pearl Harbor, the US colony of the Philippines, and the British colonies of Malaya, Singapore and Hong Kong.

The agreement to carry out the policy of the 'open door' in China which was accepted in Washington is a formal admission of the equality of the privileges of the imperialist robbers in the plundering of China, and is directed against Japan, who is the biggest competitor of American imperialism in the Far East. In return, Japan [has been] given the privilege to continue her exploitation of Korea, Shandong[2] and Manchuria and to extend her dominions in the direction of autonomous Mongolia, (this with the aid of her tool Zhang Zuolin), and Soviet Russia.

The Washington Conference should put an end to the last illusion entertained by the broad masses of Korea, China and Mongolia, to the effect that they can [count for the least help] on the part of the imperialists, and should prove to them that only by their own solidarity and organised struggle against all aggressors, and in union with the international proletariat and Soviet Russia, can they gain independence and freedom.

II. The defeat of tsarist Russia in 1905 [gave] a free hand to imperialist Japan in Korea. The seizure of Korea was carried out with the full agreement of the great powers, including America, who in 1883[3] had pledged herself to uphold the independence of Korea. At first, on the pretext of building highways and railroads, the best arable land was expropriated; then followed the wholesale confiscation of property of citizens of Korea, who were executed on the pretext of being political offenders. The press was gagged, the whole country was placed under martial law, and a regime of bloody terror was established. In 1910, Korea was formally annexed. [The] Japanese authorities [began] a campaign of duping the minds of the broad masses of Korea with opium and morphine and [by] spreading prostitution with all its concomitants widely over the country. The Japanese trust company Chen-Behoy-Sua has been systematically seizing peasant land and passing it over to Japanese landlords and capitalists. The Korean peasants have become farm-hands of the Japanese landlords. The entire Korean population has been burdened with unbearable taxes. The peasants have been shamelessly robbed of their products, which [are] shipped wholesale to Japan. In 1916, 42 million yen worth of farm produce was pumped out of Korea, and in 1919, the export of farm produce to Japan amounted to 137

---

2 Sovereignty over Shandong was formally returned to China in a bilateral treaty with Japan agreed at the Washington Conference. But because of China's internal chaos, the crucial Qingdao-Jinan railway, and with it economic primacy within Shandong, remained in Japanese hands until after World War Two. The Japanese also continued to station troops in the province. See Elleman 2002, p. 161; Fenby 2004, pp. 176–8.
3 The treaty between the United States and Korea was signed in 1882.

million yen. The speculation on the rice harvest reached its zenith in Korea. In 1917, 27 million yen's worth of rice was exported, and in 1919, it amounted to 113 million.

Poverty and starvation became the lot of the Korean toiling masses. Consciously aiming at the physical annihilation of the Korean people, the Japanese plunderers at the same time established in Korea a number of schools for the training of the Korean youth in the spirit of servitude to their violators under the pretext of advocating 'Pan-Mongolianism'.

In March 1919, the Korean people, having been brought to a point of desperation by the incessant tortures, violations and vilifications, rose to a man, unarmed, and [proclaimed] the declaration of independence.

This passive revolution of protest, which was aimed at [a] so-called 'civilized' bourgeois society, was drowned in rivers of blood, with the tacit encouragement of the conference that was then taking place in Versailles. But the toiling masses of Korea, after this horrible bloody lesson convinced themselves of the total hopelessness of expecting assistance from any of the international highwaymen, and have openly started on the road of revolution.

III. The Washington Conference, in the name of the Alliance of the Four Bloodsuckers, has come out solidly for the predatory policy of Japanese imperialism, so that now the enslaved and subjugated masses of Korea are fully aware that only the victory of the international proletariat, in union with the oppressed nations of the whole world, will guarantee them freedom and independence.

China, with her 400 million-strong population, has [effectively] been turned into a colony of the big plundering powers, and the Washington Conference has given its official consent to this.

The taming of China started with her defeat in the war of 1839–41 with England, when English capital forced upon the Chinese people the free import of opium. In 1858, the right of extraterritoriality was forced upon China, which means special privileges [for] foreigners on Chinese territory. Each new attack on China was followed by the exaction of all kinds of contributions from the people of China and the extortion of new concessions and privileges. With the coming of foreign merchants, warships, and troops, the Chinese people became virtual slaves on their own territory. The European, American and Japanese newcomers captured and divided among themselves all the ports, important points of communication, and the political administrative centres of China.

The crushing of the Boxer Rising of 1901 was a signal for the overt invasion of China by England, Russia, Japan, Germany and America with their punitive expeditions, and the partition of China into spheres of influence.

Until the revolution of 1911, the imperialist vultures utilized in their own interests the much-hated Manchu dynasty, but after the fall of the latter, they imposed their influence over the Chinese military clique, converted it into a pliant tool in their hands and transformed China into an arena of incessant civil strife. Japanese imperialism, taking advantage of the imperialist war of 1914, which temporarily diverted the attention of European and American capital from China, forced the latter, by means of military and diplomatic trickery, and by means of bribes to the Chinese militarists, to transfer to Japan all the rights and privileges of the former German concessions in China, which include the most fruitful land, the province of Shandong, rich in natural resources, and the whole Peninsula of Jiaozhou.[4] In 1915, Japan presented her well-known ultimatum of 21 points, the fulfilment of which would [have] reduced China to complete political, military, financial and administrative subjection to Japan. South as well as North China were destined to become a sphere of domination of the Japanese aggressors. Imperialistic diplomacy drew China into a fictitious participation in the world war for the purpose of more freely exploiting her.

Having been unable to agree with Japan during the Versailles Conference, the American imperialists attempted to carry out their economic policy in China by means of a Consortium[5] thus giving the entire country over to the rule of a bank trust in which America would play the leading part. The Consortium was proposed for the purpose of enslaving the Chinese peasantry by taking over the right of collecting land taxes, and strangling Chinese industry by obtaining a state monopoly of financing all industrial enterprises in China.

The reasons why Japan failed to carry out her 21 points in full, and why America failed to organise the Consortium were, on the one hand, the imperialist rivalry among the plunderers themselves, and on the other, the unanimous outburst of protest of the Chinese people and the struggle of the Southern revolutionists.

---

4 Jiaozhou, now known as the Qingdao peninsula, is in Shandong Province. Jiaozhou bay on the southern coast of the peninsula was seized by Germany in November 1897, on the pretext of the murder of two Catholic missionaries. In fact, the Germans had been seeking a port and naval base in the area for several decades, and Admiral Tirpitz had recommended the occupation of Jiaozhou bay a year before the murders. In March 1898, the Chinese surrendered the bay and the surrounding area to Germany on a 99-year lease. Under German rule, the village of Qingdao was transformed into a modern city. In November 1914, the Japanese, supported by British forces, took Qingdao after a two-month siege.

5 Woodrow Wilson, who had initially opposed the international banking consortium, reversed his decision and urged American banks to take part in order to counter Japanese expansion in China. See Sutter 2010, p. 32.

At the Washington Conference, America made another attempt to establish the Consortium, with more chance of success because she managed to isolate Japan by means of the Quadruple Alliance. At the present moment, when China has the greatest opportunities for development, she is being torn to pieces by the mercenary *dujun* in Manchuria and northern China, where the Japanese hireling Zhang Zuolin dominates. Most of the Chinese industries, timber and other [resources] are in the hands of foreigners. Revolutionary South China, carrying on a struggle for its national existence, is in constant danger of attack from the northern militarists and cannot hope to strengthen its position without the victory of the national-democratic revolution all over the country. The Chinese peasant, the Chinese working man and coolie, is the unwilling slave of foreign capital. The Chinese people are not the masters of their own destiny; they are dependent upon Tokyo, Washington, London and Paris. They cannot rid themselves of the barbarous rule of the middle ages, because their poverty, weakness and unorganised state are an encouragement to imperialist plunder.

The Washington Conference exposed before the world the true meaning of the politics of the great powers, and the Chinese toiling masses in their struggle for national and social emancipation cannot count on any other allies except the toiling and exploited masses of the entire world, who have already started a determined fight against imperialism with the Russian Socialist Federative Soviet Republic at their head.

IV. Having made Mongolia its prey, Japanese imperialism, which at the Versailles Conference could not settle the point as to whether it alone should exploit Mongolia, or whether it should divide its mission with America, is trying to get special rights to exploit and pillage Mongolia and her riches by means of excluding the latter from the sphere of influence of the Consortium of the international banking trust.

Japanese imperialism, at the beginning of 1919 and at the end of 1920, took up active operations in Mongolia through their agents: the leader of the Anfu Club and their plenipotentiary on Mongolian territory – 'Little Xu',[6] and their other creature – Baron Ungern, who made it his aim to enslave the Mongolian people in the interests of Japan, and to turn her into a base in the struggle of Japanese imperialism against the first Republic of the toilers – Soviet Russia. The further penetration of Japanese militarism into Mongolia was carried out by its obedient agent – the Northern Chinese militarist, General Zhang Zuolin. His

---

6 General Xu Shuzheng, see previous note.

Mongolian expedition, his plan of organising a Japanese Zhang Zuolin bank in Mongolia, with himself and the Japanese millionaire Okura[7] as the chief shareholders, the substitution of General Tzin-Dun – Zhang Zuolin's hireling – for Junstude in the province of Tu-Tupa Shahai,[8] and the instigation of China [to carry out] new adventures in Mongolia, are the most characteristic symptoms of the next stage of the offensive of Japanese imperialism in Mongolia.

Having freed herself, by an armed struggle and co-operation with the Red Army of friendly Soviet Russia, from the yoke of foreign oppressors, i.e. the Russian white guards and Chinese imperialists who are the guides of Japanese imperialism, Mongolia finally secured the opportunity [to arrange] her own affairs in her own way. Friendly relations between the Mongolian and Chinese peoples are dictated by their common interests, which are trodden upon by the international imperialists and the northern militarists. The people of Mongolia know that the imperialist plot in Washington is directed against their life interests.

v. The predatory policy of Japanese imperialism in the Far East is in irreconcilable conflict with the interests of the toiling masses of Japan. The governing clique of the military, *genro*, and plutocracy are making use of it, not only in order to enslave Korea, China and Mongolia, but also to oppress the Japanese workers and peasants. The rapid development of Japanese capitalism during the war resulted in an acute crisis immediately the favourable war situation disappeared. Japanese capitalism cannot mitigate this crisis by further annexationist policies. The working class and peasants of Japan, who are deprived of all rights, are beginning to see more clearly that only the overthrow of imperialist rule will enable them to emerge out of their state of poverty and slavery. The Japanese proletariat is becoming an independent revolutionary power which knows well that the enemy is in their own land. International proletarian duty demands of the Japanese workers that they consider the struggle for the liberation of China and Korea as their own task.

---

7   The Okura *zaibatsu* was established by Okura Kihachiro (1837–1928) and inherited by his son Okura Kishichiro (1882–1963).
8   It is not clear who General Tzin-Dun was. Junstude is a mangled transcription of a military title. Tu-Tupa Shahai possibly refers to the Special Administrative Region of Chahar, the *chaha'er tequ* within Zhili Province. Chahar roughly comprised eastern Inner Mongolia. In May 1921, the Beijing government appointed Zhang Zuolin high commissioner for Mongolia, gave him control over the Special Administrative regions of Chahar, Jehol and Suiyuan, and directed him to recapture the Mongolian capital Urga, but Zhang never carried out the plan. See Bisher 2005, p. 279; see also McCormack 1977, pp. 54–5.

The Washington Conference only temporarily postponed the new world imperialist war in the Far East. If the Japanese toiling masses do not want to be cannon fodder for the ruling classes, [but want to] save themselves [from a] repetition of the bloody war of 1914–18 on the Pacific Ocean, they must come out [as one] against their class enemies. [Nearly half] of the Japanese budget is spent on war expenditures. The working class of Japan lives under more terrible conditions than the working class of any other capitalist country. The terrorism of the ruling class ruthlessly strangles any activity of the working class. Seventy percent of the Japanese peasants are semi-proletarians working for landlords and capitalists. The Japanese imperialists hypocritically [try] to justify their annexationist policies by [citing] the over-population of their islands. In reality, the robbery of foreign lands only aggravates the conditions of the toiling masses of Japan. A people that oppresses other peoples cannot itself be free. The sword of Japanese imperialism must be broken by the Japanese proletariat itself.

VI. The imperialist plot of the four robbers of Washington [has thrown together] the destinies of all the peoples of the Far East. The struggle for national emancipation of the masses of China, Korea, and Mongolia is, at the same time, a struggle for the international proletariat, headed by the workers and peasants of Soviet Russia, against the world imperialists; it is, at the same time, a struggle for the freedom and independence of all oppressed nations. The plot of the four bloodsuckers in the Far East must be counteracted by the revolutionary union of the toilers of the Far East with the international proletariat, under the banner of the Communist International. The toiling masses of the Far East will be able to free themselves from the position of slaves, and avail themselves of the inexhaustible natural resources of their countries, only when they are able to break the chains of imperialist oppression and establish a free [regime] based upon the [fraternal] union [of] the workers and the peasants. The experience of revolutionary construction in the R.S.F.S.R. proves that the Soviet system of government suits not only the interests of the working class, but those of the peasants as well, for it establishes democracy for the toilers in the genuine and fullest sense of the word. In Japan, China, and Korea, the peasant masses, equally suffering the miserable lot of semi-tenant farmers and semi-labourers, suffer from land hunger and exploitation by the large landowners (in Korea, chiefly Japanese landlords, in China, from the exploitation of the foreign owners of large plantations and concessions), and also [by] merchant and usurers' capital. The slogan of expropriation of untilled land should find a lively response in [their] ranks. The Chinese peasants, who suffer most of all from the disorder in the country and from unbearable taxation, are in great need of a single, [low-cost] democratic government that would protect their interests, and of a system of uniform taxation and a well-organised, [elected] local administration. The chief enemy of the Korean peasants is the foreign invader, and he is not only his national oppressor but also his class enemy.

In Japan, in the very near future, the proletariat will decide the political destiny of the country. In China and Korea, the working class, as a conscious organised force, is still in an embryonic stage. Nevertheless, even in those places, class organisation is the most important condition for the political and economic emancipation of the toiling masses.

Only after the triumph [over] imperialism, achieved in conjunction with the world proletariat, will the toiling masses of the Far East be able to [establish] economic co-operation among themselves and, [together] with the advanced proletarian republics, in their own interests, ensure their free development by availing themselves of the conquests of contemporary science and [technology].

The true road to the freedom and independence of the oppressed peoples of the Far East lies through the union of the toiling masses, and with them only, against all imperialists.

The masses of workers and peasants of the Far East make up 'the last reserves of mankind'. Their revolutionary awakening will be a mortal blow to the entire world rule of oppression and exploitation.

Resolution Proposed by Comrade Chow on the Report of Comrade Safarov

Having learned of the decisions of the Comintern Congresses on the national and colonial questions, the Congress of the Toilers of the Far East:
1. Declares its complete solidarity with them.
2. Emphasizes particularly the necessity of a clear understanding of the inter-relations between the various national revolutionary movements and the struggle of the toilers for their social emancipation, recognizing that only by union with the international proletariat will the toiling masses of the Far East, oppressed by imperialism, be able to achieve their national and social emancipation.
3. Welcomes the revolutionary awakening of the proletarians of Japan, China, and Korea, and considers it an assurance of the success of the struggle.

Final Session

Held Jointly with the Petrograd Soviet at the Uritsky Palace, Petrograd, on February 2, 1922

(*Session opens at 7.20 p.m.*).

Zinoviev. Comrades, I declare the session, called in honour of the Congress of the Toilers of the Far East, opened. Comrade *Smirnov* will greet the Congress on behalf of the Petrograd Communists.

Smirnov.[1] Comrades, today, for the first time since the great proletarian revolution, we are meeting with the peoples of the Far East. On behalf of the Communist organisation of Petrograd, on behalf of the 25,000 Communists of Petrograd and their [leadership], the Petrograd Committee of the Russian Communist Party, I greet the representatives of the peoples of the Far East who have come here from a distance of thousands of miles. (*Applause*). Here, the historic Russian proletarian forces meet the peoples of the Far East; we meet here, in the building where the proletariat of Petrograd liquidated the last bourgeois government. Here we meet the representatives of those 300–400 million people around whose neck foreign capital has thrown its noose and laid its heavy hand; we meet the representatives of these countries for which the capitalists have recently been bargaining at Washington, and about which there will be some more talk in the near future in Genoa. The revolution was accomplished in Russia under the leadership of the Communist Party. Under the leadership of the Communist Party, the peoples of the near and Far East are rising. Nowhere do the toilers suffer such destitution as in the far outlying parts of Asia. The proletariat there [faces] a much harder struggle for its life, for its welfare, than in Europe. We are now [witnessing], so to speak, the last reserves of the oppressed

---

1 Ivan Nikitich Smirnov (1881–1936) joined the RSDLP in 1899. He was active on the Eastern Front in the civil war and organised the capture of the Baron von Ungern-Sternberg (an incident he refers to in his speech). At the time of the Congress, he was serving on the Petrograd committee of the Bolshevik party. He was a supporter of Leon Trotsky and the opposition from 1923. In 1927, he was dismissed from his post as People's Commissar for Post and Telegraph, and exiled. After recanting, he was appointed to posts in heavy industry, but was rearrested and jailed in 1933. In August 1936, Smirnov was tried and executed along with Zinoviev, Kamenev and others in the case of the 'Trotskyite-Zinovievite Terrorist Centre'. He was rehabilitated by Gorbachev in 1988. http://www.marxists.org/history/ussr/government/law/1936/moscow-trials/, retrieved 3 February 2014.

rising against capital. We, the Communists, have raised the banner of revolt against capital, relying on the European proletariat on the one hand, and calling the peoples of the Far East to the struggle against capital, on the other. And it is not only [in words] that we call them to this struggle – we have fought together with them in the East with arms in our hands.

We [see assembled] here four great [nations] of the East – Mongolia, Korea, China, and Japan. Not so very long ago, only a few months back, our Red Army, hand in hand with the Mongolians, carried on a struggle against the Russian white guards, who, having been armed by French, English and Japanese imperialism, attempted to create in Mongolia a counter-revolutionary bulwark against Soviet Russia and the Far Eastern Republic. Together with the Mongolians, the Red Army and the People's Revolutionary Army of the Far Eastern Republic marched over a distance of 300 versts to Urga and destroyed Ungern's army, captured Ungern himself and sentenced him to be shot. Thus Mongolia was freed from this white guard who had escaped from the Russian proletariat. Mongolia [was] freed, to a great extent, [thanks to] the assistance of the Russian peasants and workers. Now, out in the Far East, an open and underground struggle is [being] carried on against imperialism; preparations [are] being made to overthrow capitalism. In October 1917, we raised the slogan of the emancipation of the toilers of the entire world, more than half of whom live in Asia, in the East. Here, for the first time today, we have met them. Comrades, we are certain that we shall not part with them on the road which we have followed and are following now. And this present day will remain in our memories as a symbol of the union of the Russian proletariat, organised in the Communist Party, with [the] 300–400 million toilers of the Far East whose representatives have come to us. Together with them, and the European proletariat, we shall bring the struggle against capital to its triumphant conclusion. Long live the World Union of the Proletariat! Long live the World Revolution! (*Applause, singing of the 'International'*).

Zinoviev. Comrade *Evdokimov* will speak on behalf of the Petrograd Trade Union Council.

Evdokimov.[2] Comrades, the Presidium of the Petrograd Council of Trade Unions has instructed me to greet our dear guests, comrades and brothers in the

---

2 Grigori Eremeievitch Evdokimov (1884–1936) was an old Bolshevik who joined the RSDLP in 1903. He was a member of the party Central Committee in 1919–20 and 1923–27. A member of the Zinoviev faction of the opposition, he recanted in 1928, but was expelled from the Communist Party in 1934. In 1936, he was tried and executed along with Zinoviev, Kamenev

great struggle, who are present here at the ceremonial session of the Petrograd proletarian organisations. (*Applause*). The Congress of the Toilers of the Far East is taking place at a significant historical moment. It marks a turning point in the relations between the First Republic of Workers and Peasants and world capital. World capital, which in the last four years has been trying to overthrow the Toilers' Republic by the force of arms, seems to be abandoning this task for the present, having learnt the bitter lesson of the four-year struggle with our victorious Red Army. In Genoa, world capital will, of course, not strive to achieve the different aims that were put out for a mere show at Cannes[3] – the restoration of the ruined industries of Western Europe and the entire world. No, just as it did during the great world struggle between labour and capital, so will world capital at this Conference make it its first aim to concoct some new scheme, to work out [a] plan [for] some new crusade against the Republic of the Workers and Peasants. We are going to this Conference [fully aware] of the complexity and difficulty of our situation, without, however, exaggerating the danger threatening us; nor do we exaggerate the forces which are backing us. Yes, world capital is stronger than [we are], both economically and militarily. But [the] material and military forces at its disposal cannot at present be used against the Republic of the Workers and Peasants. Why? Because behind the Republic of the Workers and Peasants stand the toilers of the entire world. And [on the eve of] this Genoa Conference, on the territory of this Republic of Workers and Peasants, a Congress of the oppressed peoples of the Far East is taking place. The Communist International unites in the struggle against world imperialism not only the power of the proletariat and the peasantry, but also all the nationalist-revolutionary forces of the oppressed [nations]. These formidable forces of the Communist International are organising for the struggle against world imperialism. [What] took place in Moscow at the Congress of the Toilers of the Far East, and is now taking place here at the concluding session of this Congress, is only one of the preliminary stages for the final battle with world imperialism. It is necessary to point out another side of this Congress. There are present here not only representatives of the oppressed nationalities, but also representatives of the toilers of imperialist Japan. Japan is one of those world imperialist sharks which harrows, oppresses and exploits the peoples of

---

and others. See http://www.marxists.org/francais/bios/evdokimov.htm, retrieved 3 February 2014; see also http://www.melgrosh.unimelb.edu.au/php/pol_individ.php?action=indinfo&indid=46, retrieved 3 March 2014.

3   The Cannes conference, 6–13 January 1922, attended by Great Britain, France, Belgium, Japan, Italy and Germany, set the scene for the Genoa conference by agreeing to Lloyd George's proposal to invite Soviet Russia and Germany to a meeting on economic issues.

the Far East. The toilers of Japan are represented at this Congress only [by] a proletarian revolutionary element. The Petrograd workers greet their comrades in Japan and express their admiration for their struggle against Japanese imperialism in the name of emancipation, not only of those toilers who are oppressed by Japanese imperialism outside of Japan, but also in the name of freedom for the Japanese toiling masses themselves. (*Applause*).

We greet the representatives of the oppressed nationalities and we say to them: comrades, you will not rid yourselves of the yoke of foreign exploitation, nor that of native exploitation, as long as you do not build a single revolutionary front directed first of all against the imperialist rulers of the globe. (*Applause*).

In greeting all our dear guests, we tell them on behalf of the Petrograd workers: The Russian working class had to overcome many obstacles on the thorny path of the civil war; difficult is the position of the Soviet Republic which this year has been stricken with the additional misfortune of the famine in the Volga region. The Russian working class is weary; the industries of the Soviet Republic [have been disrupted]. But despite all that, in [this] most complex and difficult situation, we have never refused, and never will refuse, to support the international revolutionary movement of the toiling masses (*Loud applause*).

I shall avail myself of the opportunity to greet, on behalf of the Petrograd Council of Trade Unions, the young trade union organisations of Japan, China and Korea. I refer particularly to the comrades of Japan, where the trade unions have already shown their capacity [to] struggle against capital, and call upon them to strengthen, by all means, the revolutionary trade union movement, to see to it that the vanguard of the toiling masses, organised in trade unions, led by the proletarian revolutionary party, [tries] to draw into the revolutionary movement the vast masses of the oppressed workers and poor peasants of Japan. I call upon the Japanese comrades to help organise and develop the trade union movement in the other countries of the Far East. In this work, our Japanese comrades and the comrades of the other countries of the Far East [can] expect all possible support, not only from the Russian trade unions, but also from the international federation of revolutionary trade unions – the Red Labour Union International.

In conclusion, I again greet our dear comrades and brothers in arms, and express my deep conviction that our comrades who are present here today will do everything possible to quickly build a up mighty united revolutionary front of the toilers of the Far East, and link up this front of the toilers of the Far East with the world united revolutionary proletarian front under the leadership of the Third Communist International, to the glory, happiness, and the triumph of the toilers, and to the doom of international capital. (*Applause, singing of the 'International'*).

Zinoviev. Comrade *Naumov* will speak on behalf of the Revolutionary Military Council of the District and of the Fleet.

Naumov.[4] Comrades, delegates of the Congress of the Peoples of the Far East, accept the greetings of the Red Army men of the Military District of Petrograd and of the sailors of the Baltic Fleet. Comrades, during the Russian revolution, it was our lot to meet the formidable forces of the Western imperialists, who compelled us to learn how to defeat them. We have learned to meet military danger boldly, proudly, and in full certainty that we shall come out victorious. We greet you here today in our Red Petrograd where not only the October Revolution began, but where our Red Army was born, where during all the revolutionary [actions] and during the October days, the Red Army men and sailors of the Baltic Fleet played a most important part. You see us now in [a] city engaged in economic reconstruction, without the pomp and glory of military show. Let this not trouble you. When you are [ready] to do what we [did] in October 1917 in Russia, and in Petrograd in particular, not only hundreds, but thousands and hundreds of thousands of workers and peasants will be found who learned to wield arms during the civil war to defeat even the mightiest of enemies. These hundreds and thousands impatiently wait for the opportunity to come to your aid and help you organise your forces. (*Applause*). Comrades, we do not doubt that sooner or later the long awaited moment will come, and you, the toilers of the Far East, will meet among your advancing ranks those comrades who [previously] fought in the ranks of the glorious Russian Red Army and Red Navy. In greeting you on behalf of the Red soldiers and sailors of the Petrograd District and the Baltic Fleets, I say you can boldly, without fear, continue the great work begun by us. From here, from the ranks of our Russian workers and peasants, many will come to your aid. Tell [the] comrades you are representing at this Congress that among the Russian workers and peasants there are many a thousand who will come to help you in the military struggle. The time is not far off when your Red Army and your Red sailors will be doing heroic deeds on the field of battle, when your workers, your peasants, your soldiers and sailors, marching under the banner of the Communist International, will cover it with greater glory, and the proletarian revolution will be reinforced by detachments who will come from the Far East. (*Applause, singing of the 'International'*).

---

4 I.K. Naumov was a member of the Petrograd committee of the Bolshevik party in 1917. His recollections of the Russian revolution were published in French as *Les Journees d'Octobre*. He was jailed in 1934 as an associate of Zinoviev. See Rabinowitch 1999, pp. 92–3; see also Medvedev and Shriver 1989, p. 347.

Zinoviev. I call upon comrade *Nikolaeva* to address you on behalf of the Petrograd working women.

Nikolaeva.[5] Comrades, in the name of the working women [of] Petrograd, I bid welcome to the representatives of the Far East. The comrades who have preceded me have already spoken of the enormous significance of your presence here in our glorious Petrograd. I should like to tell our Far Eastern comrades about the part the Petrograd working women played in our revolution, and also about the difficult and painful conditions under which the Petrograd working women, as well as the working men, have had to carry on the struggle. We know that the proletariat cannot win any victories without the active participation of working women in the revolutionary struggle. We know this [from] our own four years' experience. The Russian working women, and especially the working women of Petrograd, have contributed a glorious page to the history of the world working class struggle. We shall never forget that golden page. One has only to remember those times when the enemy was nearing Petrograd in the days of Yudenich, and also in last year's Kronstadt days. During those terrible days, the working women took an active part in the struggle and fulfilled every task which was allotted to them in this revolutionary struggle. But comrades, when we look upon the working women of the Near and the Far East, as I remember them at last July's women's conference, we realise that they have not yet grasped the full significance of the proletarian struggle. In the hall where the conference was held, they appeared covered with thick veils, from behind which they were timidly looking round. This is a sign that the women of the East are not yet familiar with the struggle of the working class. Among the 200 Far Eastern delegates here, we see only seven women. This is a sign that the working women in the East have not been sufficiently drawn into the workers' movement. Nevertheless, it seems that these seven women are taking an active part in the working class struggle. I think that, having seen the Petrograd and all the Russian working women taking part in the revolution together with the men, they will also endeavour to draw the working women of their countries into the revolutionary struggle. Comrades, four years ago we seemed to be standing alone, and it seemed that our Western comrades were not giv-

---

5   Klavdia Ivanovna Nikolaeva (1893–1944) was the daughter of a worker and took part in the 1905 and 1917 revolutions. She was the editor of Rabotnitsa (Woman Worker) and a leading figure in the first All-Russian Congress of Women Workers and Peasants in 1918. She later served on the Central Committee of the Communist Party, the Central Executive Committee of the Soviet Union, and the Presidium of the Supreme Soviet. She is buried in the Kremlin Wall. See 'Nikolaeva, Klavdiia Ivanova', in *The Great Soviet Encyclopedia* (1979 edition).

ing us sufficient support in our struggle. But today we witness the awakening of the East and are rejoicing, notwithstanding our misery and our weariness.[6] Our comrades from the Far East will see with their own eyes our great misery – perhaps they already noticed it when they set foot on the territory of Soviet Russia. Nevertheless, regardless of this poverty and misery, we, the Petrograd working men and women, are now convinced of the final victory of the world proletariat. If four years ago we seemed to be lonely, we have now side by side with us the wakening east. This will give us more energy, courage and boldness, and will be an incentive to go forward on the revolutionary path, and to raise still higher the banner of the Communist International, until the final proletarian victory [is] achieved. Comrades, I am convinced that the women of the East will play the same role as the Russian working women in the victory of the world proletariat. (*Applause, singing of the 'International'*).

Zinoviev. Comrades, now I will call on the representatives of the biggest delegations taking part in the Far Eastern Congress. The first to address you will be a railwayman from the Beijing-Mukden[7] Railway, the Communist comrade *Lang-Tsa-Sin*.

Lang-Tsa-Sin.[8] Comrades, in the name of the Chinese toiling masses I wish to say a few words to you. The toiling masses of the Far East have been oppressed and exploited by the foreign imperialists and capitalists for many years. As we had no experience in fighting the imperialists and capitalists, they were able to oppress us far more than any other people. We were able to learn many things from the Russians after the Revolution. Now we know how to organise ourselves and how to conduct the fight against our oppressors. Now we have come to organise and to fight together with you against our enemies – world imperialism and capitalism. Our Congress, which was held in Moscow and had eleven sessions, has decided many important questions and has adopted the resolutions and programme of the Second Congress of the Communist International. This shows that the Far Eastern toiling masses are now working under the banner of the Communist international and are uniting with Soviet Russia and with you comrades. We are finishing our Congress here in Red Petrograd, the starting point of the world revolution, the proletarian revolution. This Congress proves our solidarity with the Communist International. It proves that the world revolution which started in Petrograd has reached all over the world.

---

6 The original says 'misery and lassitude'.
7 Now Shenyang.
8 Perhaps Zhang Guotao or Deng Pei. Both were railworkers' leaders.

It proves that the proletarian world revolution is victorious on a worldwide scale and that we have joined with you, our Russian comrades, in fighting world imperialism and in creating a new economic life.

We have learned much here and we [will] go back to our homes to carry on practical work for the revolution against capitalism and imperialism.

Long Live the Third International! Long Live Soviet Russia! Long live the union of the toiling masses of the world!

Zinoviev. Comrades, we will now call upon a man who personifies a large part of the history of the world's labour movement, and is at the same time the representative of the proletarian movement of the Far East. I am speaking of the historical leader of the Japanese labour movement, comrade Katayama. (*Cheers*). Comrade Katayama was the founder of the first labour union in Japan, the Railway Workers' Union, for he was himself a railway worker. During several decades afterwards, he was in the front ranks of the old Second International. During the Russo-Japanese war he fulfilled his sacred duty as a revolutionary internationalist, fighting against the Japanese bourgeois Government. Everybody recollects the part he played at the Amsterdam International Congress when, in the midst of war between Russia and Japan, he voiced his protest against the Japanese Government and held out the hand of fellowship to the then representative of the Russian revolutionary workers, the late Plekhanov.[9] Many of the leaders of the Second International, as you know, upon the outbreak of the imperialist war, betrayed the cause of the working class. Not so comrade Katayama. He was, and has remained, in the ranks of the militant proletariat. Now he is a member of the Executive Committee of the Communist International, as the representative of Japan. We are all happy to see in our midst this oldest and most devoted herald of Communism in the Far East. (*Prolonged cheers*). Comrade Katayama has the floor.

Katayama. Comrades, fellow workers of Petrograd! I bring to you the hearty greetings of the Japanese workers and the Japanese Communist Party. Comrades, it gives me great pleasure to tell you that the Japanese workers are dissatisfied with the present Japanese Government, though they are compelled to fight against Siberia now. We know that the Japanese workers are heart and soul with you, comrades and workers of Petrograd. The Japanese workers, for many years, have been oppressed and exploited by foreign capitalists and also

---

9 Katayama shook hands with Plekhanov in a symbolic gesture of internationalism at the Sixth Congress of the Second International held in Amsterdam 14–18 August 1904 in the midst of Russo-Japanese war.

by the Japanese Government. But I bring you news that the Japanese workers are already beginning to awaken, to organise labour unions, and we have already organised a Communist Party,[10] influenced by the Comintern and the Russian revolution. It gives me great pleasure to be here and to tell you that we, the Japanese workers, are greatly influenced by the Russian revolution. You are the ones that sacrificed most; you have fought hardest against imperialism, not only in its policy towards Russia, but also against its world policy. You have fought against your counter-revolutionary General Yudenich, [who was] supported by European capitalism, and you have beaten him. Comrades, we are here today because we want to get experience [to help us] in the fight against imperialism in the Far East. We came to Moscow to get ready for this fight and to establish a united front against imperialism and capitalism, to advance the social revolution in the Far East. Today in Washington, they have organised to exploit the Far East by joint efforts. But I am glad to come here when the European capitalists are trying to hold a conference at which Soviet Russia will be present. They tried to oppress you and to starve you by the economic blockade, but today they are inviting you to come to Genoa. It may be that they wish to exploit you further. But I think you stand victorious before the world and can now fight the imperialism of the whole world. Comrades, I will not take up more of your time. I only wish to add that the Japanese workers will fight against Japanese imperialism and the Japanese army together with the Koreans and our other brothers of the Far East. (*Applause. Exclamations 'Long live comrade Katayama!'*).

Zinoviev. I will now call upon the famous Chinese authoress, the organiser of the women's movement in China, and a member of the Canton Parliament, our comrade Wong.

Wong [Huang Bihun]. Comrades, I represent the Chinese Women's Union. I came many thousands of miles from Asia to Europe, and am very glad indeed to speak to you. When I came to Russia I was impressed with the spirit of the Russian people. Soviet Russia has suffered many years from the blockade of the Western imperialist countries, yet she is still progressing without hesitancy

---

10   The Japanese Communist Party was not formally established until a few months after the Congress, on 15 July 1922, at a secret meeting in Takase Kiyoshi's house in Tokyo. The party had just a few dozen members. Takase's father-in-law Sakai Toshihiko was elected party chairman. Among seven chosen to from the executive committee was Kondo Eizo, who, in August 1921, had formed the short-lived Enlightened People's Communist Party. See Beckmann and Okubo 1969, p. 49.

or fear. The women of the Eastern world have suffered economic oppression by imperialism and capitalism. The women of the Eastern countries will unite with the Russian women to struggle against the capitalists and imperialists oppressing the women of the Far East, and they will go [forward] hand in hand with the Russian women in the struggle against world capitalism and imperialism.

Zinoviev. I will now call upon Comrade *Khem* to speak on behalf of the Korean delegation.

Khem. Comrades, it is a great honour for me to be present at such an unusual occasion. I bring you greetings from the toiling masses of Korea, who have suffered under the yoke of Japanese imperialism, and from the revolutionary people of Korea who are working for the overthrow of this Japanese yoke. How glad we are to see you face to face, fighting not only for Russia but for the proletarian revolution of the world. That is the cause you are championing. The delegates of the Far East held a great Congress at Moscow, and we discussed ways and means of carrying on the Far Eastern revolutionary movement, and now we are on our way home. There has also been a conference at Washington. What are the results of the Washington Conference? In a word, it is the union of the imperialists against the proletarian peoples of the Far East, for their exploitation and oppression. What are the results of the Congress in Moscow? I can also tell you in a word. It is the union and the establishment of an international [bond] between the East and the West. Which of these unions will ultimately prevail? Not the imperialist union, but the proletarian union. The imperialists have lost out. They will [fall] to pieces because of [their] quarrels among themselves. But what is our union? It is the union of the proletariat; it is the testimony of the faith of great masses of people in the emancipation of mankind, showing that we are all brothers and we will fight together to the very end.

Zinoviev. I will now call upon the representative of the Mongolian delegation, member of the Central Committee of the Mongolian Popular Revolutionary Party, a worker in the printing trade, Comrade *Tan-Zam*. (*Stormy applause*).

Tan-Zam [Danzan].[11] Comrades, in 1921, with the mighty aid of the valiant Red Army of Soviet Russia, the Mongolian toilers overthrew the yoke of Japanese

---

11   Ajvaagiyn Danzan (1895–1932), known as 'Japanese Danzan' because he had visited Japan in 1916, was the leader of the Mongolian delegation. He was party chairman from 1923–24. He died in prison in 1932 after being accused of spying for Japan.

and Chinese militarism. I am very glad to greet the Petrograd workers, who were the first to raise the banner of liberation of the toilers of Russia and of the whole world. Under this red banner, our Mongolian toilers are establishing their life in accordance with their own wishes, hoping that the world revolution proclaimed by the Communist International will become ever wider and stronger.

I am happy to exclaim together with you: Long live the Communist International! Long live the Union of the Peoples of the Far East! (*Applause*).

Zinoviev. Comrades, a great number of representatives of the youth of the Far Eastern peoples have taken part in all delegations of the Congress. [The] youth had [their] own special conference. I will call upon Comrade *Li* to speak on behalf of all the delegations of the youth that participated in the Far Eastern Congress.

Li. Comrades, we began [in] Moscow, and are concluding [in] Petrograd, the discussion of the only question, the question or life or death, the question of the overthrow of capitalism and the establishment of the power of the proletariat. I represent the youth of one of the most oppressed peoples of the Far East, namely Korea. Korea, and her youth in particular, is at the present time under the yoke of Japan. The Japanese authorities have taken upon themselves the task of educating our youth without consulting their wishes; the arbitrariness of the Japanese authorities is rampant everywhere. It is our present aim to unite with the youth of the West. This is to us the all-important question, the question of life or death. Today, we had the great honour and joy to solve this question. The Congress has resolved that the Japanese workers and proletarians pursue the same interests as those of Korea and China. After the close of the Congress it will be particularly necessary to go and explain this to the Japanese proletarians, so that they may become convinced and join us, and this [should] be followed by a union of the proletarians of the West and of the Far East and also of all countries. The Manifesto drawn up by the Young People's League, having been distributed among all delegations on behalf of the Presidium, has met with unanimous approval. (*Applause*).

Gordon. Long live the Youth of the East! Hurrah! (*Loud cheers*).

Zinoviev. Comrades, along with the delegates of the toilers of the Far Fast we have also some representatives of Western Europe and America. I will call upon the representative of the French Communist Party, a comrade who has arrived from Paris and is the Secretary of the Party and a member of the Central Committee of one of the greatest European Communist Parties. Our comrade *Ker* will now address you.

Ker. Comrades, I am happy, as a French Communist, to greet the proletariat of Petrograd which has been fighting [for] the last five years against world imperialism under the most trying conditions, and which is bearing upon its own shoulders, in the pains of hunger and cold, the entire burden of the struggle against the sharks of world imperialism. The heroic Russian proletariat could reproach the Western proletariat, which abandoned it in the struggle without aiding and joining in the fight. Yet the Western proletariat has tried to struggle and is struggling against imperialism. The French proletariat has gone through three great battles which have considerably shaken and weakened it. In March 1917, the Communists declared [a] general strike in order to force the Government to open peace negotiations. In 1918, revolutionary feeling in France ran so high that the bourgeoisie realised that it [would] soon have to give an account of its deeds before the toiling masses. In the same year, the railway workers declared [a] general strike, but this strike was broken like its predecessors. The workers suffered defeat [and were] unable to emerge victorious like their Russian comrades have done. Why? Because the working class in France was under the influence of the opportunists, under the influence of the bourgeoisie; because the French workers were not sufficiently revolutionary; because the toiling masses of France were still in the grip of illusory national pride, believing that the bourgeoisie, in the event of victory, would on its own [initiative] mitigate their living conditions. But now the situation [is beginning] to change. The consequences of the war are asserting themselves. France wished to conquer Germany. She did conquer and ruin her enemy, but the catastrophe that has overtaken Germany is dragging the whole of Western Europe into misery. The Entente wished to subject Russia to an economic blockade, and has maintained this blockade for quite a long time. But now they realise that without Russia they will not be able to reconstruct their economic life, that they will not be able to vanquish Russia. And thus now, in spite of all their proud boasts that they would have no dealings with the Soviet Government, they have actually opened economic relations.

The bourgeoisie of the Entente has concluded peace, but it is a peace that smacks of war. The bourgeoisie proved unable to reconstruct the economic life of Europe after the war, and this is the stimulus which [is stirring] the consciousness of the workers. 'Who will pay [the cost of] the war?' the workers are asking. And the bourgeoisie, maintaining control of the governmental machine and of the armed forces, declares that it will force the workers to pay the war expenses. The bourgeoisie of the whole of Europe has, of late, taken the offensive against the working class; everywhere there is a reduction of wages, extension of working hours etc. If the workers until now had entertained any illusion that the bourgeoisie would mitigate their conditions, they now see quite clearly that in order to secure their most vital requirements they must declare resolute war on the bourgeoisie. There is no other way out. A few months ago, the French textile workers had to strike for ten weeks for an increase of twenty centimes on their wages; the coal miners downed tools for the most elementary demands; and both these strikes ended in failure. This demonstrates that the French workers must enter the path of a more determined [fight]. They are gradually progressing from petty struggles for elementary demands to the decisive struggle against the French bourgeoisie which will unite them with the Russian proletariat. Comrades, I bring to you the warm greetings of the French proletariat. (*Applause*).

Zinoviev. I will now call upon comrade *Carr*, the representative of the American Communist Party.

Carr [L.E. Katterfeld]. Comrades and workers of Petrograd! It is indeed an inspiration to stand in your presence this evening. It is a double inspiration for one who comes from a country where a Communist cannot at present stand up publicly and say what he is publicly, but has to speak under a camouflage. I come from a land where the Communists have to meet in secret, as you did under the Tsar. So I say that it is an inspiration to be in a country where one can openly proclaim his faith. It makes one feel very humble also to speak before you when one remembers that here is the only country in the world where the workers have as yet had the strength to achieve power, where they have not only achieved power but maintained it against the armed attacks of the imperialist world, where they have not only achieved and maintained power but where the workers are now organised to solve the problems of building a new society.

Comrades, the special occasion of this meeting is one of great significance. You have here delegates to the Congress of the Far East. I come from the country of the Far West as a fraternal delegate. Here we have representatives of many lands; lands that are exploited not only by their own bourgeoisie but now are divided by the imperialists of the world. Here we have been planning to meet the decisions made at Washington. Here we are organising for the world revolution. You know, we in America know, that the time is coming when the American capitalist class will try to set us at the throats of the Far Eastern countries. It shall be our endeavour, I pledge you, so to organise, and so to propagandise, that when that day comes we can say to them: No, we shall not fight our brother workers of the Far East! If you make us fight, if we must fight, we shall fight our own foes robbing us at home and join hands with our brothers in order to overthrow the imperialists of the world. And we know that we can depend upon you to join hands with us, and that only then will the capitalists and imperialists be abolished from the face of the earth.

Zinoviev. I will now call upon comrade *Safarov* to read the manifesto that has been adopted by the Congress.

(*Safarov reads the manifesto*).

Zinoviev. Comrades, the Congress of the Peoples of the Far East has concluded its labours. Permit me, in a few words, to sum up the results. At this Congress there were the representatives of four countries.[12] The bourgeoisie of these countries resorts to every possible means to sow discord among the toilers of these countries, just as was the practice of Russian tsarism in its time. The Japanese bourgeois government tries to cultivate irreconcilable hatred between the populations of Japan, China, and Korea. A part of the counter-revolutionary bourgeoisie tries to sow permanent discord between the Mongolian and the Chinese populations. Behind the bourgeoisies of these countries are the European and American imperialist robbers who, while putting them at loggerheads, pose in the role of arbitrators. The principle of *divide et impera* bolsters up the imperialist oppression of all these countries.

The Executive Committee of the Communist International has done everything necessary to remove all differences between the toiling populations of these countries. I must declare, at the close of this Congress, that the consciousness of the toiling population of these countries has extremely lightened the task of the Communist International. The Congress, on the whole, has been carried through without any appreciable friction.

It is also the task of the Communist International to erect a bridge between the vanguard of the West European and American proletariat and the hundreds of millions of the masses of the Far and Near East. The Comintern accomplished this task last year at Baku, and is now accomplishing this task at Moscow and Petrograd.

We are profoundly convinced that the time is not far distant when all the acts deemed by the bourgeoisie to be [of] historical [importance], will be forgotten.

---

12   China, Japan, Korea and Mongolia. Oddly, Zinoviev did not include the Dutch Indies, which was also represented, albeit only by one delegate, but had the biggest Communist Party in Asia at the time. The manifesto of the Congress was addressed to the four countries listed by Zinoviev, plus the Pacific islands, Indochina and the Dutch Indies.

Brest-Litovsk will be forgotten, and so will Versailles, Trianon,[13] Washington, and perhaps even Genoa will be forgotten, although there is so much talk about it just now. But Moscow will not be forgotten, Baku will not be forgotten, Petrograd, and this night's session, will not be forgotten in the history of mankind. Trianon will be forgotten, but the Kremlin will not be forgotten, nor the Uritsky Palace, where we are now holding our session.

We are profoundly convinced that the power of the Comintern will grow along with the growth of consciousness not only of the foremost proletarians of Western Europe and America, but also with the growth of consciousness among the toilers and oppressed peasants of China, Japan, Korea and Mongolia. The junction of forces between the vanguard of the proletarian movement and the popular liberation movement against imperialism has now been completed. The peoples of China, Korea and Mongolia know imperialism not merely from books, not merely from hearsay, not merely as a result of the imperialist war. They have experienced the scourge of imperialism upon their very own backs. They are called upon to accomplish the work that was initiated by the vanguard of the world proletariat of Europe and America.

We have a perfect right to declare that the East is awakening. If the revolution of 1905 caused the first awakening in Turkey and Persia, the first feeble manifestations of revolutionary movement in the East, then our present revolution of 1917–22 has reverberated throughout the world like a thunderclap, arousing hundreds of millions of those human masses which seemed to be in a lethargic sleep. *Ex oriente Lux* – the ray of hope dawns in the East. We have a perfect right to say that the sun of world revolution is rising at this very moment, because, knowing events, it cannot[14] be considered as decisive if confined to Europe alone. To be victorious, the revolution must embrace the peoples of the Far East, must arouse the 400 million-strong population of China, the young and vigorous working class of Japan. All this is beginning to take shape before our eyes. The Communist International was the first to enter into close contact with the Japanese labour movement.[15] This brings new forces into the Communist International, this warrants the assurance that the Communist International will not be an organisation for Europe and America alone, but a worldwide organisation, such as it aims to be.

---

13 The Treaty of Trianon between the World War One allies and the Kingdom of Hungary. It was signed on 4 June 1920, in the Grand Trianon Palace, Versailles.
14 The original text says 'can'.
15 This presumably means the Comintern took the initiative to establish links with the Japanese labour movement.

In closing this Congress, we are profoundly convinced that this small handful of people, about two hundred delegates who have travelled many thousands of miles to come to us, will now carry to all the towns and villages of the four principal countries of the Far East the ideas of brotherhood, the ideas of Communism. Among the delegates there are people who never professed to be Communists, but who have engaged in the fight against alien oppressors, against foreign capitalists, because these aggressors do not permit them to speak their native tongue, to live their own free lives.

These two streams are converging before our eyes. One stream is the movement of the oppressed peoples who seek independence, the right of free development and the removal of the imperialist yoke. The other stream is the far mightier current of the conscious proletarian movement. The confluence of these two streams vouchsafes the confidence that our revolution will be triumphant.

I declare the session closed.

Long live the Communist International!

Long live the enfranchisement of the peoples of the Far East, and down [with] world imperialism!

(*Loud applause; orchestra plays the 'International' accompanied by the entire assembly. Japanese delegates sing Japanese revolutionary songs*).

The Congress was concluded at 9.45 p.m.

Manifesto of the Congress

Manifesto of the First Congress of the Communist and Revolutionary Organisations of the Far East to the Peoples of the Far East.

Toilers of the Far East!

Workers and peasants of China, Korea, Japan, Mongolia, of the Pacific Isles, Indochina and the Dutch Indies!

Enslaved nations of the Far East!

You [have been] suffering [for] dozens of years from the savage and arbitrary actions and the depredations of European, American and Japanese bandits. The Japanese oppressors have bespattered Korea with blood from end to end. The Japanese, American, French and English robbers are plundering and tearing to pieces China with her 400 million-strong population, and building their own welfare on the blood and tears of the Chinese people. They do not look upon the representatives of the oppressed nations as human beings. They want gold that glitters, profits and riches, and in order to obtain [them], they are ready to sacrifice hundreds of millions of human lives. [Chinese] and Koreans are not allowed to enter the gardens and other public places in the foreign quarters of Beijing, Shanghai, Tianjin, Hong Kong, Seoul and Chemul'po – [they are] on a par with dogs. In these quarters, foreign bourgeois, fattened on other men's perspiration and blood, ride about in carriages drawn by man-horses, the rickshaws, hastening them up with kicks and sticks. The most oppressed and brow-beaten slave of the rich of the world – the Chinese coolie – works for these parasites to a state of deadly extenuation. The Chinese peasant does unbearable labour, toiling 16 and 18 hours a day at a stretch, and nevertheless, the produce of his labour is null, for it goes only to enrich the foreign money-lenders and bloodsuckers and filters into the pockets of their mercenary lackeys. The Korean pauper has no land wherewith to gain his daily bread. The land is in the hands of the Japanese [planter], the landowners and capitalists who, with their bayonets and [gunfire], force the refractory to work. Every word of protest, every cry of desperation is smothered by the rattle of mass shootings; in the Philippines, the Isle of Formosa, Indochina, and the islands of the Dutch Indies, as well as in neighbouring British India, long since become a terrible prison for a people of 300 million. Millions of labouring lives are bowed down [over] the earth on rice, coffee, cotton and other plantations and cruelly exploited. Only the other day, Mongolia freed herself from Japanese and white-guard clutches. The dominating classes of Japan [are known as the hangmen of the Far East.] The factory workers and the peasants, including [day] labourers on rented land, lead an existence [fit only] for lower animals. The heavy groans of hundreds of enslaved millions are heard everywhere.

The oppressors will hear nothing of freedom and independence for the oppressed nations, nor of their human rights. They have met lately in the halls of the American Exchange in Washington, in order to come to an understanding on the subject of the further plunder of the countries of the Far East. There they have signed their Alliance of the Four Bloodsuckers. Korea, the Russian Far East and Manchuria have been given over to be robbed and pillaged by Japan. The principle of equal rights [to] robbery in China was [established], leaving the leading role in this base affair to American capital. The universal bloodsucking machine – the Consortium of 1918 – invented by America, was intended to make all the Chinese peasants tributaries of American capital; they were to pay a [hefty] tax to the American bankers. Chinese industry was to become an American workshop. Nothing came of this enterprise in 1918, owing to differences among the oppressors and the unanimous protest of the masses of the Chinese people. It is now [planned] to arrange a new consortium – an international firm for the military, financial and industrial robbery of China. Japan, America, England and France have, for the time being, put off a war which was [about] to break out for dominion over the Pacific Ocean. They have put it off, but not [indefinitely]. They have put it off in order to be able to continue to rob in unison for some time [longer].

The world war of 1914 undermined their strength. The workers' revolution [took] them by the throat in Europe on the very [scene] of their bloody crime. They struggled for four years against the Soviet Republic, the promised land of all the oppressed and exploited, [but] must now openly acknowledge its strength, and their own impotence to defeat the Soviets. They hope to re-establish their [failing] power in the Far East at the price of our lives, our blood and our labour. They bring new chains, new horrors, and a still more terrible [form of slavery] to the patient and resigned peoples of the Far East.

This must not be, this shall not be! We [will] become the masters of our own fate and [cease] being the playthings of greedy appetites and imperialist vanity.

The cause of the freedom of mankind is our cause.

The Russian worker began the work, the European worker continued it, and we shall victoriously end the bitter strife between the parasites and the workers, [for the benefit] of [all] hard-working hands and backs bent in labour!

The Communist International has issued a great appeal: World proletarians and all oppressed nations of the world – unite!

We will carry [this message] to our destroyed villages, to the slave-plantations, to the factories, schools and barracks.

We have met in the Red capitals of the Soviet Republic – Moscow and Petrograd – in order to raise our voices, from this world tribune, against the world executioners and against the Washington Union of the Four Bloodsuckers.

We are the representatives of the four hundred million oppressed [people] of China, the representatives of the national organisations of workers and peasants and the working intellectuals, as delegated by the Kuomintang[1] of Southern China, of the revolutionary organisations of:
   The provinces of Shandong, Hunan. Anhui, Guangdong and Zhejiang.[2]
   The towns of Hankou, Shanghai, Harbin, Hangzhou, Tianjin and Tangshan.[3]
   The National Revolutionary Society, Young China.
   The Trade-Union organisations.
   The Union of the Railroad Workers.
   The Chinese Communist Party.
   The Women's Patriotic League.
   The National press, represented by the *Republican Gazette* and the review: *The Pacific Conference and China*.

We are the representatives of the oppressed toiling masses of imperialist Japan sent by:
   The organisation Rodosha.[4]
   The Federation of the left wing of the Trade Unions of Japan.
   The Union of Printers of Tokyo, Osaka and Kyushu.[5]

---
1 The original text says Koushinda.
2 The original text says Shantung, Hunan, An-Houp, Canton, Tche-Dzian.
3 The original says Han Keou, Shanghai, Ha-Yuan, Han-Dzk, Tian-Tsin, Tian-Shan.
4 Rodosha was a left-wing faction of the Nihon Rodo Sodomei (Japan Federation of Labour). It was mainly based among miners and engineers.
5 Tokyo, Osaka and Kin-Shin in the original. The introduction to the German edition of the

The Miners' Federation of Kei-Sui-Kai.
The Labour press of Japan.
The Japanese Communist Party.

We are the representatives of oppressed Korea, groaning under the yoke of Japanese imperialism, as delegated by:
The General Labour Federation of Korea.
The Trade Union of Workers of the province of Shi-Do, belonging to the Communist Party.
The Union of Communist Youth of Korea.
The Revolutionary-Patriotic League of Korean Christians.
The organisation: The Restoration of Korea.
The Revolutionary Korean Troops.
The Amalgamated Union of the organisations of the Korean Youth.
The Union of Youth: New Korea.
The Union of Korean Students in China.
The Club of Korean Students in Japan.
The Central Union of Korean Students.
The editors of the paper: *The Independence of Korea*.

We are the representatives of Mongolia, as delegated by:
The People's Revolutionary Party of Mongolia.[6]
The Revolutionary Union of Youth of Mongolia.

We are the representatives of the workers of the Dutch Indies, oppressed by the American, British and Dutch imperialism, as delegated by:
The left wing of the organisation Sarekat-Islam.
The Red Federation of Trade Unions of the Dutch Indies.
The Communist Party of the Dutch Indies.

We demand equality, freedom and independence.

We call to a just struggle on the just path, all those who are not traitors to their people, to whom the paramount interests of the oppressed are near and dear, to those who are themselves slaves, and desire to be slaves no more!

---

minutes says an Association of Print Workers in Kiusiu (presumably Kyushu) sent a delegate to the Congress.
6 Officially called the Mongolian People's Party.

We know that our executioners will grant us no liberty.

We know that the struggle for freedom is a hard and strenuous one.

But we wish to live, and will take by force all that is ours by right, for we are the majority – there are hundreds of millions of us, and our strength is in our unity!

We declare war to the death to the Japanese, American, British, French and all other world rapacious plunderers. We declare war to the death to the mendacious *dujun* and the lackeys of our oppressors in China. We declare war to the death to Japanese militarism and [plutocracy].

We declare war to the death to hypocritical and thievish American imperialism and the greedy British usurpers. Out with them from China and Korea, the Pacific Isles, Indochina and the Dutch Indies! Out of the Far East!

The Japanese working class stretches out a brotherly hand to the workers of China and Korea. It takes its place in our general revolutionary union for the freedom of the peoples of the Far East. The sword of Japanese imperialism will snap in the hands of the Japanese proletariat.

The world proletariat is with us. Our cause is its own cause. Its cause is the cause of our lives.

We conclude, from now on, an indissoluble union of the workers of the Far East under the flag of the Communist International. We will attain our freedom. We will overthrow the oppressors and establish a just workers' order by seizing the land of the idle parasites and handing over the power to our own men, [drawn] from the ranks of the workers and peasants.

Organize! Rally to our fighting ranks! Form workers' and peasants' unions for the struggle [against] capitalism and imperialism! Make ready for the struggle!

Down with the Washington plotters!
Down with the Union of the Four Bloodsuckers!
Long live the Alliance of the Workers of the Far East!
Long live the Communist international!
Workers and Oppressed Peoples of the World – Unite!

Greetings to the President of the All-Russian Central Executive Committee M.I. Kalinin

Greetings sent by the Congress to the President of the All-Russian Central Executive Committee, comrade M.I. Kalinin.

The Presidium of the Congress of the Toilers of the Far East [sends] fraternal greetings to the supreme legislative and administrative organ of the first Workers' Republic in the world – the supreme session of the All-Russian Central Executive Committee.

The Presidium of the Congress, as well as the workers of the Far Eastern countries, are fully aware that the Russian workers and peasants had to tread a thorny path before gaining the power of being the arbiters of their own fate and of building up their Soviet Republic. This conviction is deep in the hearts of all the delegates of the Congress who will take it home into their own countries in order to instil it into their own workers and peasants.

At the same time, the Congress fully appreciates and endorses the foreign policy of the Russian Soviet Republic which, while safeguarding the sovereign rights of the Workers' and Peasants' Republic, has forced the world imperialists to conduct negotiations with Soviet Russia.

Report of the Credentials Committee

Standing Orders of the Credentials Committee.

1. Every mass national-revolutionary, Socialist, or Communist organisation (party, union, co-operative society, military organisation) is entitled to a representation at the Congress of the Peoples of the Far East.

2. Each one of the organisations mentioned in paragraph 1, having a membership of not over one hundred is entitled to two decisive votes and not over three consultative ones. For every one hundred members of an organisation above the first hundred, it is entitled to one decisive and not over two consultative votes.

3. Representatives of groups not included in paragraph 1 are entitled to send delegates only with a consultative vote, the number of such delegates in each case to be decided upon by the Credentials Committee.

4. In order to be represented at the Congress with a decisive as well as a consultative vote, it is necessary to present credentials of the respective organisation, duly certified. But, considering the conspirative conditions of delegates that have arrived for the Congress, the Credentials Committee is empowered, in individual cases, to make exceptions to this rule.

Comintern Representative *B. Shumyatsky*.

The various delegations have the following representation:

With decisive votes		With consultative votes	
1. Korean Section	52	1. Indian Section	2
2. Chinese	37	2. Japanese	3
3. Japanese	13	3. Yakut	3
4. Mongolian	14	4. Buryat, R.S.F.S.R. and Far Eastern Rep.	4
5. Buryat	8[1]	5. Chinese Section	5

---

1 This section was blank in the English text, but Zand-Bei's verbal report to the congress says eight Buryats had decisive votes. The German edition of the minutes also records eight Buryats with decisive votes.

(*cont.*)

With decisive votes		With consultative votes
6. Java (Islands)	1	
7. Kalmyk	2	

Note: The Mongolian and Buryat Sections (4. and 5. in the left-hand column form one section, as also do the Buryat. R.S.F.S.R. and the Far Eastern Republic Sections (4. in the right-hand column)).

In addition, decisive votes have been allocated to 2 representatives of the Communist University for Eastern Workers and to 2 representatives of the Korean students in Moscow.

Classification of Delegates

Korean Section

No. del. born in		Social position		Education		Party membership	
1867	1	Intell.	13	Higher	10	Commun.	37
1879	1	Workers	3	Interm.	29	Y.C.L.	5
1880	1	Peasants	25	Elem.	9	Y.S.L.	–
1881	2	Others	2	Illiter.	–	An.-Comm.	–
1882	2					Nat. Par.	–
1833	3					Non.-Par.	6
1885	2						
1886	1						
1887	2						
1889	2						
1890	2						
1891	1						
1892	5						
1893	3						
1894	2						
1895	1						
1896	4						
1897	1						
1898	1						
1899	6						
1900	3						
1902	2						
	48						

From 20 to 55 years of age.

Chinese Section

(Data re 39 delegates).

No. del. born in		Social position		Education		Party membership	
1885	1	Intell.	20	Higher	9	Commun.	14
1886	2	Workers	9	Interm.	26	Y.C.L.	–
1887	2	Peasants	9	Elem.	4	Y.S.L.	11
1891	1	Others	1	Illit.	–	An.-Com.	–
1892	1					Nation. P.	–
1893	1					Non-Par.	14
1895	1						
1896	5						
1897	1						
1898	4						
1899	3						
1900	6						
1901	4						
1904	2						
	39						

From 18 to 37 years of age.

Japanese Section

(Data re 16 delegates)

No. del. born in		Social position		Education		Party membership	
1859	1	Intell.	4	Higher	5	Commun.	9
1872	1	Workers	12	Interm.	5	Y.C.L.	–
1881	1	Peasants	–	Elem.	5	Y.S.L.	
1884	1	Others	–	Illit.	1	An. Com.	4
1891	1					Nat. Par.	–
1894	3					Non-Par.	3
1895	1						
1896	1						
1897	2						
1899	3						
1901	1						
	16						

From 21 to 63 years of age.

Mongol-Buryat Section

(Data re 16 delegates)

No. of del. born in		Social position		Education		Party membership		Remarks
1872	1	Intel.	4	Higher	4	Commun.	1	The intellectuals
1877	1	Workers	–	Interm.	8	Y.C.L.	1	include lamas and
1878	1	Peasants	12	Elem.	4	Y.S.L.	1	princes. There are no
1882	1	Others	–			An-Com.	–	data concerning [the
1888	1					Nat. Party	10	eight] Buryats.
1892	1					Non-Par.	3	
1897	2							
1899	1							
1901	4							
1902	1							
1903	1							
1905	1							
	16							

Summary

No. of del. born in		Social position		Education		Party membership		Remarks
1859	1	Intel.	46	Higher	28	Commun.	61	The majority of delegates are either intellectuals or peasants, and have intermediate or higher education.
1867	1	Workers	24	Interm.	68	Y.C.L.	6	
1872	2	Peasants	46	Elem.	22	Y.S.L.	12	
1877	1	Others	3	Illit.	1	An. Com.	4	
1878	1					Nat. Par.	10	
1879	1					Non-Par.	26	
1880	1							
1881	3							
1882	3							
1883	3							
1884	1							
1885	3							
1886	3							
1887	4							
1888	1							
1889	2							
1890	2							
1891	3							
1892	7							
1893	4							
1894	5							
1895	3							
1896	15							
1897	6							
1898	8							
1899	10							
1900	9							
1901	9							
1902	3							
1903	1							
1904	2							
1905	1							
	119							

From 18 to 63 years of age.

APPENDIX 1

Organisations Represented at the Congress

Japan[1]

Workers' organisation of Kansai[2] has 13,000 members in state-owned factories, arms manufacturing, the steel industry, the print union in Osaka, and the Workers Association of Kobe. They use strikes and sabotage to improve the economic situation of the workers. Shipbuilding workers are the most active and militant and have engaged in many strikes. Their slogans and demands include the right to vote. The Kansai organisation belongs to the General Workers Federation[3] (the former Yuaikai) which is influenced by the Japanese compromisers, especially the Yuaikai leader Suzuki Bunji. The progressive wing of Kansai has freed itself from the influence of the trades unions but uses the legal status of these organisations to engage in revolutionary propaganda and spread the message of class struggle.

Rodosha. Rodosha is based in Tokyo and has 500 members. Its members are all delegates from workers' organisations in Tokyo. It is Anarcho-Syndicalist and renounces political struggle, especially parliamentarism. It conducts its work among the lower layers of the working class. It engages in strikes and sabotage and is presently fighting wage cuts. It is under the influence of the anarchist Osugi. Its leaders are all workers and it is very popular among the workers. Now it has fused with the Japanese Communist Party and is changing its strategy. It sent one delegate – one of its leaders from the steel industry – to the Congress.

Tokyo Print Workers Association. Founded in 1917, it has 1,000 members. It fights for the economic and political liberation of the workers, using direct action. Like Rodosha,

---

1 The information in this appendix is taken from the Comintern's German language report of the Congress and a memorandum by the Korean delegation dated 8 February 1922. See *Der Erste Kongress der Kommunistischen und Revolutionären Organisationen des Fernen Ostens*, Moskau, Januar 1922, pp. 3–11, and from *Information Relative to the Korean Delegation to the Congress of the Communist and Revolutionary Parties of the Far East*, memorandum from the Korean delegation to the People's Commissariat of Foreign Affairs. Russian State Archive of Socio-Political History 495-154-175.
2 An area including Osaka, Kobe and Kyoto. The organisation was also called the Kanzai League.
3 That is, the Japan Federation of Labour (Nihon Rodo Sodomei).

it is influenced by Anarcho-Syndicalism and the anarchist Osugi, although it also includes a number of Marxists. It led a big print strike in Tokyo shortly after its foundation. It sent one delegate to the Congress.

Kyushu Print Workers Association. This organisation is similar to Rodosha and the Tokyo Print Workers Association. It sent one delegate to the Congress.

Japanese Communist Party. The party has a women's section that carries out propaganda work. The party actively takes part in Mayday demonstrations and all working class struggles. Its influence is growing.

Korea

General Labour Federation of Korea [Chosŏn nodong taehoe]. Founded in Seoul in November 1919, it has 85,000 members and many affiliated trades unions throughout Korea, but is mainly centred in Seoul. It has also created many unions under its auspices. Transport and railway workers, coolies and rickshaw men and miners are all represented. As well as in Seoul, it has a strong presence in industrial port cities. Its actions are aimed at achieving Korean independence. It has organised several major strikes and its next goal is the formation of factory committees. It has always fought for national liberation, despite repression and surveillance by the Japanese. The ideas of proletarian revolution have solid roots among the workers. The Federation sent six delegates to the Congress.

Federation of Korean Youth [Chosŏn ch'ŏngnyŏn yŏnhap'oe] is an influential grouping within Korea, formed in April 1920. It has 13 provincial sections, 210 branches and 57,000 members. It was formed by a fusion of various youth organisations. Its objectives are the spiritual development of Korean youth, the introduction of foreign knowledge and technology, and national liberation. It has links with young factory workers. It is one of the most influential organisations in the national liberation struggle and publishes newspapers, magazines and books. It sent two delegates to the Congress.

The Korean Student League was founded in April 1920 in Korea, and has 13,000 members. Its goals are the spiritual development of its members, and spreading knowledge and education. It takes an active part in revolutionary struggle. It has a close relationship with Korean student organisations in Korea and Japan. It carries out agitprop work and organises evening classes and debates. It sent two delegates to the Congress.

Korean Cooperative Association [Chosŏn Kongjedan]. A secret organisation for revolutionary undertakings established in April 1919. Its membership was around 27,000 and it sent three delegates to the Congress.[4]

Korean Women's Patriotic Society was formed in Seoul in March 1919. It has 3,000 members in Korea. Its goals are to fight for national liberation and the emancipation of women. It took part in the March 1919 uprising. It co-operates with other revolutionary groups. It fights against traditions of Korean society that are oppressive towards women. It also has branches in Shanghai, Japan and the United States, and has links with the Korean Women's Organisation of Siberia. It publishes newspapers and magazines, and carries out agitation, as well as legal work such as organising night classes, seminars and outings for women. It plays an important role in the national liberation movement. Most of its members are students.

General HQ of the Korean Restoration Army [Taehan kwangbokkun ch'ongyŏng] was formed on 1 January 1920 and has 30,000 members. Its objective is the arming and training of Korean troops to fight for independence. Its membership mainly consists of Korean exiles in Manchuria who have, for 10 years, taken up arms against the Japanese in various formations. They are mainly farmers and workers. Troops are organised in units of 50–100 and are active in partisan warfare. It fights mainly on the border between Manchuria and Korea. It includes prominent Communists and sent two delegates to the Congress.

League of Korean Young People's Associations [Taehan ch'ŏngnyŏndan yŏnhap'oe] was founded in October 1919 in the Kwantung (Guandong) leased territory in Manchuria. It has 20,000 members. Its objective is arming troops for national liberation. It was formed by the fusion of 150 youth organisations. It takes an active part in revolutionary and military actions against the Japanese. The majority of its members are immigrant farmers settled in southern Manchuria. It also has intellectuals and farmers inside Korea. It is one of the most active independence organisations and differentiates itself from other youth organisations by its active and direct participation in the revolutionary struggle. It sent two delegates to the Congress.

Korean Independence League [Taehan tongniptan] was founded in April 1919 in Manchuria, and focuses on military training of its members for actions against Japan. It has 8,600 members, most of whom are farmers and workers who emigrated to Manchuria

---

4 The description of the Cooperative Association as a secret revolutionary organisation seems at odds with both its name and large membership.

after the occupation. They engage in partisan warfare. Some of its leaders are Communists. It sent two delegates to the Congress.

Korea Restoration League [Kwanghandan] was formed in February 1920. It has three sections and 1050 members. Its goals and tasks are the same as the Korean Independence League. It sent one delegate to the Congress.

Young People's Party of New Korea [Sinhan ch'ŏngnyŏndang] was formed in Shanghai in November 1918. It also has a branch in the USA. It has 126 members consisting of major and minor leaders of the liberation movement – which explains the small membership. It was established to coordinate the activities of the various revolutionary groups. It is made up of revolutionary intellectuals, many of whom used to be in the Provisional Government but withdrew to take part in the revolutionary struggle against Japan. It spreads propaganda abroad to build support for Korean independence and organises riots and other revolutionary actions inside Korea. It has socialistic leanings and some Communist members. It sent one delegate to the Congress.

Yi-pal Club/Organisation of Korean Returned Students from Japan was formed in February 1920 in Shanghai and has 55 members. It was previously the Youth League for the Independence of Korea which was formed in February 1919 in Japan. It published a Declaration of Independence in Japan and pursued its activities despite persecution. It played an active part in the preparation of the March First uprising, after which its members returned to Korea and from thence to Shanghai. It publishes newspapers, magazines and books and remains very influential. It also acts as a link between Korean students in Japan and youth in Korea. It sent one delegate to the Congress.

League of Korean Students in China was formed in August 1921. It has 165 members and its objectives are the spiritual development of Korean youth and the introduction of new education methods. It sent two delegates to the Congress.

Red Star Union [Chŏksŏngdan]. Secret revolutionary organisation established in Tokyo in 1919. It had 368 members and sent one delegate to the Congress.

Representatives of Korean Christian Churches represents 400,000 Korean Christians. It began to organise in 1905 when the Japanese protectorate was established, and set up secret political organisations to stir the masses to fight against the occupation. It uses churches as legal cover to carry out political work. It plays a significant role in the liberation movement. It sent one delegate to the Congress.

Communist Party of Korea was founded in Russia under the direct leadership of the Comintern. It has established deep roots, among Korean émigrés as well as in Korea, in the short period of its existence. It exerts a great influence on the revolutionary liberation struggle. It needs to carry out a firm struggle against both adventurists and compromisers who have a bad influence on the young liberation movement. Another task is to educate the Korean masses in the class struggle. Its growth shows that it is set to become the leading force in the liberation movement. It sent six delegates to the Congress.

All-Russia Korean Labour Union based in Moscow had 1,032 members and sent two delegates to the Congress.

South Russia Korean Labour Union based in the Donbas region sent one delegate.

Korean Communist Party Women's Section sent four delegates – three from Shanghai and one from Moscow.

Korean Communist Party Youth Section sent two delegates from Irkutsk and two from Shanghai.

Korean Brigade in Irkutsk sent seven delegates.

Korean students in Moscow (there were 54) sent two delegates.

Korean Independence News, a Shanghai-based journal, was represented by one delegate.

The memorandum from the Korean delegation also stated that two representatives of the Korean Provisional Government had arrived late to the Congress and that representatives of the Ch'öndogyo religion and the Beijing-based Korean Military Unification Council were on their way.

China

The Chinese delegates came from Socialist, Nationalist and Workers organisations.

The Socialists comprised: the Renewal Organisation from Shandong, the Socialist Youth League from Tangshan and Taiyuan, the Mutual Aid Organisation and the Workers League from Hankou, the Organisation for the Study of Theory and Practice of

Socialism from Hunan, the Marxist Institute from Canton, Young China, and the Association for the Study of Trade Union Construction.

The National-revolutionaries comprised: the Teachers Association from Shandong, Hankou and Anhui, the Students Association from Shandong, Anhui and Hunan, the Kuomintang, and media representatives from Shandong, Hunan and Hubei, as well as the Union of Chinese Women.

The Workers organisations comprised: the Union of Mechanics from Shanghai and Canton, Rail workers from the Beijing – Mukden (Shenyang) line, Construction workers from Canton, Print workers from Hangzhou and Zhejiang, the Workers Association of Hunan, the Workers Association of Shandong, and the Farmers Associations of Hunan and Zhejiang.

The Communist movement was represented by delegates from Beijing, Shanghai, Sichuan and Canton.

APPENDIX 2

Timeline of Events

1839–42	First Opium War.
1850–64	Taiping Rebellion.
1853–54	Commodore Perry shells the Japanese harbour town of Uraga. Signs Convention of Kanagawa between United States and Japan.
1856–60	Second Opium War.
1866	Korea executes French missionaries and many Korean Christians. US armed merchantman General Sherman is destroyed near Pyongyang. French punitive expedition against Korea.
1868	Meiji Restoration begins Japan's modernisation.
1871	US punitive expedition against Korea.
1876	Japan-Korea Treaty of Amity and Commerce.
1882	United States-Korea Treaty of Peace, Amity, Commerce and Navigation.
1883–85	Sino-French War.
1884	Kapsin coup by Korean reformers, supported by Japan, suppressed by Chinese troops.
1894	Tonghak Uprising in Korea, government asks China for help. Outbreak of Sino-Japanese War. Sun Yat-sen forms Revive China Society.
1895	*April:* Treaty of Shimonoseki ends Sino-Japanese war. China cedes Taiwan and the Liaodong Peninsula to Japan. Triple Intervention by Russia Germany and France forces Japan to return Liaodong. *October:* Japanese minister in Korea organises the assassination of the Korean Queen.
1898	Scramble for Concessions in China. Russia takes Port Arthur, Britain takes Weihaiwei, Germany takes Qingdao and France takes Guangzhouwan. Failure of the Hundred Days Reform movement in China. Kang Youwei and Liang Qichao flee China. Beginning of the Boxer Uprising. The United States annexes Hawaii and seizes the Philippines and Guam in the Spanish-American war.
1899	The United States begins a three-year counterinsurgency campaign in Philippines that claims 200,000 lives. US Secretary of State, John Hay, announces the Open Door Policy in diplomatic notes to the major powers.
1900	Occupation of Beijing by Eight-Nation Alliance. Looting of Summer Palace.
1902	Anglo-Japanese Alliance signed.
1904–05	Russo-Japanese War. Japan imposes protectorate on Korea. Sun Yat-sen forms Tongmenghui. 1905 Revolution in Russia.

1905–11   Korean Righteous Armies revolt against Japanese rule. Revolt strengthened by influx of army officers after Japan disbands the Korean army in 1907.
1910   Japan annexes Korea.
1910–11   Japan Treason Trial. Twelve radicals hanged for alleged plot to assassinate the emperor.
1911   Chinese Revolution overthrows last emperor. Mongolia declares independence under the Bogda Khagan.
1912   *August:* Kuomintang formed in Beijing. *December:* Kuomintang wins national assembly elections.
1913   Yuan Shikai organises the assassination of Kuomintang leader Song Jiaoren and disperses parliament.
1914   On the outbreak of World War One, Japan seizes Qingdao and the Yap archipelago from Germany. Henk Sneevliet and others form Indies Social Democratic Association, forerunner of the Indonesian Communist Party.
1915   Japan presents 21 demands to China.
1917   *February–October:* Russian Revolution. *April:* United States enters the World War. *July:* Coup in Beijing briefly restores Qing dynasty. *August:* China declares war on Germany and Austria-Hungary. *December:* Bolsheviks issue appeal to the Muslims of Russia and the East.
1918   *January:* Woodrow Wilson sets out his Fourteen Point Peace Plan in a speech to Congress. *March:* Treaty of Brest-Litovsk is signed. *May:* Revolt of Czech Legion in Siberia. *July–September:* Rice riots in Japan lead to resignation of government. Arrival of Intervention forces in Russia. *November:* Kiel Mutiny, outbreak of the German Revolution, Kaiser abdicates.
1919   *January:* Spartacist uprising in Germany. Rosa Luxemburg and Karl Liebknecht murdered. *March:* First Comintern Congress. March First Movement in Korea. *May:* May Fourth Movement in China. *June:* Versailles Treaty signed. *July:* Soviet foreign minister Karakhan renounces Tsarist-era unequal treaties with China. *October:* Mongolian Revocation of Autonomy, Chinese Army retakes Urga. Sun Yat-sen re-launches Kuomintang.
1920   *February:* Capture and execution of Admiral Kolchak. *April:* American Expeditionary Force leaves Siberia. Formation of Far Eastern Republic. Comintern agent Grigory Voitinsky travels to China for discussions with Chen Duxiu on establishing a communist party. *May:* Indies Social Democratic Association changes name to Communist Union of the Indies and appoints Semaun party chairman. *July:* Second Comintern Congress adopts Lenin's theses on the national and colonial questions.
1920–21   White General Roman von Ungern Sternberg occupies Mongolia.
1921   *March:* Defeat of March Action in Germany. Kronstadt rebellion. New Economic Policy approved. *June:* Free City Incident, clash between Korean

communist factions in Siberia. Henk Sneevliet arrives in China as Comintern representative. *June–July:* Third Comintern Congress. *July:* Chinese Communist Party holds founding congress in Shanghai. Mongolian People's Party ousts Sternberg regime with help from Red Army. *November:* Washington Conference opens. *December:* Henk Sneevliet arrives in Guilin to meet with Sun Yat-sen.

1922   *January:* Comintern calls for United Front of the Proletariat. *January–February:* Congress of the Toilers of the Far East. *January–May:* Hong Kong seafarers strike. *April–May:* Genoa Conference. Russia and Germany sign Treaty of Rapallo. *June:* Chen Jiongming carries out coup against Sun Yat-sen in Canton. *July:* Japanese Communist Party founding congress. Joffe and Sneevliet leave for China. *August:* At the Hangzhou Plenum of Chinese Communist Party Central Committee, Sneevliet pushes through motion on entry into Kuomintang. *November–December:* Fourth Comintern Congress. *November:* Far Eastern Republic absorbed into Soviet Russia. *December:* Formation of the Soviet Union.

1923   *January:* Sun-Joffe Manifesto includes clause that soviet system is not appropriate for China. *February:* Sun Yat-sen returns to power as Grand Marshal of military government in Canton. *September:* Great Kanto earthquake in Japan is followed by a massacre of leftists, Koreans and Chinese. *August:* Henk Sneevliet leaves China. *October:* Mikhail Borodin arrives in China.

1924   *January:* First National Congress of the Kuomintang. *March:* Japanese Communist Party dissolves itself. *May:* Opening of the Soviet-funded Whampoa Military Academy in Canton. *June–July:* Fifth Comintern Congress.

1925   *March:* Sun Yat-sen dies. *April:* Korean Communist Party formed in Seoul. *May:* 30 May Incident – British police shoot down students in Shanghai, sparking a revolutionary upsurge. *June:* Chinese workers begin Hong Kong boycott. *November:* Korean Communist Party arrested.

1926   *March:* Chiang Kai-shek carries out coup in Canton forcing out the Left Kuomintang leader Wang Jingwei. *July:* Chiang launches Northern Expedition to reunify China. *November:* Failed Communist uprising in the Dutch East Indies (Indonesia).

1927   *April:* Chiang Kai-shek coup and massacre of workers in Shanghai. *April–May:* Mass killings of leftists in Canton and Changsha. *July:* Wang Jingwei, head of Left Kuomintang government in Wuhan, purges Communists. *August:* Nanchang uprising by Communists ends in failure and destruction of their army. *December:* Canton Commune, thousands massacred after botched uprising.

1928   *February:* First Japanese elections under manhood suffrage. *March:* Japanese Communist Party wiped out in mass arrest of leftists.

APPENDIX 3

Congress Delegates

Name[1]	Dates	Notes
Mongolian Buryat and Far Eastern Republic		
Arkhincheeva, Agapia Stepanovna	born 28 Dec 1901	One of seven female delegates. A Buryat born in Russia of peasant background. An official of the Russian Young Communist League, and a delegate from its Buryat Oblast committee.
Ayushi	age 19	Delegate of the Central Committee of the Mongolian Revolutionary Youth League. Also working as an official.
Bagator	age 25	A delegate from the Central Committee of the Mongolian Revolutionary Youth League.
Boyan-Nemekhu/ Sonombaljiryn Buyannemekh		An official and a delegate of the Central Committee of the Mongolian Revolutionary Youth League. A poet and playwright, executed in 1937 accused of spying for Japan. See biographical note in main text.
Danzan, Ajvaagiyn	1876–1932	Ajvaagiyn Danzan, leader of the Mongolia delegation to the congress. He was known as 'Japanese Danzan' because he visited Japan in 1916, was chairman of the Mongolian People's Party from January 1923–August 1924 and continued as deputy chairman until 1925. He was then sent on various diplomatic postings. In 1932 he was accused of spying for Japan and died in prison.
Danzan, Nyaraw	age 34	An accountant, educated in in a monastery.
Dashepylov	born 1903	A herder who came to Russia to study in 1919.
Davazhev	age 25	One of seven female delegates. Working for the Women's Committee of the Central Committee of the Mongolian People's Party. A delegate from the Central Committee.
Dendev	age 40	Dendev was one of the founder members and leaders of the Mongolian People's Party. He was executed a few months after the Far East Congress. For a fuller biography see footnote in main text.
Dylgyrov, Balzhinima	age 49	A teacher from a peasant background. A delegate from the Buryat Mongol Far Eastern Republic. Speaks Tibetan and Russian. Aim is to realise the socialist ideal as soon as possible.

---

1 This is not a complete list of delegates. It comprises those who completed questionnaires plus a few names from other sources.

CONGRESS DELEGATES 323

(cont.)

Name	Dates	Notes
Gombo	age 21	An official in the Mongolian Finance Ministry and a delegate from the Mongolian Revolutionary Youth League.
Gombozhap	age 21	Official and delegate of the Central Committee of the Mongolian Revolutionary Youth League
Lepekhin, Aleksandr	born 1889	Commander of the Primorskaya Oblast. Delegate from the Far Eastern Secretariat of the Central Committee of the Russian Communist Party
Losol Daryzavin	age 30, died 1940	A former 'soldier-lama' now an official and delegate from the Central Committee of the Mongolian People's Party. Losol was a founder member of the Consular Hill group and one of the seven-member delegation that, with the blessing of the Bogda Khagan, sought aid from Soviet Russia. He was purged by Choibalsan in 1939 and died in prison the following year.
Mishidorzhi	age 18	A delegate of the Central Committee of the Mongolian Revolutionary Youth League.
Namzhilon, Badma		A student of working class Buryat background. A member of the Chita Youth League and a candidate member of the Russian Communist Party.
Ochiron, Zhamchi	age 20	A herdsman and a teacher, delegate from the Far Eastern Regional Committee of the Russian Young Communist League
Purbozhap/ Purewjab	age 45	Official of the Justice Ministry of Mongolia and a delegate of the Central Committee of the Mongolian People's Party. A Duke of the Sixth Grade.
Sosor-Daba	born 1904	A translator and interpreter, delegate from the Mongolian Revolutionary Youth League.
Sundarovu	born 1895	A Buryat born in the Pribaikal Oblast. A delegate from the Far Eastern section of the Russian Young Communist League.
Tsydenzhabun	age 24	A herder born in Russia. Said his aim was to liberate humanity from the yoke of slavery.
Zhamsaran	age 21	An official, and delegate, of the Central Committee of the Mongolian Revolutionary Youth League.
Zodboyev, Tsypil	age 28	A teacher born in Russia who said his aim is the destruction of world capitalism.

(*cont.*)

Name	Dates	Notes
		India
		(Although India was not considered part of the 'Far East', two Indian delegates were allowed to attend with consultative votes)
Abani Mukherji	(1891–1937)	Founder of the Indian Communist Party, along with Roy. Later Roy's factional rival. Mukherji was executed during the Great Purges. See note in introduction for biography.
M.N. Roy (1887–1954)		Founder of the Indian Communist Party. See note in main text for biography.
		Indonesia
Semaun / Semaoen	born Feb 1897	Semaun was the first chairman of the Indonesian Communist Party. At the Congress he represented three organisations – the Communist Party of the Indies (he wrote Indian Communist Party), Red Sarekat Islam, and the Federation of Transport, Petroleum and Fabric workers. For a fuller biography see footnote in main text.
		China
Deng Pei	1885–1927	A delegate from the Tangshan Railway Workers' Union and member of the Communist Party. Deng was tortured and executed by the Kuomintang in 1927. For a fuller biography see footnote in main text.
Deng Youming	born 15 Oct 1900	A student. Member of the Shandong branch of the Chinese Communist Party.
Feng Jupo, He wrote it as Cook Pou Funk	1899–1957	Feng describes himself as student and newspaperman. He set up an anti-imperialist youth movement in 1923. He was later a member of the Communist Party's Guangdong executive committee.
Gao Shangde aka Gao Junyu	1896–1925	Delegate from the Young China Society. Gao was one of the student leaders of the May Fourth Movement and later an editor of Guide Weekly, the Communist Party journal. He died of illness at the age of 29.
Hao Tianzhu	born Oct 1896	A journalist who studied in Japan. Represents a Japan returned students patriotic organisation, an Anhui comrades association, an Anhui patriotic organisation, etc. His political affiliations are to the above organisations and to a Chinese-Korean mutual aid society.
He Shu	1899–1947	A teacher, delegate from a Teachers Association in Hunan, and a member of the Communist Party. He Shu joined the Socialist

CONGRESS DELEGATES 325

(cont.)

Name	Dates	Notes
		Youth League set up by Mao Zedong in Changsha in 1920. In 1926 he was appointed propaganda chief in the political department of the sixth division of the National Revolutionary Army. After the Kuomintang coup he worked underground. In 1929 he was appointed provincial secretary of the Communist Party in Jiangxi. He died of illness.
He Zhonghan	1900–72	He Zhonghan initially worked as a journalist (he was employed by the *Dahan bao* at the time of the Congress) but later joined the Whampoa (Huangpu) Military Academy and rose through the ranks of the Kuomintang military as a political officer. Initially considered a fellow-traveller by the Communists, by the mid-1920s he had moved to the right. He left for Taiwan in 1949.
Huang Bihun	1886–1923	One of seven female delegates. Addressed Congress on women's rights. Arrested and executed by the Kuomintang in 1923. See introduction and footnote in main text for fuller biography.
Huang Lingshuang	1897–1982	Huang Lingshuang was one of China's leading anarchists and an activist in the May Fourth Movement. In 1919 he and Chen Duxiu set up a group called the socialist alliance which became one of the nuclei of the future Communist Party. He described himself on his delegate questionnaire (in English) as 'proletarian (middle class)', and a member of the Communist Party, but this was corrected, in Russian to 'sympathiser'. His credentials were from the Mechanical Labourers' Union of Guangdong but Deng Pei and other working class members of the delegation complained to the mandate commission that he was not a genuine trade unionist. In 1923, after Chen Duxiu claimed he had become a Bolshevik, Huang published an open letter insisting he was still an anarchist.
Jiang Fosheng	born 24 June 1898	A teacher, but a delegate from the Hunan Peasants Association. A member of the Shanghai Socialist Youth League.
Li Jichu	8 Feb 1900	Newspaper editor from Changsha. A delegate from the Hunan newspaper offices' association (written in English). A member of the Communist Party.
Liang Botai*[2]	1899–1935	Liang arrived in Russia in 1921 to study. He held senior posts in China's Soviet Republic after the 1927 coup. In 1935 he was wounded in battle, captured and executed by the Kuomintang.

---

2 Chinese delegates marked * have no delegate questionnaires but are listed as delegates in Yang 1994.

(cont.)

Name	Dates	Notes
Liang Pengwan	1898–1951	A delegate from the Tangshan Socialist Youth League, Liang joined the Chinese Communist Party while in Moscow. After returning to China he was active in the trade union movement. He was arrested by the Kuomintang in 1931 and 1934 and defected from the Communist Party. He later joined an underworld gang and spied on the Kuomintang underground for the Japanese. He was executed as a traitor in 1951.
Lin Yunan	1898–1931	A relative of Lin Biao, Lin Yunnan was one of the founders of, and a delegate from, the *gongcunshe* a socialist propaganda group. He later joined the Communist Party. In January 1931 he was arrested and severely tortured by the Kuomintang but refused to submit. He was executed with 24 others on February 7 that year.
Liu Yihua	born 27 Jan 1901	A student delegate from the Union of Students and Workers in Changsha.
Ma Nianyi	born 1900	A journalist delegated from the Wuhan journalists' association. Also a member of the Communist Party.
Ma Zhanglu	born 30 Nov 1900	A teacher from Anhui delegated to the Congress by the Wuhu Professional Teachers' Association. Ma wrote his date of birth in the old style, saying he was born in the 27th year of the reign of the Guangxu Emperor. He later wrote that most delegates were opposed to Mongolian independence but Zhang Guotao made them toe the line.
Ni Youtian		A printer, delegate from Workers Mutual Aid Society. No party affiliation.
Ouyang Diyu	1894–1931	Metal worker, delegate from the Shanghai Metal Workers Union. Ouyang was born into a scholarly family, but in 1919, he took a job in a Shanghai factory and became a trade union organiser. He later worked as an organiser for the Communist Party in various places. He was arrested and killed by the Nationalists in 1931.
Peng Shuzhi	1896–1983	Peng Shuzhi was studying in Moscow when the Congress took place. He was secretary of his branch of the Communist Youth League and signed a request for three delegates to the Congress using his pseudonym Petrov.[3] Peng was a member of the Central Committee of the Chinese Communist Party from 1925 and editor of its main publication during the 1925–27 revolution. He was expelled from the party in 1929 along with Chen Duxiu. He

---

3 Russian State Archive of Socio-Political History 495.154.175.

CONGRESS DELEGATES 327

(cont.)

Name	Dates	Notes
		was later a leading member of the Fourth International. He died in Los Angeles. Peng left an interesting account of the Congress in his memoirs.
Ren Bishi*	1904–50	According to Professor Yang Kuisong, Ren Bishi was one of the student delegates referred to by the Congress credentials committee. Ren later became one of the Communist Party's most senior leaders – a Red Army commander and a member of the Politburo. He died of a cerebral haemorrhage.
Song Weinian	born 22 Oct 1899	Student delegate from the Anhui Provincial Students Association.
Tang Daohai	born 13 Aug 1901	A student delegate from the Workers Mutual Aid Society in Wuhu, Anhui.
Wang Fuyuan	born 1899	A printer; a member of the Shandong branch of the Communist Party and a delegate from a Shandong Labour Union.
Wang Guanghui	born 1896	A worker delegated from the Hunan Labour Union.
Wang Hanjin	Oct 1888–194?	Wang was a carpenter, a delegate from the Canton Construction Workers Union. He fled to Hong Kong and then Singapore after the April 1927 Kuomintang coup. In Singapore he was active in various patriotic movements. He died in Hong Kong sometime during World War Two.
Wang Jinmei	1899–1925	A journalist on a Shandong labour newspaper, delegated from the Shandong Journalists' Association. Wang was a founder member of the Communist Party. He attended the first national congress of the Kuomintang in 1924. He died of a chronic lung disease the following year.
Wang Juyi	13 Sept 1887	A teacher and a member of the Shandong branch of the Communist Party.
Wang Xiaojin	1899	A student and a member of the Shandong branch of the Communist Party.
Wang Zhenyi	1901–31	A student delegated from the Taiyuan Socialist Youth League. Wang took part in the Nanchang uprising. He was elected an alternate member of the Chinese Communist Party Central Committee at its Sixth Congress, held in Moscow in 1928. He was arrested in 1930 and died in prison.
Xia Kuisheng	born 14 Oct 1900	A farmer; delegate from the Wuhu Industry and Commerce Promotion Society and a member of the Communist Party.
Xia Xi	born 14 July 1901	A student; delegate from the Hunan Student Association and a member of the Communist Party.

(cont.)

Name	Dates	Notes
Xu Chiguang	born 9 June 1899	A mechanic/machine worker. A delegate from the Chinese Labour Secretariat which was established in August 1921 on Sneevliet's initiative. Zhang Guotao was its president.
Xuan Zhonghua	born 5 Oct 1898	A delegate from a peasant association. A student leader in Hangzhou during the May Fourth Movement, Xuan was a teacher at the time of the Congress. He joined the Communist Party in 1924. He was arrested and killed by the Kuomintang during the April 1927 coup in Shanghai.
Yu Shude	1893–1982	Yu Shude joined the Communist Party after returning to China from the congress, but dropped out of politics in 1927. He was later appointed to the standing committee of the Chinese People's Political Consultative Committee. For a fuller biography see footnote in main text.
Yu Xiusong *	1899–1939	Yu was one of the pioneers of Chinese Communism. During the May Fourth movement he launched a radical magazine and organised demonstrations in Hangzhou. He joined China's first Communist 'small group' set up by Chen Duxiu in Shanghai in 1920, and was the first leader of the party's youth league. In 1925, while studying in Moscow, Yu clashed with China's arch-Stalinist Wang Ming. In 1932, he was assigned to work in Xinjiang. In 1937, Wang accused Yu of Trotskyism and conspired with Xinjiang's Soviet-backed warlord, Sheng Shicai, to arrest Yu and deport him to Russia where he was executed in February 1939.
Zhang Guotao	1897–1979	Zhang was appointed leader of the Communist delegation by Chen Duxiu. He wrote that he was an official of the metal workers' union. A May Fourth leader, founder member of Communist Party and later a rival to Mao, Zhang Guotao defected to the Kuomintang in 1938 and died in Canada after converting to Christianity. For a fuller biography see the introduction and footnote in the main text.
Zhang Qiubai	1887–1928	The Kuomintang representative, Sun Yat-sen's envoy to the Congress. He was assassinated in Nanjing in 1928. For a fuller bio see introduction and main text.
Zhao Zijun	born 23 Mar 1886	Transport worker, a delegate from Wuhan Socialist Workers League.
Zhu Zhenxin	born 1 Nov 1904	A journalist. Said he studied at St. Chong's (St. John's?) College in Shanghai.

(cont.)

Name	Dates	Notes
		Japan
Katayama Sen		One of the founders of the Japanese labour movement and a prominent figure in the Comintern. For a fuller biography see the footnote in the main text.
Kitamura Eiji	born 19 Oct 1896	An Anarchist Communist printer.
Kobayashi Shinjiro	20 June 1898	A printer, member of a print workers union and the Japanese Communist Party.
Maniwa Suekichi*[4]		Travelled from United States to the congress. Maniwa was a sailor who jumped ship in America and worked for a while as a cowboy.
Mizutani Kenichi	born 12 Sept 1894	A lawyer, delegate of the Japanese Communist Party. One of the main Japanese speakers at the Far East Congress.
Nikaido Umekichi*		Also arrived from the United States.
Nonaka Masayuki*		Also arrived from the United States.
Oba Kako*		Attended the congress with speaking rights only. Also arrived from the United States.
Shima Gonta		Listed on the same mandate as Mizutani Kenichi and Umeda Ryozo. The mandate, dated 13 October 1921 is typed in English and signed by the General Secretary of the Communist Party of Japan. See Russian archive of Socio-Political History 495.154.176.
Suzuki Mosaburo*		Also arrived from the United States, Suzuki was a journalist. He later joined the Nihon Ronoto – the Japan Labour-Farmer Party, a leftist party outside the Comintern fold, and became the leader of its successor, the Musan Taishuto (Proletarian Mass Party).
Taguchi Unzo	5 May 1894	At the time of the Congress, Taguchi was working in the Japanese section of the Comintern in Irkutsk. In 1919, he and Katayama established the Japanese Socialist Group in America (later the Japanese Communist Group in America) in New York. He attended the Third Comintern Congress as a delegate from that organisation.

---

4 I could find no questionnaires or mandates for the Japanese delegates marked *. They are listed as delegates by Beckmann and Okubo 1969, pp. 39–40. A note in the Comintern archive relates that some Japanese delegates lost their mandates on their way to the congress and told some Korean delegates they were planning to reproduce them. The Koreans advised them not to try to do so. See Russian State Archive of Socio-Political History 495.154.176.019.

(*cont.*)

Name	Dates	Notes
Takase Kyoshi*		A delegate from the Enlightened People's Communist Party, he was the chair of its publications committee. After returning from the congress, Takase played a key role in establishing the Japanese Communist Party.
Tokuda Kyuichi*	1894–1953	A delegate from the Wednesday Society, a Marxist study group in Japan. Tokuda was a lawyer, a founder of the Japanese Communist Party in 1922, and a member of its central committee. He was jailed from 1928–45 under the Peace Preservation law. On his release, he was elected general secretary of the party and retained the post until his death, in exile in China. In 1946, he was elected to Japan's House of Representatives but in 1950 he was banned from public office by the US occupation authorities.
Watanabe Haruo*		A member of Katayama's circle in New York, Watanabe had studied chemistry and industrial management. He later wrote two books about his experiences in the Communist movement.
Umeda Ryozo	born 10 Oct 1901	Umeda's questionnaire, completed in English, says he is employed as Secretary of the Communist Party and is a proletarian.
Wada Kiichiro	7 May 1898–1924	An Anarchist Communist miner delegated from the Federation of Kyushu Workers. Kiichiro was a prominent anarchist. He shot himself in 1924.
Yoshida Hashime	1895–1966	An engineering worker. Member of the revolutionary union Rodosha. An Anarchist-Communist, he converted to Communism while at the congress. For a fuller biography see footnote in the main text.

Korea

47 of the Korean names are taken from delegate questionnaires. In addition, there were also seven representatives of the Shanghai faction, according to a 1999 paper by Professor Im Kyŏngsŏk.

Name	Dates	Notes
Ch'ae Tongsun	born 1892	A delegate from the First Korean Brigade (presumably of the Red Army). Ch'ae had been in Russia since 1899 and was a member of the Russian Communist Party. He spoke at the Congress using the pseudonym Kor-Khan. For a fuller biography see note in main text.
Chang Tŏkchin	20 April 1898–1924	A delegate from the HQ of the Great Korea Restoration Army (Taehan Kwangbokkun), and the Korean Communist Youth League. A member of the Korean Communist Party in Shanghai. Chang fled to Manchuria after the March First movement. In 1920, together with a group of comrades he carried out an armed attack in Pyongan province. In 1922, he moved to Shang-

CONGRESS DELEGATES 331

(cont.)

Name	Dates	Notes
		hai and worked with the Korean Provisional Government. He was shot and killed in Shanghai in 1924.
Cho Tongho	4 Aug 1893–1954	Cho studied to be a teacher at Jinling College in Nanjing. He later worked as a journalist and was regional secretary of Korean Communist Party in Shanghai. He was a delegate from the Far Eastern Council of the Korean Communist Party.
Ch'oe Ch'angsik	1892	A delegate from Korean Communist Party in Shanghai. Employed as an editor by the party, Ch'oe was also a teacher. He moved to Shanghai after the March First movement and worked with the provisional government. In 1930, he was imprisoned by the Japanese.
Ch'oe Chindong	17 July 1882–1945	A member of Righteous Army (Ŭibyŏng). Ch'oe was a police official in Manchuria. After the March First movement, he organised an armed group that carried out attacks inside Korea that killed hundreds of Japanese. He was arrested in 1924.
Ch'oe Koryŏ	27 Sept 1893	Ch'oe was a delegate from the First Korean Brigade of the Red Army. He was one of the leaders of the Irkutsk faction of Korean communists and while at the Far East Congress he met Lenin.
Chŏn Chŏnggwan	15 March 1899	A student, delegate from the Korean Mutual Aid Society.
Chŏn Hŏn	14 Feb 1899	A peasant. A delegate from Korean Mutual Aid Society and a member of the Communist Party.
Chŏng Kwangho	22 Aug 1900	A representative of the East China Korean Students Union and a member of the Korean Communist Youth organisation in Shanghai. Chŏng described himself as a member of the gentry.
Chŏng Sujŏng	28 Sept 1896	One of seven female delegates. Representing the Women's Patriotic Assembly. She wrote that her aim was world proletarian revolution, especially women's revolution.
Chŏng T'aehwa	5 Jan 1896	A student. Delegate from Korean Communist Mutual Aid.
Han Myŏngse	29 May 1885	A delegate from the Central Committee of the Korean Communist Party and a leader of the Irkutsk faction. Han was born in Russia. He fought on the Russian side in the Russo-Japanese war and took part in the 1905 Revolution. He joined the Socialist Revolutionaries in 1917 but switched to the Russian Communist Party in 1920. In 1921, he was employed by the Far Eastern Bureau of the Comintern. He was a delegate to the Third and Fourth Comintern Congresses and while at the Far East Congress he met Lenin. He was expelled from the party in 1929, recanted and was readmitted, but was arrested during the Great Purges and disappeared.

(cont.)

Name	Dates	Notes
Hong Chin-u[5]		Delegated by the All-Russia Korean Labour Union. One of seven supporters of the Shanghai faction among the Korean delegates.
Hong Pŏmdo	27 of eighth month (lunar) 1867	A delegate from the First Korean Brigade of the Red Army. Hong was a veteran of the Righteous Army (Ŭibyŏng). He wrote that his aim was the liberation of Korea. Hong carried out many assaults on the Japanese beginning in 1907. In 1910, he moved to Kando and became a commander of the Korean Independence Army. He took part in the battle of Qingshanli in 1920. In 1921, after the Free City Incident, he joined the Red Army. He joined the Soviet Communist Party in 1927. Along with other Koreans in the Soviet Union, he was exiled to Kazakhstan by Stalin in 1937. He died there at the age of 76.
Kang P'ilsu	15 Nov 1893	A trade union delegate and candidate member of the Korean Communist Party. Kang said his aim was to turn the world red.
Kim Chaebong	19 May 1891	A delegate from a trade union in Seoul. Kim took part in the March First movement. In 1921, he was jailed for six months and on his release moved to Manchuria, Beijing and Moscow. He joined the Irkutsk faction of Korean communists and moved to Vladivostok in 1923. When the Korean Communist Party was re-founded in 1925, he became its general secretary, but in December that year he was arrested by the Japanese and jailed for six years.
Kim Chŏngha[6]		A delegate from the Korean student union in Moscow. One of seven supporters of the Shanghai faction among the Korean delegates.
Kim Dong-han[7]		One of seven supporters of the Shanghai faction among the Korean delegates.
Kim Hasŏk	19 Sept 1886	A Professor and a member of the gentry according to his questionnaire. A delegate from the Korean Communist Party. He wrote that his aim was world proletarian revolution. Kim was one of the leaders of the armed wing of the Irkutsk faction at the time of the 1921 Free City Incident.

---

5 Im 1999.
6 Ibid.
7 Ibid.

(cont.)

Name	Dates	Notes
Kim Iktong	21 July 1885	A trade union delegate. His aims are Korean independence and world communism.
Kim Kilpak Arkadii	born 1894	A member of Korean section of the Russian Communist Party. Has been in Russia since 1902. Delegate from the First Korean Brigade of the Red Army.
Kim Kyu	16 Jan 1900	Secretary and delegate of the Korean Communist Youth League in Shanghai. Also a member of the Communist Party. Speaks Japanese, English, Chinese and Esperanto. Doctor Owen Miller suggested Kim Kyu is the same person as Kim Tanya, a March First activist who joined the Irkutsk faction of Korean communists and met Lenin while at the Far East Congress. He was imprisoned on returning to Korea and later worked as a journalist in Korea and Shanghai. In 1937 he was arrested in the Soviet Union, accused of spying for Japan and was executed in 1938.
Kim Kyuch'an[8]		A delegate from the Korean student union in Moscow. One of seven supporters of the Shanghai faction among the Korean delegates.
Kim Kyu-sik	29 Jan 1881–10 Dec 1950	One of Korea's most prominent independence activists. Kim was delegated from the New Korea Young Men's Society.
Kim Sangdŏk	10 December 1894	A delegate from the Korean Student Union in East China and a member of the 28 Club.
Kim Sihyŏn	9 June 1883	Kim studied Law at Meiji University in Tokyo. A trade union delegate to the Congress. Following March First, Kim went to Manchuria. He joined the Irkutsk faction of the Korean Communist Party in 1921. He later joined the resistance group Ŭiyŏltan and set up a training school in Nanjing. He was jailed for five years for killing a traitor. He was elected to the Korean national assembly in 1950. In 1952, he was sentenced to death – commuted to life imprisonment – for allegedly plotting to assassinate Syngman Rhee. (The incident, in which the attacker's gun failed to fire, may have been staged by Rhee). After Rhee fled Korea in 1960, Kim was again elected to the national assembly.
Kim Sŭnghak	12 July 1880–1964	A graduate of Seoul Normal University. An editor of Korea Independence News. Member of Korean Communist Party in Shanghai.
Kim Tŏk'yong Woman	11 Oct 1882	One of the seven women delegates. A teacher delegated by the Korean Communist Party Shanghai branch.

---

8 Ibid.

(cont.)

Name	Dates	Notes
Kim Won'gyŏng	22 Sept 1899	One of the seven women delegates. Secretary and delegate of the Korean Communist Party's Shanghai branch. A member of the Korean Women's Patriotic Society.
Kwon Aera	1 February 1899	One of the seven women. A kindergarten teacher and member of the Shanghai branch of the Korean Communist Party. See also the footnote in the main text.
Kwon Chŏngp'il	10 Feb 1890–1935	A peasant delegate from the Korean Youth Assembly. He wrote that his aims were Korean independence and communism. In 1919, Kwon left Korea for Manchuria and joined the armed group Ŭiyŏltan. He smuggled arms into Korea several times. In 1929, he was arrested in Manchuria and jailed for five years. He died of illness.
Min Uyŏng	16 July 1877	A member of the Jingcheng Labour Union and the Korean Communist Party. Said his aims were Korean Independence and World Communist Revolution.
Mun Do	21 Oct 1892	A law student at Mingzhi University, delegated from Tokyo Student Union. Also a member of the Korean Communist Party.
Mun Si'hwan[9]		One of seven supporters of the Shanghai faction among the Korean delegates.
Paek Namjun	29 July 1883	A peasant delegated by the HQ of the Kwangbokkun – the Restoration Army.
Pak Ch'angnae	19 July 1899	A former student. Pak Joined the Red Army in 1919, and was in its Third Division at the time of the congress. He was a delegate from the Far East People's Revolutionary Congress and the Far East Youth Congress. His aim was world revolution and communism.
Pak Hŭigon	7 May 1895	A peasant delegated from the Korean Independence Union which, he said, is linked to the Communist Party.
Pavel Alexandrovich Park (Pak-Ppapel Alleksandŭr-obich'i)[10]		Delegated by the All-Russia Korean Labour Union. One of seven supporters of the Shanghai faction among the Korean delegates.
Ra Yonggyun (Na Yongkyun)	25 Nov 1899	Ra described himself as a professional revolutionary. He studied politics at Waseda University. He was delegated by the Korean Returned Japan Students Political Party (his own English). Also

9   Ibid.
10 Ibid.

Name	Dates	Notes
		a member of the 28 Club in Shanghai. His aims were Korean independence and world peace.
Rim Wŏn-gŭn (Im Wŏn-gŭn)	10 April 1900–63	A journalist on the Shanghai newspaper Independence News. Delegated from the newspaper and the Communist Youth League. A member of the Communist Party in Shanghai. An Esperanto speaker. Rim came from a bourgeois family. In 1917, he went to study in Tokyo and joined the socialist movement. He joined the Communist Youth League in 1921 and became a member of its central committee. Although based in Shanghai he was aligned with the Irkutsk faction. He was arrested in April 1922 while trying to enter Korea. After his release he worked as a journalist. He drifted away from the socialist movement in the early 1930s and moved to the right. According to some sources, he supported the 1961 coup d'état in South Korea.
Son Kongnin	14 Nov 1902	A delegate from the Korean Students Union.
Sŏng Yuhwan	10 June 1888	Sŏng studied at military school in Korea. He was a delegate from a Seoul trade union.
Sŭng Chin	20 Sept 1889	A peasant, delegate from the Kwangboktan (Restoration League).
Tok Kojŏn	10 Feb 1892	A delegate from the Sinŭiju Dockers Union and a member of the Communist Party. Tok said he was a trader and his aims were independence and communism. He was born in P'yŏng'an province. After a spell as a grain trader he left Korea for Harbin in 1919. In 1921, he went to Chita where he joined the communist movement. In 1924, he returned to P'yŏng'an as a Comintern organiser and attended the (re-)founding congress of the Korea Communist Party in April 1925. He was imprisoned in December the same year and released in 1929.
Yi Chaegon	25 May 1902	Law student and candidate member of the Communist party.
Yi Hwaryong	1879	Peasant. A delegate from the First Korean Brigade of the Red Army.
Yi Mu	5 Nov 1890	Peasant. A delegate from a Korean youth organisation.
Yi Sŏn'gu	14 April 1899	A Red Army soldier who said his aim was world proletarian revolution. He arrived in Russia in 1918 from China.
Yi Sŏk-ki[11]		One of seven supporters of the Shanghai faction among the Korean delegates.

---

11 Ibid.

(cont.)

Name	Dates	Notes
Yi Wanung	17 Sept 1896	A peasant delegated from a Korean Independence organisation. Also a member of the Korean Communist Party in Shanghai.
Yi Yŏngsŏn / Ri Yŏngsŏn	22 May 1887	A miner delegated from the Communist Party of the Ukraine and the South Russia Korean Labour Union Yi represented Korean miners who had been sent to the Donbas region by the Tsarist regime during World War One, and had become stranded by the civil war. Yi was apparently trying to negotiate their return to the Russian Far East. Remarks on his questionnaire record he was 'revolutionary worker' who spoke Russian, Chinese and Japanese in addition to Korean. In an archive photograph of the congress. Yi is picked out by four crosses. On the back of the photograph is a handwritten note describing him as a 'provocateur [unclear] by the organs of the NKVD'.[12]
Yŏ Unhyŏng. He signed his name in English W.H. Lyuh	1881–1947	A delegate from the Central Committee of the Korean Communist Party. Although Yŏ was based in Shanghai, he was aligned with the Irkutsk faction. Yŏ was one of the leading figures in Korea's independence movement. He was born into a wealthy yangban family, became a Christian and studied English literature in China, where he joined the Korean Communist Party in 1920 or 1921, and the Kuomintang in 1924. He was jailed in Korea from 1929 to 1932 and in Japan in 1942. In 1945, the Japanese colonial authorities selected him as a credible politician to hand power to. Yŏ established the Committee for the Preparation of Korean Independence (CPKI / *Kŏn'guk chunbi wiwonhoe*) and organised people's committees across the country. The CPKI declared the People's Republic of Korea (PRK), with a programme of nationalisation of major industries, confiscation of collaborators' land, and an eight-hour working day. When US forces landed in South Korea they suppressed the PRK and established a military government. In the north, the people's committees fell under Soviet control. Yŏ was assassinated by a right-wing extremist on 19 July 1947.
Yu Kŏnhyŏk	11 Feb 1892	A peasant farmer, delegate from the Korean Youth League and a member of the Communist Party.
Yun Wonjang	17 Jan 1896	A metal worker, delegate from the Korean Youth League. Yun said his aim was Korean independence and peace in the East.

---

12   495-154-181a, Russian State Archive of Socio-Political History, Moscow. The word seems to be "rassrel". There is no date on the note.

Bibliography

Adle, Chahryar and Madhavan K. Palat 2005, *History of Civilizations of Central Asia, Volume VI*, Paris: UNESCO.
Akimova, Vera Vladimirovna Vishniyakova 1971, *Two Years in Revolutionary China, 1925–1927*, Cambridge, MA: East Asian Research Center, distributed by Harvard University Press.
Archief Henk Sneevliet. International Institute of Social History, Amsterdam.
Argenbright, Robert 2011, 'Vanguard of "Socialist Colonization"? The Krasnyi Vostok Expedition of 1920', *Central Asian Survey*, 30(3–4): 437–54.
Atwood, Christopher Pratt 2004, *Encyclopedia of Mongolia and the Mongol Empire*, New York: Facts on File.
Barnouin, Barbara and Changgeng Yu 2006, *Zhou Enlai: A Political Life*, Hong Kong: Chinese University Press.
Batbayar, Bat-Erdene and Christopher Kaplonski 1999, *History of Mongolia*, Ulaanbaatar: Monsudar Publ.
Batbayar, Ts 2005, 'The Mongolian People's Revolution of 1921 and the Mongolian People's Republic (1924–46)', in *Towards the Contemporary Period: From the Mid-nineteenth to the End of the Twentieth Century*, edited by Chahryar Adle, Paris: UNESCO.
Bawden, C.R. 2009, *The Modern History of Mongolia*, London. Routledge.
Becker, Jasper 2008, *City of Heavenly Tranquillity: Beijing in the History of China*, London: Allen Lane.
Beckmann, George M. and Genji Okubo 1969, *The Japanese Communist Party 1922–1945*, Stanford, CA: Stanford University Press.
Benton, Gregor 1996, *China's Urban Revolutionaries: Explorations in the History of Chinese Trotskyism, 1921–1952*, Atlantic Highlands, NJ: Humanities Press.
Benton, Gregor (trans. and ed.) 1997, *An Oppositionist for Life: Memoirs of the Chinese Revolutionary Zheng Chaolin*, Atlantic Highlands, NJ: Humanities Press.
Benton, Gregor 2007, *Chinese Migrants and Internationalism: Forgotten Histories, 1917–1945*, London: Routledge.
Bergére, Marie-Claire 1994, *Sun Yat-sen*, Stanford, CA: Stanford University Press.
Berton, Peter 2006, 'From Enemies to Allies. The War and Russo-Japanese Relations', in *The Impact of the Russo-Japanese War*, edited by Rotem Kowner, Leiden: Brill, 78–87.
Berton, Peter 2012, *Russo-Japanese Relations, 1905–1917: From Enemies to Allies*, Abingdon: Routledge.
Billingsley, Phil 1988, *Bandits in Republican China*, Stanford, CA: Stanford University Press.
Bing, Dov 2009, 'Lenin and Sneevliet: The Origins of the Theory of Colonial Revolution in the Dutch East Indies', *New Zealand Journal of Asian Studies*, 11(1): 153–77.

Bisher, Jamie 2005, *White Terror: Cossack Warlords of the Trans-Siberian*, London: Frank Cass.

Boorman, Howard L., Richard C. Howard and Joseph K.H. Cheng 1967, *Biographical Dictionary of Republican China*, New York: Columbia University Press.

Bradley, James 2009, *The Imperial Cruise: A Secret History of Empire and War*, New York: Little, Brown and Co.

Brandt, Conrad 1958, *Stalin's Failure in China, 1924–1927*, Cambridge, MA: Harvard University Press.

Brandt, Conrad, Benjamin I. Schwartz and John King Fairbank 1952, *A Documentary History of Chinese Communism*, Cambridge, MA: Harvard University Press.

Buckley, Sandra (ed.) 2002, *Encyclopedia of Contemporary Japanese Culture*. London: Routledge.

Buell, Raymond Leslie 1922, *The Washington Conference*, New York: D. Appleton and Co.

Buzo, Adrian 2002, *The Making of Modern Korea*, London: Routledge.

Cadart, Claude and Cheng Yingxiang 1983, *Memoirs de Peng Shuzhi: L'Envol du communisme en Chine*, Paris: Gallimard.

Cain, P.J. and A.G. Hopkins 2002, *British Imperialism, 1688–2000*, Harlow: Longman.

Carr, Edward Hallett 1952, *The Bolshevik Revolution: 1917–1923*, London: Macmillan.

Chan Lau, Kit-ching 1990, *China, Britain and Hong Kong, 1895–1945*, Hong Kong: Chinese University Press.

Chattopadhyaya, Gautam 1976, *Abani Mukherji, a Dauntless Revolutionary and Pioneering Communist*, New Delhi: People's Publishing House.

Chattopadhyay, Kunal 2009, 'Manabendra Nath Roy (1897–1979)', in *The International Encyclopedia of Revolution and Protest, Volume 6*, edited by Immanuel Ness, Malden, MA: Wiley-Blackwell.

Chesneaux, Jean 1968, *The Chinese Labour Movement, 1919–1927*, Stanford, CA: Stanford University Press.

Chicherin, G.V. 1922, 'The Washington Conference', *Soviet Russia*, 6(1), January.

Chung, Young-Iob 2006, *Korea Under Siege, 1876–1945: Capital Formation and Economic Transformation*, Oxford: Oxford University Press.

Cohen, Stephen F. 1973, *Bukharin and the Bolshevik Revolution: A Political Biography, 1888–1938*, New York: Alfred A. Knopf.

Congress of the Toilers of the Far East 1922, *Der Erste Kongress der Kommunistischen und Revolutionären Organisationen des Fernen Ostens, Moskau, Januar 1922*. Verlag der Kommunistischen Internationale, Auslieferungsstelle für Deutschland, Hamburg: C. Hoym Nachf.

Congress of the Toilers of the Far East 1970, *The First Congress of the Toilers of the Far East, held in Moscow, January 21st–February 1st 1922, closing session in Petrograd, February 2nd 1922*, London: The Hammersmith Bookshop, Ltd.

Conroy, Hilary 1960, *The Japanese Seizure of Korea, 1868–1910: A Study of Realism and*

Idealism in International Relations, Philadelphia: University of Pennsylvania Press.

Cornell, Richard 1982, *Revolutionary Vanguard: The Early Years of the Communist Youth International, 1914–1924*, Toronto: University of Toronto Press.

Craft, Stephen G. 2003, *V.K. Wellington Koo and the Emergence of Modern China*, Lexington: University Press of Kentucky.

Crane, Daniel M. and Thomas A. Breslin 1986, *An Ordinary Relationship: American Opposition to Republican Revolution in China*, Gainesville, FL: University Presses of Florida.

Dalin, Sergei 1928, Очерки революции в Китае (Sketches of the Revolution in China), Moscow.

Degras, Jane 1971, *The Communist International, 1919–1943 Documents*, London: Routledge.

Dirlik, Arif 1989, *The Origins of Chinese Communism*, New York: Oxford University Press.

Dirlik, Arif 1991, *Anarchism in the Chinese Revolution*, Berkeley, CA: University of California Press.

Dickinson, Frederick R. 1999, *War and National Reinvention: Japan in the Great War, 1914–1919*, Cambridge, MA: Harvard University Press.

Dukes, Paul 2012, *The USA in the Making of the USSR: The Washington Conference, 1921–1922, and 'uninvited Russia'*, London: Routledge.

Dunscomb, Paul E. 2011, *Japan's Siberian Intervention, 1918–1922: A Great Disobedience Against the People*, Lanham, MD: Lexington Books.

Duus, Peter and Irwin Scheiner (eds) 1989, *The Cambridge History of Japan, Volume 6: The Twentieth Century*, Cambridge: Cambridge University Press.

Edwards, Louise P. 2008, *Gender, Politics, and Democracy: Women's Suffrage in China*, Stanford, CA: Stanford University Press.

Elleman, Bruce A. 2002, *Wilson and China: A Revised History of the Shandong Question*, Armonk, NY: M.E. Sharpe.

Elleman, Bruce A. 2009, *Moscow and the Emergence of Communist Power in China, 1925–30: The Nanchang Uprising and the Birth of the Red Army*, London: Routledge.

Esherick, Joseph and C.X. George Wei 2014, *China: How the Empire Fell*, London: Routledge.

Fairbank, John King and Kwang-Ching Liu 2008, *The Cambridge History of China, Volume 11*, Cambridge: Cambridge University Press.

Far Eastern Republic 1922, *A Short Outline of the History of the Far Eastern Republic. Published by the Special Delegation of the Far Eastern Republic to the United States of America*.

Fenby, Jonathan 2004, *Chiang Kai-shek: China's Generalissimo and the Nation He Lost*, New York: Carroll & Graf.

Fink, Carole 1993, *The Genoa Conference: European Diplomacy 1921–1922*, Syracuse: Syracuse University Press.

Finley, John H. and James Sullivan 1919, *American Democracy from Washington to Wilson: Addresses and State Papers*, New York: The Macmillan Company.

Fuller, Pierre 2013, 'North China Famine Revisited: Unsung Native Relief in the Warlord Era, 1920–1921', *Modern Asian Studies*, 47(3): 820–50.

Gale Research Inc. 1998, *Encyclopedia of World Biography*, Detroit: Gale Research.

Ganin, A.V. 2004, *Chernogorets na russkoi sluzhbe: general Bakich*, Moskva: Russkii put'.

Gerwarth, Robert and Erez Manela 2014, *Empires at War: 1911–1923*, Oxford: Oxford University Press.

Goldman, Merle and Andrew Gordon 2000, *Historical Perspectives on Contemporary East Asia*, Cambridge, MA: Harvard University Press.

Goodman, David S.G. 1990, *China and the West: Ideas and Activists*, Manchester: Manchester University Press.

Gragert, Edwin H. 1994, *Landownership Under Colonial Rule: Korea's Japanese Experience, 1900–1935*, Honolulu: University of Hawai'i Press.

Gray, Jack 2002, *Rebellions and Revolutions: China from the 1800s to 2000*, Oxford: Oxford University Press.

Hall, John Whitney 1988, *The Cambridge History of Japan*, Cambridge: Cambridge University Press.

Hopkirk, Peter 2001, *Setting the East Ablaze: On Secret Service in Bolshevik Asia*, Oxford: Oxford University Press.

Houtsma, M.Th. 1993, *E.J. Brill's First Encyclopaedia of Islam, 1913–1936*, Leiden: E.J. Brill.

Hunter, Janet 1984, *Concise Dictionary of Modern Japanese History*, Berkeley, CA: University of California Press.

Hwang, Kyung Moon 2010, *A History of Korea: An Episodic Narrative*, Basingstoke: Palgrave Macmillan.

Im, Kyŏngsŏk 1999, 'Kŭktong Minjok Taehoe-wa Chosŏn Taep'yodan', *Yŏksawa Hyŏnshil*, Han'guk Nyŏksa Yŏn'guhoe. ('The Korean delegation to the Far East People's Congress', *Quarterly Review of Korean History*, Korean History Research Association), 54–7.

Isaacs, Harold R. 1938, *The Tragedy of the Chinese Revolution*, London: Secker & Warburg.

Jacobson, Jon 1994, *When the Soviet Union Entered World Politics*, Berkeley, CA: University of California Press, http://ark.cdlib.org/ark:/13030/ft009nb0bb/.

Jansen, Marius 1980, 'Japan and the Chinese Revolution of 1911', in *The Cambridge History of China, Volume 11*, edited by John King Fairbank and Kwang-Ching Liu, Cambridge: Cambridge University Press.

Ji, Zhaojin 2003, *A History of Modern Shanghai Banking*, Armonk, NY: M.E. Sharpe.

Johnson, Kay Ann 2009, *Women, the Family, and Peasant Revolution in China*, Chicago: University of Chicago Press.

Katayama Sen 1918, *The Labor Movement in Japan*, Chicago: C.H. Kerr & Co.
Kennedy, Malcolm 1957, *A History of Communism in East Asia*, New York: Praeger Publishers.
Kilgroe, Louisa E. 1999, 'Banker as Diplomat, Thomas W. Lamont in Post-World-War I Japan'.
Kim, Djun Kil 2005, *The History of Korea*, Westport, CT: Greenwood Press.
Kim, Richard S. 2011, *The Quest for Statehood: Korean Immigrant Nationalism and US Sovereignty, 1905–1945*, Oxford: Oxford University Press.
Korean Mission to the Conference on the Limitation of Armament, Washington, DC, 1921–1922, *Korea's Appeal to the Conference on Limitation of Armament*, Washington, DC: GPO.
Kotkin, Stephen and Bruce A. Elleman 1999, *Mongolia in the Twentieth Century: Landlocked Cosmopolitan*, Armonk, NY: M.E. Sharpe.
Lai, H. Mark 2010, *Chinese American Transnational Politics*, Urbana, IL: University of Illinois Press.
Lan, Mei-Hua 1999, 'China's "New Administration" in Mongolia', in *Mongolia in the Twentieth Century: Landlocked Cosmopolitan*, by Steven Kotkin and Bruce A. Elleman, New York: M.E. Sharpe, 39–58.
Large, Stephen S. 1977, *The Labour Movement in Japan, 1912–1919: Suzuki Bunji and the Yuaikai*, Ann Arbor, MI: University Microfilms International.
Large, Stephen S. 1981, *Organized Workers and Socialist Politics in Interwar Japan*, Cambridge: Cambridge University Press.
Lattimore, Owen 1955, *Nationalism and Revolution in Mongolia*, Leiden: E.J. Brill.
Lazitch, Branko M. and Milorad M. Drachkovitch 1986, *Biographical Dictionary of the Comintern*, Stanford, CA: Hoover Institution Press.
Lee, Chong-Sik 1963, *The Politics of Korean Nationalism*, Berkeley, CA: University of California Press.
Lee, Peter H. (ed.) 1993, *Sourcebook of Korean Civilization, Volume 1*, New York: Columbia University Press.
Lee, Peter H. (ed.) 1996, *Sourcebook of Korean Civilization, Volume 2*, New York: Columbia University Press.
Lee, Peter H. and William Theodore De Bary 1997, *Sources of Korean Tradition*, New York: Columbia University Press.
Lenin, V.I. 1975, *Collected Works*, Moscow: Progress Publishers.
Lenin, V.I. 1977, *Collected Works*. Moscow: Progress Publishers.
Lewis, Ben, Lars T. Lih, Grigory Yevseyevich Zinovyev and L. Martov 2011, *Martov and Zinoviev: Head to Head in Halle*, London: November Publications.
Li, Chien-Nung, Ssu-yü Teng and Jeremy Ingalls 1967, *The Political History of China, 1840–1928*, Stanford, CA: Stanford University Press.
Li, Xiaobing 2012, *China at War: An Encyclopedia*, Santa Barbara, CA: ABC-CLIO.

Libbey, James K. 1977, *Alexander Gumberg and Soviet-American Relations, 1917–1933*, Lexington: University Press of Kentucky.

Linden, Marcel van der and Jürgen Rojahn 1990, *The Formation of Labour Movements, 1870–1914: An International Perspective*, Leiden: E.J. Brill.

Liu, Xiaoyuan 2006, *Reins of Liberation: An Entangled History of Mongolian Independence, Chinese Territoriality, and Great Power Hegemony, 1911–1950*, Washington, DC: Woodrow Wilson Center Press.

Lowe, Cedric James and Michael L. Dockrill 1972, *The Mirage of Power, 2 volumes*, London: Routledge & Kegan Paul.

MacKenzie, Frederick Arthur 1920, *Korea's Fight for Freedom*, London: Simpkin, Marshall & Co.

Martin, Bradley K. 2013, *Under the Loving Care of the Fatherly Leader: North Korea and the Kim Dynasty*, New York: St. Martin's Press.

McCauley, Martin 1997, *Who's Who in Russia since 1900*, London: Routledge.

McCormack, Gavan 1977, *Chang Tso-lin in Northeast China, 1911–1928: China, Japan, and the Manchurian Idea*, Stanford, CA: Stanford University Press.

McVey, Ruth Thomas 2006, *The Rise of Indonesian Communism*, Jakarta: Equinox Pub.

Medvedev, Roj Aleksandrovič 1989, *Let History Judge: The Origins and Consequences of Stalinism*, Oxford: Oxford University Press.

Mitter, Rana 2000, *The Manchurian Myth Nationalism, Resistance and Collaboration in Modern China*, Berkeley, CA: University of California Press.

Mitter, Rana 2004, *A Bitter Revolution: China's Struggle with the Modern World*, Oxford: Oxford University Press.

Moltchanoff, Victorin Mikhailovich and Boris Raymond 1972, *The Last White General: An Interview*, Berkeley, CA: University of California, Bancroft Library, Regional Oral History Office.

Morton, Leith 2004, *Modernism in Practice: An Introduction to Postwar Japanese Poetry*, Honolulu: University of Hawai'i Press.

Naumov, V.P., A.A. Kraiushkin and N.V. Teptsov 2005, *Stalin's Secret Pogrom: The Post-War Inquisition of the Jewish Anti-Fascist Committee*, New Haven, CT: Yale University Press.

Ness, Immanuel 2009, *The International Encyclopedia of Revolution and Protest: 1500 to the Present*, Malden, MA: Wiley-Blackwell.

Nicolle, David 1990, *Attila and the Nomad Hordes: Warfare on the Eurasian Steppes 4th–12th Centuries*, London: Osprey.

Nimura, Kazuo 1990, 'Japan', in *The Formation of Labour Movements, 1870–1914: An International Perspective*, edited by Marcel van der Linden and Jürgen Rojahn, Leiden: Brill.

Nimura, Kazuo and Andrew Gordon 1997, *The Ashio Riot of 1907: A Social History of Mining in Japan*, Durham, NC: Duke University Press.

Olsen, Edward A. 2005, *Korea, the Divided Nation*, Westport, CT: Praeger Security International.
Palace, Wendy 2004, *The British Empire and Tibet 1900–1922*, New York: Routledge.
Palmer, James 2009, *The Bloody White Baron: The Extraordinary Story of the Russian Nobleman Who Became the Last Khan of Mongolia*, New York: Basic Books.
Pantsov, Alexander 2009, 'Zhang Guotao (1897–1979)', in *The International Encyclopedia of Revolution and Protest, Volume 7*, edited by Immanuel Ness, Malden, MA: Wiley-Blackwell.
Pantsov, Alexander 2013, *The Bolsheviks and the Chinese Revolution, 1919–1927*, Oxford: Routledge.
Pasvolsky, Leo 1922, *Russia in the Far East*, New York: Macmillan.
Perry, Elizabeth J. 1993, *Shanghai on Strike: The Politics of Chinese Labor*, Stanford, CA: Stanford University Press.
Pratt, Keith L., Richard Rutt and James Hoare 1999, *Korea: A Historical and Cultural Dictionary*, Richmond: Curzon Press.
Prokhorov, A.M. 1980, *Great Soviet Encyclopedia*, New York: Macmillan.
Pye, Lucien W. and May W. Pye 1984, *China: An Introduction*, Boston: Little Brown.
Rabinowitch, Alexander 1991, *Prelude to Revolution: The Petrograd Bolsheviks and the July 1917 Uprising*, Bloomington, IN: Indiana University Press.
Rabinowitch, Alexander 1999, *Prelude to Revolution: The Petrograd Bolsheviks and the July 1917 Uprising*, Indiana: Indiana University Press.
Reinsch, Paul S. 1922, *An American Diplomat in China*, Garden City, NY: Doubleday, Page & Co.
Rhoads, Edward J.M. 2000, *Manchus and Han Ethnic Relations and Political Power in Late Qing and Early Republican China, 1861–1928*, Seattle: University of Washington Press.
Riddell, John (ed.) 1993, *To See the Dawn, Baku, 1920: First Congress of the Peoples of the East*, New York: Pathfinder.
Rubenstein, Joshua and Vladimir Pavlovich Naumov 2001, *Stalin's Secret Pogrom: The Postwar Inquisition of the Jewish Anti-Fascist Committee*, New Haven, CT: Yale University Press.
Russian State Archive of Socio-Political History, Moscow.
Safarov, Georgii Ivanovich 1923, *Natsional'nyii vopros i proletariat*, Moskva: Izdatel'stvo 'Krasnaia Nov'', Glavpolitprosvet.
Safarov, Georgii Ivanovich 1935, *The Far East Ablaze*, New York City: Workers' Library.
Safarov, Georgii Ivanovich and A.K. Bochagov 1996, *Kolonial'naia revoliutsiia: opyt Turkestana*, Almaty: Zhalyn.
Saich, Tony 1991, *The Origins of the First United Front in China: The Role of Sneevliet (alias Maring)*, Leiden: Brill.

Saich, Tony and Bingzhang Yang 1996, *The Rise to Power of the Chinese Communist Party: Documents and Analysis*, Armonk, NY: M.E. Sharpe.

Saich, Tony and Hans J. Van de Ven 1995, *New Perspectives on the Chinese Communist Revolution*, Armonk, NY: M.E. Sharpe.

Sanders, Alan J.K. 2010, *Historical Dictionary of Mongolia*, Lanham, MD: Scarecrow Press.

Scalapino, Robert A. 1975, *Democracy and the Party Movement in Pre-war Japan: The Failure of the First Attempt*, Berkeley, CA: University of California Press.

Scalapino, Robert A. 1983, *The Early Japanese Labour Movement: Labour and Politics in a Developing Society*, Berkeley, CA: Institute of East Asian Studies, University of California, Berkeley, Center for Japanese Studies.

Scalapino, Robert A. and Chong-Sik Lee 1961, 'The Origins of the Korean Communist Movement (II)', *Journal of Asian Studies*, 20(2): 149–67.

Scalapino, Robert A. and Chong-Sik Lee 1972, *Communism in Korea*, Berkeley, CA: University of California Press.

Schimmelpenninck Van Der Oye, David 2005, 'The Immediate Origins of the War', in *The Russo-Japanese War in Global Perspective: World War Zero*, edited by John W. Steinberg et al., Boston: Brill.

Seaman, Louis Livingston 1905, *From Tokio through Manchuria with the Japanese*, New York: D. Appleton and Company.

Serge, Victor 2002, *Memoirs of a Revolutionary*, Iowa City: University of Iowa Press.

Seth, Michael J. 2011, *A History of Korea: From Antiquity to the Present*, Lanham, MD: Rowman & Littlefield.

Shaw, Carole Cameron 2007, *The Foreign Destruction of Korean Independence*, Seoul: Seoul National University Press.

Smith, S.A. 2000, *A Road is Made: Communism in Shanghai, 1920–1927*, Honolulu: University of Hawai'i Press.

Smith, S.A. 2002, *Like Cattle and Horses: Nationalism and Labour in Shanghai, 1895–1927*, Durham, NC: Duke University Press.

Soedjatmoko 2007, *An Introduction to Indonesian Historiography*, Jakarta: Equinox Pub.

Stanley, Thomas A. 1982, *Ōsugi Sakae, Anarchist in Taishō Japan: The Creativity of the Ego*, Cambridge, MA: Council on East Asian Studies, Harvard University.

Steinberg, John W. 2005, *The Russo-Japanese War in Global Perspective: World War Zero*, Leiden: Brill.

Sun Yat-sen 2014, *The International Development of China*.

Sutter, Robert G. 2010, *US-Chinese Relations: Perilous Past, Pragmatic Present*, Lanham, MD: Rowman & Littlefield.

Tang, Peter S.H. 1959, *Russian and Soviet Policy in Manchuria and Outer Mongolia, 1911–1931*, Durham, NC: Duke University Press.

Tanner, Harold Miles 2008, *China: A History of One of the World's Oldest Civilizations*, Indianapolis, IN: Hackett.
Tarasov, Michael 2008, 'The Yenisei Cossacks in Mongolia during the Civil War Period', *Journal of Siberian Federal University: Humanities & Social Sciences*, 1(1): 104–14.
Tarasov, Michael 2011, Eniseĭskoe kazachestvo v gody revoliūtsii i grazhdanskoĭ voĭny, 1917–1922: monografiiā. Moskva: Flinta.
Taylor, Richard 1991, 'Ideology as Mass Entertainment: Boris Shumyatsky and Soviet Cinema in the 1930s', in *Inside the Film Factory: New Approaches to Russian and Soviet Cinema*, edited by Richard Taylor and Ian Christie, New York: Routledge, 193–216.
Taylor, Richard and Ian Christie 1991, *Inside the Film Factory: New Approaches to Russian and Soviet Cinema*, London: Routledge.
Trotsky, Leon and Ahmed Shawki 2009, *History of the Russian Revolution*, New York: Haymarket Books.
Trotsky, Leon, John G. Wright and Richard Chappell 1973, *The First Five Years of the Communist International*, London: New Park Publications.
Trotsky, Leon, Leslie Evans and Russell Block 1976, *Leon Trotsky on China*, New York: Monad Press.
Wang, Fanxi 1991, *Memoirs of a Chinese Revolutionary*, New York: Columbia University Press.
Weiner, Michael 1989, *The Origins of the Korean Community in Japan, 1910–1923*, Manchester: Manchester University Press.
Whiting, Allen Suess 1954, *Soviet Policies in China, 1917–1924*, New York: Columbia University.
Whitney Griswold, A. 1938, *The Far Eastern Policy of the United States*, New York: Harcourt Brace and Company.
Wilbur, C. Martin 1984, *The Nationalist Revolution in China, 1923–1928*, Cambridge: Cambridge University Press.
Wilbur, C. Martin and Julie Lien-ying How 1989, *Missionaries of Revolution: Soviet Advisers and Nationalist China, 1920–1927*, Cambridge, MA: Harvard University Press.
Williams, Michael 1980, 'Sneevliet and the Birth of Asian Communism', *New Left Review*, I/123: 81–90.
Wittfogel, Karl A. 1960, 'The Legend of "Maoism"', *China Quarterly* (January–March; April–June): 72–86; 16–31.
Wohl, Robert 1966, *French Communism in the Making, 1914–1924*, Stanford, CA: Stanford University Press.
Xu, Guoqi 2005, *China and the Great War: China's Pursuit of a New National Identity and Internationalization*, Cambridge: Cambridge University Press.
Yang Kuisong 1994, 'Yuandong geguo gongchandang ji minzu geming tuanti daibiaodahui de zhongguo diabiao wenti' (The question of the Chinese delegation to the con-

gress of far eastern communist parties and revolutionary organisations), *Jindaishi yanjiu*, 2: 269–84.

Yao, Jin'guo and Hang Su 2007, *Zhang Guotao zhuan* (Biography of Zhang Guotao), Xi'an: Shanxi renmin chubanshe.

Yi, Ki-baek 1984, *A New History of Korea*, Cambridge, MA: Published for the Harvard-Yenching Institute by Harvard University Press.

Zhang, Qiao 2011, *An sha wang Wang Yaqiao quan zhuan*, Nanjing: Feng huang chu ban she.

Zhang, Guotao 1971, *Wo de huiyi*, Hong Kong: Mingpao Monthly.

Zhao, Suisheng 1996, *Power by Design: Constitution-making in Nationalist China*, Honolulu: University of Hawai'i Press.

Index

Africa 125, 129, 130
Alimin, Indonesian Communist leader 36, 36n87
All-Russia Korean Association (Chŏnlo hanin hoe) 142
All-Russia Korean Labour Union 317
All-Russian Central Executive Committee 50, 84, 304
Alliance of Four Bloodsuckers 71, 277, 300, 301, 303
   See also Four Power Treaty
Alshus, Mongolian tribe 160
Altan Khan 162n10
Amakasu Masahiko, murderer of Osugi Sakae 199n61
Amalgamated Union of the organizations of Korean Youth 302
Amban Sando 9, 170, 170n27
Amur Society   *See* Black Dragon Society
An Chunggŭn
   assassinates Ito Hirobumi 125n13
Anarcho-syndicalists 7, 197, 199, 199n61, 200, 235, 236
Anfu (Peace and Happiness) Club 90, 90n5, 90n6, 166, 166n19, 167, 168, 279
Anglo-Japanese Alliance 6, 48n4, 123n7, 124, 124n10, 204, 204n4, 275, 319
Anhui clique 4, 90n6, 115n38, 167n21
Annam 252
Asahara Kenzo 195n50
Ashio copper mine strike 194
Association of Enlightened People 198n55
Australia 205

Bakich, General Andrei Stepanovich 169, 169n25
Baku Congress of the People's of the East 2, 2n3, 15, 47, 47n3, 48, 268, 296, 297
Balfour, Lord Arthur James 204n4
Balkans 69
Bank of Chosen 175
Banking Consortium 92n9, 101, 103n5, 278n5, 300
Beijing-Hankou railway strikes 38, 88n1, 90n5, 93, 93n12
Beiyang Army 107n13, 110n23, 110n24, 113n31

Bela Kun 2n3, 16, 49
Bertrand Russell 231
Black Dragon Society
   plans conquest of China 225, 225n4
Blagoveshchensk 154, 154n72
Bodoo, Dogsomyn, Prime Minister of Mongolia 31, 159n1
Bogda Khagan 9, 164n15, 167, 167n22, 320, 323
Borodin, Mikhail 39, 61n15, 321
   reorganization of Kuomintang 39
   Soviet representative in China 39
   works with Katayama in Mexico 49n5
Bosporus and Dardanelles 69
Boxer uprising 76n19, 77, 77n21, 100, 106, 135, 277, 319
Briand, Auguste, French PM 20, 68, 68n8, 71
Britain 3, 26, 57n11, 77n21, 285n3
   alliance with Japan 124, 125n15, 204n4
   coal reserves 227
   Opium wars 89n2
   proposes triple alliance 203, 204n4
   takes Weihaiwei 319
Buddhism 9n20, 133n25, 160n3
Bureau of military affairs 152
Buryats 160n6, 166n18, 305, 306, 322, 323
Buyannemekh, Sonombaljiryn 65, 213, 213n19, 322

Cai E, leads revolt against Yuan Shikai 110n21, 248n9
Canada 43, 88n1, 107n9, 185, 205, 216n23, 227, 328
Cannes Conference 19, 20, 285, 285n3
Canton Commune 321
Cao Rulin
   Chinese foreign minister, attacked by May Fourth protesters 114
cattle raising 30, 162, 164, 262
Ch'ae Tongsun, Korean delegate Kor-Khan 17, 240, 240n1, 242n3, 330
Ch'oe Che-u
   founder of Tonghak religion 134n26
Ch'ŏndogyo (Heavenly Way religion) 128n21, 143, 143n41, 144, 146

Ch'onggunbu (General Army Headquarters) 153
Ch'ŏngnyŏndan yŏnhap'oe (Young Men's Federation) 156
Chahar 280n8
Charles Evans Hughes, U.S. Secretary of State 204n4
Chemul'po 176, 299
Chen Duxiu
    accepts job from Chen Jiongming 26
    approves decisions of Toilers' Congress 38
    editor of *New Youth* 26
    employs Huang Bihun 57n11
    first leader of Chinese Communist Party 10, 93n11
    May Fourth commander in chief 10
    meets Osugi Sakae 29
    neutral on Chen Jiongming coup 27n63
    opposes Sneevliet's bloc within 38
Chen Jiongming 8n18
    aim was a federal China 26
    coup against Sun Yat-sen 26, 38
    employs Chen Duxiu 57n11
Chen Yi 166, 167
Chiang Kai-shek -12, 37, 40, 40n103, 61n15, 72n13, 75n18, 104n6, 114n35, 230n9, 321
Chianju 147
Chicherin, Georgy (Soviet foreign minister)
    accepts invitation to Genoa 19
    offers to honour Tsarist debt 19
    protests against Russia's exclusion from Washington Conference 3
    seeks normalization of relations 73n14
    signs Treaty of Rapallo 20n53
    stresses difference between Comintern and Russian government 19
    warns Lenin about Toilers' Congress 19
child labour 90, 95
China
    1911 Xinhai Revolution, fall of Qing dynasty 2, 7, 46, 72n13, 91, 92, 92n9, 101, 103n5, 111n25, 115, 128, 141, 161, 210, 224, 278
    Beijing government 4, 8, 10, 23, 91n7, 93n11, 167, 210, 211, 256, 280n8
    Canton government 8n18, 22, 48n4, 115, 210–212, 216, 248, 250, 261
    invasion of Mongolia, 1919 10, 279
    May Fourth Movement 10, 72n13, 88n1, 91n7, 93, 93n11, 110n23, 112n30, 113n32, 114, 320, 324, 325, 328
    war with Japan 1894–95 7, 100, 100n2, 106, 135, 136
    Wuhan government 41
Chinese Communist Party 2, 37, 38, 66n5, 301, 321
Chinese Eastern Railroad 275
Chita 166, 323, 335
Cho Tongho (delegate Kho) 35, 173n30, 331
    report on economic situation in Korea 173
Choibalsan, Khorloogiin, Mongolian dictator 11n26, 159n1, 323
Chosŏn Nodong Taehoe *See* General Labour Federation of Korea
Christians
    and Japanese labour movement 49n5, 200n62, 234n14
    in China 77, 92
    in Korean independence movement 9, 137–139, 142, 144, 146, 151
Chung, Henry 242n2
Communist International (Comintern)
    calls for soviets in colonial and semi-colonial countries 217, 231
    centralism 1
    debates within 1
    planned invasion of British India 15
    Second Congress resolution on anti-colonial struggle 1, 37, 48, 83–85, 221, 243, 260, 289
Confucianism
    and oppression of women 25, 119
    in Korea 133n25, 174
Constitutional Protection War 91n7
Consular Hill group, Mongolian nationalists 30n71, 159n1, 323
coolies 90, 96, 126, 131, 256, 314
Corporation Law of 1911 253n20
Crimea 19, 56, 207n8, 208, 208n10
Cuba 63
Curzon, Lord, British foreign secretary 204n4

Dalai Lama 9n20, 162n10, 167n22
Dalin, Sergei 65, 66n6

Danzan, Ajvaagiyn "Japanese" leader of Mongolian delegation   15, 292
Danzan, Soliin, Mongolian party leader   30, 30n71, 159n1
Declaration of Independence by Korean students in Tokyo   145
Declaration of Independence in Seoul, March 1, 1919   9, 128, 146
delay of world revolution   218
Dendev (delegate Din-Dib)   30, 31n71, 49, 159n1, 172, 220, 240, 271n3, 273, 274n6, 322
   biographical note   159n1
   executed   30
   report on Mongolia   159
   says Mongolian People's Party neither communist nor socialist   171
Deng Pei (delegate Wong Kien-ti)   88n1, 94n13, 96n16, 105n7, 324
   biographical note   94n13
   meeting with Lenin   94n13
   objects to Huang Lingshuang's trade union credentials   14
   on exploitation of women workers   24
   report on Chinese labour movement   94
   tortured and executed by Kuomintang   94n13
Derbeis, Mongolian tribe   160
disarmament   50, 69, 71, 205
disbanding of Korean army   125, 137, 320
Duan Qirui   91n7, 110, 110n23, 111n27, 112n28, 113n31, 113n32, 115, 115n38, 166n19, 167n21
dujun (military governors/warlords)   76, 226, 229, 230, 256, 261, 262, 264, 279, 303
Dutch East Indies   11, 59n13, 215n22, 321
   See also Indonesia
Dutch imperialism
   "little boy" of imperialism   214
duty to support oppressed nations   46–48, 223, 269

earthquake in Japan, 1923
   massacre of immigrants and leftists   28, 199n61, 321
East Urga group, Mongolian nationalists   159n1

ECCI   See Executive Committee of the Communist International
economic crisis of 1920   220
Egypt   74, 275
Eight-Nation Alliance   100, 319
Eisenstein, Sergei   65n1
Emperor of Korea   124, 233
Enlightened People's Communist Party   28, 198n55, 291n10, 330
Entente   5, 216, 270, 294
European revolution   7, 45, 81, 83
Evdokimov, Grigori   284, 284n2
Executive Committee of the Communist International   45, 45n1, 47, 274, 290, 296
extraterritoriality   8, 224, 277

famine in the Volga region   20, 286
Far East masses "last reserves of humanity"   86, 282, 283
   main force that will overthrow imperialism   217
Far Eastern Bureau of the Comintern   17, 65n1, 66n5, 331
Far Eastern Republic   4, 17, 43n3, 48n4, 54, 65n1, 65n3, 65n4, 159, 242n3, 275, 284, 306, 320, 322
   created in April 1920   20
   delegation to Washington   20, 207n8
   unites with Soviet Russia January 1922   321
Federation of Korean Youth (Chosŏn ch'ŏngnyŏn yŏnhap'oe)   314
Feng Guozhang   111n26, 113, 113n31, 113n32
feudalism
   in China   223, 224, 229
   in Korea   132–134
   in Mongolia   161, 162, 165, 169–171
   remnants of in Japan   234
Fifth Army of Soviet Russia Korean brigade   155
Finland   56
Five Power Naval Treaty   6, 48n4
Foreign Missions Board   150
Formosa   See Taiwan
Four-Power Treaty   6, 20, 203, 204, 206, 209
France
   aims to crush Soviet Russia   207
   and failure of Genoa conference   20, 73n14

350 INDEX

attack on Korea   8, 319
concessions in China   77n21, 319
Indochinese colonies   74, 252
involvement in Siberia   206
secret agreement with Japan   20, 207, 207n8, 208
war with China   319
World War One casualties   5n12, 68n9
Free City Incident   32, 154, 154n72, 320, 332
Fukumoto Kazuo   30
Fusataro Takano   192n46

Gelugpa school of Tibetan Buddhism   9n20, 162n10, 167n22
Gemingdang, forerunner of KMT   116, 116n42
General HQ of the Korean Restoration Army (Taehan kwangbokkun ch'ongyŏng)   315
General Labour Federation of Korea (Chosŏn Nodong Taehoe)   156, 302, 314
Genghis Khan   9, 9n20, 160, 160n4, 162n10, 167n22
Genoa conference   19, 20, 48, 68, 73, 73n14, 86, 283, 285, 285n3, 291, 297, 321
genro (Japanese elder statesmen)   183, 233, 280
Georgia   84n24
Germany
  a colony after World War One   270
  buys Yap archipelago from Spain   74n16
  invited to Genoa conference   19
  seizes Qingdao   278n4
  signs treaty of Rapallo with Russia   20, 21n53, 321
ginseng monopoly   179, 253
Girgeni, nomadic tribe   160
Gonghedang (Republican Party)   109n18, 248n9
Graves, General William S.   166n18
Great Shabi   11n25, 167n22
guilds   96, 96n16, 176

Hague Peace Conference   124, 124n12, 209
Han Chinese colonization of Mongolia   9, 23, 163
handicrafts destroyed by cheap imports   102, 176, 223
Hangzhou   38, 99n1, 170n27, 301, 318, 321, 328

Hangzhou plenum, 1922   38, 321
Hankou   38, 88n1, 90n5, 93, 93n12, 111n25, 301, 317, 318
Harbin   125n13, 301, 335
Harding, President Warren G.   22, 203, 205
Hawaii   72n13, 139, 142n34, 143, 319
Hideyoshi invasions   121
historical stages, impossible to skip   85, 262
Hong Kong and Canton seafarers' strike, 1922   37, 249n12, 321
Honghuzi (Red Beards)   76, 76n19, 264
Huang Bihun (Chinese delegate Wong)   26, 26n63, 49, 57, 57n11, 291, 325
  report on position of women in China   118
Huang Lingshuang, Chinese anarchist delegate   14, 325
Hubei   91, 318
Hunan   91, 96, 110, 110n21, 301, 301n2, 318, 324, 325, 327
Hunchun incident, 1920   130, 130n23, 153, 210n14

Ilchinhoe (Korean collaborationist organization)   140, 140n31
Imperialism as block on development   224
independence of Communists and labour movement   230–231, 259–261
India   43, 43n3, 59, 61, 61n15, 74, 160, 204, 214n21, 218, 228, 232, 245, 246, 252, 267, 275, 299
Indies Social Democratic Association (ISDV)   12, 59n12
Indochina   43, 43n5, 74, 296n12, 299, 303
Indonesia   35, 37, 41
Indonesian Communist Party
  origins of   12
  uprising and destruction   36, 37
International Seamen's Union of America   249n12
Ireland   78, 80, 245
Ito Hirobumi   125n13, 233n11
IWW (Industrial Workers of the World)   249n12

Jaisohn, Philip (Sŏ Chaep'il)   242n2
Japan Federation of Labour (Nihon Rodo Sodomei)   30, 200n62, 234n14, 301n4, 313n3

INDEX 351

Japan-Korea Treaty of Amity and Commerce, 1876   123n7, 319
Japan-Korea Treaty of Defensive and Offensive Alliance, 1904   123n7, 124
Japan Labour Union Council (Nihon Rodo Hyogikai)   30
Japan Metalworkers Union (Tekkokumiai)   192n46
Japan railway strike of 1898   193
Japan
   21 demands on China   5, 89n4, 93n10, 114n36, 320
   annexes Korea   8, 123, 125, 139, 140, 276, 320
   assassination of Korean Queen   8, 122
   atrocities in Korea   151
   role of proletariat   82, 264, 265
   domination of Korean economy   174, 176, 177
   fictitious role in World War One   220, 278
   imposes protectorate on Korea   8, 124, 125n13, 136, 137, 139, 319
   key to revolution in East Asia   81, 263
   Prussia of the East   80, 185, 233
   rice riots of 1918   81n22, 194, 195, 235, 320
   seeks puppet states in Siberia and Mongolia   10
   seizes Qingdao   5, 320
   semi-feudal plutocracy   234
Japanese Communist Party
   formation   28, 197, 198
   virtually wiped out by arrests   29
   votes to dissolve itself   29, 321
Jeam-ri massacre   151, 151n57
Jiaozhou bay, Qingdao   278, 278n4
Jibzundamba Khutugtu   *See* Bogda Khagan
jihad   2n3
Joffe, Adolph   23n57, 38, 52n7, 72n13, 247n7, 321
   concludes alliance with Sun Yat-sen   38
   doubts on Mongolian independence   23

Kalgan-Urga-Kyakhta caravan route   163
Kalinin, Mikhail Ivanovich   50, 50n6, 304
Kalmykov, Ataman Ivan Pavlovich   10
Kalmyks   13, 160, 160n5, 213, 267

Kamchatka   4, 4n9, 206, 207
Kando
   Korean settlement and guerrillas in   129, 142n34, 143, 149, 152–154, 332
Kang Youwei   107n9, 108, 108n14, 319
Kangxi emperor   107n12, 161, 162
Katayama Sen
   anti-war gesture with Plekhanov   290
   biographical note   49n5
   founder of Japanese labour movement   192, 192n46
   other speeches   49, 50, 66, 271, 272, 290
   report on political and economic problems of Japan   182
   report on the Four Power Pact and the Far East   203
Katterfeld, Ludwig Erwin (U.S. delegate John Carr)   43n1, 49, 62, 62n16, 295
Kazantsev, Cossack captain   168, 168n24
Kenseikai (Japan Constitutional Party)   183, 183n40, 185n41
Ker, Antoine (French delegate)   268, 268n1, 269, 271, 294
Khem (Korean delegate)   292
Kho-Syl-Mon (Korean delegate)   271, 273
Khobdo   161, 161n8
Kim Chow   *See* Yi Chaegon
Kim Il-Sung   35n84
Kim-Khu   *See* Rim Won-gun
Kim Kyu-sik
   biographical note   55n10
   Christian, educated in USA   10
   denounces Yi Tong-hwi   33
   foreign minister of Korean Provisional Government   14
   greeting to the congress   55
   Korean envoy to Paris Peace Conference   10
   remains in Moscow to seek aid after Far East Congress   33
   report on Korean revolutionary movement   132
Kim Won'gyŏng (Korean delegate Flore)   211
KMT   *See* Kuomintang
Koguryŏ (ancient Korean kingdom)   133n25
Kokuminto (Japan Constitutional Nationalist Party)   183, 183n40, 184

Kokuryukai   *See* Black Dragon Society
Kolchak, Admiral Alexander Vasilyevich   4n9, 20, 168, 169n25, 206, 320
Kolokolov   251
Kondo Eizo   28, 198, 198n55, 291n10
Koo (delegate)
  speech   250
Kor-Khan   *See* Ch'ae Tongsun
Korani, Mongolian tribe   160
Korea Labour Service and Relief Association (Nodong Kongjehoe)   156
Korea Restoration League (Kwanghandan)   316
Korea
  anti-Japanese guerrillas   143, 151–153, 295
    See also Righteous Army, *also* Kando
  bombardment by imperialists   122, 122n4
  Commission to Europe and America   149
  emigration and diaspora   9n19, 126, 126n18, 142, 176
  intense nationalism   137
  Josŏn dynasty   8, 133, 133n25
  Koryŏ dynasty   133, 133n25
  March First Movement   9, 128, 145–148, 210, 277
  mission to Washington Conference   242, 242n2
  sangnom class (commoners)   133
  situation of peasants   178, 179
  situation of workers   181
  Three Kingdoms era   133, 133n25
  Tonghak rebellion   8, 100n2, 122n5, 134, 134n26, 135, 136, 143n41, 144, 174, 178, 182, 319
  yangban (hereditary elite)   133, 133n25, 134, 135, 174, 176, 336
  See also Japan annexes Korea
  See also Japan imposes protectorate
Korean Communist Party
  armed conflict between factions   *See* Free City Incident
  Comintern description of   317
  origins   32, 35, 157, 254
  refounded inside Korea   35
  Shanghai and Irkutsk factions   32, 32n75, 33, 154n72, 242n3
  virtually wiped out by arrests   85

Korean Cooperative Association (Chosŏn Kongjedan)   315
Korean Independence League (Taehan tongniptan)   315
Korean Independence News   317
Korean miners in Donbas region   336
Korean National Council (Taehan kungmin ŭihoe)   33, 142, 154
Korean Provisional Government   9, 14, 32, 33, 55n10, 128, 128n21, 148, 149, 149n53, 150, 154n72, 155, 157, 242, 242n2, 316, 317
Korean Student League   314
Korean Women's Patriotic Society   157, 315, 334
Korean Youth Independence Corps (Josŏn Ch'ongnyon Tongniptan)   145n43
Kublai Khan   160n4, 162n10
Kuku, Mongolian tribe   160
Kungmin'gun (National Army)   153
Kuomintang
  Alliance with Chinese Communist Party   2, 16, 23, 37, 38
  and labour movement   248, 249, 260
  and Southern Chinese government   115, 116
  and Versailles treaty   113
  and Yuan Shikai   109
  attitude to Mongolian independence   22, 173, 212, 215
  attitude to soviets and parliaments   247
  attitude to United States   229
  land reform policy   24, 247, 261
  massacre of Communists   40
  name changes   116
  opposition to monarchist reformists   108
  relaunched in 1919   10
  reorganization on Soviet lines   39
  Soviet aid to   39
  Wang Jingwei and Kuomintang "left wing"   41
  wins 1912 election   8
Kuusinen, Otto   31, 33
Kwangbokkun (Korean Independence Restoration Army)   153
Kwangboktan (Korean Restoration League)   141, 335
Kwon Aera (Korean delegate Khwong)
  biographical note   243n5
  speech   243

INDEX   353

Kwŏnŏp'oe (Industrial Association, Korea)   142
Kyrgyzstan   264
Kyushu steel strike 1920   195, 195n50

lamas
  40 percent of Mongolian population   164
  among Mongolian delegates   18, 18n45, 310, 323
Lamont, Thomas W.   204, 205n5
land nationalization   229, 236, 247, 250, 260, 261–262
Lang-Tsa-Sin (Chinese delegate)   289
League of Korean Students in China   316
League of Korean Young People's Associations (Taehan ch'ŏngnyŏndan yŏnhap'oe)   315
League of Nations   70n12, 74n16, 129, 150, 150n56, 165
Lenin, V.I.   18, 19, 41, 45n1, 61n15, 84n24, 86, 88n1, 94n13, 213n19, 220n1
  lauds Sun Yat-sen's nobility and heroism   2
  May 1917 calls for uprising in Asia   3
  meets Kuomintang delegate to Far East Congress   24, 105n7
  theses on national and colonial questions   1, 2, 21
Li Dazhao   66n5, 75n18
Li Yuanhong   111, 111n25, 112n28, 113n31, 248n9
Li, congress speaker   293
Liang Qichao   107n9, 108, 108n14, 109n18, 111n25, 248n9, 319
Liaodong peninsula   5n13, 68n7, 74, 77n21, 100, 100n2, 106n8
Liebknecht, Karl   47, 270, 320
Lin Biao   27, 27n64, 326
Liu Shaoqi   13n32, 18
Lloyd George   19, 204, 204n4, 208, 285n3
Lozovsky, Solomon Abramovich
  biographical note   52n7
  speech   52
Lu Zhengxiang (Lou Tsieng-Tsiang)   113n35
Lu Zongyu   114, 114n36
Lushunkou   See Port Arthur
Luxemburg, Rosa   270, 320

Malaya   248, 275n1
Manchu
  nationality of Qing dynasty ruling house   160, 160n7
  one of the "five peoples" of Republican China   22
Manchuria
  imperialist rivalry over   62
  Japanese encroachment   5, 48n4, 68n7, 103, 125, 226, 254, 276, 300
Mao Zedong   14, 27, 28n65, 88n1, 325, 328
Marine Transport Workers Union   249n12
Marx, Karl   7, 80, 81, 186, 227
Mexico   49n5, 61n15, 143
Mikado   126, 127, 141, 183, 234, 237, 256, 264
Ming Dynasty   121n3, 133n25, 160n4
Ming Pao (Kuomintang newspaper)   108, 108n16
missionaries   150n55
  executed in Korea in 1866   319
  expose Japanese atrocities in Korea   151
  famine relief work in China   91n8
  influence on March 1 Movement in Korea   210
  murder used by Germany as pretext to seize Qingdao   278n4
  number of converts in China   76
  protect dishonest Chinese converts   92
Mississippi Bubble   175
Mitsui Corporation   253
Miura Goro
  organizes murder of Korean Queen   122, 122n5
Mizutani Kenichi
  (Japanese delegate Yoodzu), speech   53
  possibly also Japanese speaker Yakiwa   197
Mongolia
  autonomy under Bogda Khagan   164, 165
  Buddhism as prop of Chinese rule   161, 162
  conquered by Qing dynasty   160, 161
  dukedoms and nobility   161
  foreign mercantile capital in   162, 163
  invaded by Chinese Republic 1919   10, 167
  invasion by Ungern-Sternberg   168

lamas riot against Amban Sando   170n27
revocation of autonomy   166
revolution of 1921   168, 169, 280, 284
Mongolian People's Party
   formed   11, 167
   purges and factionalism   30
   said neither communist nor socialist
      171
Moon, Lottie (missionary)   150n55
Morrow, Colonel Charles H.   166n18
Mukden (Shenyang)   123, 289, 318
Musso (Indonesian Communist leader)   36, 36n87

Nagano (delegate)   253, 257
Nanjing   8, 72n13, 108n13, 109n18, 111, 111n25, 111n26, 113n31
national question in Soviet Russia   84
Naumov, I.K.   287, 287n4
Naumov, S.N.   26n63
Neo-Confucianism   133n25
Netherlands   3, 39n98, 48n4, 215n22
New Economic Policy   18, 20, 29, 197n53, 320
Nihon Rodo Sodomei   *See* Japan Federation of Labour
Niislel Khuree (Urga)   10
Nikolaeva, Klavdia
   biographical note   288n5
   remarks only seven delegates are women   24
   speech   288
Nine Power Treaty   48n4
Nobel Peace Prize   68n7, 68n8, 70n12
North China famine   91, 91n8, 103

Oghuz, Mongolian tribe   160
Olash, Mongolian tribe   160
Open Door Policy   6n15, 22, 48n4, 72, 100, 204, 208, 276, 319
Opium Wars   89n2, 277, 319
oppressed nations should unite around Soviet Russia   83
Oriental Development Company   126, 126n16, 175, 178, 178n36, 209, 209n13, 253n24
Osugi Sakae
   anarchist   28
   biographical note   199n61

contacts with Comintern   29
denounces Japanese Communists   29
murdered by rightists   28

Paekche kingdom   133n25
Pak Chin-sun
   attacked by Kim Kyu-sik   33
   executed during Great Purges   34
   founder member of Korean Communist Party   32
   speech at Second Comintern Congress   34
Pak Hŏnyŏng
   at refoundation congress of Korean Communist Party   35
   executed by Kim Il-Sung   35n84
Pak-Kieng   *See* Kim Kyu-sik
pan-Asianism   225n4
Pan-Mongolianism   277
   Chita conference 1919   166
Paris Peace Conference   9, 114n36, 149
   See also Versailles Conference
Peace Preservation Law   28, 125, 125n14, 185n41
peasant revolution   134–136, 217, 229–231
Peng Shuzhi
   delegate from Chinese students in Moscow   13, 18, 24, 326
Persia   46, 297
Petrograd Council of Trade Unions   284, 286
Philippines   43, 43n5, 63, 74, 74n16, 74n17, 275, 275n1, 299, 319
Ping-Tong   *See* Yu Shude
Plekhanov   28, 49n5, 290, 290n9
Poincaré, Raymond, French PM   20, 68, 68n9, 69n9
Poland   56, 207
Port Arthur   124, 319
Progressive Party (Jinbudang)   108n14, 111n25, 248, 248n9
Puerto Rico   63
Pumindan (Korean People's Association)   143
Pyongyang   122n4, 147, 319

Qianlong Emperor   107n12, 162
Qing dynasty   7, 9, 72n13, 76n19, 107n10, 107n13, 108n14, 109, 111n26, 114n35, 167n22, 170n27, 320

INDEX 355

Qingdao 77n21, 278n4, 319
  Japanese seizure of 5, 320
Qu Qiubai 18
Quadruple Alliance 54, 216, 228, 275, 279
  See also Four-Power Treaty

Rathenau, Walter (German foreign minister) 21n53
raw materials 97, 102, 163, 221, 223, 224, 227–229
Red Federation of Trade Unions of the Dutch Indies 302
Red International of Trade Unions 52n7
Red Star Union, Korea (Chŏksŏngdan) 316
religious organizations and revolution 135, 143–144, 232
Ren Bishi 327
Representatives of Korean Christian Churches 316
Republican Gazette 301
Revive China Society (Xingzhonghui) 72n13, 107n10, 108n15, 319
Revolutionary Korean Troops 302
Revolutionary-Patriotic League of Korean Christians 302
Righteous Army (Ŭibyŏng) 31, 124, 124n13, 137–139, 141–143, 153, 154, 331, 332
Rim Wŏn-gŭn (Korean delegate Kim Khu)
  speech 212
  and founding of Korean party 34
  biography 212n18, 335
Rodosha, Japanese anarchist group 199, 199n58, 200, 301, 301n4, 313, 314, 330
Romania 207
Roosevelt, Theodore 68n7, 74n17, 125n15
Roy, M.N.
  biographical note 61n15
  debates Lenin at Second Comintern Congress 2
  founder of Indian Communist Party 15
  plans invasion of British India 15
  speech to Far East Congress 61
ruined peasants joining bandit gangs and armies 92
Russian Asiatic Bank 275
Russian Communist Party 240n1, 283, 323, 330, 331, 333
Russian revolution of 1905
  echoes in Turkey, Persia and China 46

Russian Revolution of 1917
  impact on Asia 128, 145, 211, 297
Russo-Japanese Protocol, 1898 123n7
Russo-Japanese War 8, 49n5, 68, 68n7, 124, 136, 137, 163, 174, 175, 209, 276, 290

sabotage
  riots and violence 256
  workplace occupations 195, 196, 313
Safarov, Georgi, Comintern spokesman
  biographical note 220n1
  clash with Kuomintang delegate 247–249, 260, 261
  professorial manner 18n46
  replies to discussion on his report 259
  report on the national-colonial question 220
  says talk of proletarian revolution in Mongolia is ridiculous 262
Saionji Kimmochi 233n11
Sakai Toshihiko
  biographical note 199n60
  dissolves party in 1924 29
  first chairman of Japanese Communist Party 28
Sakhalin
  Japan gets southern half after war of 1904–5 68n7
  Japan occupies northern half 20n52, 207
Samuel Gompers 192n46, 234n14
Santo Domingo 63
Sarekat Islam 12, 15, 35, 36, 59, 59n12, 59n13, 324
Sarekat Islam Merah (Red Sarekat Islam) 59n12
Sarekat Rakjat (Union of the People) 35, 36
Schüller, Richard (Comintern youth representative Schiller)
  speech 60
Seafarers
  role in Chinese revolution 250n12
Second International 1, 2, 46n2, 48, 290
secret agreement to divide Mongolia 165n16
Seiyukai (Japanese political party) 183, 183n40, 184, 185n41, 234

Semaun (Indonesian delegate Simpson)
  biographical note   58n12
  calls Sneevliet his guru   16n39
  exile in Soviet Union   35
  returns to Indonesia, deported   35
  speeches   58, 214
  urges Indonesian party to abandon ultra-left course   36
Semenov, Ataman Grigori   10, 166, 166n18, 208n10
Seoul   9, 14, 34, 55n10, 100n2, 122, 122n4, 124, 124n11, 125n13, 128n21, 134n26, 138, 146, 147, 152, 175, 175n32, 181, 299, 314, 315, 321, 332, 333, 335
Shandong Province
  and 21 demands   89n4
  and May Fourth Movement   93n11
  Boxer uprising starts in   77n21
  German concessions in   278n4
  secret agreement of Duan Qirui govt. with Japan   112n30
  Versailles treaty hands to Japan   113
  Wellington Koo pleads for return of   114n35
  workers' organizations from   317
Shanghai Industrial Workers' Union   249
Shanghai Machine Manufacturing Workers' union   249n11
Shenyang   *See* Mukden
Shibusawa Eiichi
  meets Vanderlip and Lamont   205
Shumyatsky, Boris
  biographical note   65n1
  described as King of Siberia   18
  on congress presidium   49
  sponsors Irkutsk faction of Korean Communists   32
Silla (ancient Korean kingdom)   133n25
Simpson   *See* Semaun
Sinch'on   147, 152
Sinhan ch'ŏngnyŏndang (Young People's Party of New Korea)   316
Sinminhoe (New People's Association)   139, 139n30, 141, 142n33
Sino-Japanese war   8, 75n18, 100n2, 122, 122n5, 134n26, 135, 185, 186, 193, 209, 319
Sneevliet, Henk
  establishes Indies Social Democratic Association   12

forms 'bloc within' Sarekat Islam   12
  instructs Chinese Communists to join Kuomintang   38
  joins opposition to Stalin   39n98
  meets Sun Yat-sen   37
  opinion of Chinese Communist leadership   38
  opposes Borodin   39n98
  shot by Nazis   39n98
Society for the Defence of the Emperor (Baohuanghui)   107, 107n9, 108, 111, 248n9
Song Jiaoren   76n19, 104n6, 107n10, 108n13, 109n19, 111n25, 114n35, 320
South Manchurian railway   5n13, 68n7, 159, 163
South Russia Korean Labour Union   317, 336
Soviet-Mongolian agreement of 1921   23, 169
soviets in predominantly peasant countries   217, 231–232
stages of revolution   251
Stalin   1, 36n87, 39n98, 45n1, 49, 51n6, 84n24, 262n2, 332
Sun (Chinese delegate)
  speech   272
Sun-Joffe Manifesto   38
Sun Yat-sen
  biographical note   72n13
  conditions on pact with Soviets   39
  opens Whampoa military academy   40
  ousted in coup by Chen Jiongming   26
  overtures to United States   22, 72
  possible role in execution of Huang Bihun   26
Syngman Rhee   -12, 48n4, 128n21, 149n53, 154n72, 242n2, 333

T'aegŭkki (the Korean national flag)   148
Taegu   147, 147n49, 152
Taejonggyo religion   144, 144n42
Taft-Katsura agreement   74n17
Taiwan   23, 88n1, 89n4, 100n2, 104n6, 116n45, 185, 185n42, 299, 319, 325
Takase Kyoshi
  founder member of Japanese Communist Party   28
  possibly Japanese speaker Yakiwa   197n52
Tan Malaka
  chairman of Indonesian party   35

INDEX   357

exiled by Dutch authorities 36
opposes uprising of 1926–27 36
Tan'gun
   mythical founder of Korea 144, 144n42
Tang dynasty 133n25
Tang Jiyao
   military governor of Yunnan province
      110n21
Tangshan 94n13, 96, 301, 317, 324, 326
Terauchi Masatake
   hardline governor of Korea 125n13
   resigns as PM due to rice riots 10
three subjections and four virtues 118
Tianjin 99n1, 299, 301
Tibet
   imperialist designs on 125
   Sun Yat-sen advocates colonization of
      23
Tokuda Kyuichi (delegate)
   founder, later general secretary of Japanese party 28
Tokyo Print Workers Association 313
Tonghak (Eastern Learning) religion
   134n26
Tonginhoe (Cooperation Association) 142
Tongmenghui (forerunner of Kuomintang)
   57n11, 72n13, 99n1, 104n6, 107n10,
   108n15, 225n4, 249n12, 319
Torghuts, Mongolian tribe 160, 160n5
Treaty of Brest-Litovsk 69, 69n11, 297, 320
Treaty of Bucharest 69, 69n11
Treaty of Kyakhta 164n15, 165n17
Treaty of Nanking 89n2
Treaty of Portsmouth 68n7, 124, 124n10
Treaty of Rapallo 21n53
Treaty of Saint-Germain-en-Laye 69
Treaty of Shimonoseki 100n2, 106n8, 123n7,
   319
Treaty of Trianon 297
Treaty of Versailles 10, 69n11, 70n12, 93n11,
   114n35, 150n56
Trilisser, Mikhail 65
Trotsky, L.D. 18, 19, 30n70, 45n1, 49, 49n5,
   52n7, 61n15, 268n1, 283n1
tuberculosis among workers 227
Turkestan 159, 161, 240n1, 264
Turkey 46, 47n3, 69n11, 297
Two-and-a-Half International 46

U-An (delegate)
   speech 252
Uchida Ryohei
   leader of Black Dragon Society 225n4
   Tongmenghui founded at his home
      225n4
Ŭibyŏng *See* Righteous Army
Uighurs 160, 160n3
Uigunbu (Headquarters of the Righteous
   Army) 153
Ukraine 207, 336
Ulan Bator *See* Urga, Niislel Khuree
Ulankosh 168
Ungern-Sternberg, Roman von
   atrocities committed by 168, 171
   captured and shot 283n1, 284
   invades Mongolia 11
Unification Party (Tongyidang) 248n9
United States
   approves Japan's conquest of Korea 124,
      125n15
   attack on Korea 8
   declines invitation, sends observer to
      Genoa 73n14
   does not ratify Versailles Treaty 150,
      150n56
   excludes Russia from Washington Conference 3
   hostility to Sun Yat-sen 22
   hypocrisy of 70, 150
   opposes Anglo-Japanese alliance 203,
      206
Urankhais, Mongolian tribe 160
Urga 164, 167, 167n22, 168, 169, 170n27,
   280n8, 284
Uriankhai region 163, 170
USA-Korea Treaty of Peace, Amity, Commerce and Navigation 123n6

Vanderlip, Frank A. 204, 204n5, 205n5
Versailles Conference 128, 129, 165, 168, 273,
   278, 279
   See also Paris Peace Conference
Voitinsky, Grigory (Comintern agent)
   on congress presidium 65
   orders Japanese to reestablish party 29
   talks with Chen Duxiu on forming party
      66n5

Walter, (German representative Jacob Walcher)
  biographical note 269n2
  speech 269
Wang Jingwei 41, 41n106, 61n15, 321
Wang Kon
  founder of Koryŏ dynasty 133n25
Wang Yingkai (Bag-Wik-Wee) 107n11
war in the Pacific inevitable 82, 209, 275, 281
Washington Conference 19, 53, 70, 72, 104, 130, 212, 228, 232, 254, 272, 273, 292
  a 'surgical operation' on peoples of the East 4
  a temporary compromise among imperialists 206, 214, 275, 281
  Britain proposes triple alliance at 204n4
  dispels illusions 74, 276, 279
  dispute over Yap islands 74n16
  Far East Congress planned to coincide with 17
  Far Eastern Republic delegation 20, 242n3
  Korea not mentioned at 71
  Kuomintang attitude to 22, 116
  Mongolia ignored at 73
  sanctions 'plunder' of China 277
  secret Franco-Japanese agreement exposed 20, 207n8
  some Korean Communists 'plan to attend' 242
Weihaiwei, British concession area 77n21, 100, 319
Wellington Koo (Gu Weijin) 114n35
Whampoa (Huangpu) Military Academy 40
Wilson, Woodrow 70n12
  fourteen point peace plan 9, 320
  hypocritical declarations 128
  opposes, then supports Banking Consortium 278n5
  supports Japan on Shangdong issue 114n35
women in the workforce 95, 192, 236
Women's Educational Society 157
women's oppression 118–120
women's sections
  call for separate organizations in movement 244

Wong-Kieng (Korean delegate)
  report on Washington Conference and Korea 121
Wong See Huang Bihun
Wŏnsan 147, 147n48
Workers Association of Hunan 318
Workers Association of Shandong 318
working class in advanced countries partly corrupted 80, 216–217
Wrangel, Pyotr Nikolaevich 19, 20, 207n8, 208, 208n9, 208n10
Wu Peifu
  backed by Britain 90
  biographical note 90n5
  courted by Soviets 4
  wins Zhili-Anhui war 115n38

Xu Shichang 113, 113n32, 115
Xu Shuzheng, Chinese general, invades Mongolia 10, 167, 167n21, 167n22, 170n27, 279n6
Xuzhou 111, 111n26

Yakova (delegate)
  speech 254
Yakutia 267
Yalu River 152
Yamagata Aritomo 233n11
Yamakawa Hitoshi
  founder member of Japanese party 28
  votes to dissolve party 29
Yap archipelago
  bought by Germany 1899 74n16
  captured by Japan 1914 5
  dispute at Washington Conference 206
  strategic position 74n16
Yi Chaegon (Korean delegate)
  speech 245
Yi-pal Club/Organization of Korean Returned Students from Japan 316
Yi Sŭng-man See Syngman Rhee
Yi Tong-hwi
  denounced by Kim Kyu-sik 33
  founder of Korean Communist Party 31
  leader of Shanghai faction 32
  prime minister of Korean Provisional Government 32

INDEX 359

Righteous Army commander 31
sent to Irkutsk to unify party 33
Yŏ Unhyŏng (Korean delegate)
   aligned with Irkutsk faction 32
   biographical note 336
   forms post World War Two Korean
      People's Republic 14
   meets with Osugi Sakae 29
   murdered by right wing extremist in 1947 14
Yongzheng Emperor 162
Yoshida Hajime (Japanese anarchist delegate Kato)
   announces conversion to Communism 200
   biographical note 199n59
   proposal for congress presidium 49
   report on the workers' organization Rodosha 199
   speech on Safarov's report 256
Young ChinaSociety 99, 301, 318, 324
Young Men's Christian Association 138
Young People's Party of New Korea 316
Yu Shude (Chinese delegate Ping-Tong)
   biographical note 99n1
   on economic situation in China 99
   on the Banking Consortium 103
   on Zinoviev's report 202
Yuaikai (Friendly Society)
   forerunner of Japan Federation of Labour 200, 200n62, 313
Yuan dynasty 133n25, 160, 160n4
Yuan Shikai
   accedes to 21 demands 89n4
   assassinates Song Jiaoren, disperses parliament 320
   biographical note 107n13
   crushes Korean rebellion 8
   declares himself emperor 109
   failed attempt to reform Qing 108
   forced to abdicate 110
   theories about his death 110n22

Yunnan province, China 108n13, 110n21, 256n28, 326
Yurin, M.I. 65

Zand-Bei (Chair of credentials committee) 266
Zhang Guotao (delegate Li-Kieng)
   account of trip to Russia 17
   biographical note 88n1
   chaired founding congress of Chinese Communist Party 88n1
   challenged Mao for leadership 14
   defected to Kuomintang 88n1
   leader of Chinese Communist delegation 2
   on congress presidium 49
   report on situation in China 88
Zhang Qiubai (Kuomintang delegate Tao)
   biographical note 105n7
   meets Lenin 105n7
   on congress presidium 49
   report on political situation in China 105
   speeches 212, 247, 249
Zhang Zongxiang 114, 114n36
Zhang Zuolin (Manchurian warlord)
   alliance with Sun Yat-sen 38
   biographical note 75n18
   conflict with Wu Peifu 38
   hireling of Japan 130, 168, 276, 279, 280
   illiterate 76
Zhejiang province, China 110n21, 170n27, 301, 318
Zhili clique 4, 113n31, 115n38
Zinoviev, Grigory
   biographical note 45n1
   opening address 45
   report on international situation and Washington Conference 67
   speeches 49, 57, 215, 283, 290, 291, 293, 296

Illustration Section

ILL. 1 Katayama Sen speaks while Zinoviev reads a document
Note: Boris Shumyatsky looks over Zinoviev's shoulder. To the left, looking on, is Bukharin, who did not officially attend the congress. Seated on the far right of the table are the Koreans Kim Kyu-sik, facing forward, and Yŏ Unhyŏng, facing sideways. The banner draped over the table reads 'Proletarians of the World Unite'.
SOURCE: PHOTOGRAPH COURTESY OF THE RUSSIAN STATE ARCHIVE OF SOCIO-POLITICAL HISTORY. (495.154.D181A)

ILLUSTRATION SECTION 361

ILL. 2   Delegates listen to a session of the congress.
SOURCE: PHOTOGRAPH COURTESY OF THE RUSSIAN STATE ARCHIVE OF
SOCIO-POLITICAL HISTORY. (495.154.D181A)

ILL. 3 A group of delegates to the congress
SOURCE: PHOTOGRAPH COURTESY OF THE RUSSIAN STATE ARCHIVE OF SOCIO-POLITICAL HISTORY. (495.154.D181A)

ILLUSTRATION SECTION 363

ILL. 4   Delegates to the congress
Note: M.N. Roy, founder of the Indian Communist Party, is in the middle of the front row.
SOURCE: PHOTOGRAPH COURTESY OF THE RUSSIAN STATE ARCHIVE OF SOCIO-POLITICAL HISTORY. (495.154.D181A)

ILL. 5 Delegates leaving the congress venue
Note: The banner above the door says 'Welcome' in Chinese.
SOURCE: PHOTOGRAPH COURTESY OF THE RUSSIAN STATE ARCHIVE OF SOCIO-POLITICAL HISTORY. (495.154.D181A)

ILL. 6   Members of the Chinese delegation in their dormitory
SOURCE: PHOTOGRAPH COURTESY OF THE RUSSIAN STATE ARCHIVE OF SOCIO-POLITICAL HISTORY. (495.154.D181A)

ILL. 7   The Chinese feminist-anarchist delegate Huang Bihun who was shot by the KMT the year after the congress
SOURCE: PHOTOGRAPH COURTESY OF THE RUSSIAN STATE ARCHIVE OF SOCIO-POLITICAL HISTORY. (495.154.D181A)

ILL. 8   M.N. Roy's request to attend the Far East Congress as a delegate from India
SOURCE: REPRODUCED COURTESY OF THE RUSSIAN STATE ARCHIVE OF SOCIO-POLITICAL HISTORY. (495.154.D175)

ILL. 9   Letter to the congress mandate commission, signed by the leader of the Korean delegation, Kim Kyu-sik
Note: This letter illustrates the intensity of factionalism in the Korean revolutionary movement. It is not clear whether Pak Chin-sun (here referred to as Pak-Din-shoon) was allowed to attend.
SOURCE: REPRODUCED COURTESY OF THE RUSSIAN STATE ARCHIVE OF SOCIO-POLITICAL HISTORY. (495.154.D175)

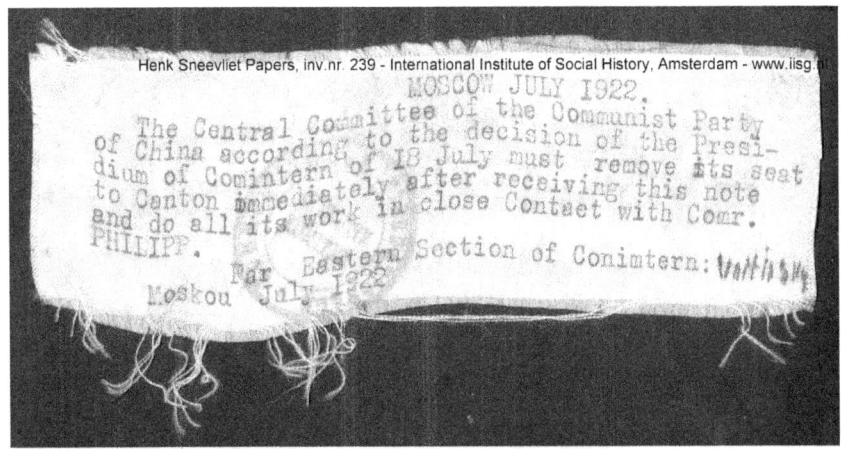

ILL. 10 Comintern order, signed by Grigori Voitinsky, directing the Chinese Communist Party to move its HQ to Canton, base of the KMT, and follow the advice of the Dutch Comintern agent Henk Sneevliet
Note: Sneevliet instructed the Communists to join the KMT as individuals, beginning the 'entrist' policy that, as implemented by Borodin, led to the disaster of April 1927.
SOURCE: REPRODUCED COURTESY OF THE INTERNATIONAL INSTITUTE OF SOCIAL HISTORY, AMSTERDAM. ARCHIEF HENK SNEEVLIET, INVENTORY NUMBER 239.

www.ingramcontent.com/pod-product-compliance
Lightning Source LLC
Chambersburg PA
CBHW071146070526
44584CB00019B/2681